TABLE OF CONTENTS

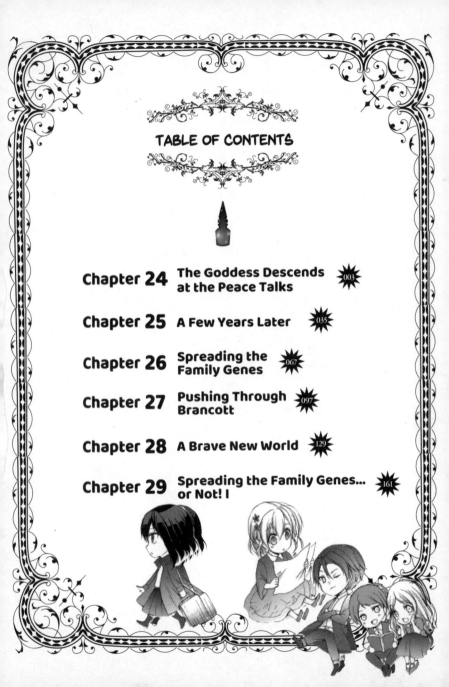

Original Work: FUNA
Manga: Hibiki Kokonoe
Character Design: Sukima

I SHALL SURVIVE USING POTIONS! 5

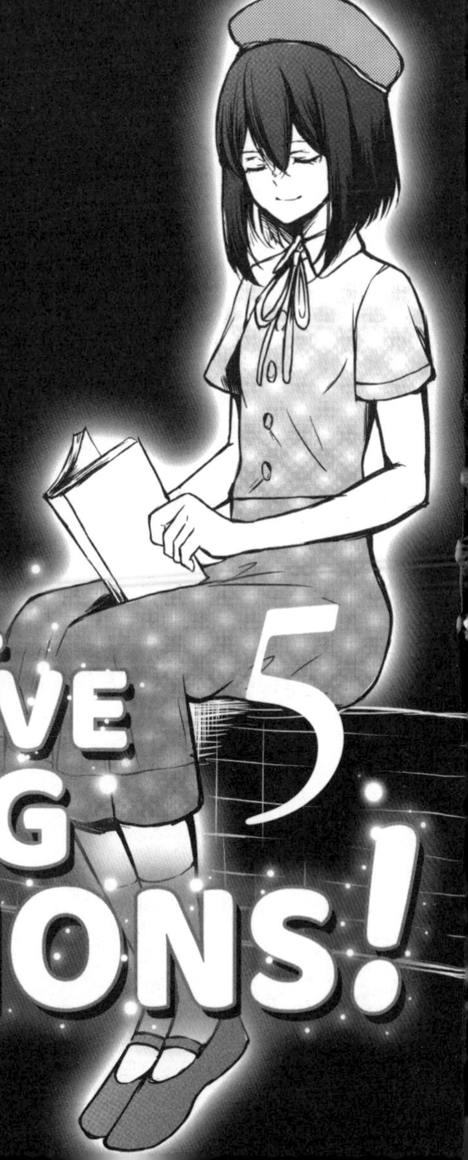

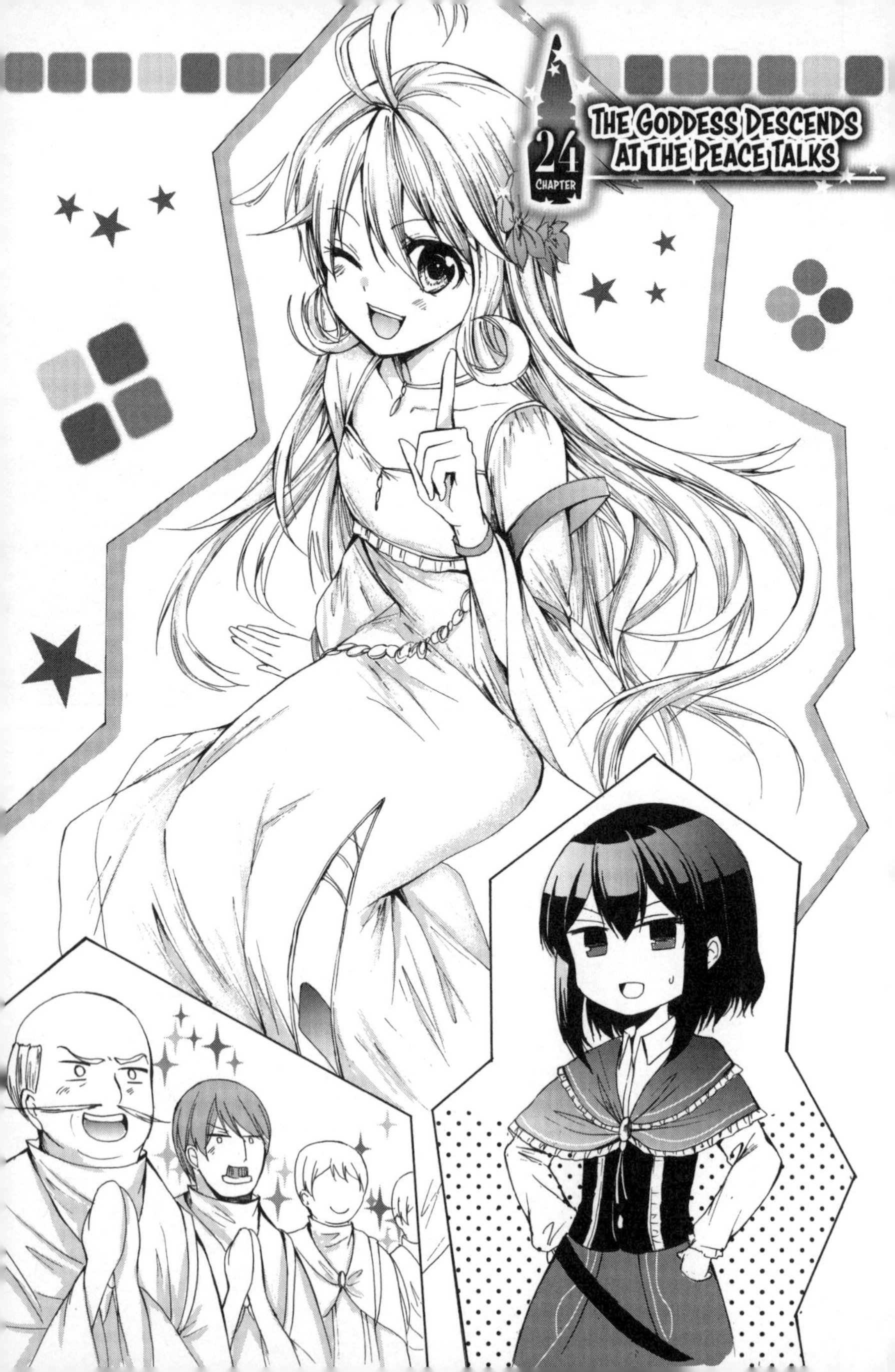
24
CHAPTER
THE GODDESS DESCENDS AT THE PEACE TALKS

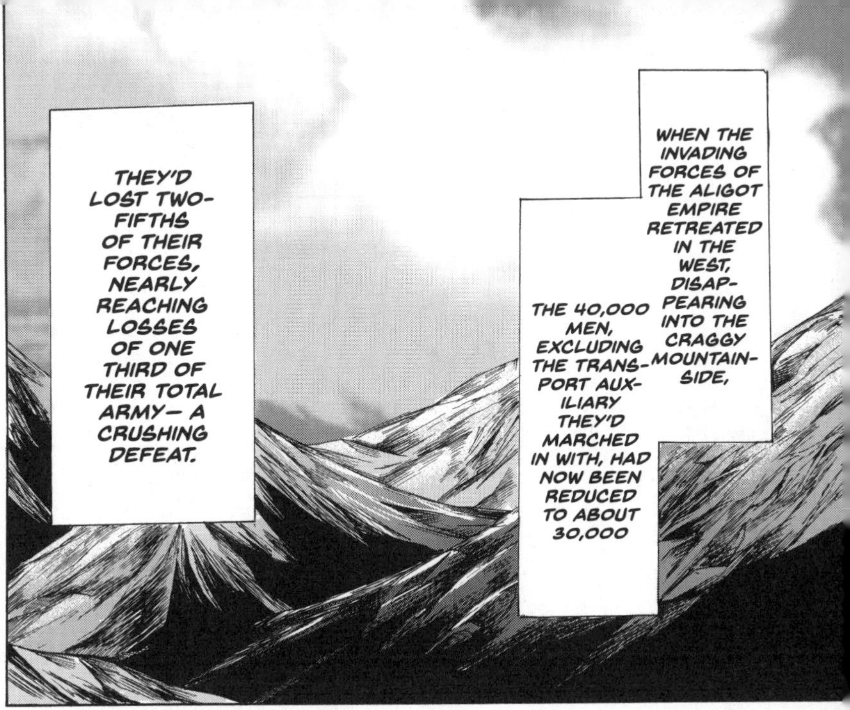
WHEN THE INVADING FORCES OF THE ALIGOT EMPIRE RETREATED IN THE WEST, DISAP-PEARING INTO THE CRAGGY MOUNTAIN-SIDE,
THE 40,000 MEN, EXCLUDING THE TRANS-PORT AUX-ILIARY THEY'D MARCHED IN WITH, HAD NOW BEEN REDUCED TO ABOUT 30,000
THEY'D LOST TWO-FIFTHS OF THEIR FORCES, NEARLY REACHING LOSSES OF ONE THIRD OF THEIR TOTAL ARMY— A CRUSHING DEFEAT.

TRANSPORT AUXILIARY: A TROOP OF TRANSPORT SOLDIERS WHICH SUPPLY THE FRONT LINES WITH MILITARY SUPPLIES, SUCH AS ARMS AND AMMUNITION.

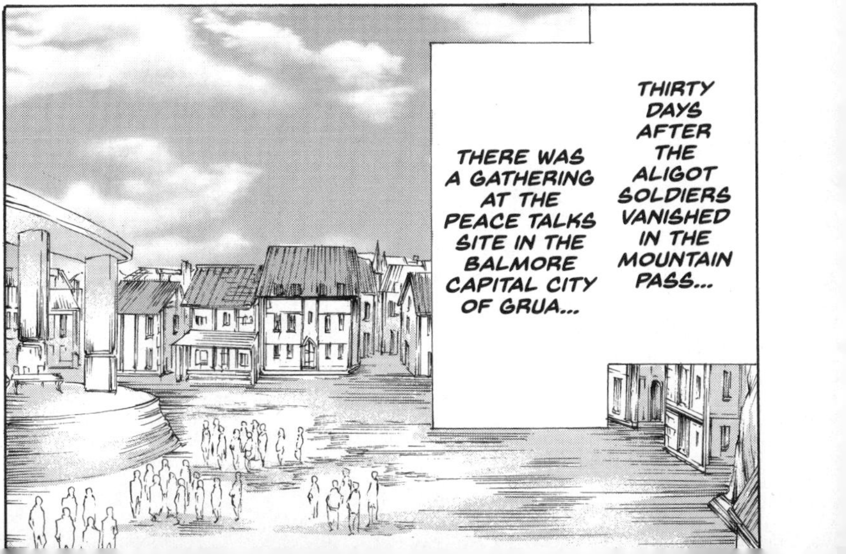
THIRTY DAYS AFTER THE ALIGOT SOLDIERS VANISHED IN THE MOUNTAIN PASS...
THERE WAS A GATHERING AT THE PEACE TALKS SITE IN THE BALMORE CAPITAL CITY OF GRUA...

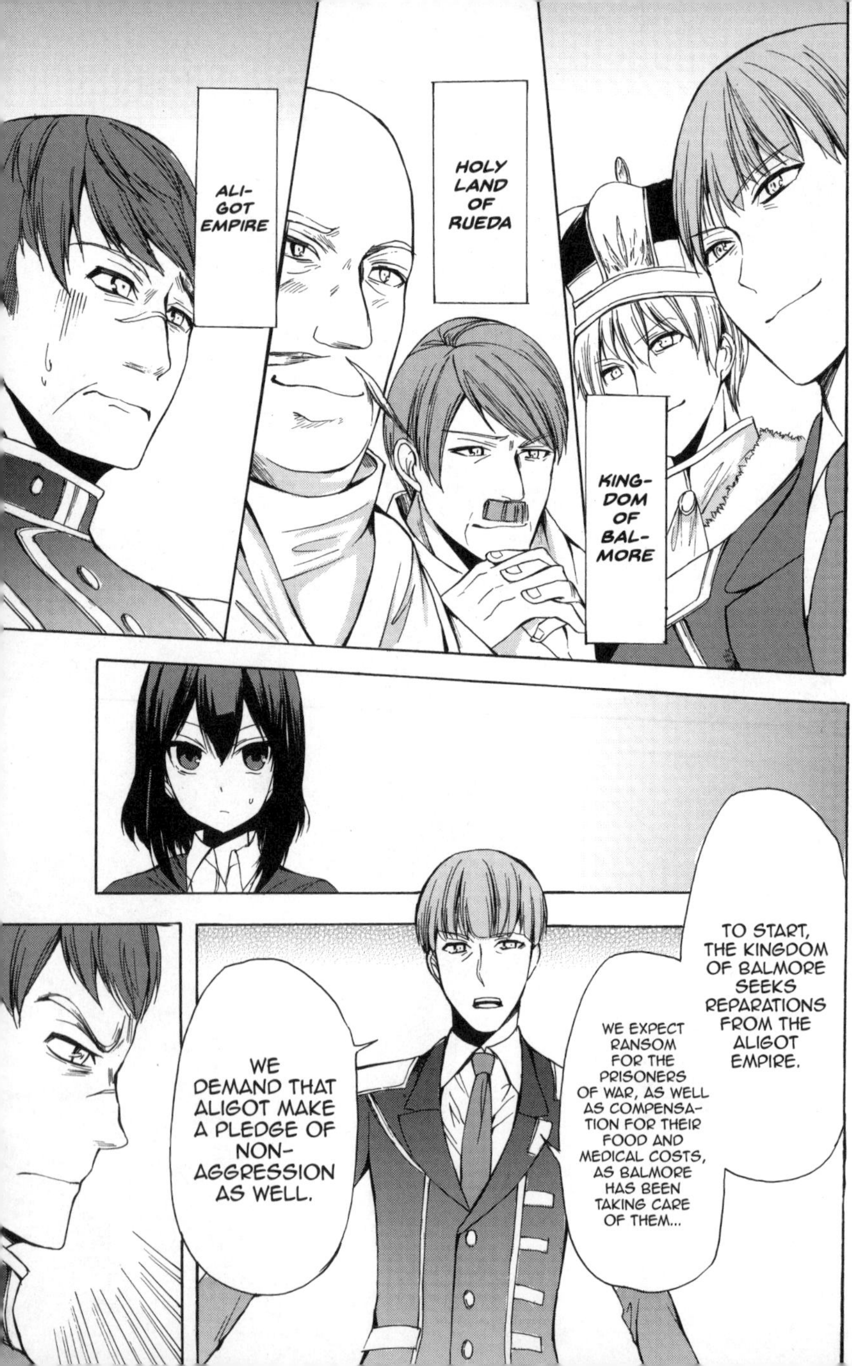
KINGDOM OF BALMORE
HOLY LAND OF RUEDA
ALIGOT EMPIRE
TO START, THE KINGDOM OF BALMORE SEEKS REPARATIONS FROM THE ALIGOT EMPIRE.
WE EXPECT RANSOM FOR THE PRISONERS OF WAR, AS WELL AS COMPENSATION FOR THEIR FOOD AND MEDICAL COSTS, AS BALMORE HAS BEEN TAKING CARE OF THEM...
WE DEMAND THAT ALIGOT MAKE A PLEDGE OF NON-AGGRESSION AS WELL.

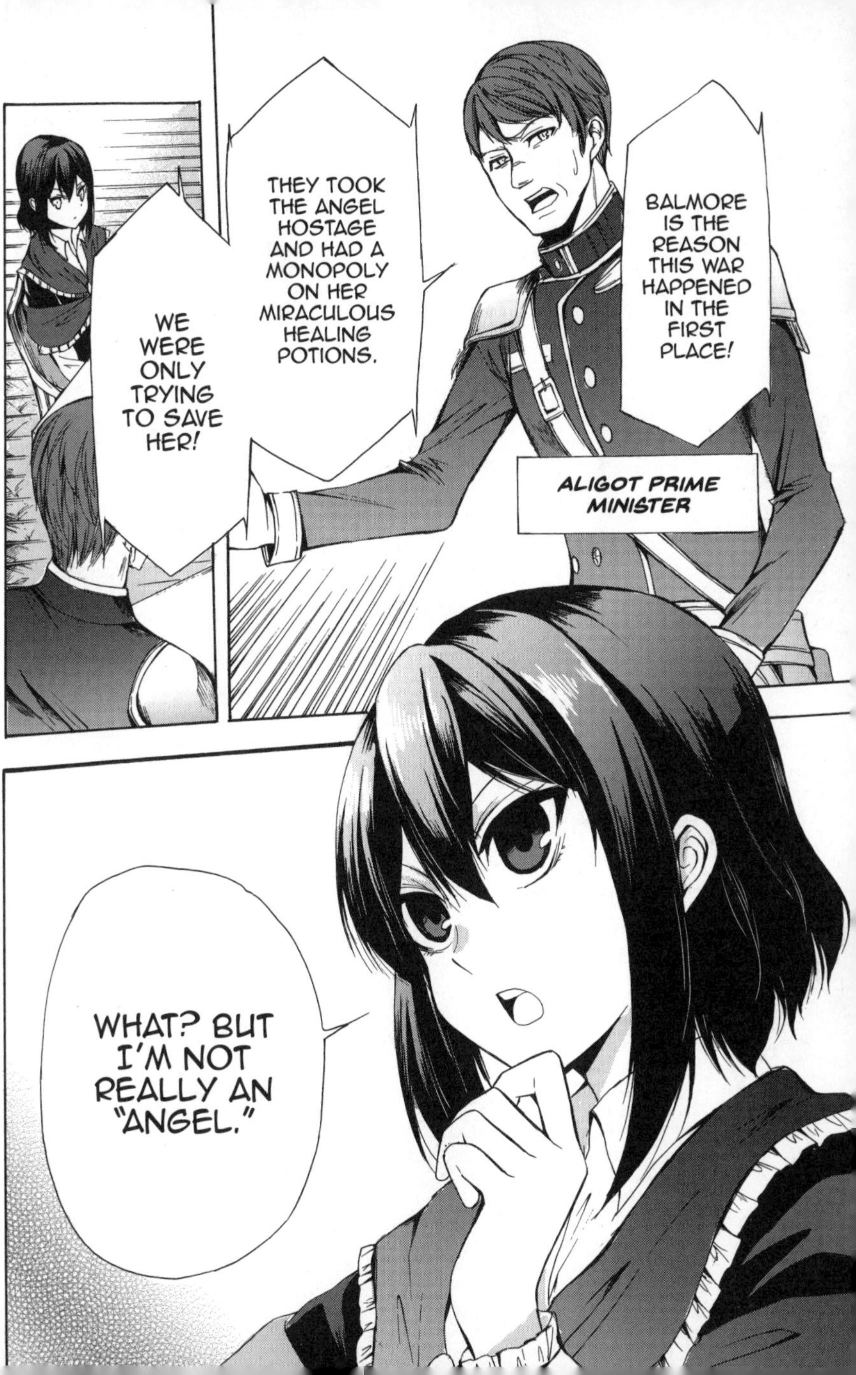
BALMORE IS THE REASON THIS WAR HAPPENED IN THE FIRST PLACE!
THEY TOOK THE ANGEL HOSTAGE AND HAD A MONOPOLY ON HER MIRACULOUS HEALING POTIONS.
ALIGOT PRIME MINISTER
WE WERE ONLY TRYING TO SAVE HER!
WHAT? BUT I'M NOT REALLY AN "ANGEL."

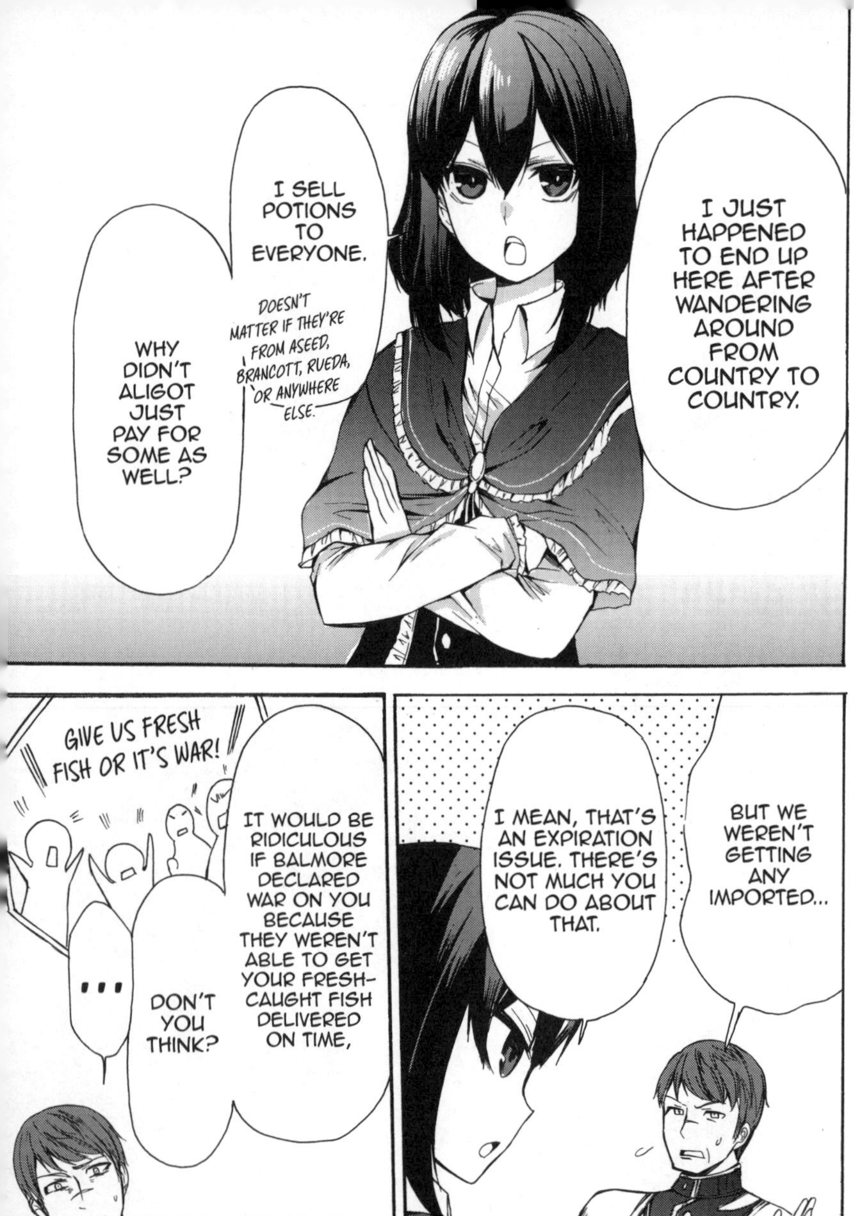
I JUST HAPPENED TO END UP HERE AFTER WANDERING AROUND FROM COUNTRY TO COUNTRY.
I SELL POTIONS TO EVERYONE.
DOESN'T MATTER IF THEY'RE FROM ASEED, BRANCOTT, RUEDA, OR ANYWHERE ELSE.
WHY DIDN'T ALIGOT JUST PAY FOR SOME AS WELL?
BUT WE WEREN'T GETTING ANY IMPORTED...
I MEAN, THAT'S AN EXPIRATION ISSUE. THERE'S NOT MUCH YOU CAN DO ABOUT THAT.
IT WOULD BE RIDICULOUS IF BALMORE DECLARED WAR ON YOU BECAUSE THEY WEREN'T ABLE TO GET YOUR FRESH-CAUGHT FISH DELIVERED ON TIME,
GIVE US FRESH FISH OR IT'S WAR!
DON'T YOU THINK?
...

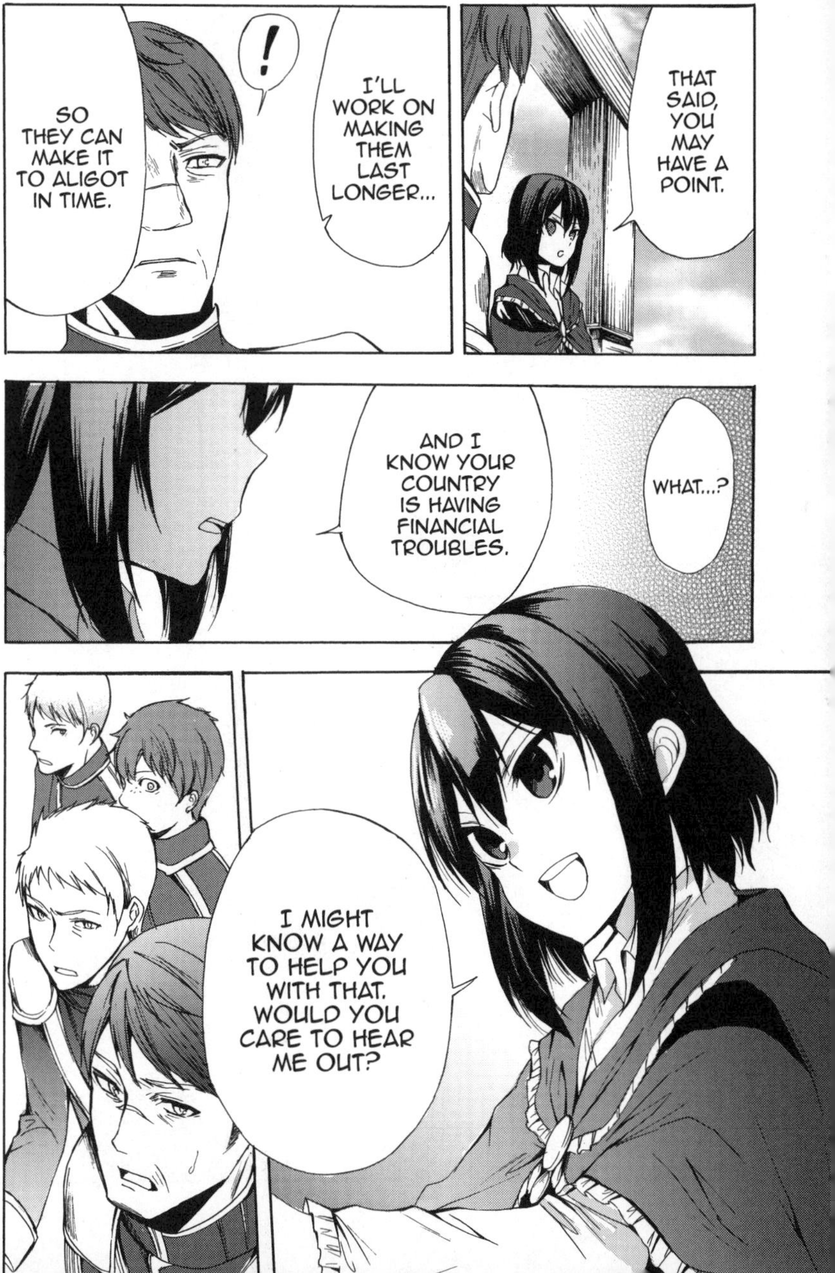
THAT SAID, YOU MAY HAVE A POINT.
I'LL WORK ON MAKING THEM LAST LONGER...
!
SO THEY CAN MAKE IT TO ALIGOT IN TIME.
WHAT...?
AND I KNOW YOUR COUNTRY IS HAVING FINANCIAL TROUBLES.
I MIGHT KNOW A WAY TO HELP YOU WITH THAT. WOULD YOU CARE TO HEAR ME OUT?

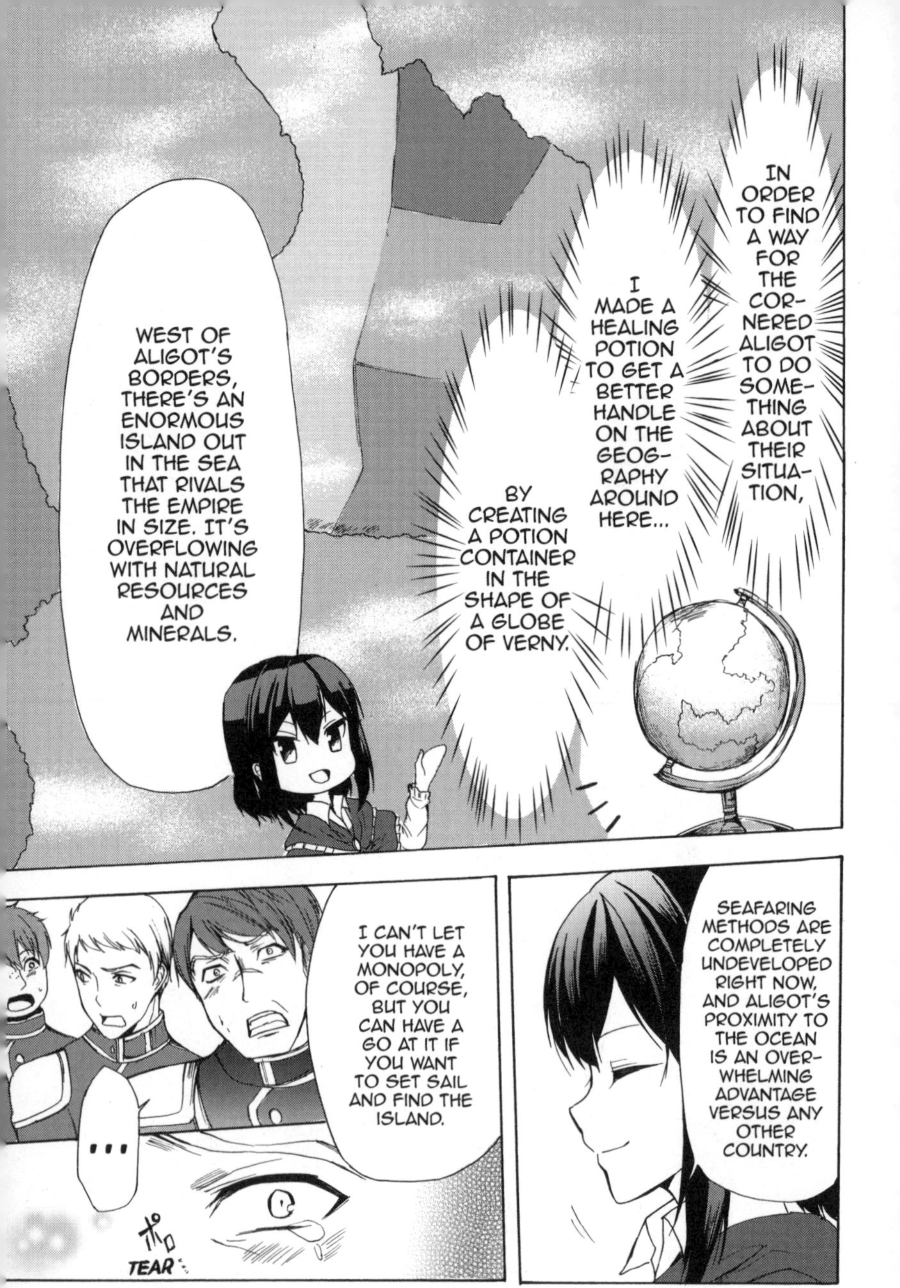
IN ORDER TO FIND A WAY FOR THE COR-NERED ALIGOT TO DO SOME-THING ABOUT THEIR SITUA-TION,
I MADE A HEALING POTION TO GET A BETTER HANDLE ON THE GEOG-RAPHY AROUND HERE...
BY CREATING A POTION CONTAINER IN THE SHAPE OF A GLOBE OF VERNY.
WEST OF ALIGOT'S BORDERS, THERE'S AN ENORMOUS ISLAND OUT IN THE SEA THAT RIVALS THE EMPIRE IN SIZE. IT'S OVERFLOWING WITH NATURAL RESOURCES AND MINERALS.
SEAFARING METHODS ARE COMPLETELY UNDEVELOPED RIGHT NOW, AND ALIGOT'S PROXIMITY TO THE OCEAN IS AN OVER-WHELMING ADVANTAGE VERSUS ANY OTHER COUNTRY.
I CAN'T LET YOU HAVE A MONOPOLY, OF COURSE, BUT YOU CAN HAVE A GO AT IT IF YOU WANT TO SET SAIL AND FIND THE ISLAND.
...
TEAR...

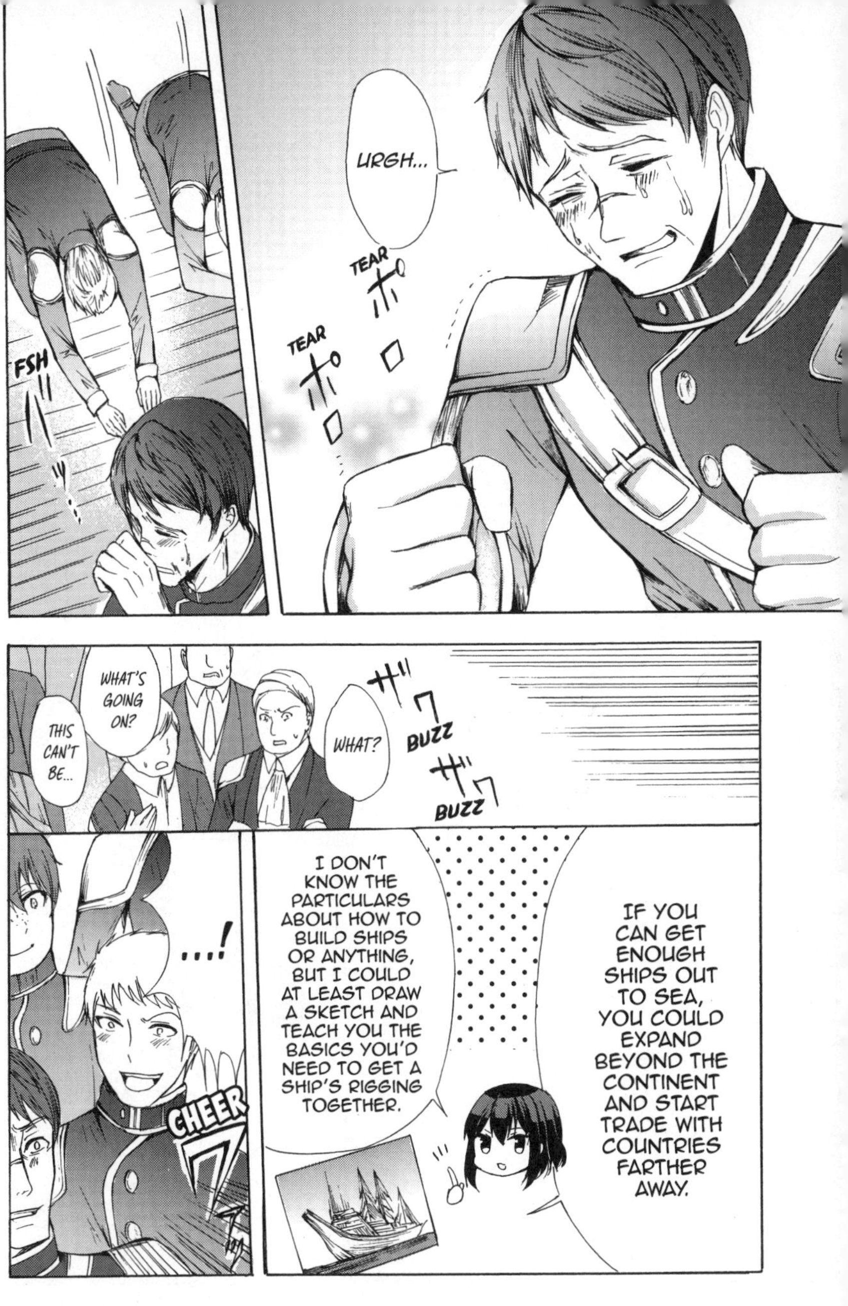
URGH...
TEAR
TEAR
FSH
BUZZ
BUZZ
WHAT?
WHAT'S GOING ON?
THIS CAN'T BE...
IF YOU CAN GET ENOUGH SHIPS OUT TO SEA, YOU COULD EXPAND BEYOND THE CONTINENT AND START TRADE WITH COUNTRIES FARTHER AWAY.
I DON'T KNOW THE PARTICULARS ABOUT HOW TO BUILD SHIPS OR ANYTHING, BUT I COULD AT LEAST DRAW A SKETCH AND TEACH YOU THE BASICS YOU'D NEED TO GET A SHIP'S RIGGING TOGETHER.
...!
CHEER

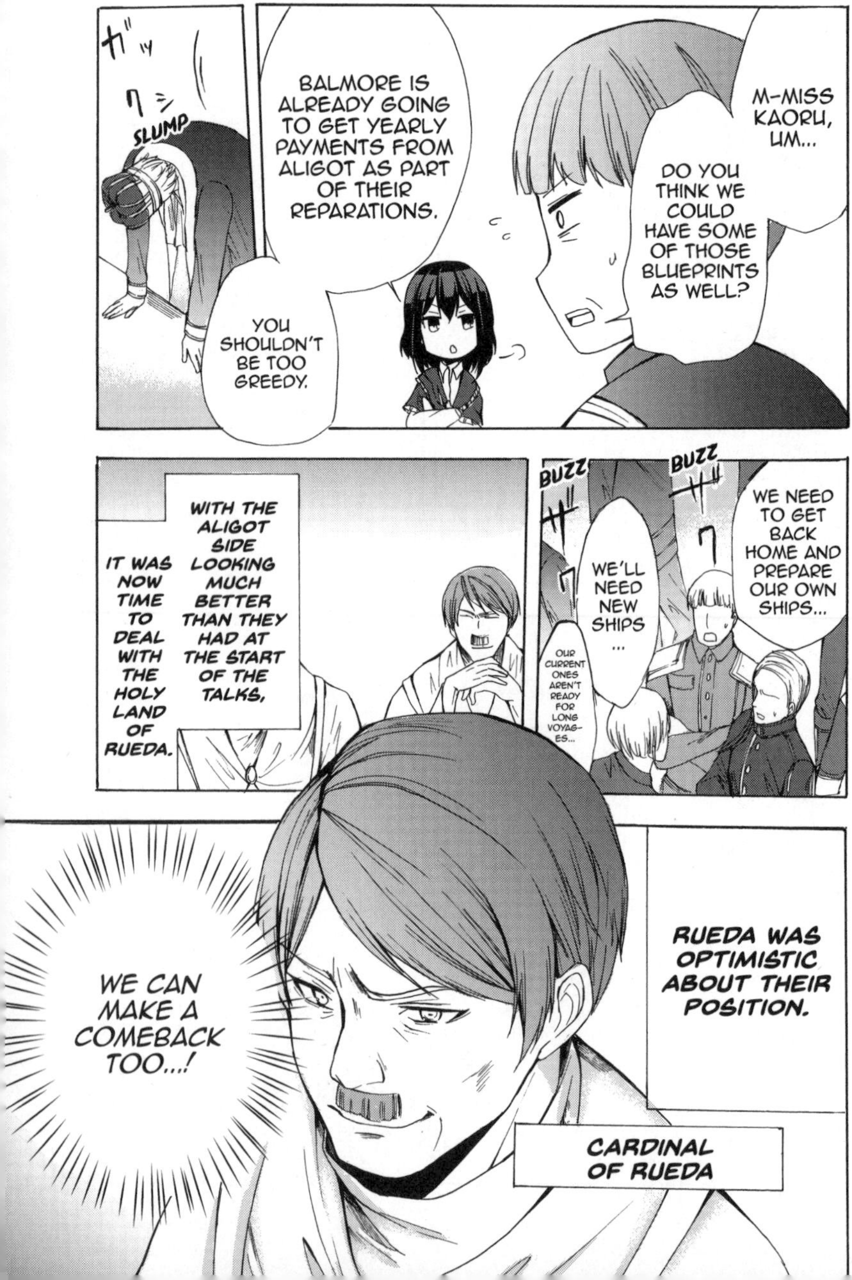
M-MISS KAORU, UM...
DO YOU THINK WE COULD HAVE SOME OF THOSE BLUEPRINTS AS WELL?
BALMORE IS ALREADY GOING TO GET YEARLY PAYMENTS FROM ALIGOT AS PART OF THEIR REPARATIONS.
YOU SHOULDN'T BE TOO GREEDY.
SLUMP
BUZZ
BUZZ
WE NEED TO GET BACK HOME AND PREPARE OUR OWN SHIPS...
WE'LL NEED NEW SHIPS...
OUR CURRENT ONES AREN'T READY FOR LONG VOYAGES...
WITH THE ALIGOT SIDE LOOKING MUCH BETTER THAN THEY HAD AT THE START OF THE TALKS,
IT WAS NOW TIME TO DEAL WITH THE HOLY LAND OF RUEDA.
RUEDA WAS OPTIMISTIC ABOUT THEIR POSITION.
WE CAN MAKE A COMEBACK TOO...!
CARDINAL OF RUEDA

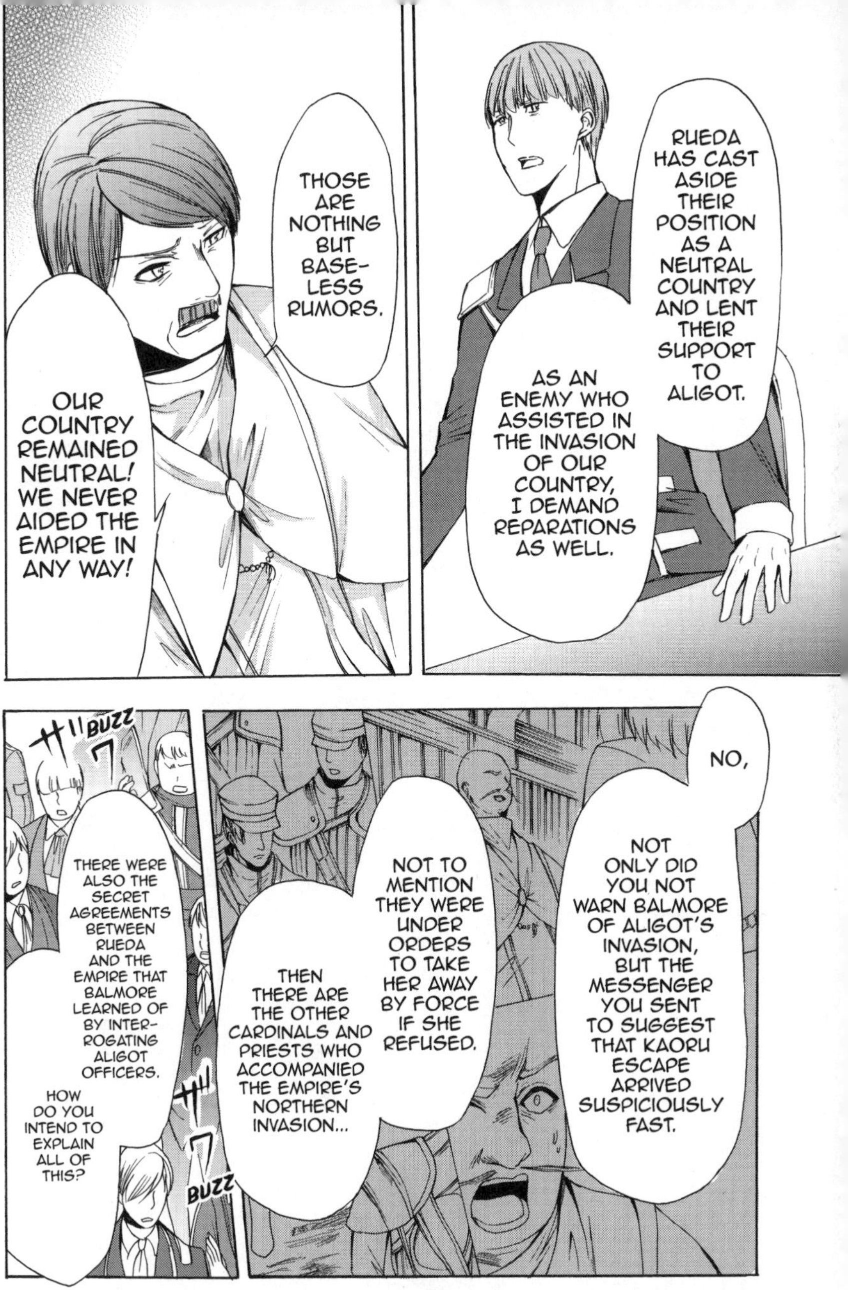
RUEDA HAS CAST ASIDE THEIR POSITION AS A NEUTRAL COUNTRY AND LENT THEIR SUPPORT TO ALIGOT.
AS AN ENEMY WHO ASSISTED IN THE INVASION OF OUR COUNTRY, I DEMAND REPARATIONS AS WELL.
THOSE ARE NOTHING BUT BASE-LESS RUMORS.
OUR COUNTRY REMAINED NEUTRAL! WE NEVER AIDED THE EMPIRE IN ANY WAY!
NO,
NOT ONLY DID YOU NOT WARN BALMORE OF ALIGOT'S INVASION, BUT THE MESSENGER YOU SENT TO SUGGEST THAT KAORU ESCAPE ARRIVED SUSPICIOUSLY FAST.
NOT TO MENTION THEY WERE UNDER ORDERS TO TAKE HER AWAY BY FORCE IF SHE REFUSED.
THEN THERE ARE THE OTHER CARDINALS AND PRIESTS WHO ACCOMPANIED THE EMPIRE'S NORTHERN INVASION...
BUZZ
THERE WERE ALSO THE SECRET AGREEMENTS BETWEEN RUEDA AND THE EMPIRE THAT BALMORE LEARNED OF BY INTER-ROGATING ALIGOT OFFICERS.
HOW DO YOU INTEND TO EXPLAIN ALL OF THIS?
BUZZ

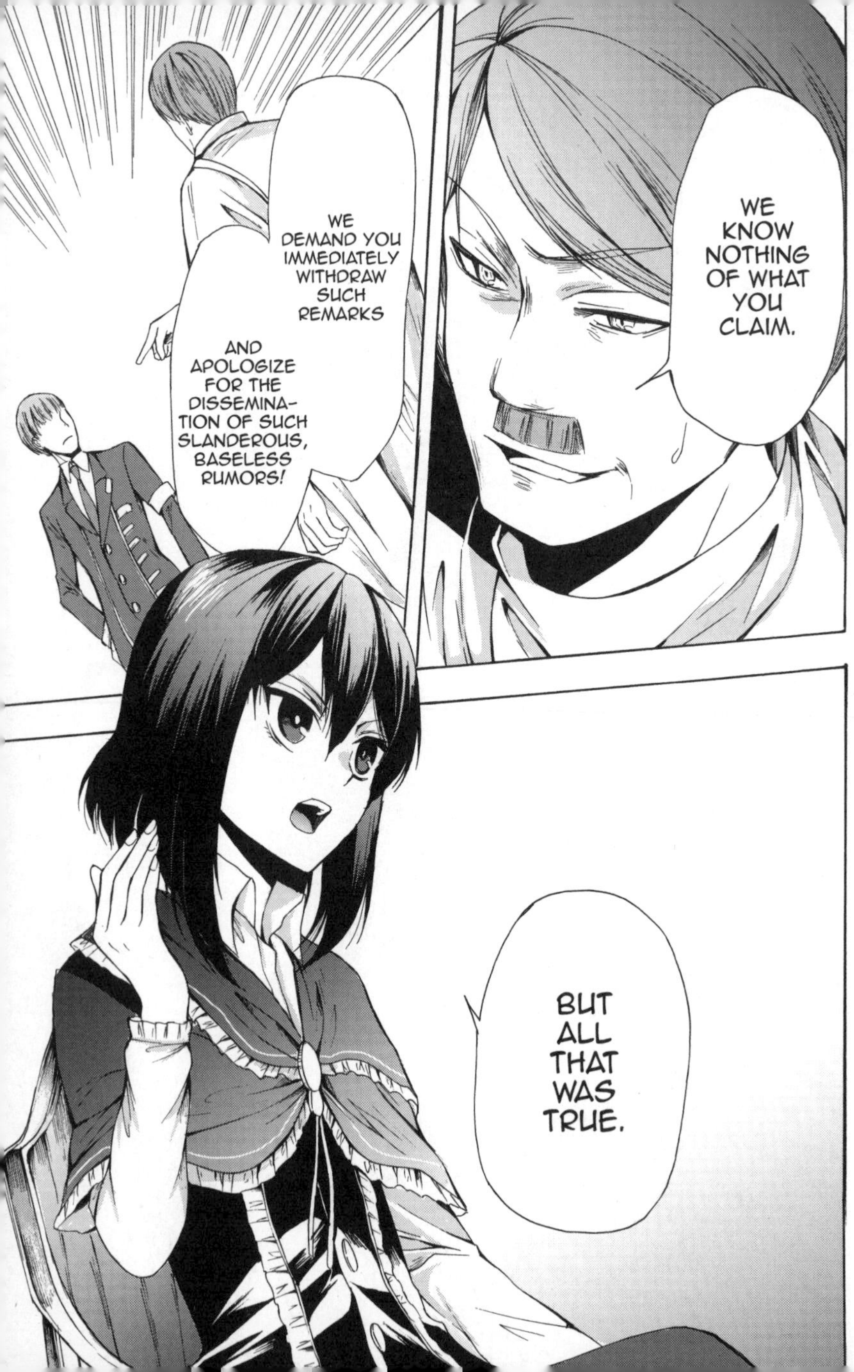
WE KNOW NOTHING OF WHAT YOU CLAIM.
WE DEMAND YOU IMMEDIATELY WITHDRAW SUCH REMARKS
AND APOLOGIZE FOR THE DISSEMINATION OF SUCH SLANDEROUS, BASELESS RUMORS!
BUT ALL THAT WAS TRUE.

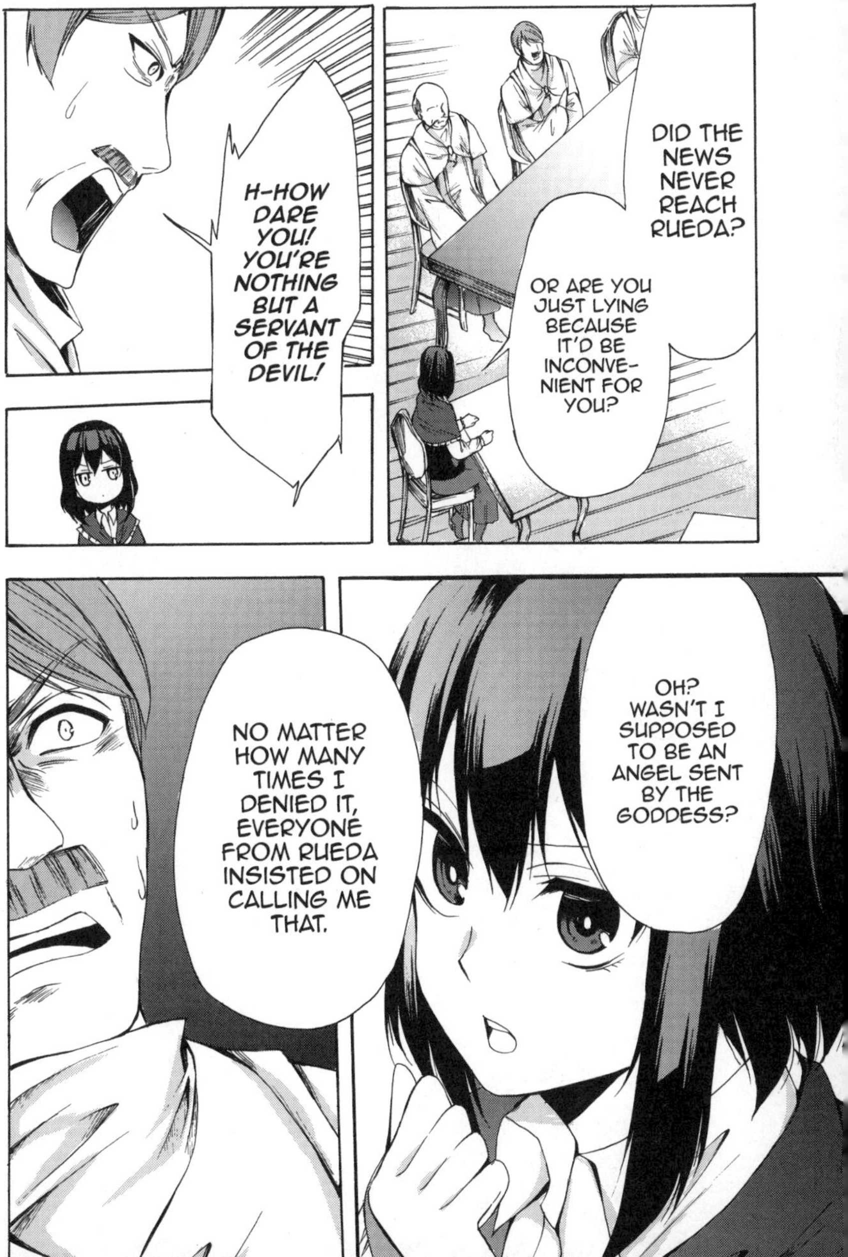
DID THE NEWS NEVER REACH RUEDA?
OR ARE YOU JUST LYING BECAUSE IT'D BE INCONVE-NIENT FOR YOU?
H-HOW DARE YOU! YOU'RE NOTHING BUT A SERVANT OF THE DEVIL!
OH? WASN'T I SUPPOSED TO BE AN ANGEL SENT BY THE GODDESS?
NO MATTER HOW MANY TIMES I DENIED IT, EVERYONE FROM RUEDA INSISTED ON CALLING ME THAT.

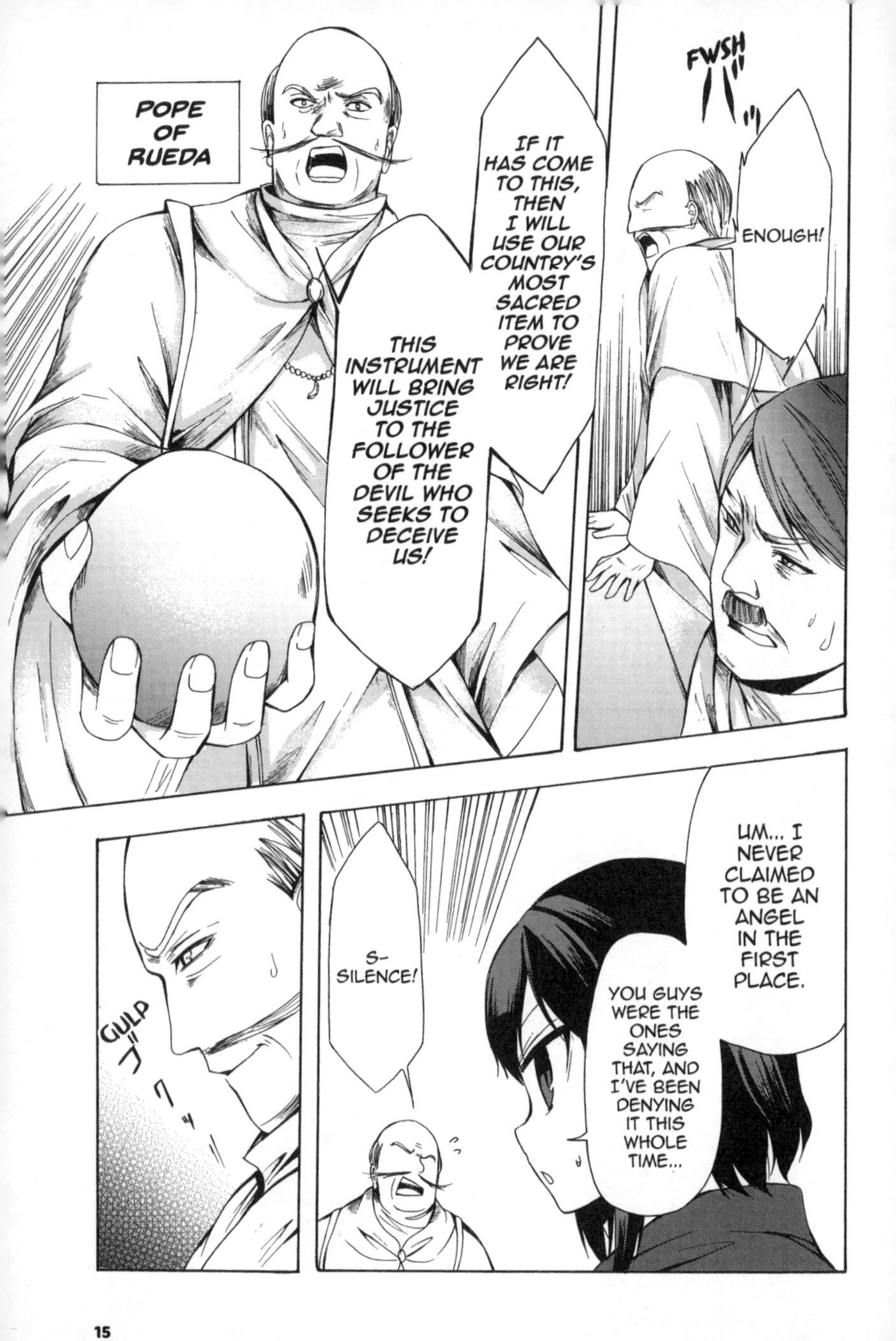
FWSH
ENOUGH!
POPE OF RUEDA
IF IT HAS COME TO THIS, THEN I WILL USE OUR COUNTRY'S MOST SACRED ITEM TO PROVE WE ARE RIGHT!
THIS INSTRUMENT WILL BRING JUSTICE TO THE FOLLOWER OF THE DEVIL WHO SEEKS TO DECEIVE US!
UM... I NEVER CLAIMED TO BE AN ANGEL IN THE FIRST PLACE.
YOU GUYS WERE THE ONES SAYING THAT, AND I'VE BEEN DENYING IT THIS WHOLE TIME...
S-SILENCE!
GULP

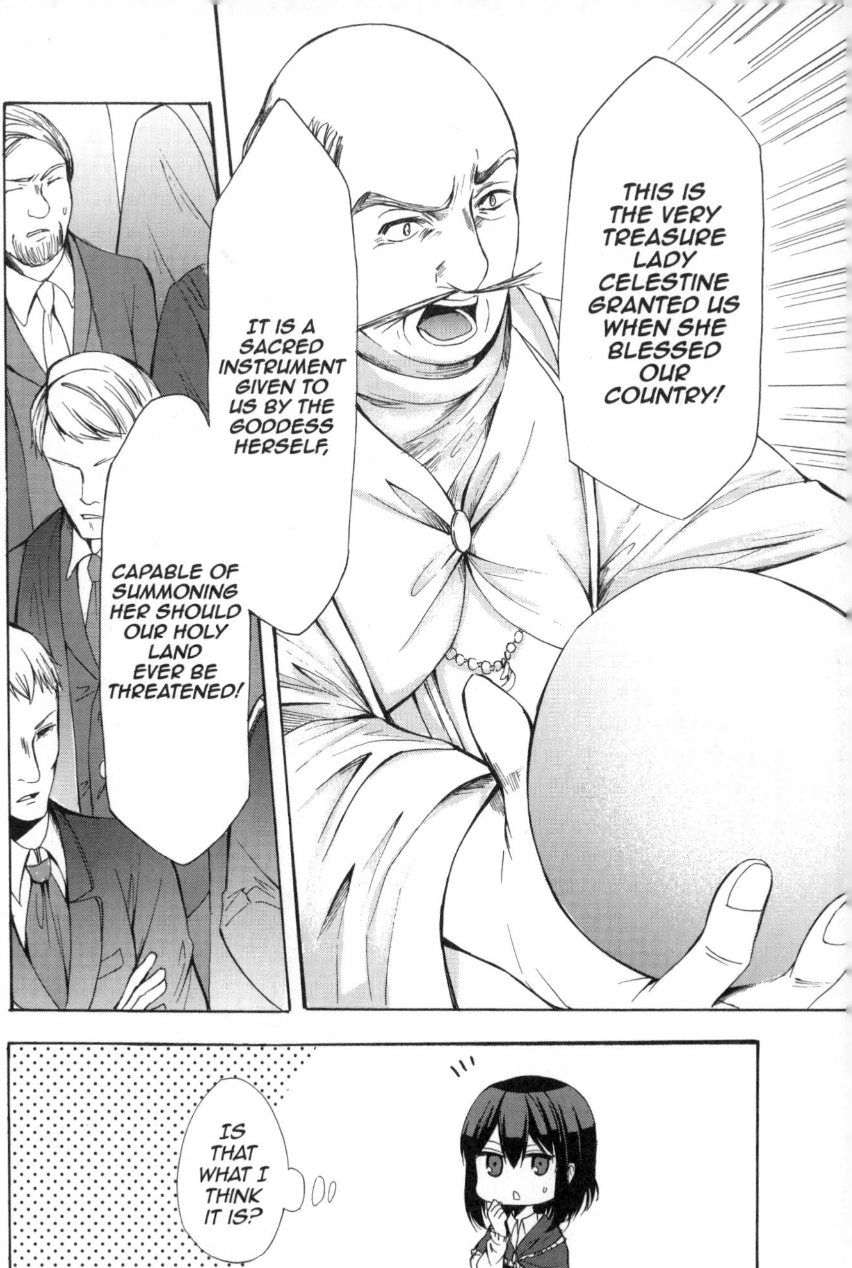
THIS IS THE VERY TREASURE LADY CELESTINE GRANTED US WHEN SHE BLESSED OUR COUNTRY!
IT IS A SACRED INSTRUMENT GIVEN TO US BY THE GODDESS HERSELF,
CAPABLE OF SUMMONING HER SHOULD OUR HOLY LAND EVER BE THREATENED!
IS THAT WHAT I THINK IT IS?

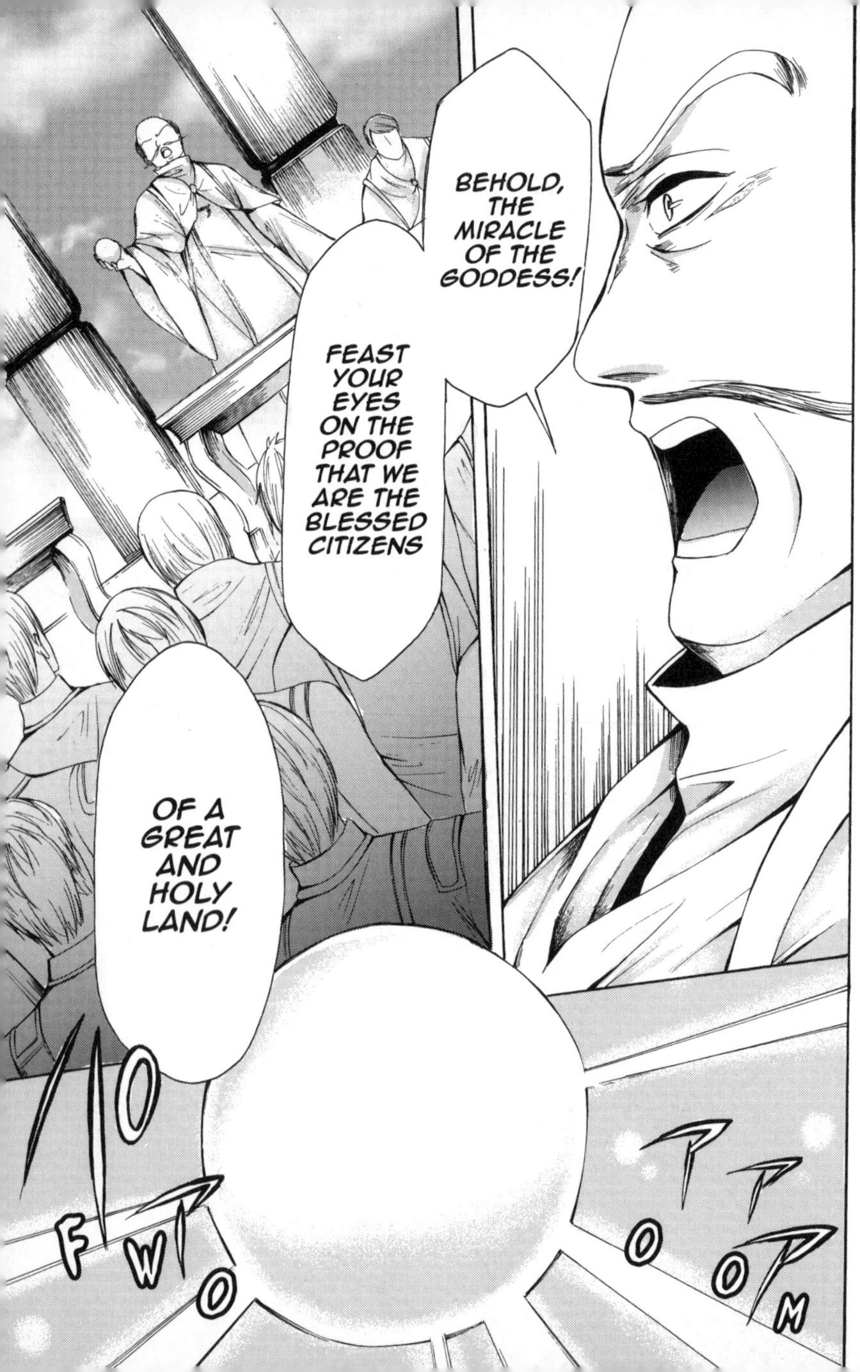
BEHOLD, THE MIRACLE OF THE GODDESS!
FEAST YOUR EYES ON THE PROOF THAT WE ARE THE BLESSED CITIZENS
OF A GREAT AND HOLY LAND!
FWO
OOM

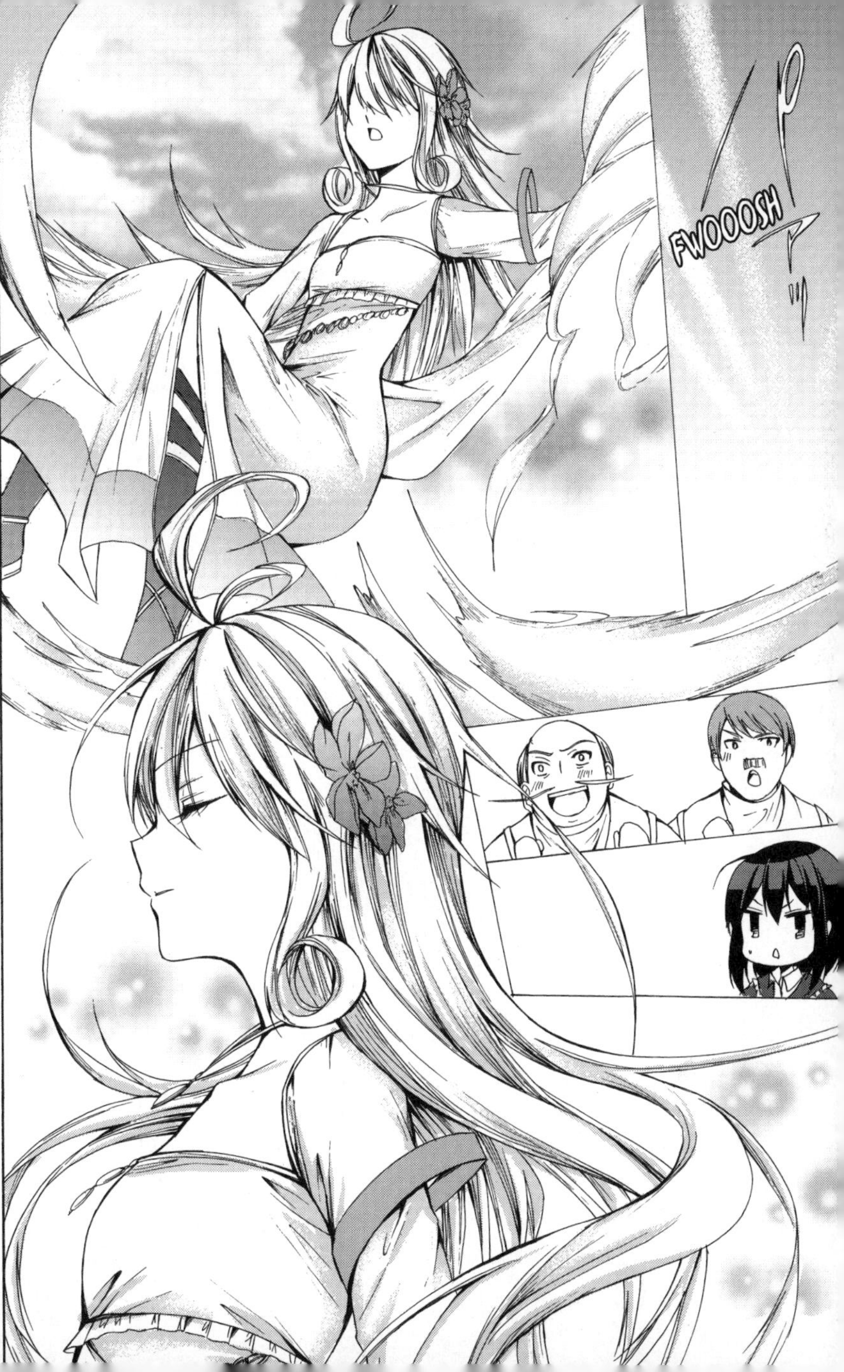
FWOOOSH

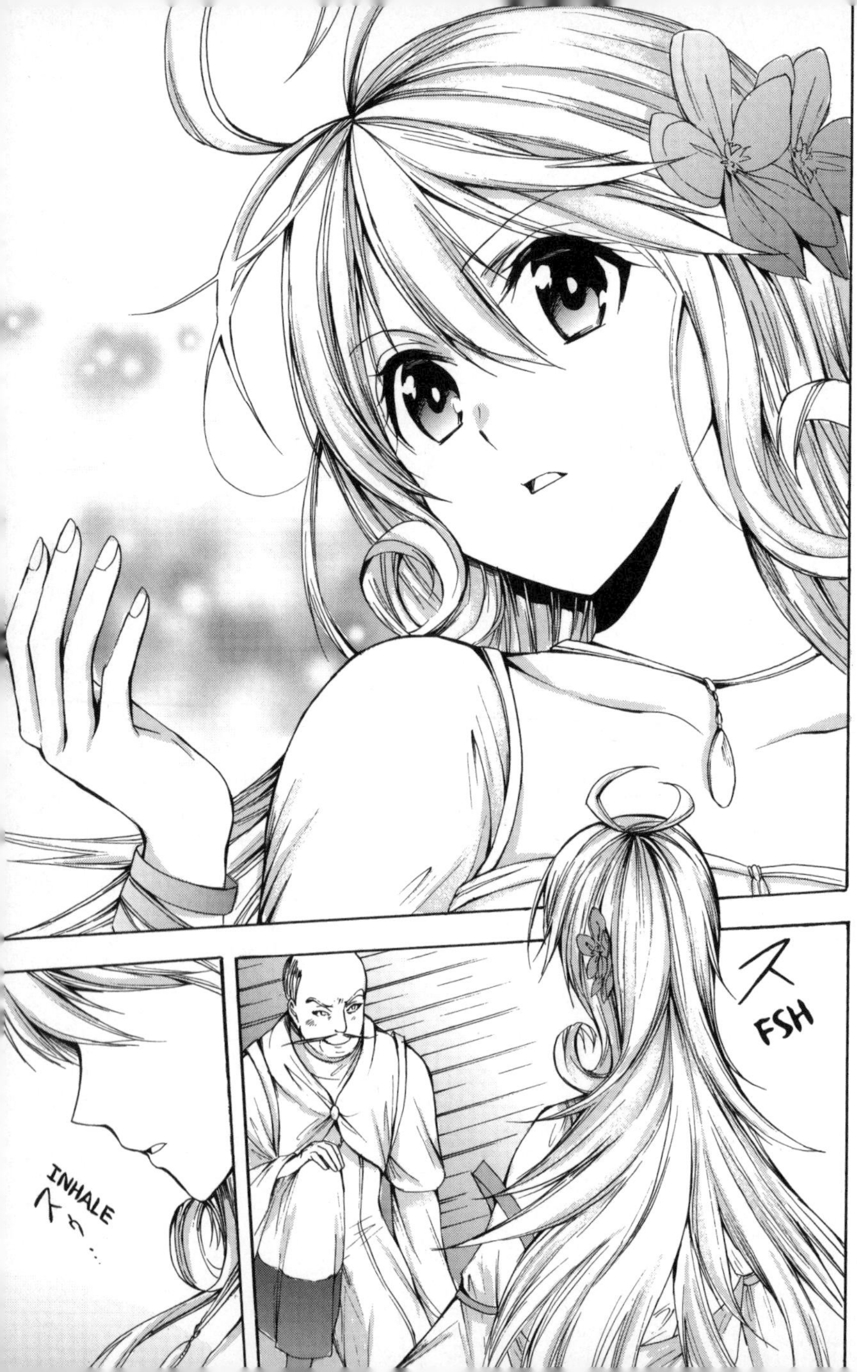
ス
FSH
INHALE

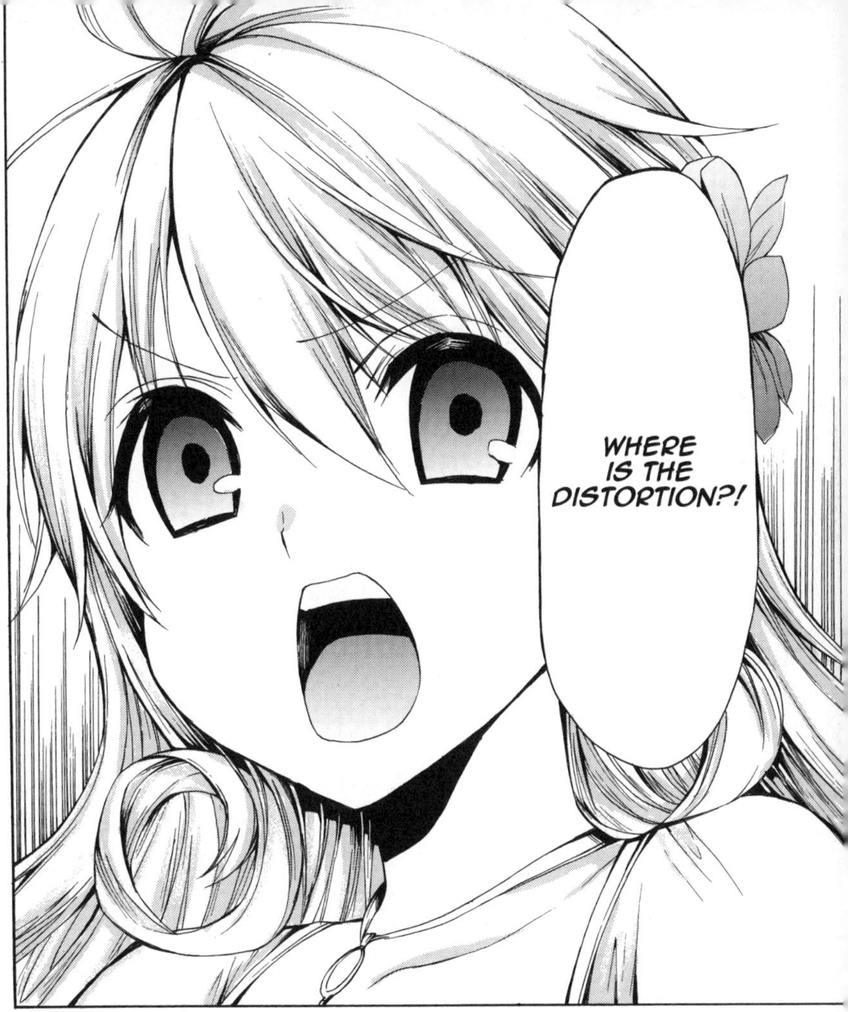
WHERE IS THE DISTORTION?!
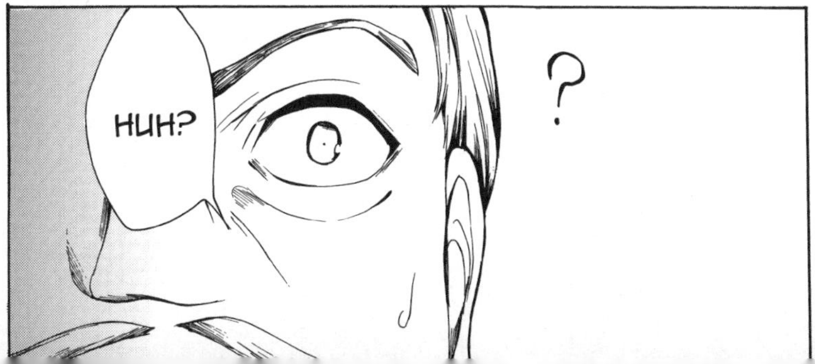
HUH?
?

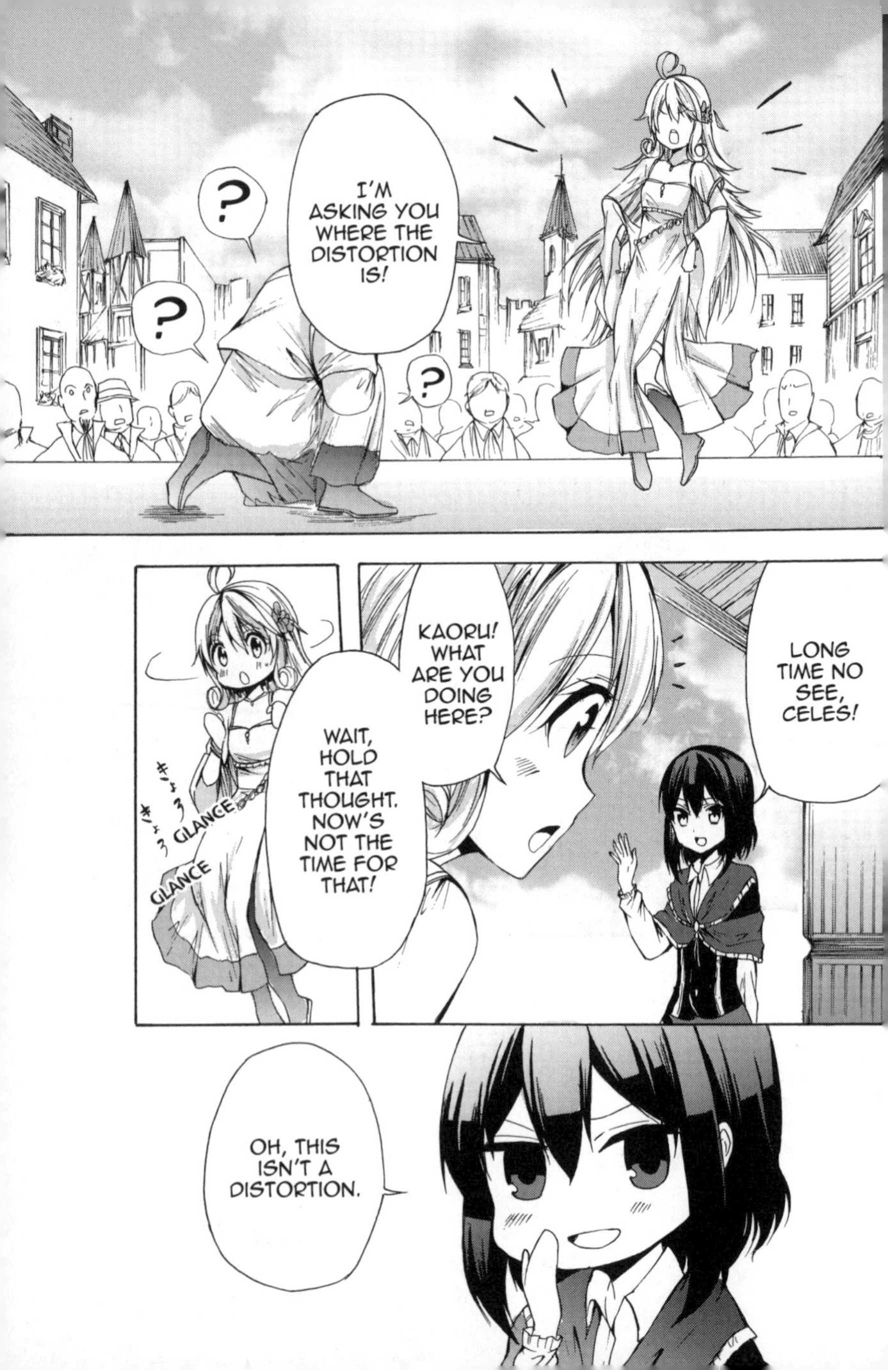
I'M ASKING YOU WHERE THE DISTORTION IS!
?
?
?
LONG TIME NO SEE, CELES!
KAORU! WHAT ARE YOU DOING HERE?
WAIT, HOLD THAT THOUGHT. NOW'S NOT THE TIME FOR THAT!
きょろきょろ
GLANCE
GLANCE
OH, THIS ISN'T A DISTORTION.

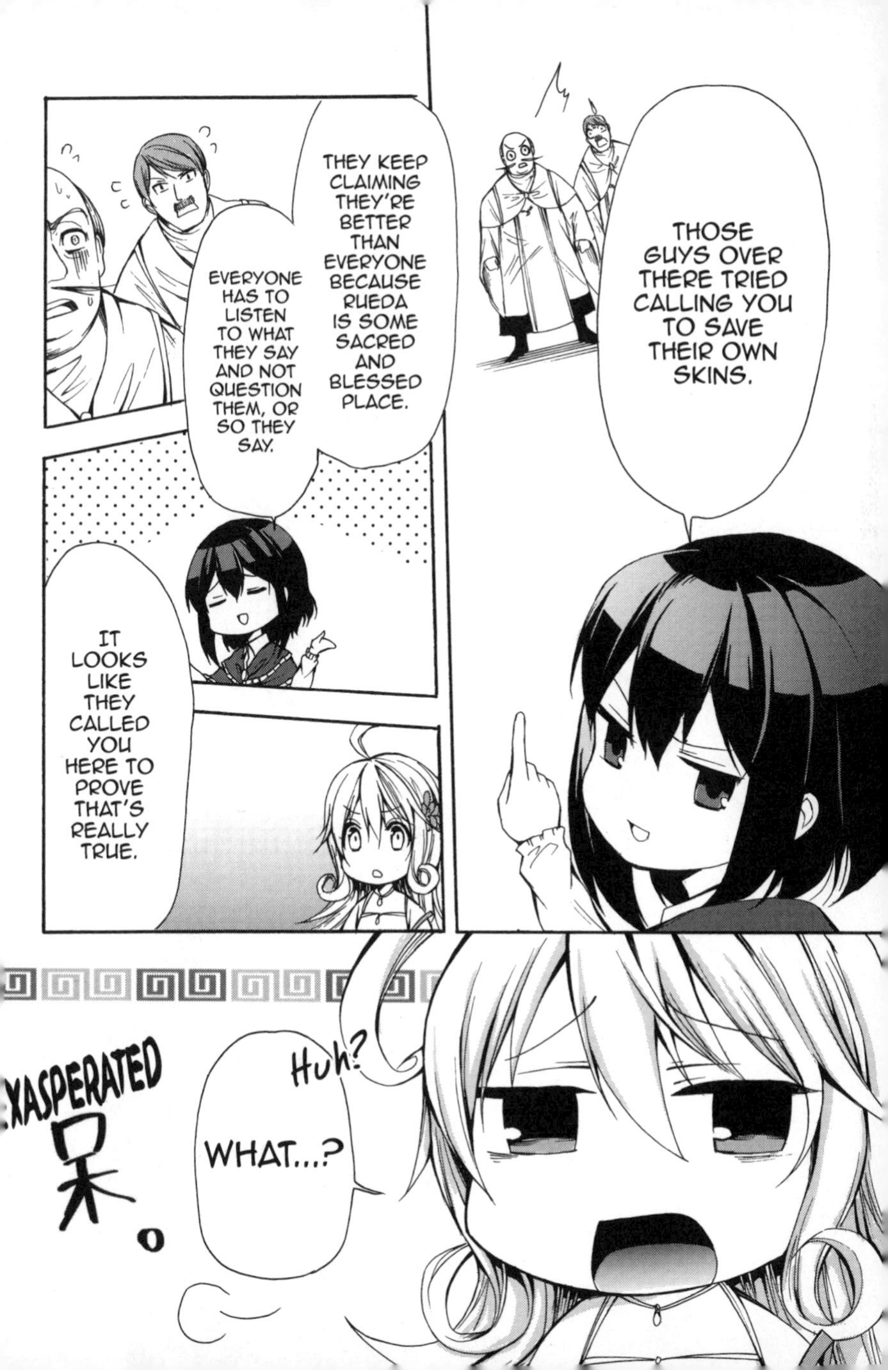
THOSE GUYS OVER THERE TRIED CALLING YOU TO SAVE THEIR OWN SKINS.
THEY KEEP CLAIMING THEY'RE BETTER THAN EVERYONE BECAUSE RUEDA IS SOME SACRED AND BLESSED PLACE.
EVERYONE HAS TO LISTEN TO WHAT THEY SAY AND NOT QUESTION THEM, OR SO THEY SAY.
IT LOOKS LIKE THEY CALLED YOU HERE TO PROVE THAT'S REALLY TRUE.
Huh?
WHAT...?
XASPERATED
呆。

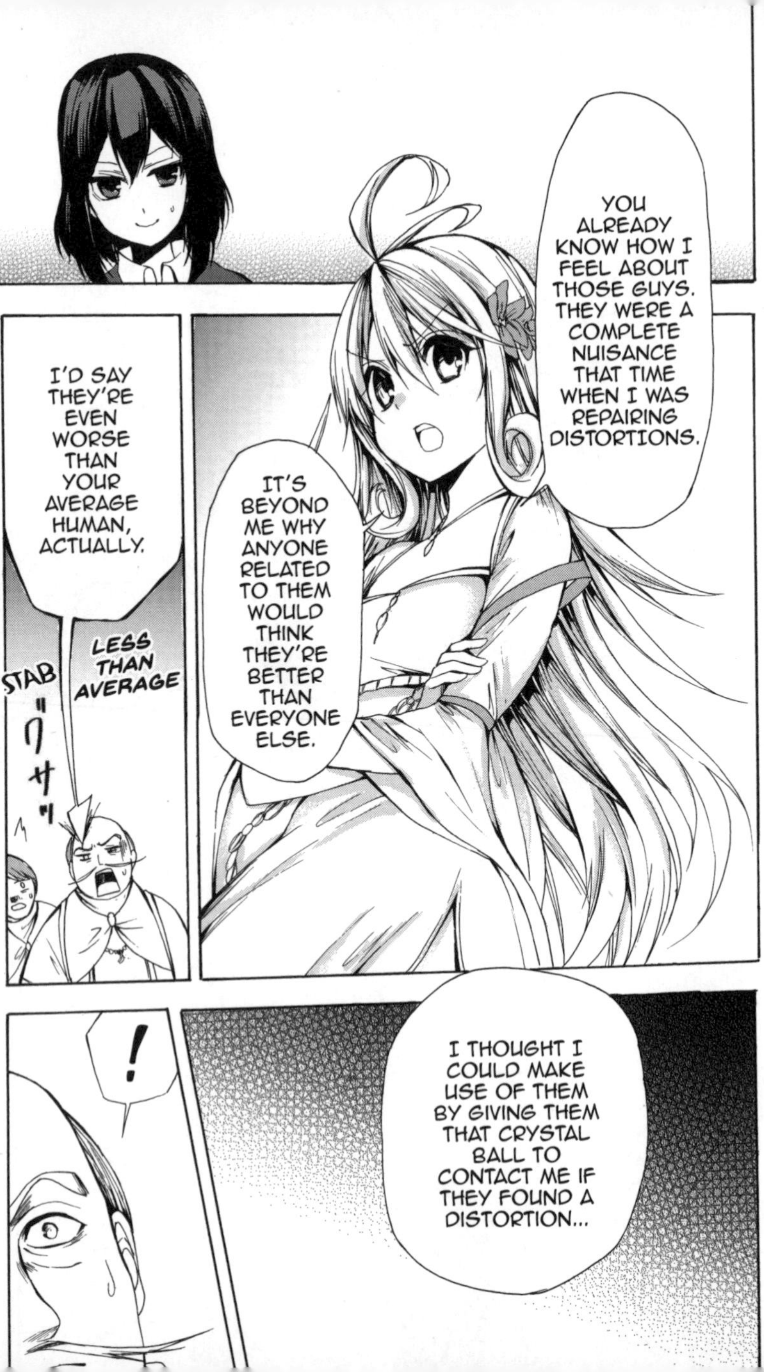
YOU ALREADY KNOW HOW I FEEL ABOUT THOSE GUYS. THEY WERE A COMPLETE NUISANCE THAT TIME WHEN I WAS REPAIRING DISTORTIONS.
IT'S BEYOND ME WHY ANYONE RELATED TO THEM WOULD THINK THEY'RE BETTER THAN EVERYONE ELSE.
I'D SAY THEY'RE EVEN WORSE THAN YOUR AVERAGE HUMAN, ACTUALLY.
LESS THAN AVERAGE
STAB
I THOUGHT I COULD MAKE USE OF THEM BY GIVING THEM THAT CRYSTAL BALL TO CONTACT ME IF THEY FOUND A DISTORTION...
!

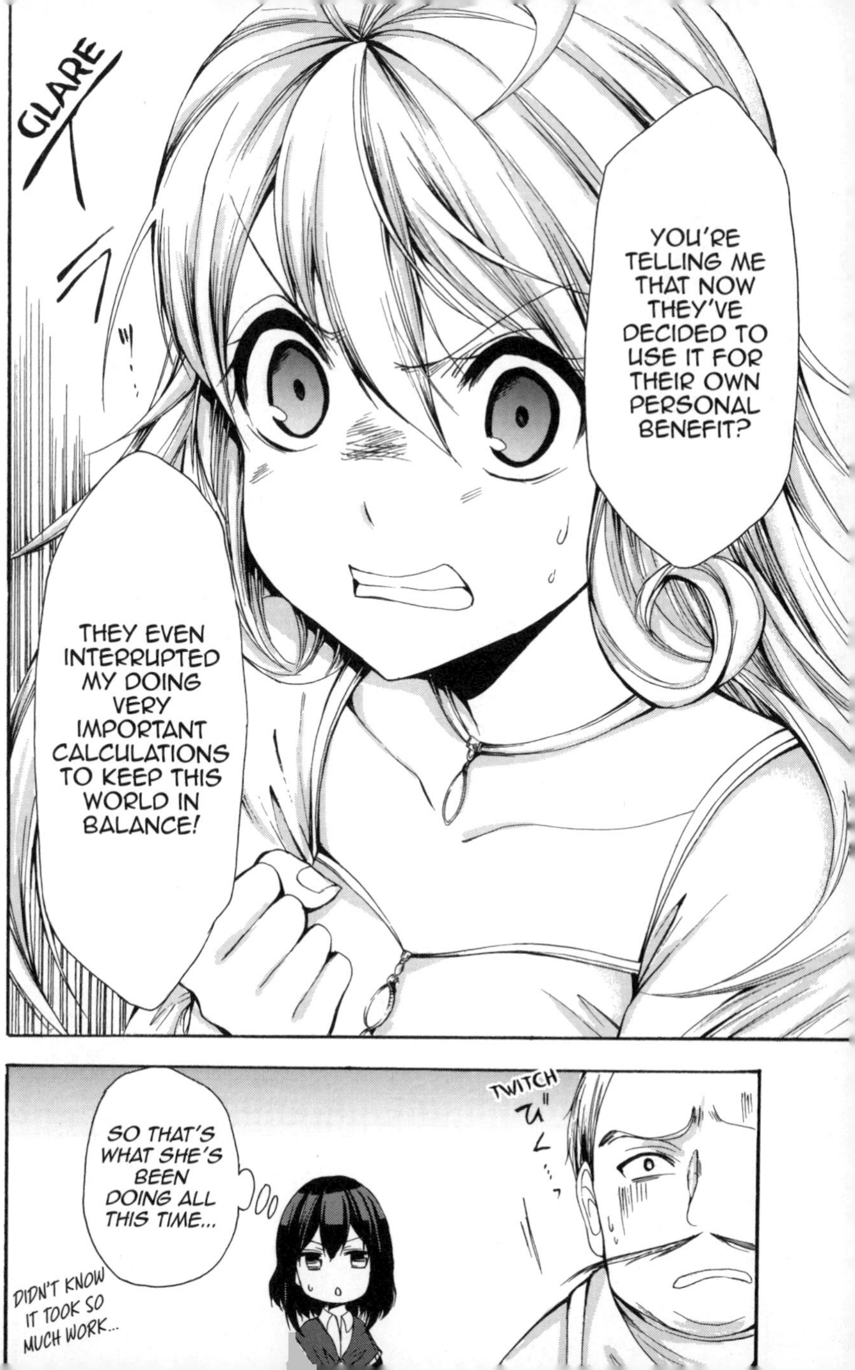
YOU'RE TELLING ME THAT NOW THEY'VE DECIDED TO USE IT FOR THEIR OWN PERSONAL BENEFIT?
GLARE
THEY EVEN INTERRUPTED MY DOING VERY IMPORTANT CALCULATIONS TO KEEP THIS WORLD IN BALANCE!
TWITCH
びく
SO THAT'S WHAT SHE'S BEEN DOING ALL THIS TIME...
DIDN'T KNOW IT TOOK SO MUCH WORK...

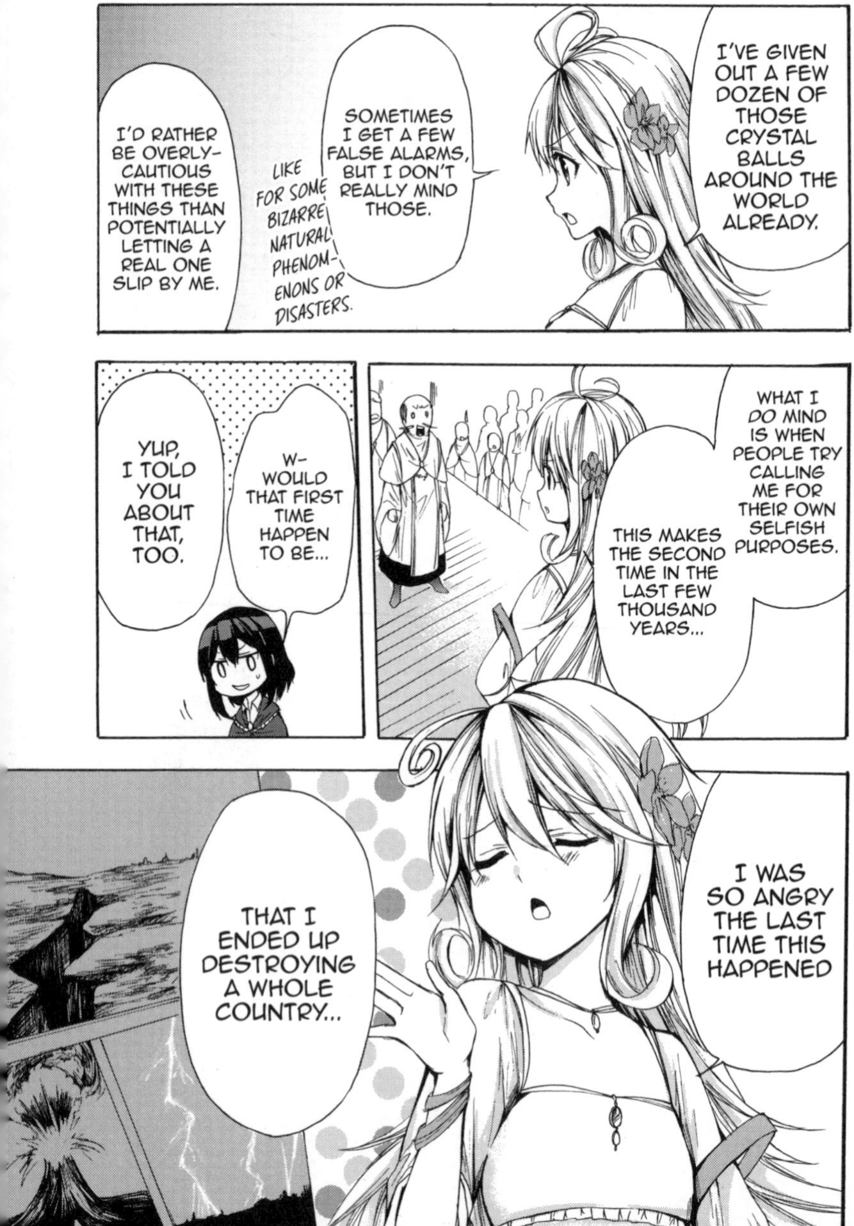
I'VE GIVEN OUT A FEW DOZEN OF THOSE CRYSTAL BALLS AROUND THE WORLD ALREADY.
SOMETIMES I GET A FEW FALSE ALARMS, BUT I DON'T REALLY MIND THOSE.
LIKE FOR SOME BIZARRE NATURAL PHENOM-ENONS OR DISASTERS.
I'D RATHER BE OVERLY-CAUTIOUS WITH THESE THINGS THAN POTENTIALLY LETTING A REAL ONE SLIP BY ME.
WHAT I *DO* MIND IS WHEN PEOPLE TRY CALLING ME FOR THEIR OWN SELFISH PURPOSES.
THIS MAKES THE SECOND TIME IN THE LAST FEW THOUSAND YEARS...
W-WOULD THAT FIRST TIME HAPPEN TO BE...
YUP, I TOLD YOU ABOUT THAT, TOO.
I WAS SO ANGRY THE LAST TIME THIS HAPPENED
THAT I ENDED UP DESTROYING A WHOLE COUNTRY...

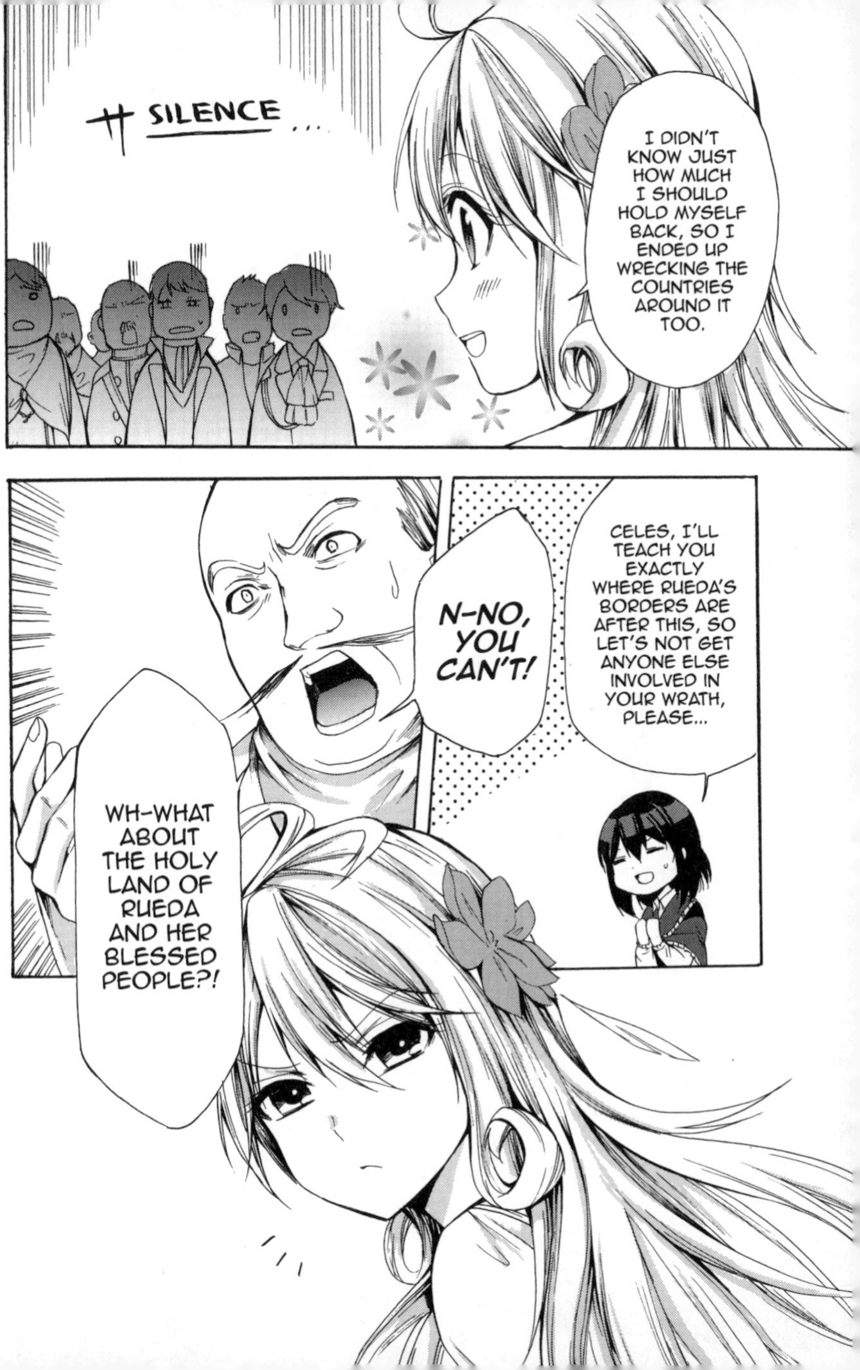
I DIDN'T KNOW JUST HOW MUCH I SHOULD HOLD MYSELF BACK, SO I ENDED UP WRECKING THE COUNTRIES AROUND IT TOO.
SILENCE...
CELES, I'LL TEACH YOU EXACTLY WHERE RUEDA'S BORDERS ARE AFTER THIS, SO LET'S NOT GET ANYONE ELSE INVOLVED IN YOUR WRATH, PLEASE...
N-NO, YOU CAN'T!
WH-WHAT ABOUT THE HOLY LAND OF RUEDA AND HER BLESSED PEOPLE?!

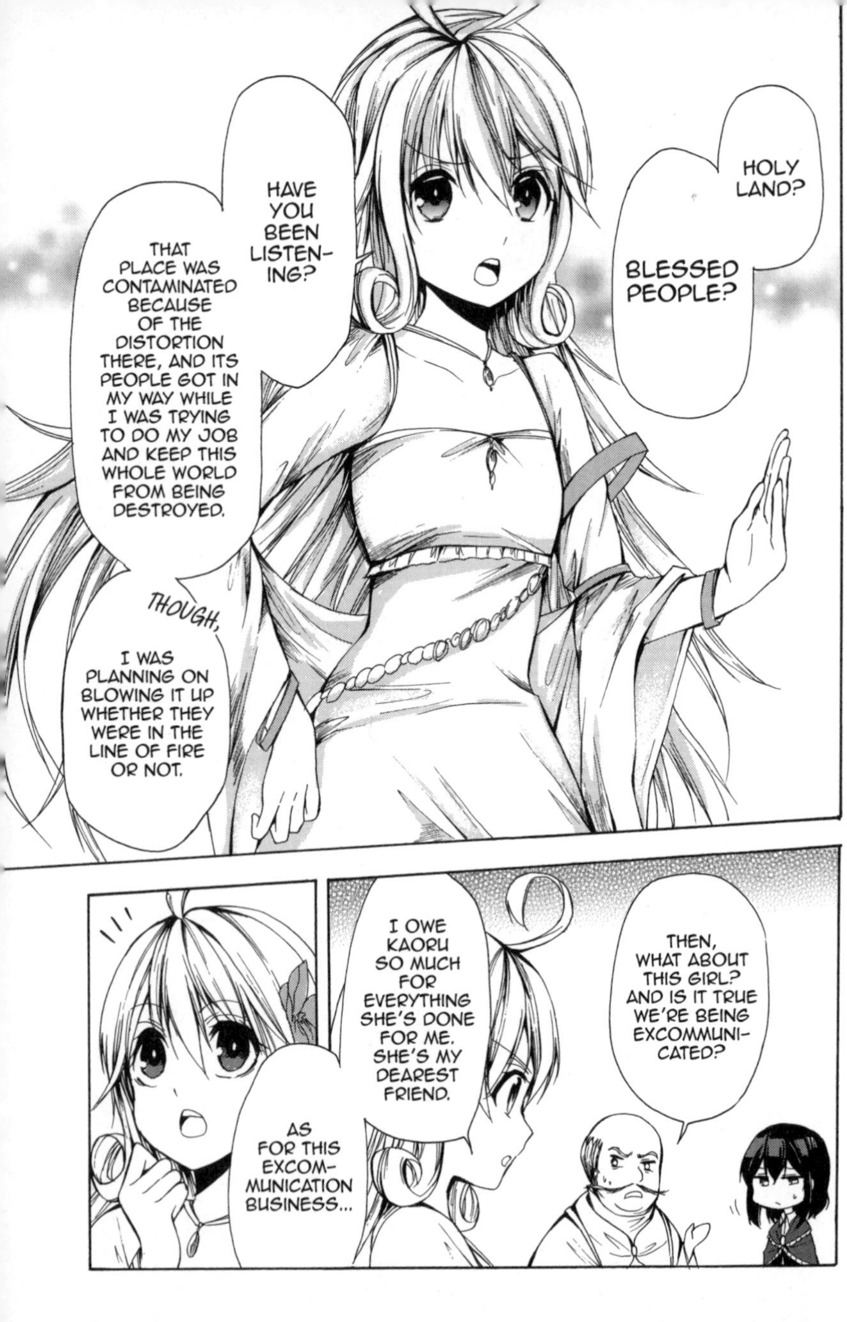
HOLY LAND?
BLESSED PEOPLE?
HAVE YOU BEEN LISTENING?
THAT PLACE WAS CONTAMINATED BECAUSE OF THE DISTORTION THERE, AND ITS PEOPLE GOT IN MY WAY WHILE I WAS TRYING TO DO MY JOB AND KEEP THIS WHOLE WORLD FROM BEING DESTROYED.
THOUGH,
I WAS PLANNING ON BLOWING IT UP WHETHER THEY WERE IN THE LINE OF FIRE OR NOT.
THEN, WHAT ABOUT THIS GIRL? AND IS IT TRUE WE'RE BEING EXCOMMUNICATED?
I OWE KAORU SO MUCH FOR EVERYTHING SHE'S DONE FOR ME. SHE'S MY DEAREST FRIEND.
AS FOR THIS EXCOMMUNICATION BUSINESS...

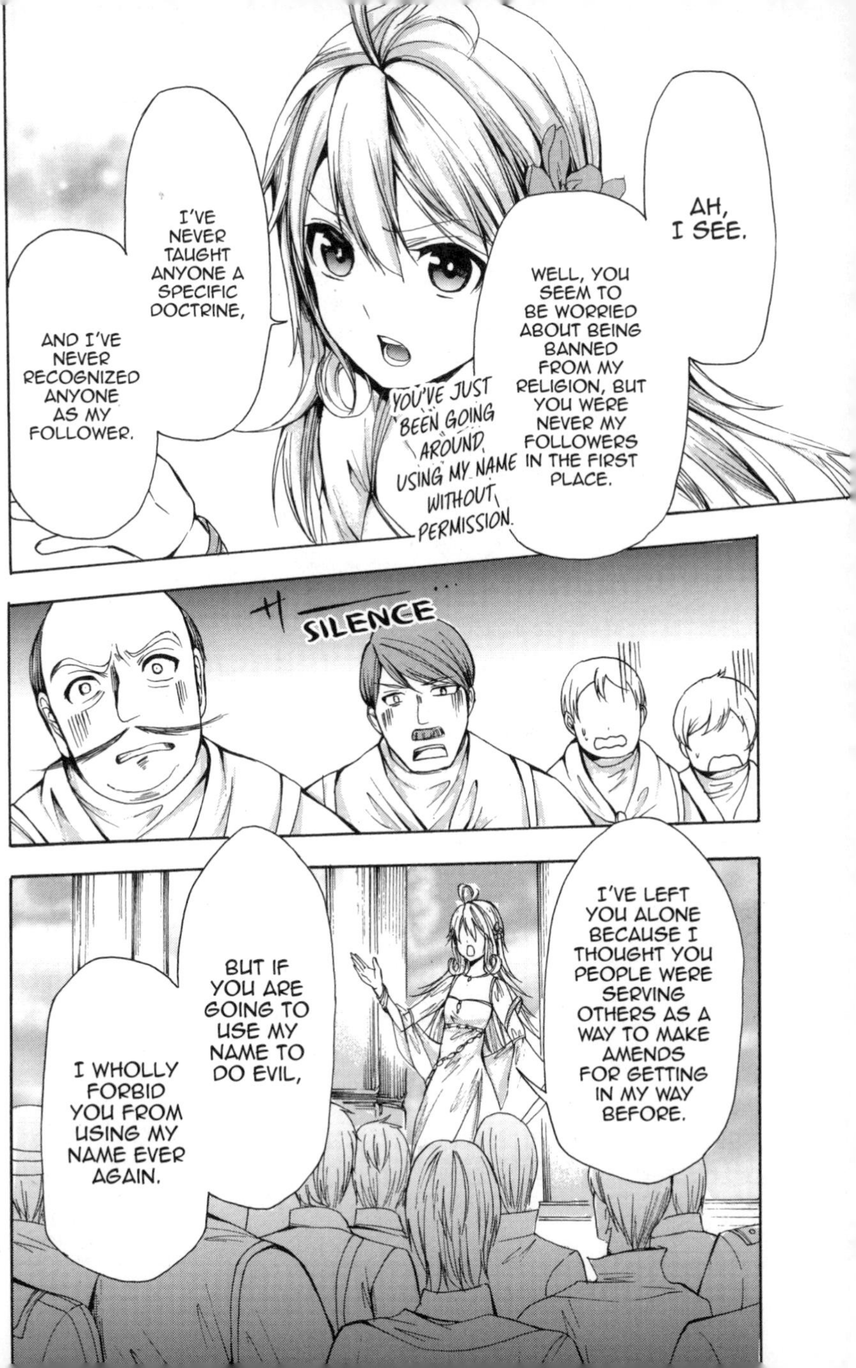
AH, I SEE.
WELL, YOU SEEM TO BE WORRIED ABOUT BEING BANNED FROM MY RELIGION, BUT YOU WERE NEVER MY FOLLOWERS IN THE FIRST PLACE.
YOU'VE JUST BEEN GOING AROUND USING MY NAME WITHOUT PERMISSION.
I'VE NEVER TAUGHT ANYONE A SPECIFIC DOCTRINE,
AND I'VE NEVER RECOGNIZED ANYONE AS MY FOLLOWER.
SILENCE
I'VE LEFT YOU ALONE BECAUSE I THOUGHT YOU PEOPLE WERE SERVING OTHERS AS A WAY TO MAKE AMENDS FOR GETTING IN MY WAY BEFORE.
BUT IF YOU ARE GOING TO USE MY NAME TO DO EVIL,
I WHOLLY FORBID YOU FROM USING MY NAME EVER AGAIN.

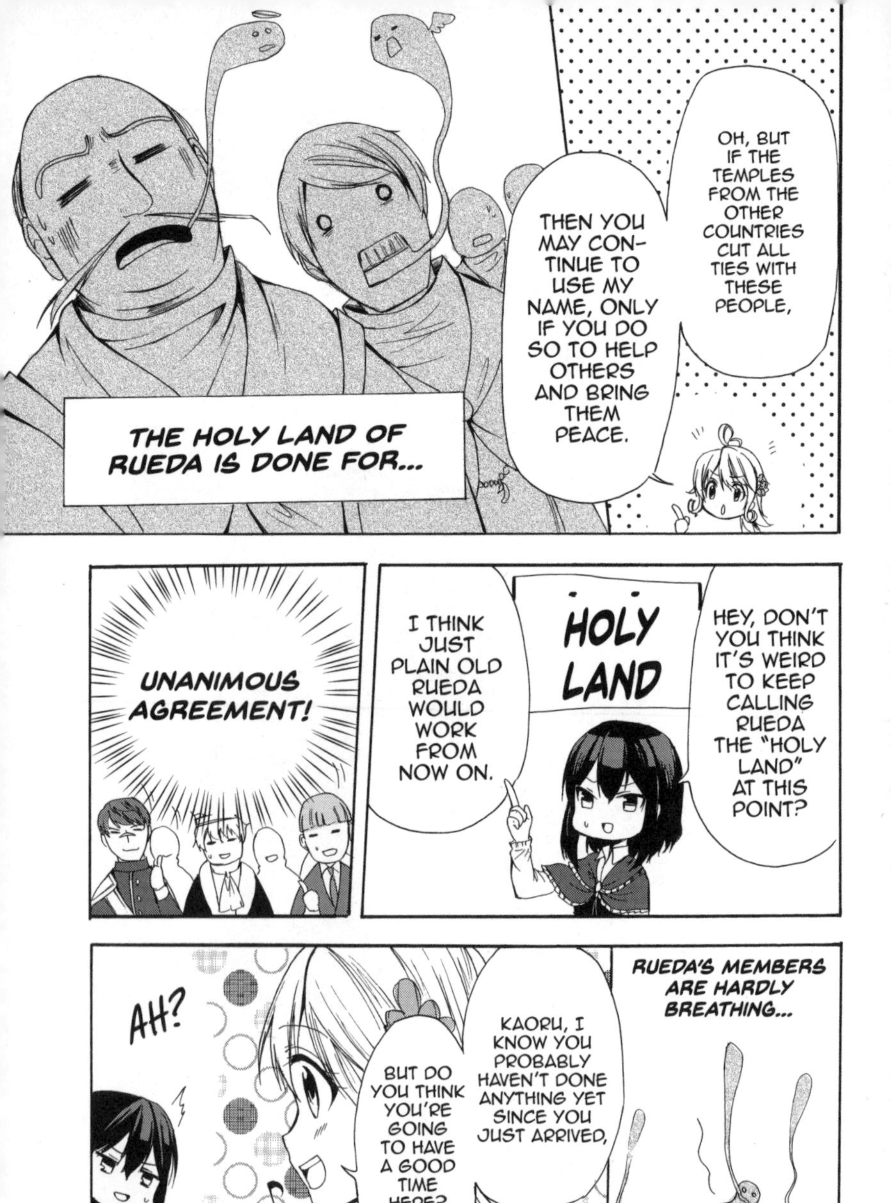
OH, BUT IF THE TEMPLES FROM THE OTHER COUNTRIES CUT ALL TIES WITH THESE PEOPLE,
THEN YOU MAY CONTINUE TO USE MY NAME, ONLY IF YOU DO SO TO HELP OTHERS AND BRING THEM PEACE.
THE HOLY LAND OF RUEDA IS DONE FOR...
HEY, DON'T YOU THINK IT'S WEIRD TO KEEP CALLING RUEDA THE "HOLY LAND" AT THIS POINT?
HOLY LAND
I THINK JUST PLAIN OLD RUEDA WOULD WORK FROM NOW ON.
UNANIMOUS AGREEMENT!
RUEDA'S MEMBERS ARE HARDLY BREATHING...
KAORU, I KNOW YOU PROBABLY HAVEN'T DONE ANYTHING YET SINCE YOU JUST ARRIVED,
BUT DO YOU THINK YOU'RE GOING TO HAVE A GOOD TIME HERE?
AH?

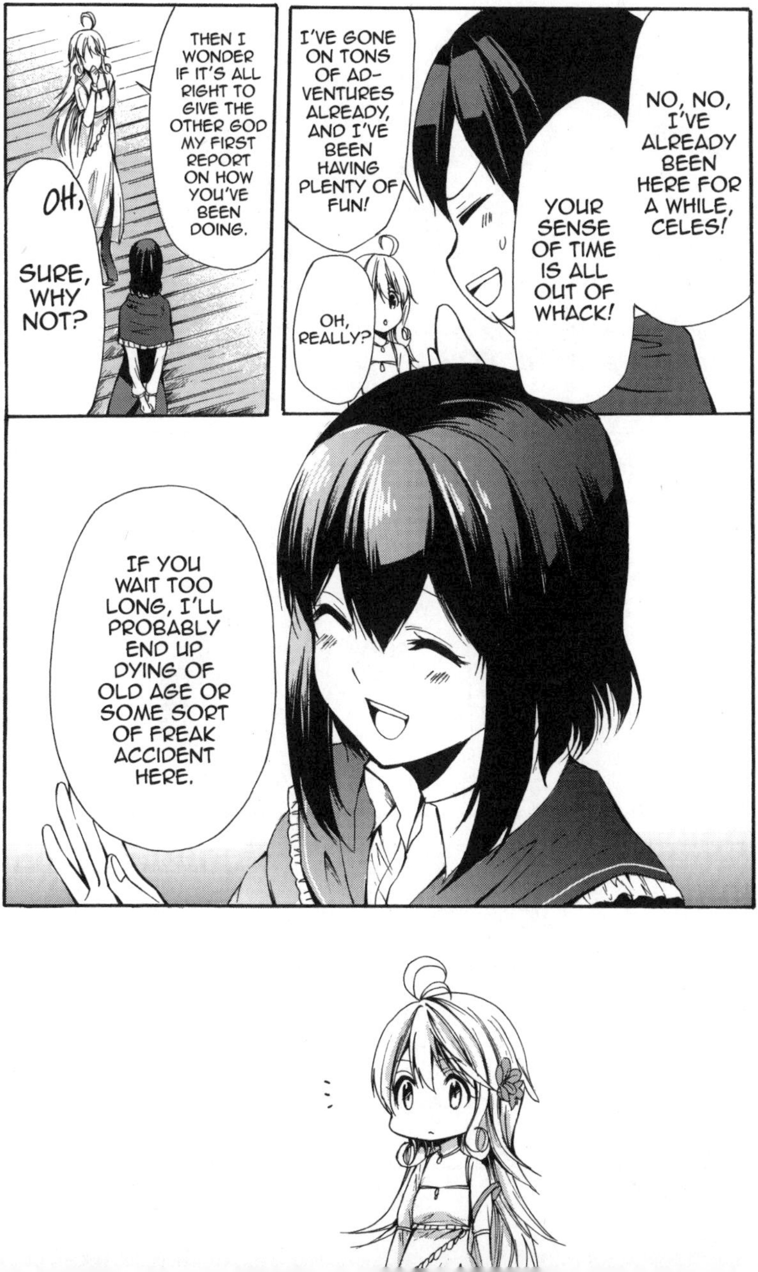
NO, NO, I'VE ALREADY BEEN HERE FOR A WHILE, CELES!
YOUR SENSE OF TIME IS ALL OUT OF WHACK!
I'VE GONE ON TONS OF AD-VENTURES ALREADY, AND I'VE BEEN HAVING PLENTY OF FUN!
OH, REALLY?
THEN I WONDER IF IT'S ALL RIGHT TO GIVE THE OTHER GOD MY FIRST REPORT ON HOW YOU'VE BEEN DOING.
OH,
SURE, WHY NOT?
IF YOU WAIT TOO LONG, I'LL PROBABLY END UP DYING OF OLD AGE OR SOME SORT OF FREAK ACCIDENT HERE.

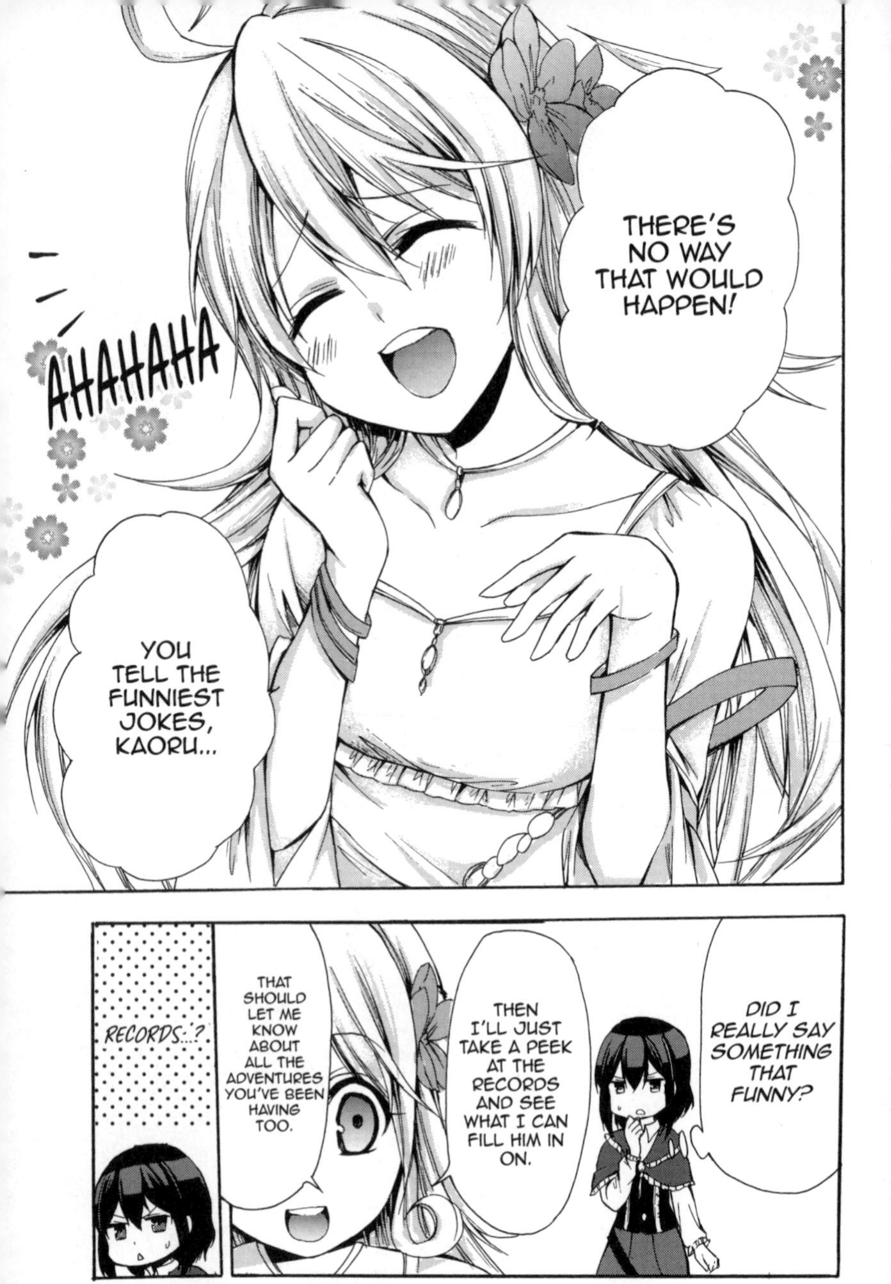
THERE'S NO WAY THAT WOULD HAPPEN!
AHAHAHA
YOU TELL THE FUNNIEST JOKES, KAORU...
DID I REALLY SAY SOMETHING THAT FUNNY?
THEN I'LL JUST TAKE A PEEK AT THE RECORDS AND SEE WHAT I CAN FILL HIM IN ON.
THAT SHOULD LET ME KNOW ABOUT ALL THE ADVENTURES YOU'VE BEEN HAVING TOO.
RECORDS...?

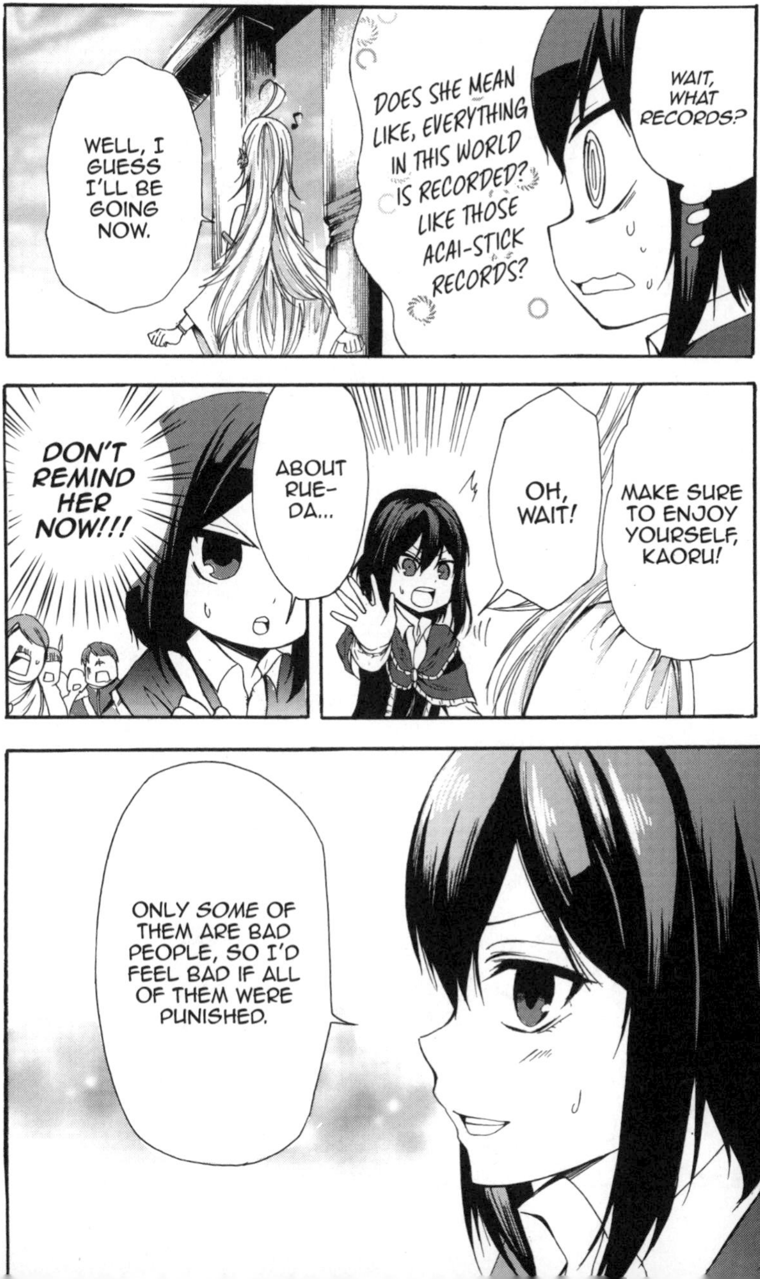
WAIT, WHAT RECORDS?
DOES SHE MEAN LIKE, EVERYTHING IN THIS WORLD IS RECORDED? LIKE THOSE ACAI-STICK RECORDS?
WELL, I GUESS I'LL BE GOING NOW.
MAKE SURE TO ENJOY YOURSELF, KAORU!
OH, WAIT!
ABOUT RUE-DA...
DON'T REMIND HER NOW!!!
ONLY *SOME* OF THEM ARE BAD PEOPLE, SO I'D FEEL BAD IF ALL OF THEM WERE PUNISHED.

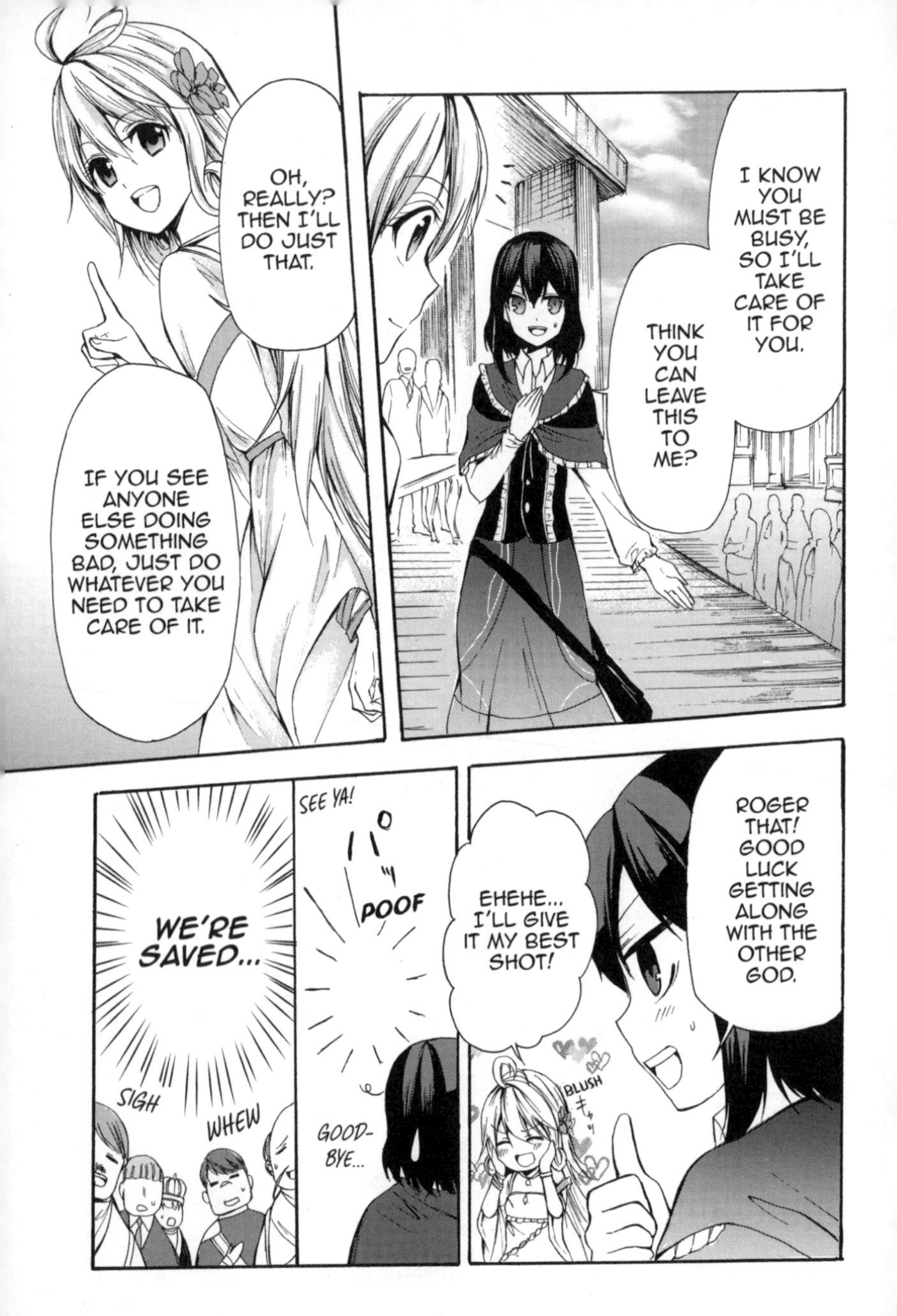
I KNOW YOU MUST BE BUSY, SO I'LL TAKE CARE OF IT FOR YOU.
THINK YOU CAN LEAVE THIS TO ME?
OH, REALLY? THEN I'LL DO JUST THAT.
IF YOU SEE ANYONE ELSE DOING SOMETHING BAD, JUST DO WHATEVER YOU NEED TO TAKE CARE OF IT.
ROGER THAT! GOOD LUCK GETTING ALONG WITH THE OTHER GOD.
EHEHE... I'LL GIVE IT MY BEST SHOT!
BLUSH
SEE YA!
POOF
GOOD-BYE...
WE'RE SAVED...
SIGH
WHEW

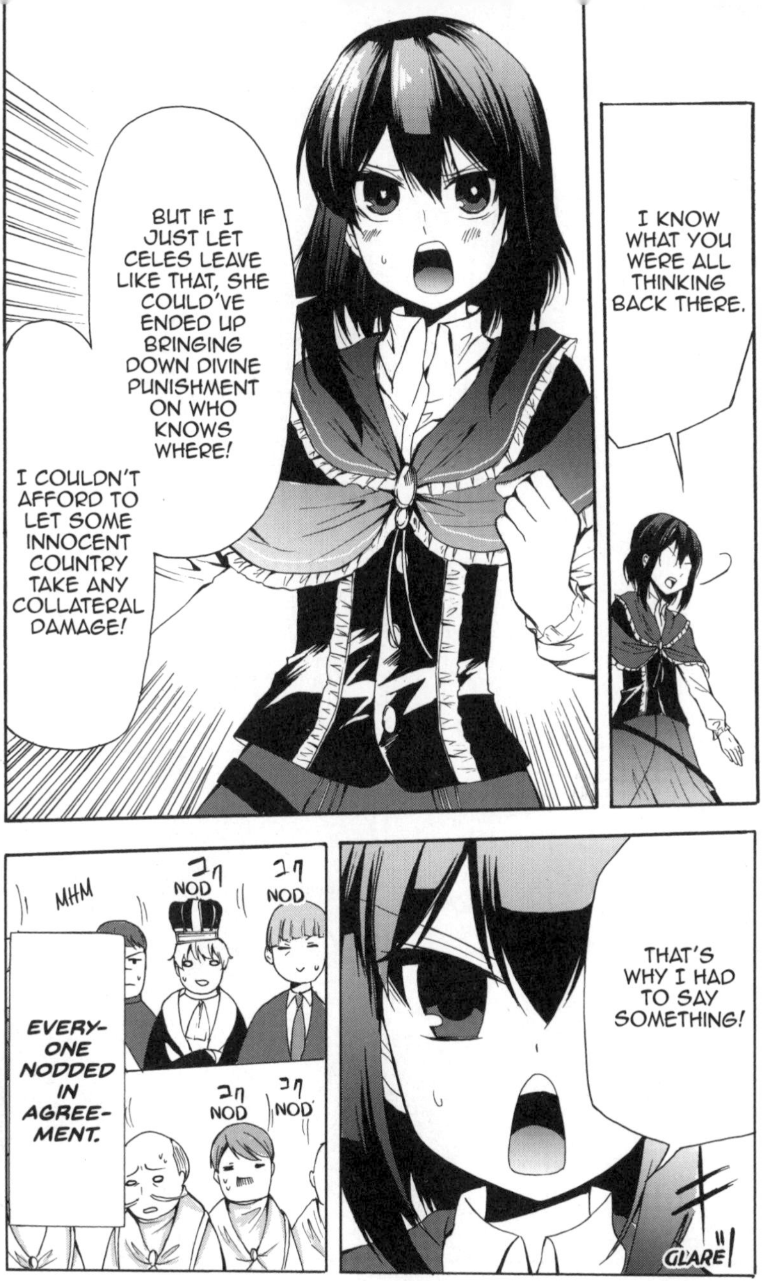
I KNOW WHAT YOU WERE ALL THINKING BACK THERE.
BUT IF I JUST LET CELES LEAVE LIKE THAT, SHE COULD'VE ENDED UP BRINGING DOWN DIVINE PUNISHMENT ON WHO KNOWS WHERE!
I COULDN'T AFFORD TO LET SOME INNOCENT COUNTRY TAKE ANY COLLATERAL DAMAGE!
THAT'S WHY I HAD TO SAY SOMETHING!
GLARE
コク NOD
コク NOD
MHM
EVERY-ONE NODDED IN AGREE-MENT.
コク NOD
コク NOD

24 CHAPTER END

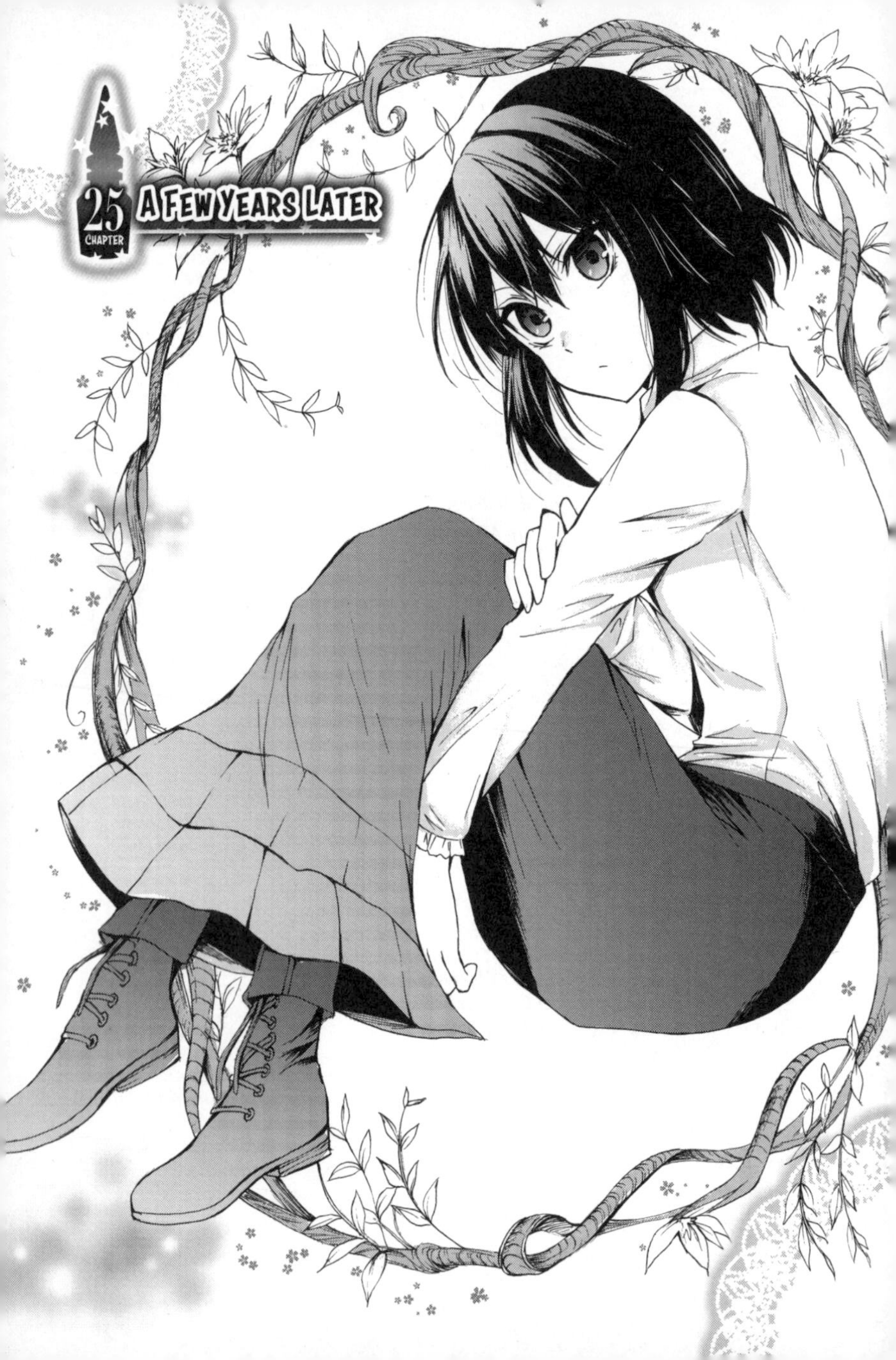
25 CHAPTER
A Few Years Later

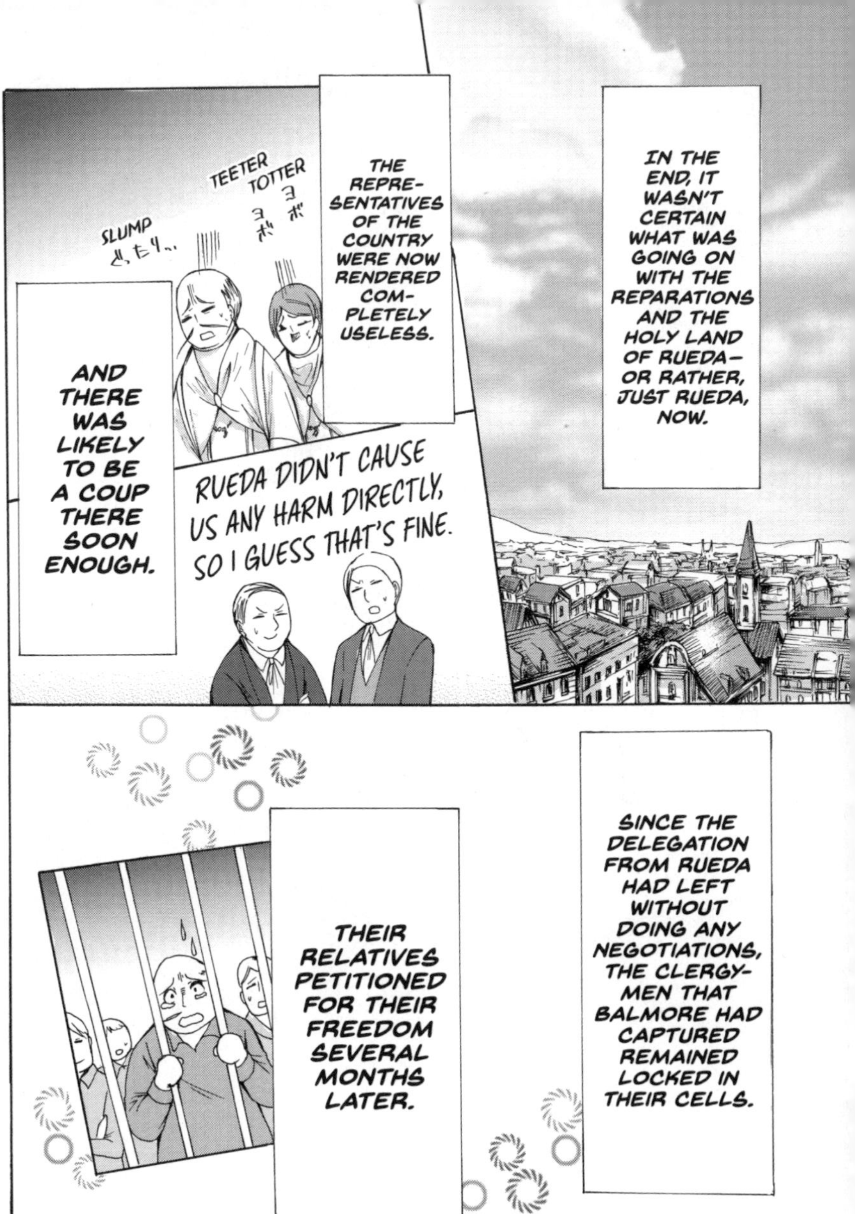
IN THE END, IT WASN'T CERTAIN WHAT WAS GOING ON WITH THE REPARATIONS AND THE HOLY LAND OF RUEDA—OR RATHER, JUST RUEDA, NOW.
THE REPRE-SENTATIVES OF THE COUNTRY WERE NOW RENDERED COM-PLETELY USELESS.
TEETER TOTTER
SLUMP
RUEDA DIDN'T CAUSE US ANY HARM DIRECTLY, SO I GUESS THAT'S FINE.
AND THERE WAS LIKELY TO BE A COUP THERE SOON ENOUGH.
SINCE THE DELEGATION FROM RUEDA HAD LEFT WITHOUT DOING ANY NEGOTIATIONS, THE CLERGY-MEN THAT BALMORE HAD CAPTURED REMAINED LOCKED IN THEIR CELLS.
THEIR RELATIVES PETITIONED FOR THEIR FREEDOM SEVERAL MONTHS LATER.

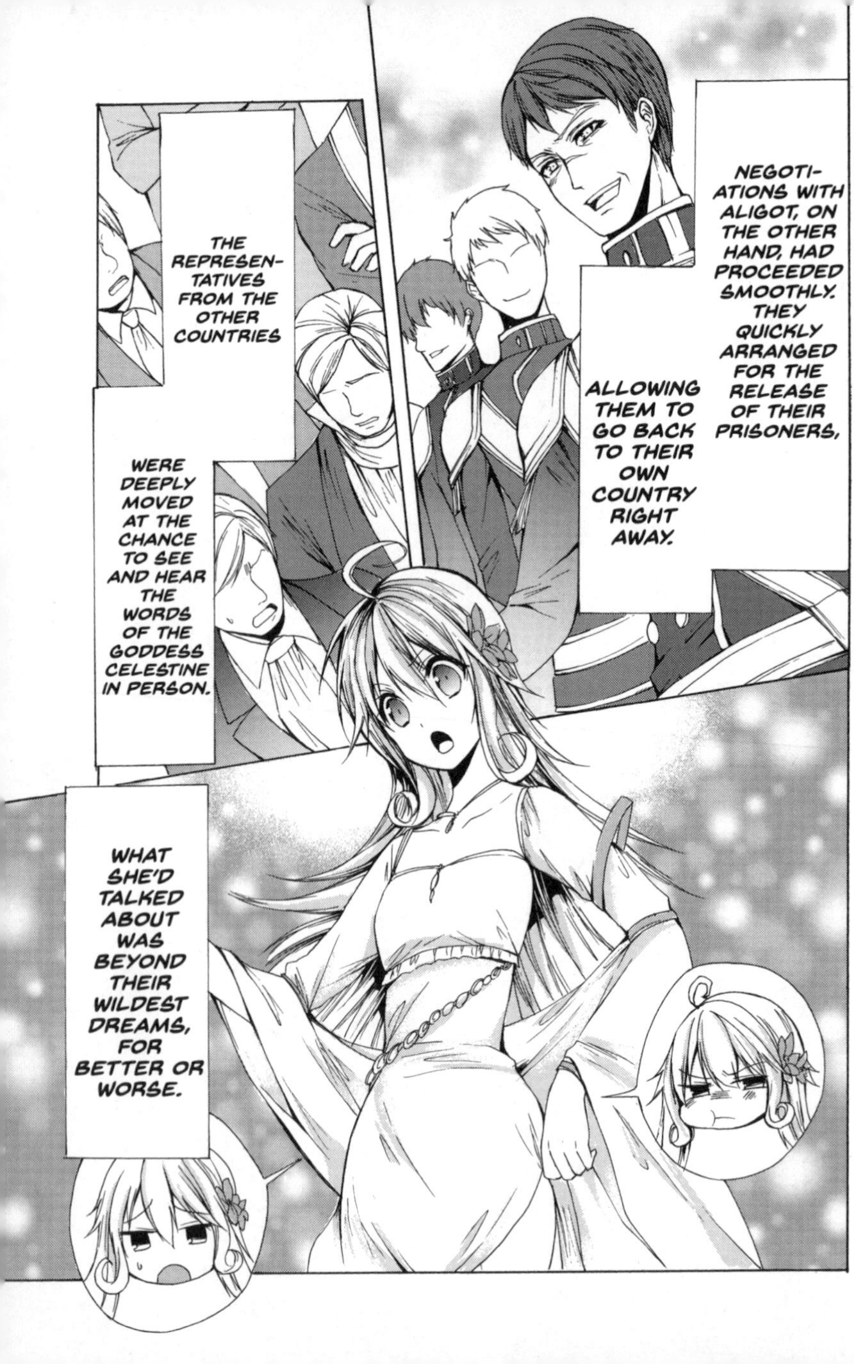
NEGOTI-ATIONS WITH ALIGOT, ON THE OTHER HAND, HAD PROCEEDED SMOOTHLY. THEY QUICKLY ARRANGED FOR THE RELEASE OF THEIR PRISONERS,
ALLOWING THEM TO GO BACK TO THEIR OWN COUNTRY RIGHT AWAY.
THE REPRESEN-TATIVES FROM THE OTHER COUNTRIES
WERE DEEPLY MOVED AT THE CHANCE TO SEE AND HEAR THE WORDS OF THE GODDESS CELESTINE IN PERSON.
WHAT SHE'D TALKED ABOUT WAS BEYOND THEIR WILDEST DREAMS, FOR BETTER OR WORSE.

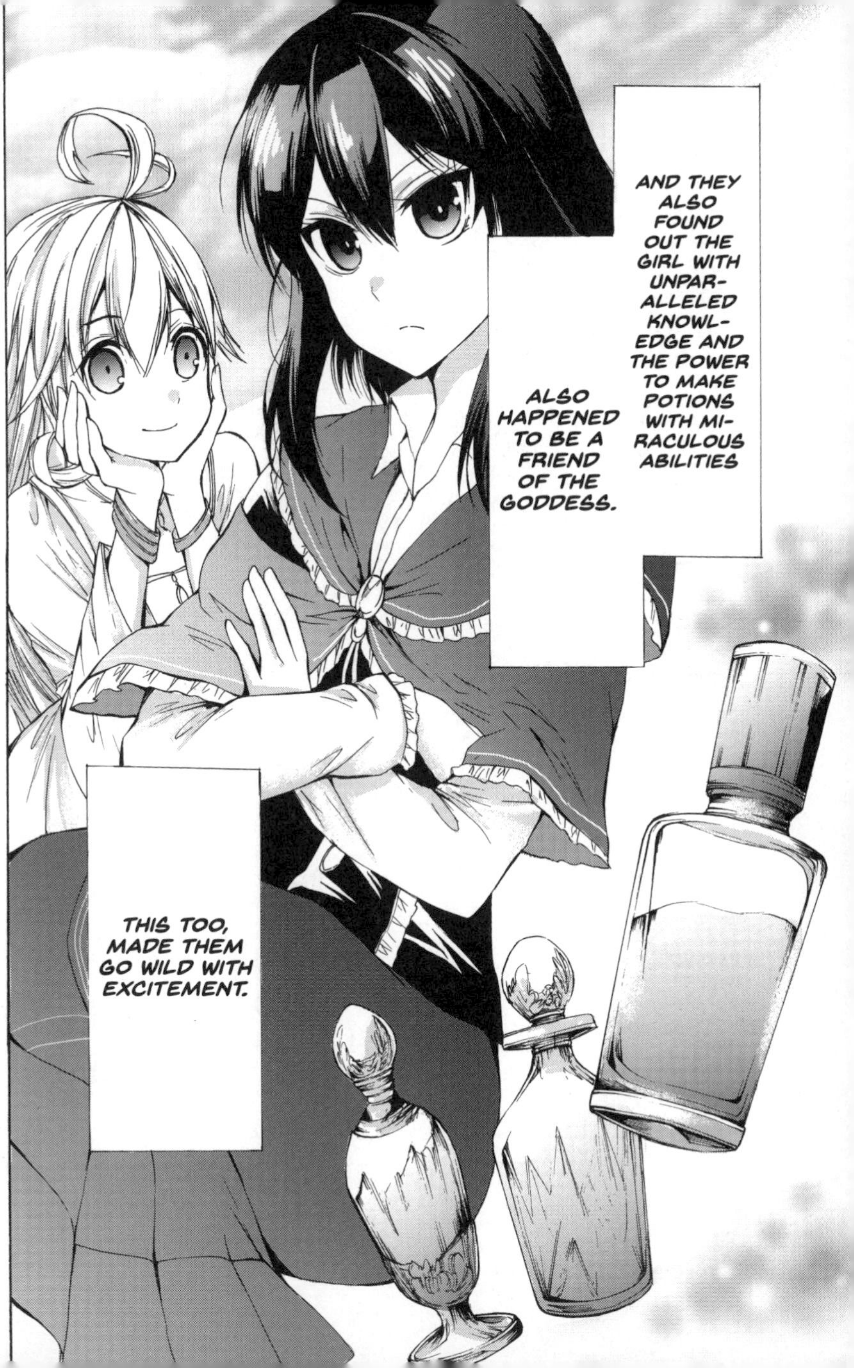
AND THEY ALSO FOUND OUT THE GIRL WITH UNPAR-ALLELED KNOWL-EDGE AND THE POWER TO MAKE POTIONS WITH MI-RACULOUS ABILITIES
ALSO HAPPENED TO BE A FRIEND OF THE GODDESS.
THIS TOO, MADE THEM GO WILD WITH EXCITEMENT.

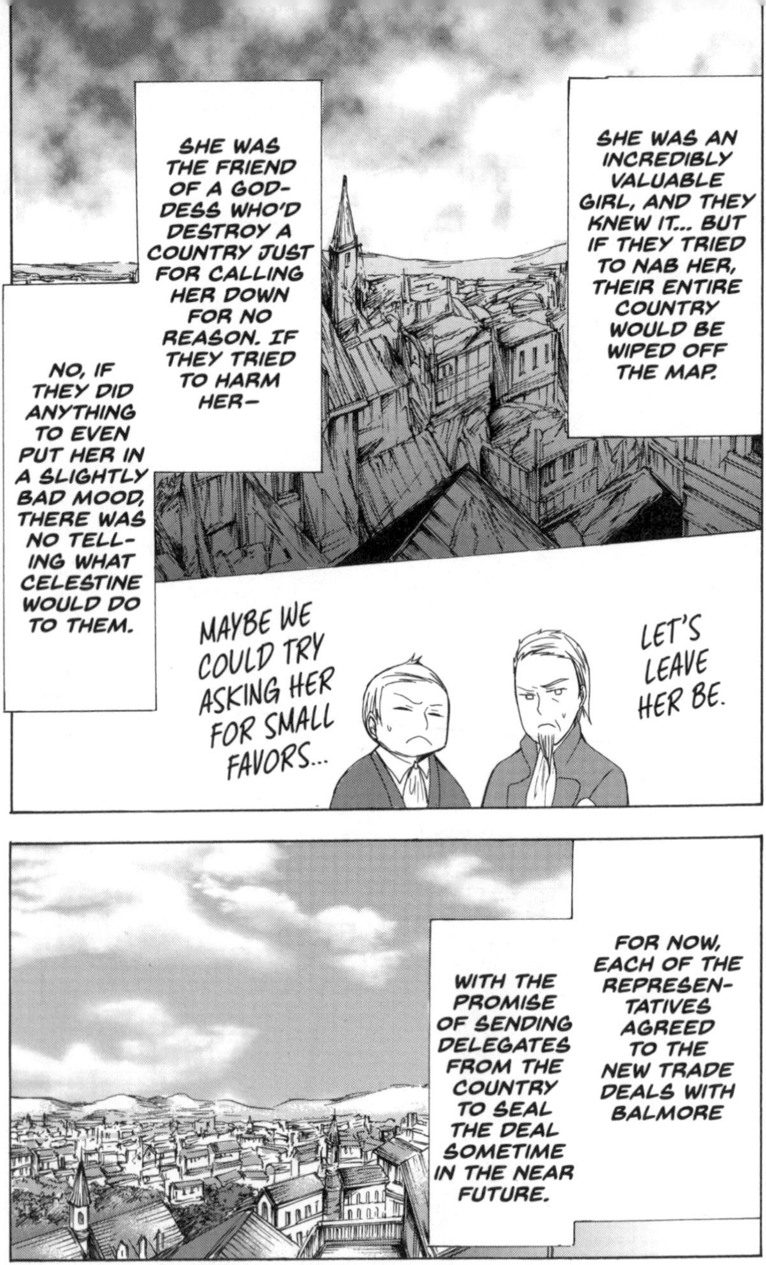
SHE WAS AN INCREDIBLY VALUABLE GIRL, AND THEY KNEW IT... BUT IF THEY TRIED TO NAB HER, THEIR ENTIRE COUNTRY WOULD BE WIPED OFF THE MAP.
SHE WAS THE FRIEND OF A GOD-DESS WHO'D DESTROY A COUNTRY JUST FOR CALLING HER DOWN FOR NO REASON. IF THEY TRIED TO HARM HER—
NO, IF THEY DID ANYTHING TO EVEN PUT HER IN A SLIGHTLY BAD MOOD, THERE WAS NO TELL-ING WHAT CELESTINE WOULD DO TO THEM.
LET'S LEAVE HER BE.
MAYBE WE COULD TRY ASKING HER FOR SMALL FAVORS...
FOR NOW, EACH OF THE REPRESEN-TATIVES AGREED TO THE NEW TRADE DEALS WITH BALMORE
WITH THE PROMISE OF SENDING DELEGATES FROM THE COUNTRY TO SEAL THE DEAL SOMETIME IN THE NEAR FUTURE.

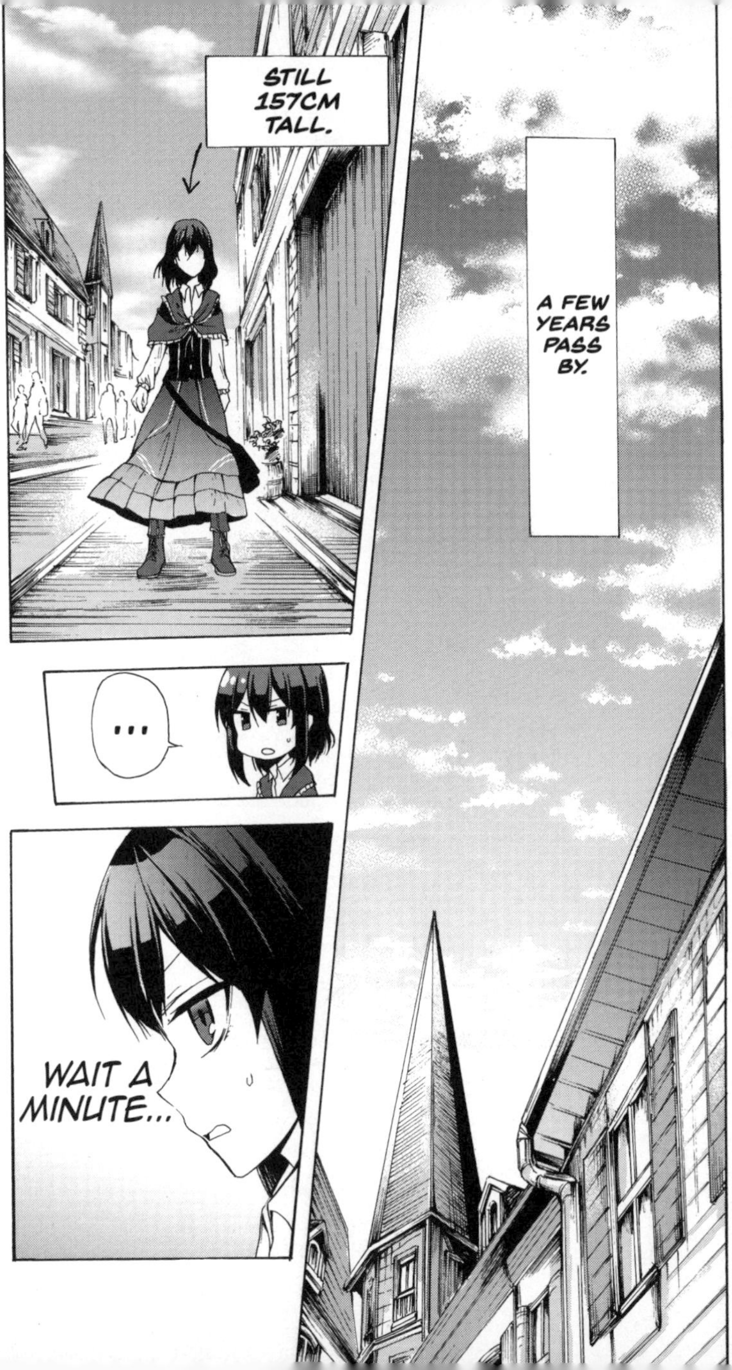
A FEW YEARS PASS BY.
STILL 157CM TALL.
...
WAIT A MINUTE...

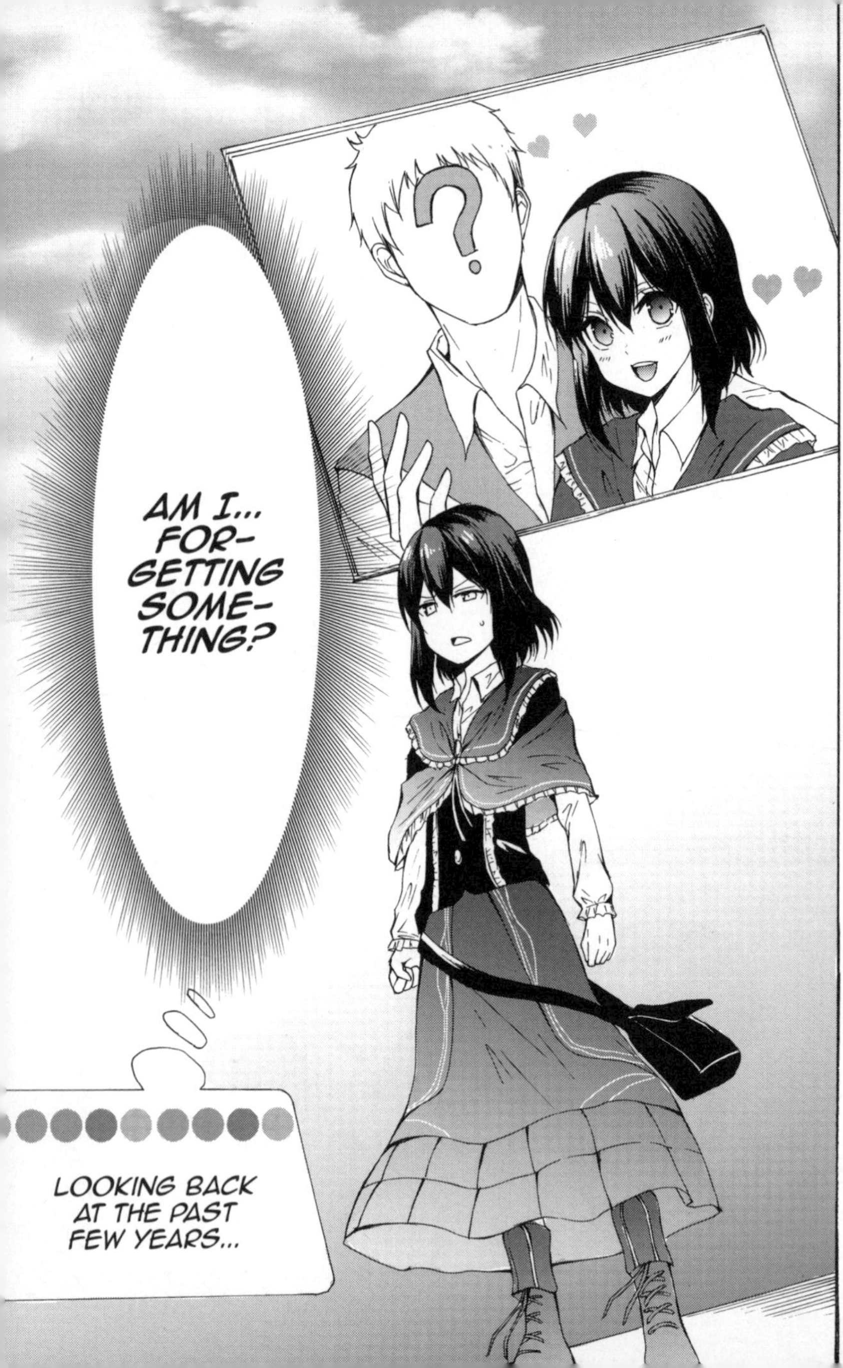
AM I... FOR-GETTING SOME-THING?
LOOKING BACK AT THE PAST FEW YEARS...

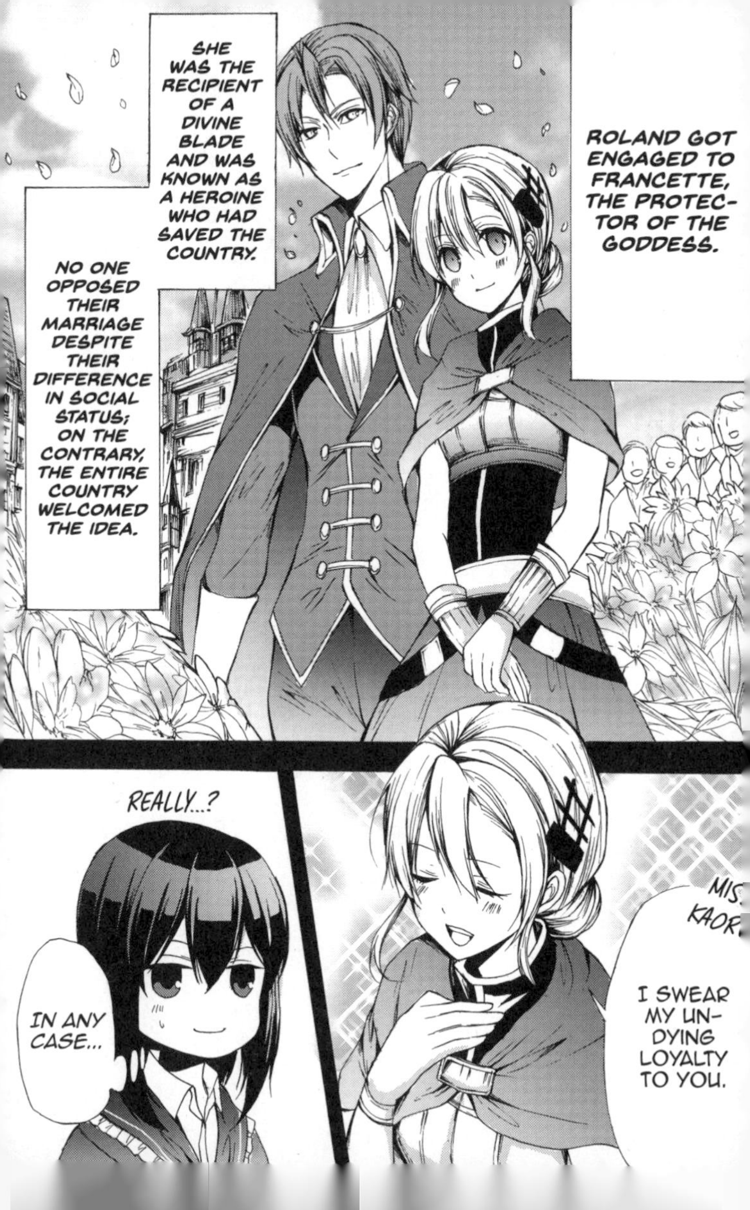
ROLAND GOT ENGAGED TO FRANCETTE, THE PROTECTOR OF THE GODDESS.
SHE WAS THE RECIPIENT OF A DIVINE BLADE AND WAS KNOWN AS A HEROINE WHO HAD SAVED THE COUNTRY.
NO ONE OPPOSED THEIR MARRIAGE DESPITE THEIR DIFFERENCE IN SOCIAL STATUS; ON THE CONTRARY, THE ENTIRE COUNTRY WELCOMED THE IDEA.
MIS KAOR
I SWEAR MY UN-DYING LOYALTY TO YOU.
REALLY...?
IN ANY CASE...

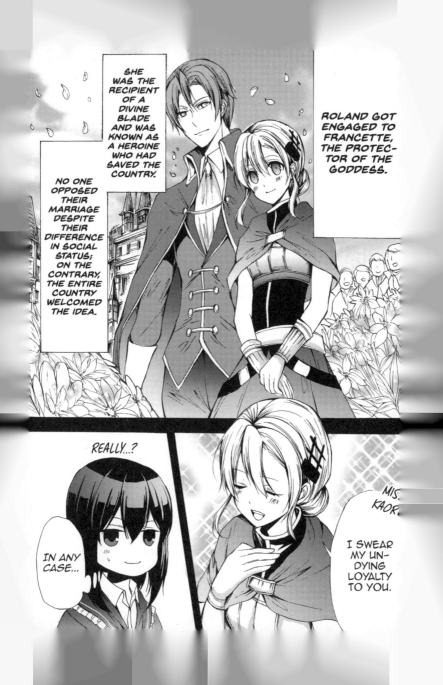

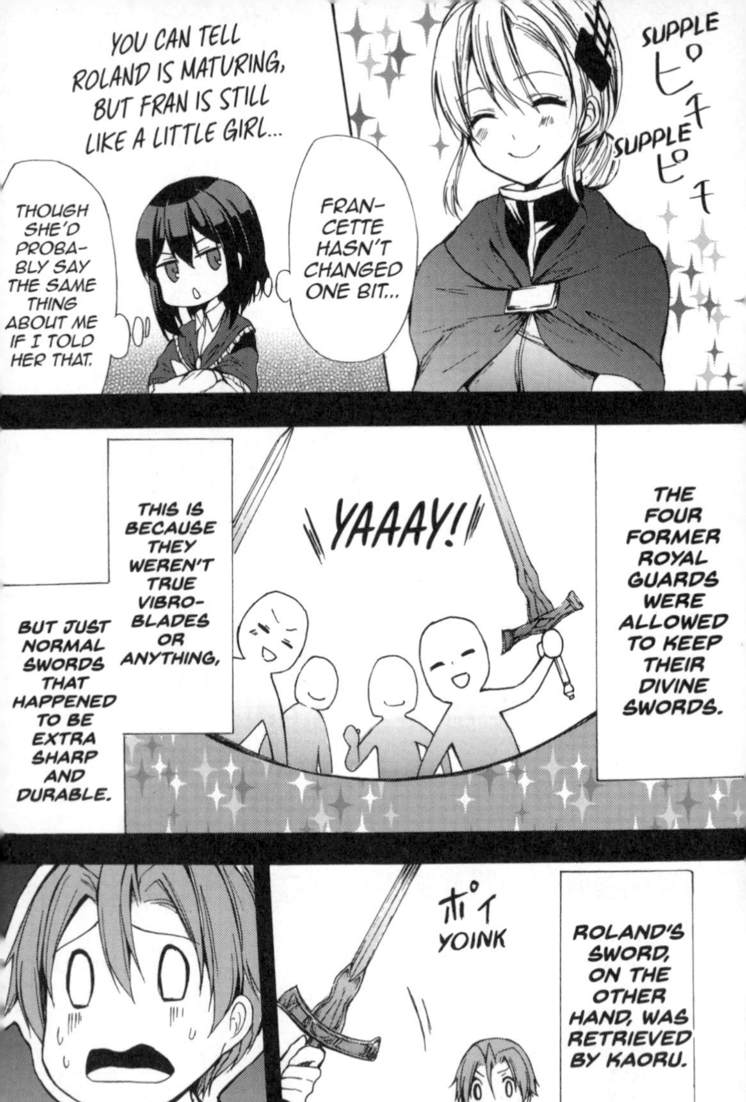
SUPPLE ピチ
SUPPLE ピチ
YOU CAN TELL ROLAND IS MATURING, BUT FRAN IS STILL LIKE A LITTLE GIRL...
FRAN-CETTE HASN'T CHANGED ONE BIT...
THOUGH SHE'D PROBA-BLY SAY THE SAME THING ABOUT ME IF I TOLD HER THAT.
THE FOUR FORMER ROYAL GUARDS WERE ALLOWED TO KEEP THEIR DIVINE SWORDS.
YAAAY!
THIS IS BECAUSE THEY WEREN'T TRUE VIBRO-BLADES OR ANYTHING,
BUT JUST NORMAL SWORDS THAT HAPPENED TO BE EXTRA SHARP AND DURABLE.
ROLAND'S SWORD, ON THE OTHER HAND, WAS RETRIEVED BY KAORU.
ポイ
YOINK

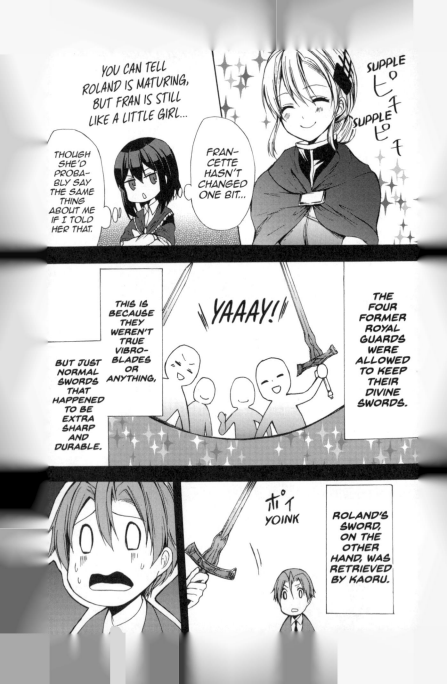

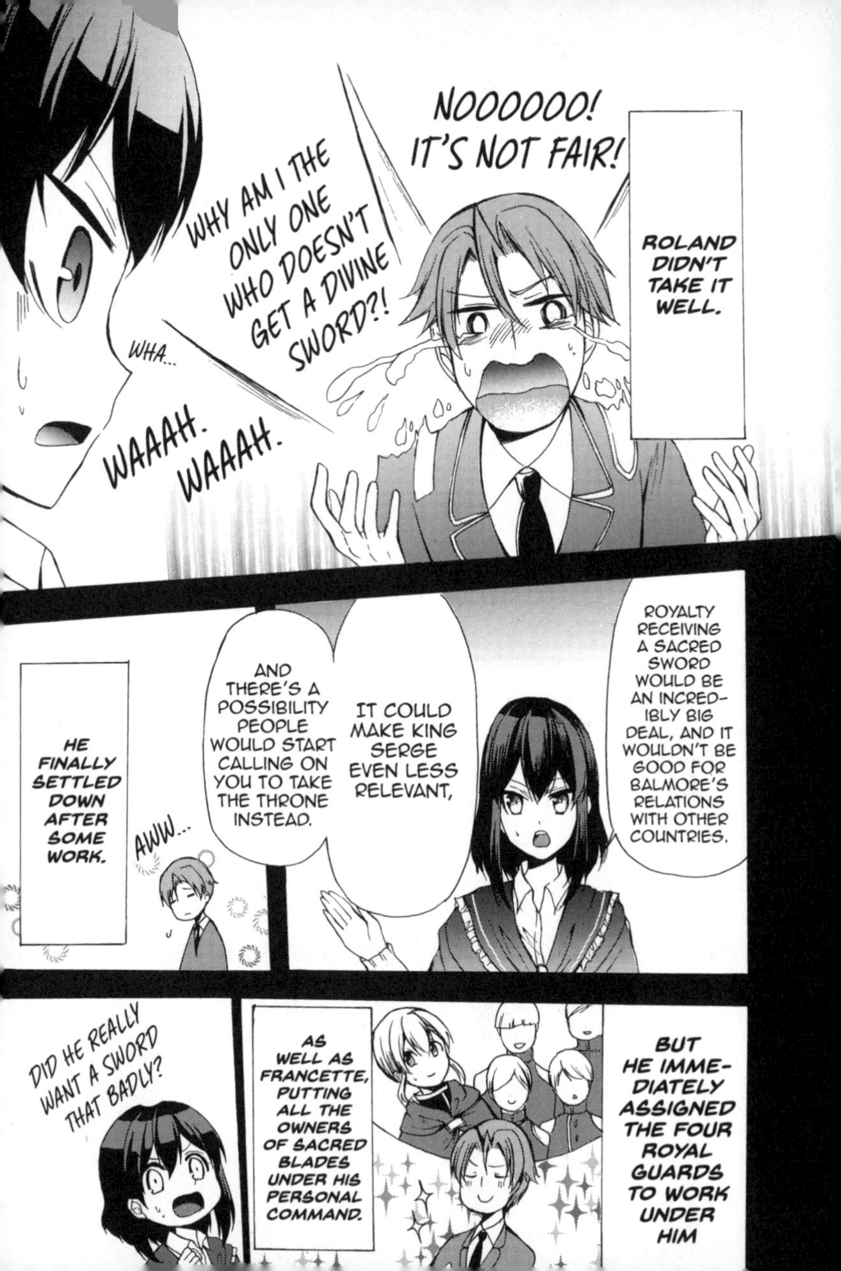
ROLAND DIDN'T TAKE IT WELL.
NOOOOOO! IT'S NOT FAIR!
WHY AM I THE ONLY ONE WHO DOESN'T GET A DIVINE SWORD?!
WHA...
WAAAH. WAAAH.
ROYALTY RECEIVING A SACRED SWORD WOULD BE AN INCREDIBLY BIG DEAL, AND IT WOULDN'T BE GOOD FOR BALMORE'S RELATIONS WITH OTHER COUNTRIES.
IT COULD MAKE KING SERGE EVEN LESS RELEVANT,
AND THERE'S A POSSIBILITY PEOPLE WOULD START CALLING ON YOU TO TAKE THE THRONE INSTEAD.
HE FINALLY SETTLED DOWN AFTER SOME WORK.
AWW...
BUT HE IMMEDIATELY ASSIGNED THE FOUR ROYAL GUARDS TO WORK UNDER HIM
AS WELL AS FRANCETTE, PUTTING ALL THE OWNERS OF SACRED BLADES UNDER HIS PERSONAL COMMAND.
DID HE REALLY WANT A SWORD THAT BADLY?

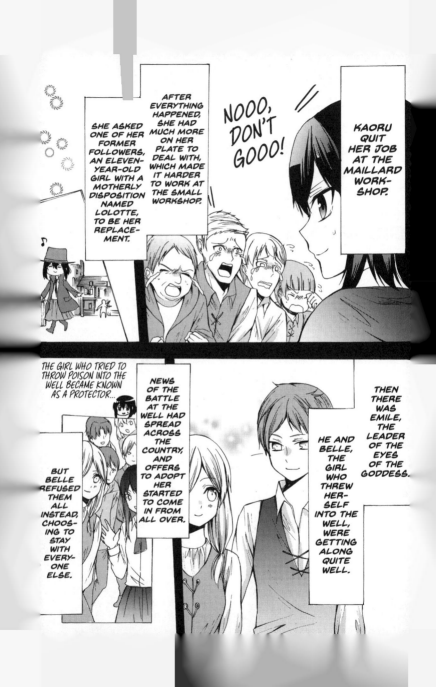

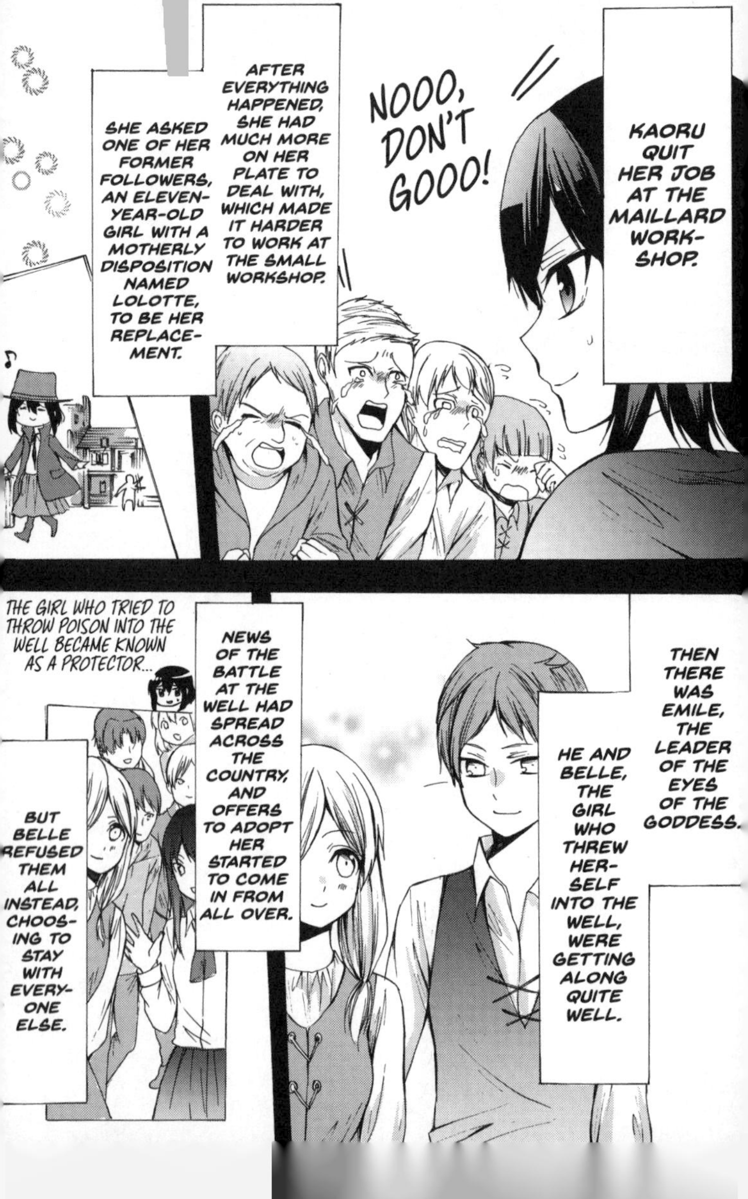
KAORU QUIT HER JOB AT THE MAILLARD WORK-SHOP.
NOOO, DON'T GOOO!
AFTER EVERYTHING HAPPENED, SHE HAD MUCH MORE ON HER PLATE TO DEAL WITH, WHICH MADE IT HARDER TO WORK AT THE SMALL WORKSHOP.
SHE ASKED ONE OF HER FORMER FOLLOWERS, AN ELEVEN-YEAR-OLD GIRL WITH A MOTHERLY DISPOSITION NAMED LOLOTTE, TO BE HER REPLACE-MENT.
THEN THERE WAS EMILE, THE LEADER OF THE EYES OF THE GODDESS.
HE AND BELLE, THE GIRL WHO THREW HER-SELF INTO THE WELL, WERE GETTING ALONG QUITE WELL.
NEWS OF THE BATTLE AT THE WELL HAD SPREAD ACROSS THE COUNTRY, AND OFFERS TO ADOPT HER STARTED TO COME IN FROM ALL OVER.
THE GIRL WHO TRIED TO THROW POISON INTO THE WELL BECAME KNOWN AS A PROTECTOR...
BUT BELLE REFUSED THEM ALL INSTEAD, CHOOS-ING TO STAY WITH EVERY-ONE ELSE.

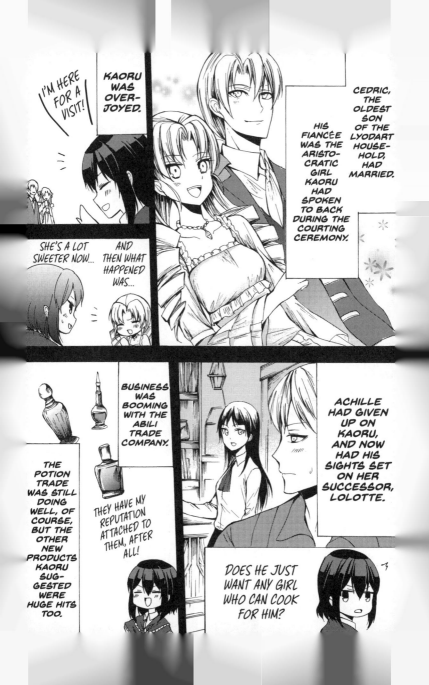

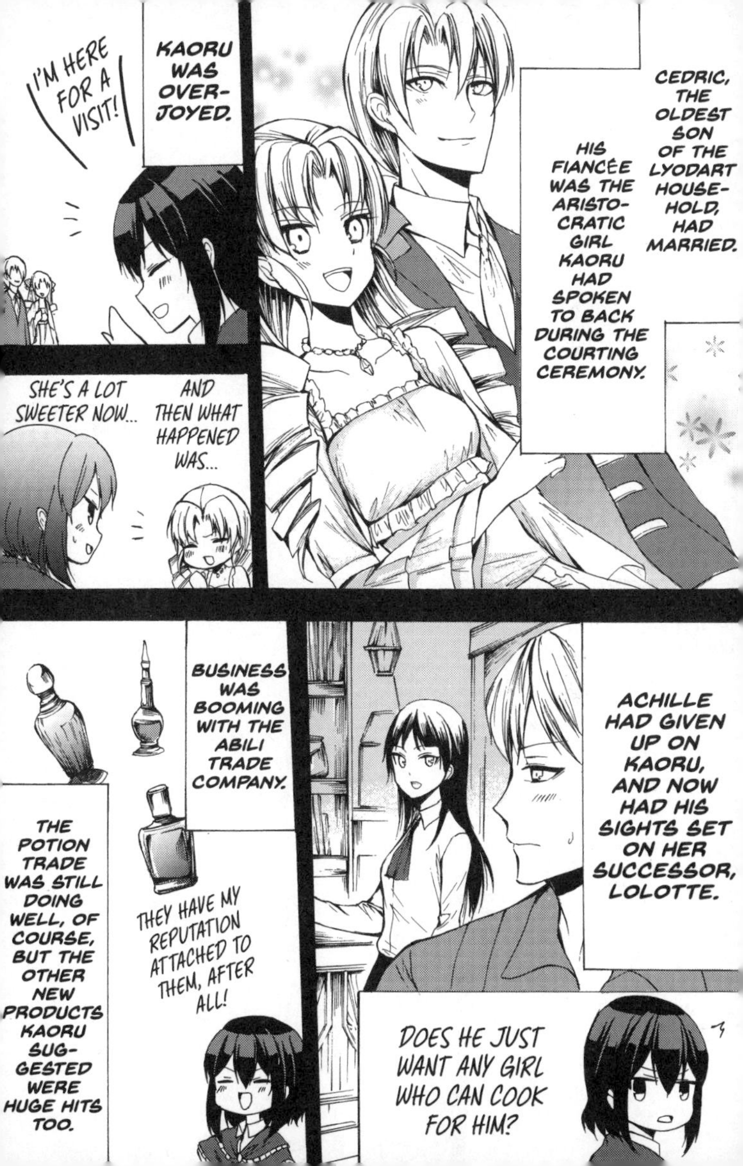
CEDRIC, THE OLDEST SON OF THE LYODART HOUSEHOLD, HAD MARRIED.
HIS FIANCÉE WAS THE ARISTOCRATIC GIRL KAORU HAD SPOKEN TO BACK DURING THE COURTING CEREMONY.
KAORU WAS OVERJOYED.
I'M HERE FOR A VISIT!
AND THEN WHAT HAPPENED WAS...
SHE'S A LOT SWEETER NOW...
ACHILLE HAD GIVEN UP ON KAORU, AND NOW HAD HIS SIGHTS SET ON HER SUCCESSOR, LOLOTTE.
DOES HE JUST WANT ANY GIRL WHO CAN COOK FOR HIM?
BUSINESS WAS BOOMING WITH THE ABILI TRADE COMPANY.
THE POTION TRADE WAS STILL DOING WELL, OF COURSE, BUT THE OTHER NEW PRODUCTS KAORU SUGGESTED WERE HUGE HITS TOO.
THEY HAVE MY REPUTATION ATTACHED TO THEM, AFTER ALL!

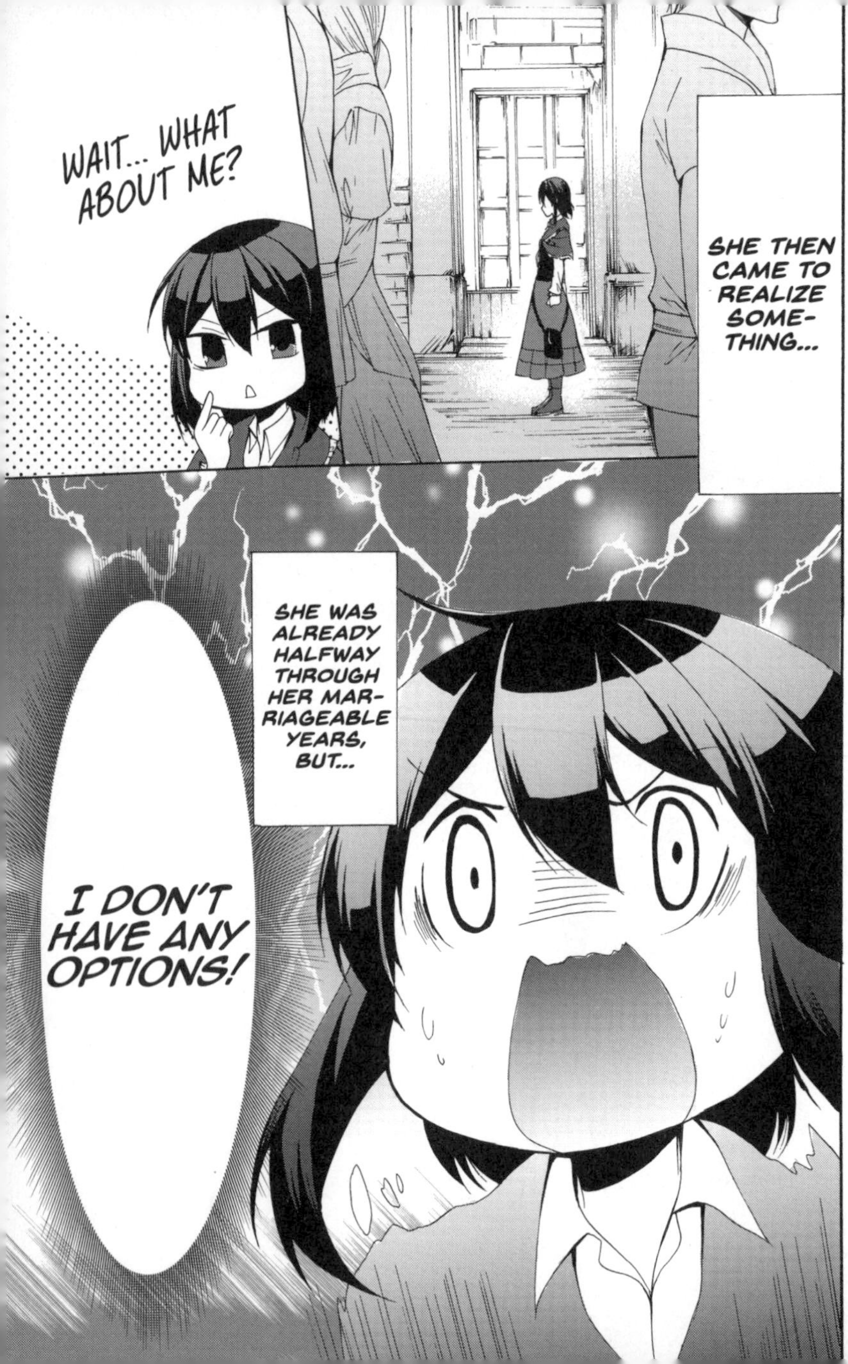
SHE THEN CAME TO REALIZE SOME-THING...
WAIT... WHAT ABOUT ME?
SHE WAS ALREADY HALFWAY THROUGH HER MAR-RIAGEABLE YEARS, BUT...
I DON'T HAVE ANY OPTIONS!

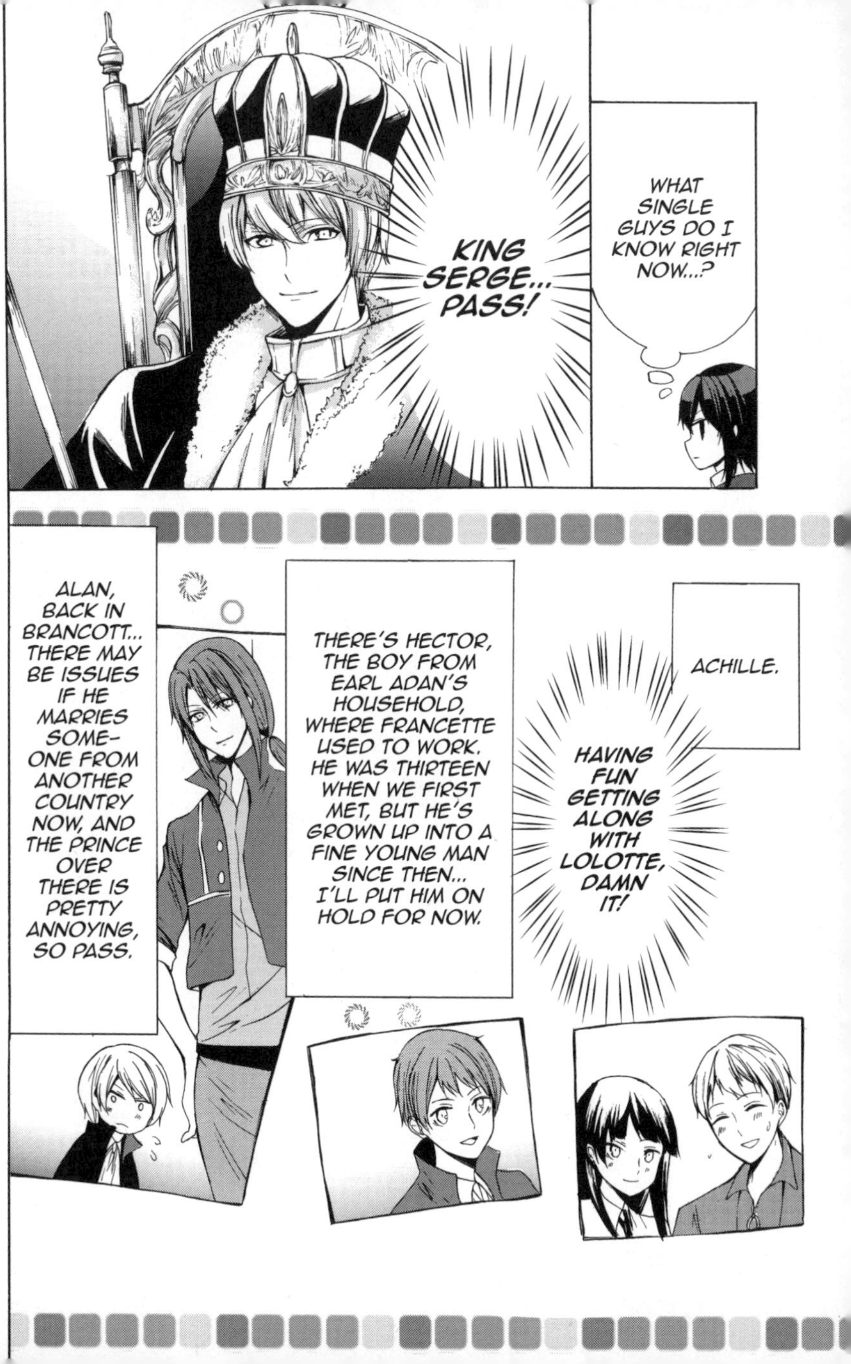
WHAT SINGLE GUYS DO I KNOW RIGHT NOW...?
KING SERGE... PASS!
ACHILLE.
HAVING FUN GETTING ALONG WITH LOLOTTE, DAMN IT!
THERE'S HECTOR, THE BOY FROM EARL ADAN'S HOUSEHOLD, WHERE FRANCETTE USED TO WORK. HE WAS THIRTEEN WHEN WE FIRST MET, BUT HE'S GROWN UP INTO A FINE YOUNG MAN SINCE THEN... I'LL PUT HIM ON HOLD FOR NOW.
ALAN, BACK IN BRANCOTT... THERE MAY BE ISSUES IF HE MARRIES SOME-ONE FROM ANOTHER COUNTRY NOW, AND THE PRINCE OVER THERE IS PRETTY ANNOYING, SO PASS.

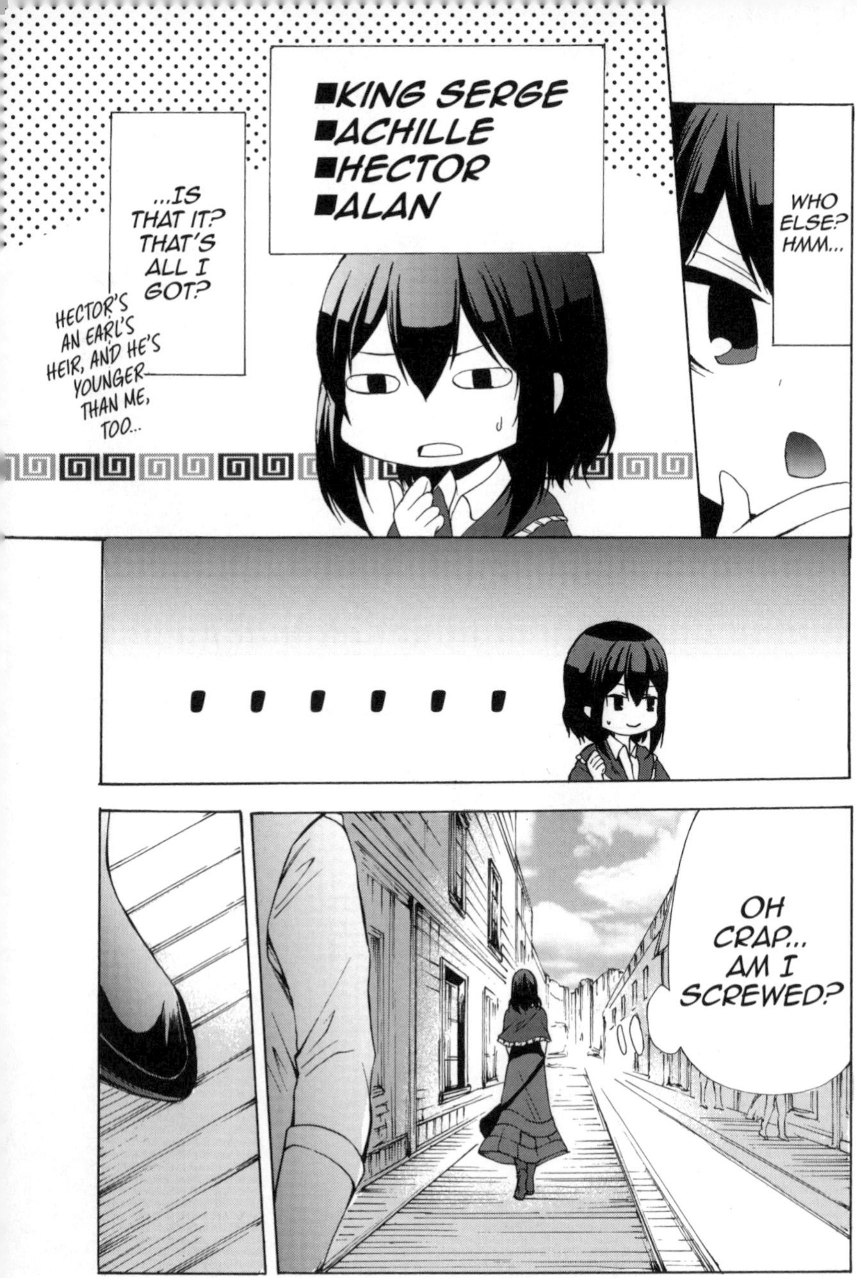
WHO ELSE? HMM...
■KING SERGE
■ACHILLE
■HECTOR
■ALAN
...IS THAT IT? THAT'S ALL I GOT?
HECTOR'S AN EARL'S HEIR, AND HE'S YOUNGER THAN ME, TOO...
......
OH CRAP... AM I SCREWED?

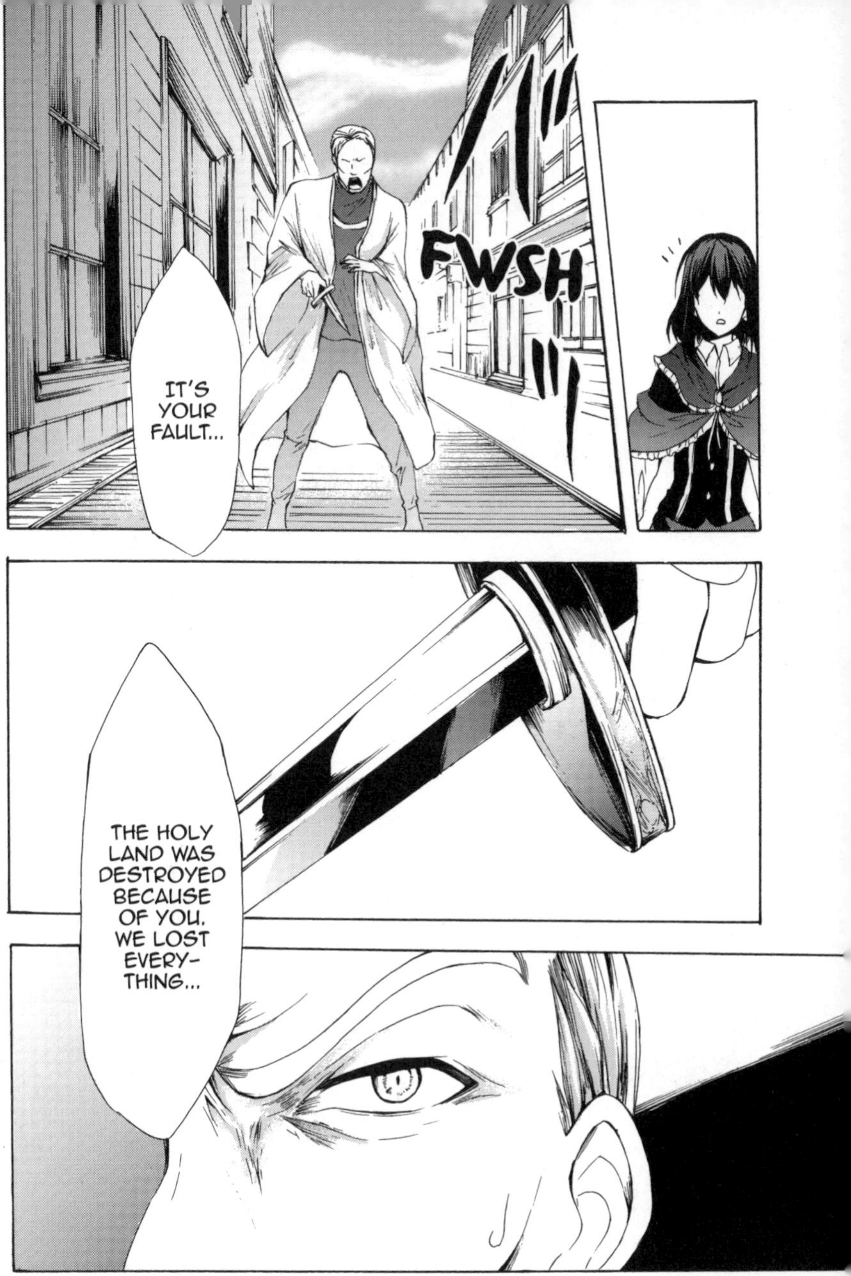
FWSH
IT'S YOUR FAULT...
THE HOLY LAND WAS DESTROYED BECAUSE OF YOU. WE LOST EVERYTHING...

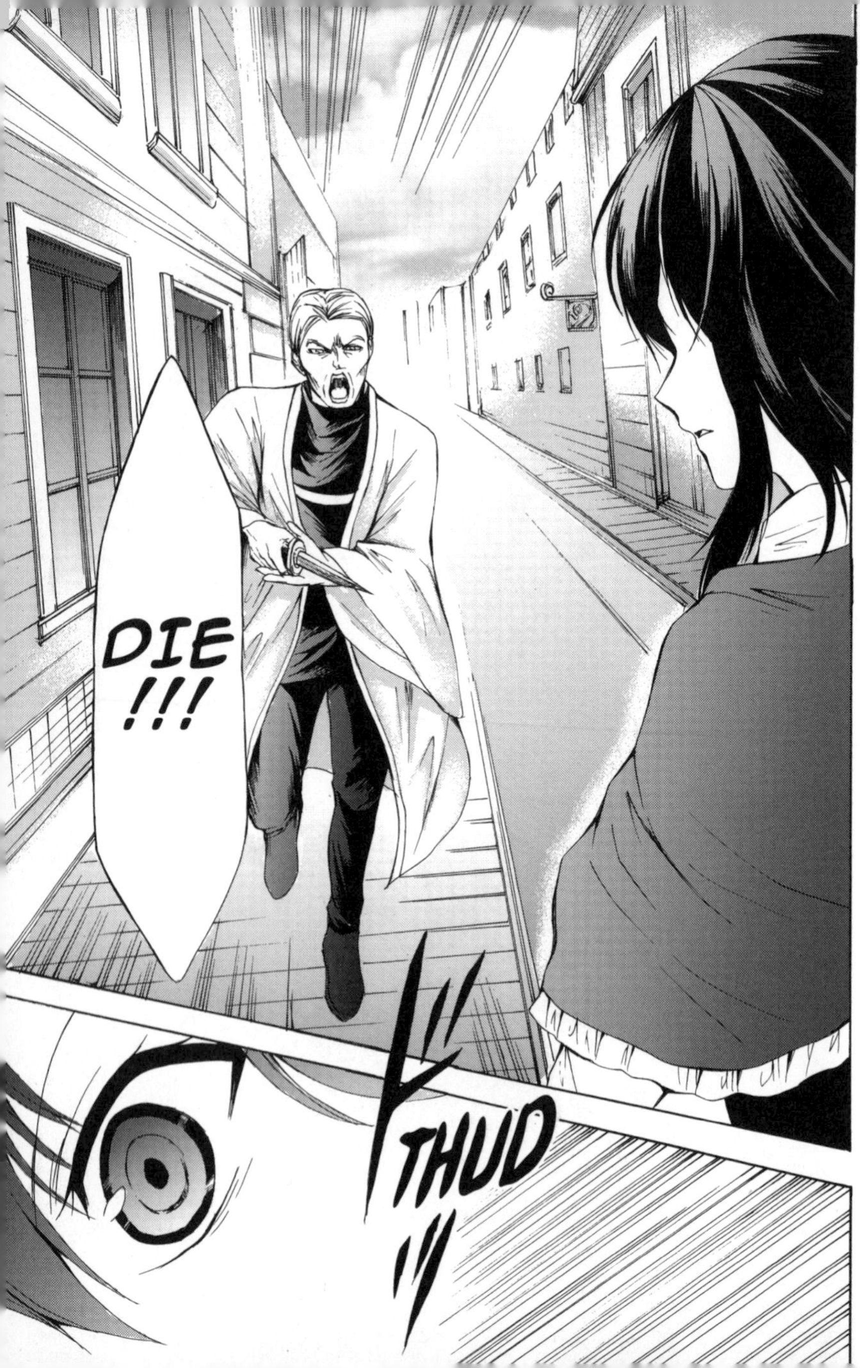
DIE !!!
THUD !!!

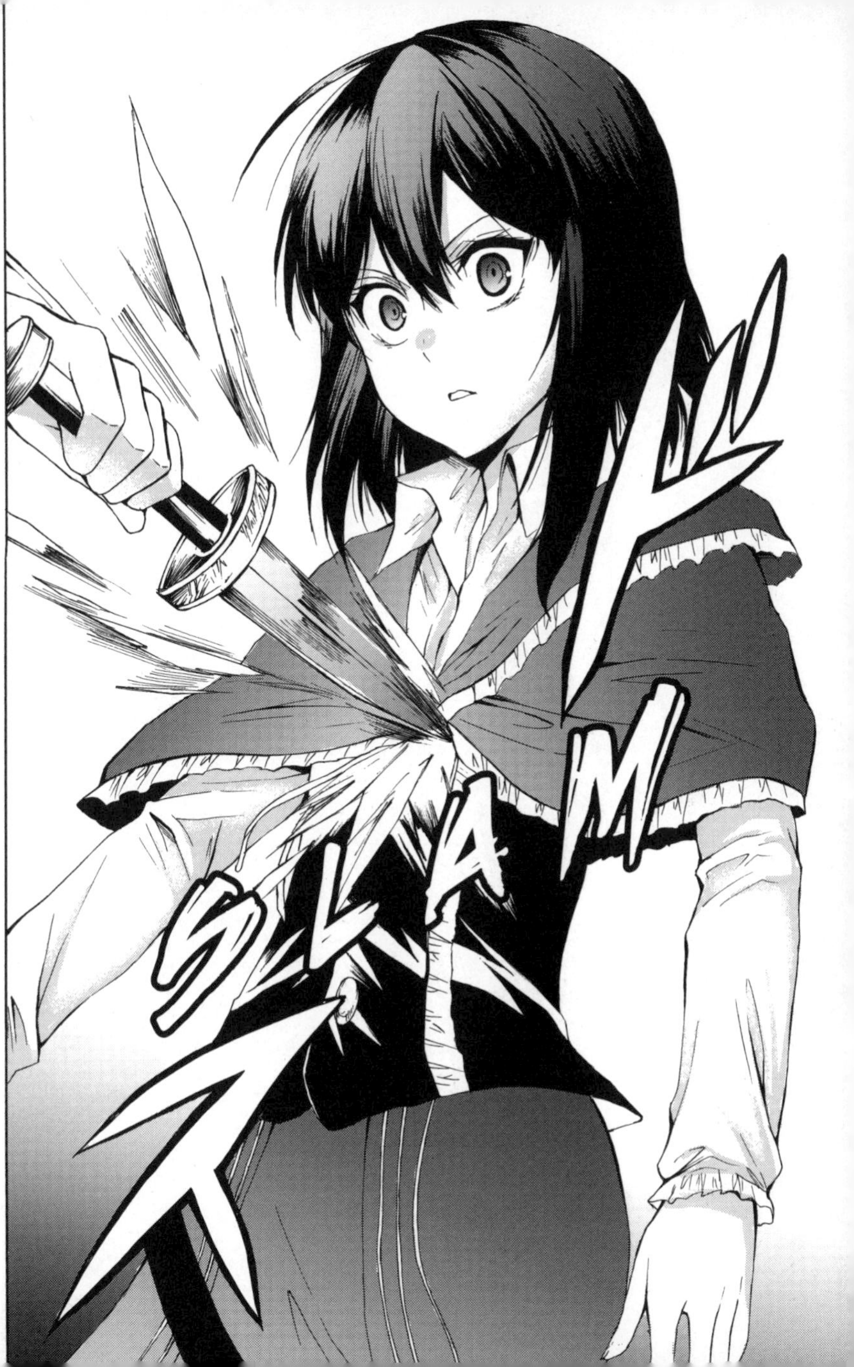
SLAM

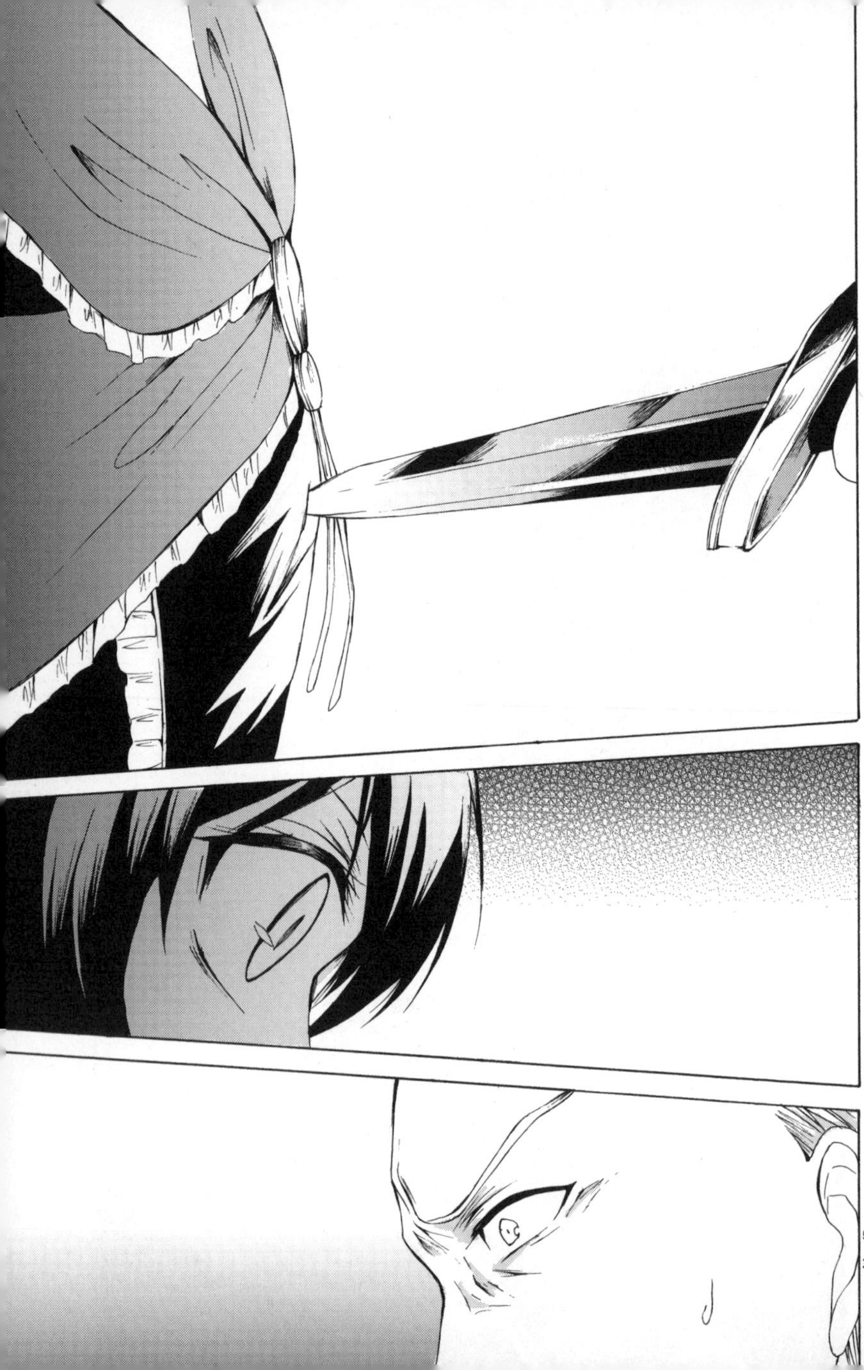

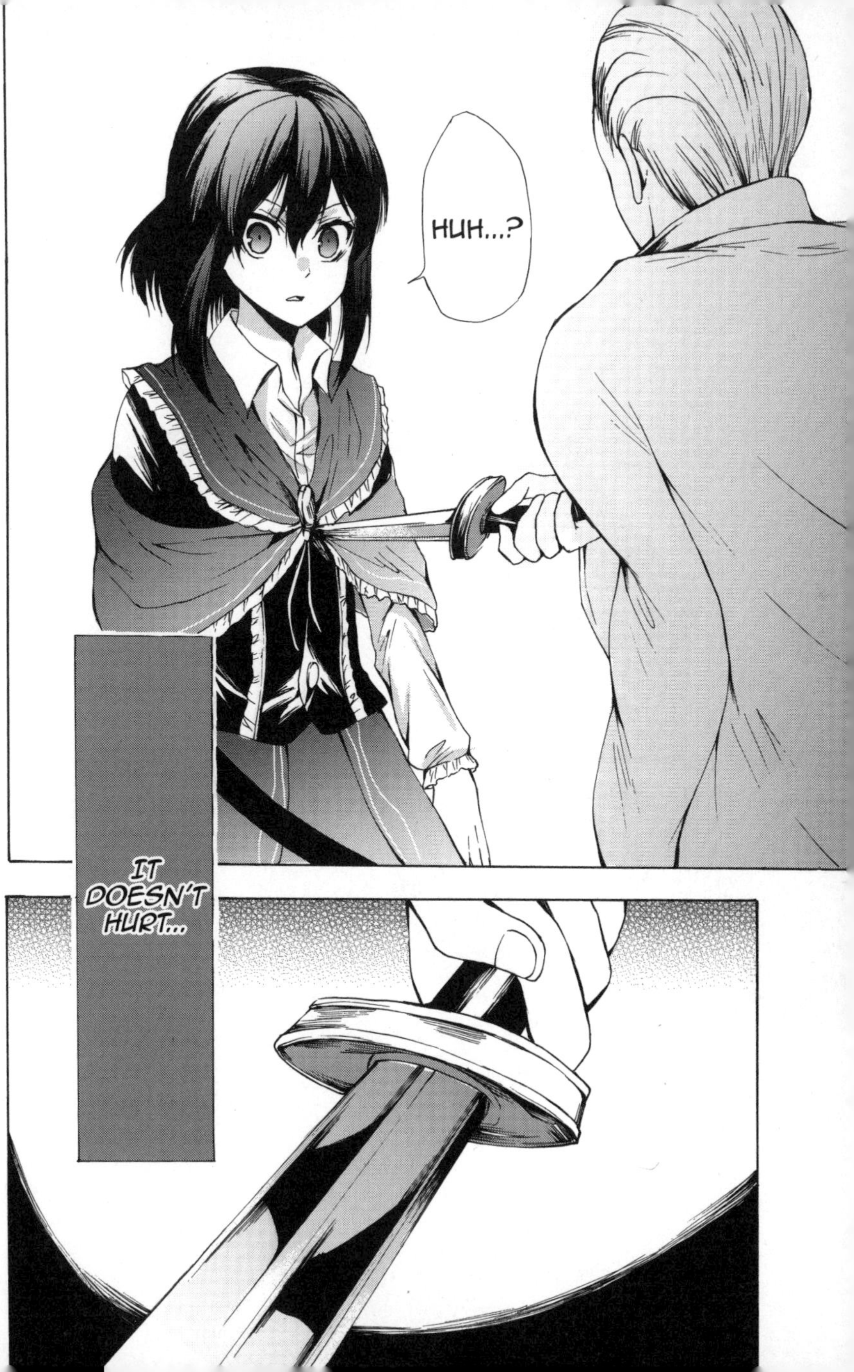
HUH...?
IT DOESN'T HURT...

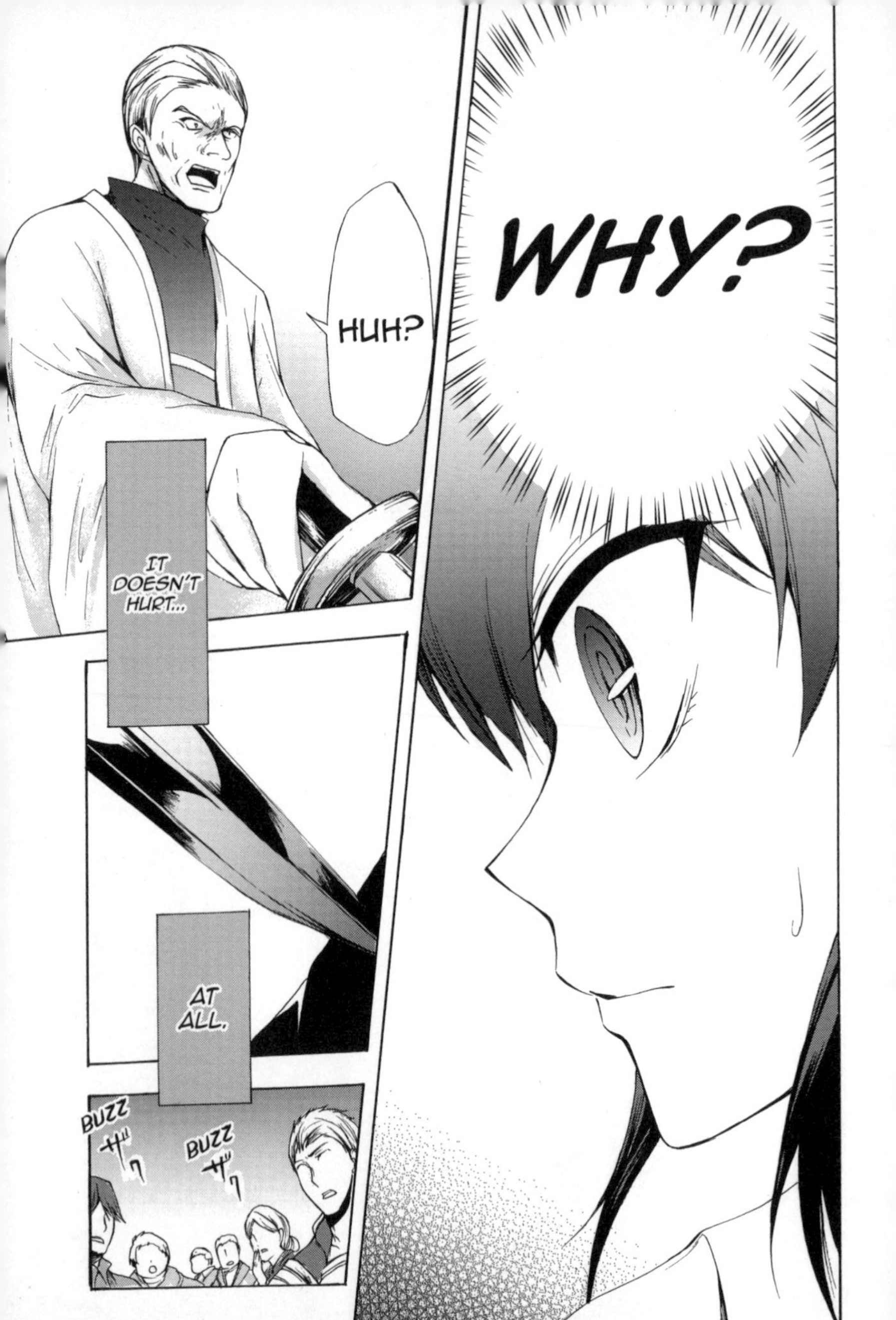
WHY?
HUH?
IT DOESN'T HURT...
AT ALL.
BUZZ
BUZZ

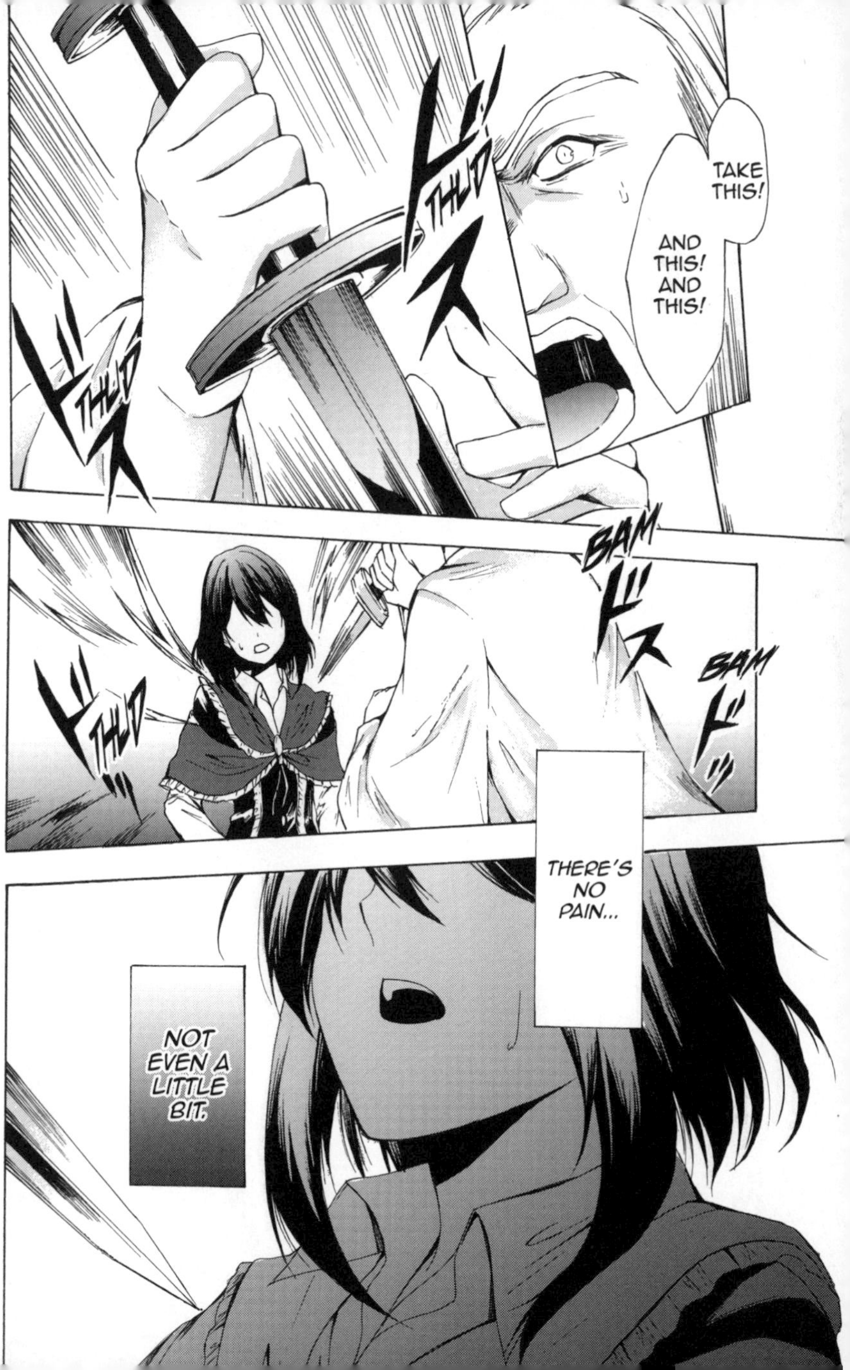
TAKE THIS!
AND THIS! AND THIS!
THUD
THUD
BAM
BAM
THUD
THERE'S NO PAIN...
NOT EVEN A LITTLE BIT.

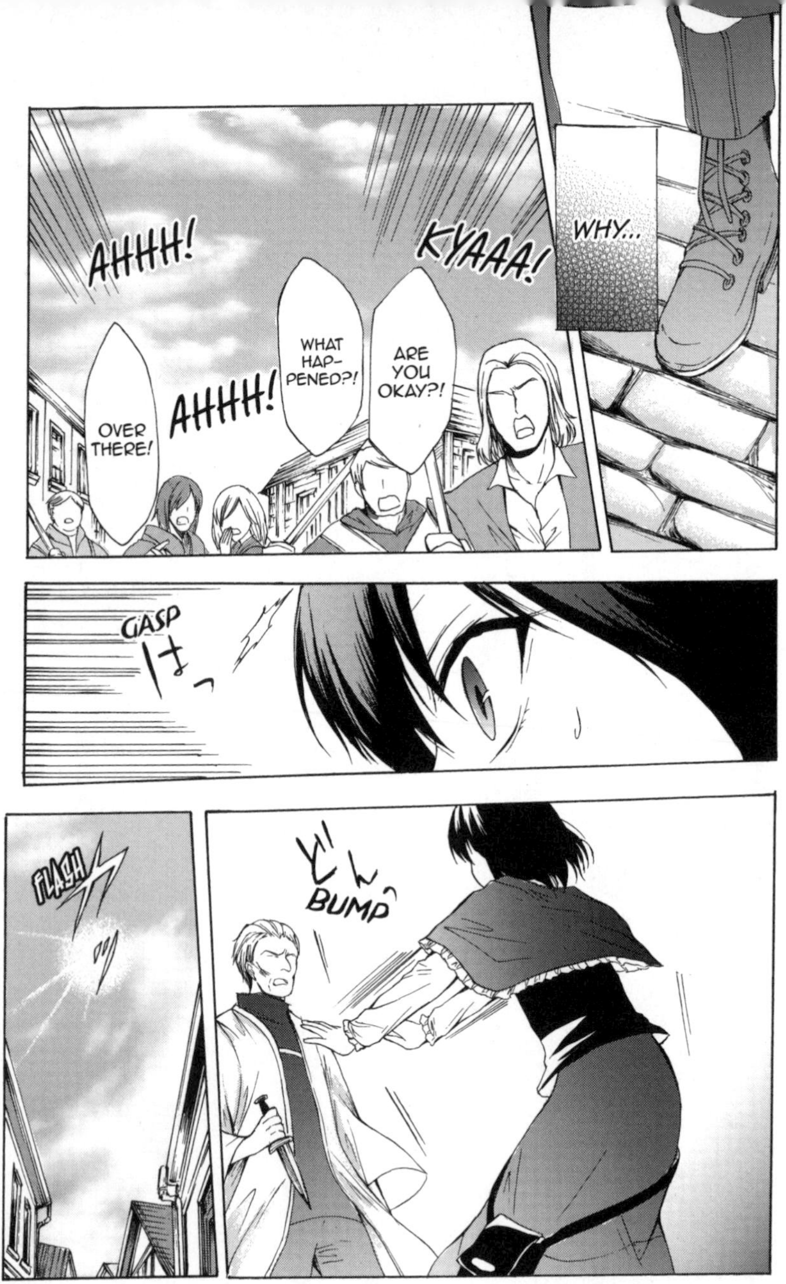
WHY...
KYAAA!
ARE YOU OKAY?!
WHAT HAP-PENED?!
AHHH!
AHHH!
OVER THERE!
GASP
はっ
どん
BUMP
FLASH

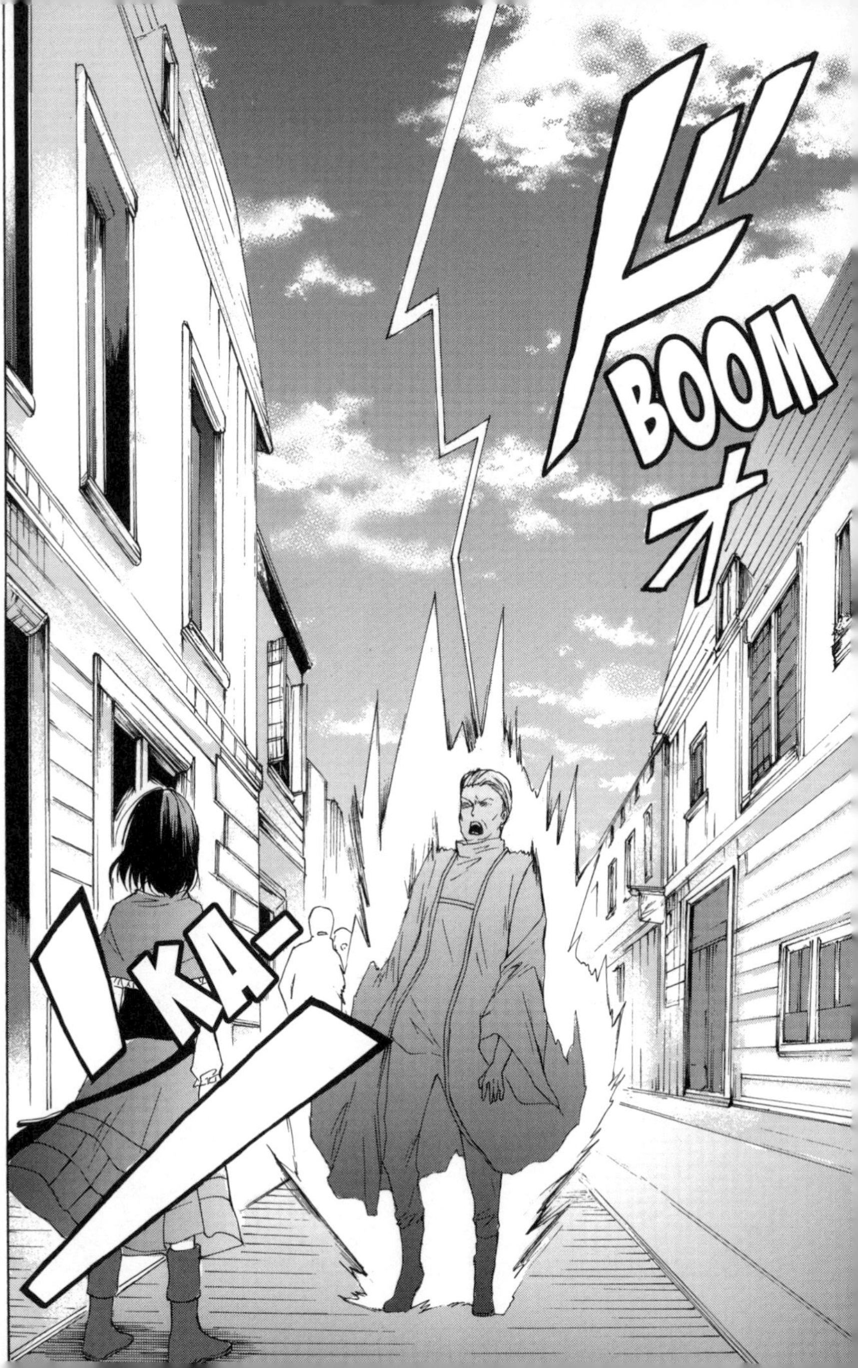
ド
BOOM
オ
KA-

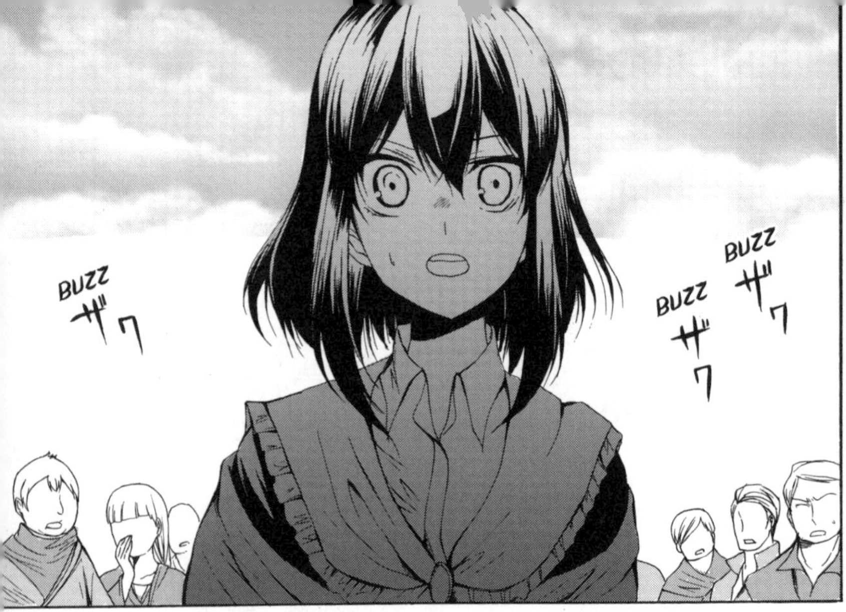
BUZZ
ザワ
BUZZ
ザワ
BUZZ
ザワ

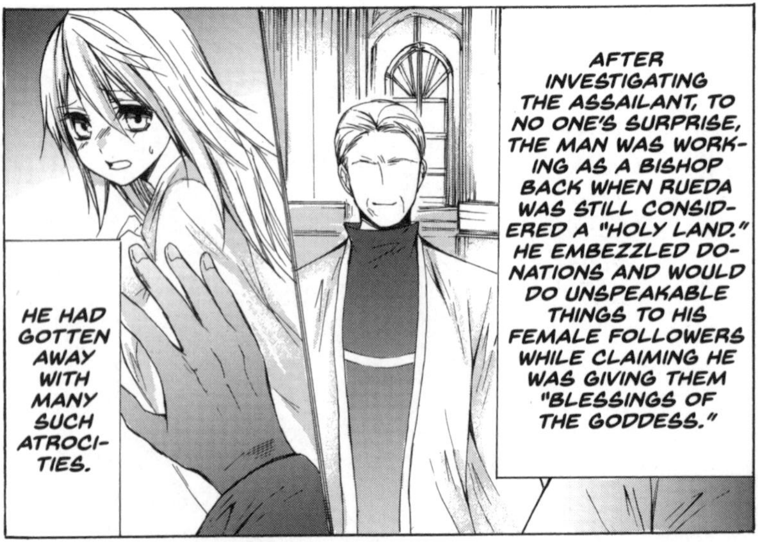
AFTER INVESTIGATING THE ASSAILANT, TO NO ONE'S SURPRISE, THE MAN WAS WORKING AS A BISHOP BACK WHEN RUEDA WAS STILL CONSIDERED A "HOLY LAND." HE EMBEZZLED DONATIONS AND WOULD DO UNSPEAKABLE THINGS TO HIS FEMALE FOLLOWERS WHILE CLAIMING HE WAS GIVING THEM "BLESSINGS OF THE GODDESS."
HE HAD GOTTEN AWAY WITH MANY SUCH ATROCITIES.

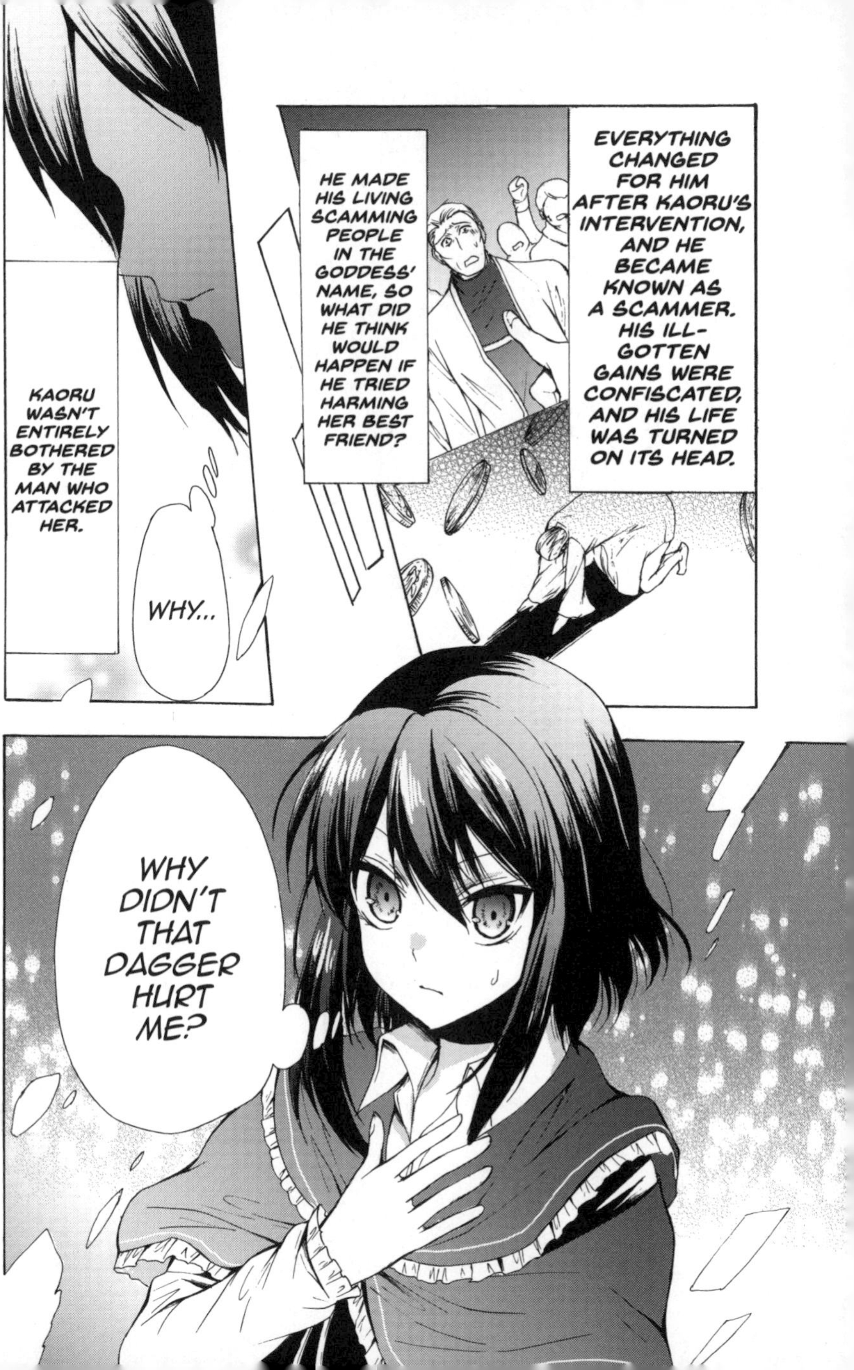
EVERYTHING CHANGED FOR HIM AFTER KAORU'S INTERVENTION, AND HE BECAME KNOWN AS A SCAMMER. HIS ILL-GOTTEN GAINS WERE CONFISCATED, AND HIS LIFE WAS TURNED ON ITS HEAD.
HE MADE HIS LIVING SCAMMING PEOPLE IN THE GODDESS' NAME, SO WHAT DID HE THINK WOULD HAPPEN IF HE TRIED HARMING HER BEST FRIEND?
KAORU WASN'T ENTIRELY BOTHERED BY THE MAN WHO ATTACKED HER.
WHY...
WHY DIDN'T THAT DAGGER HURT ME?

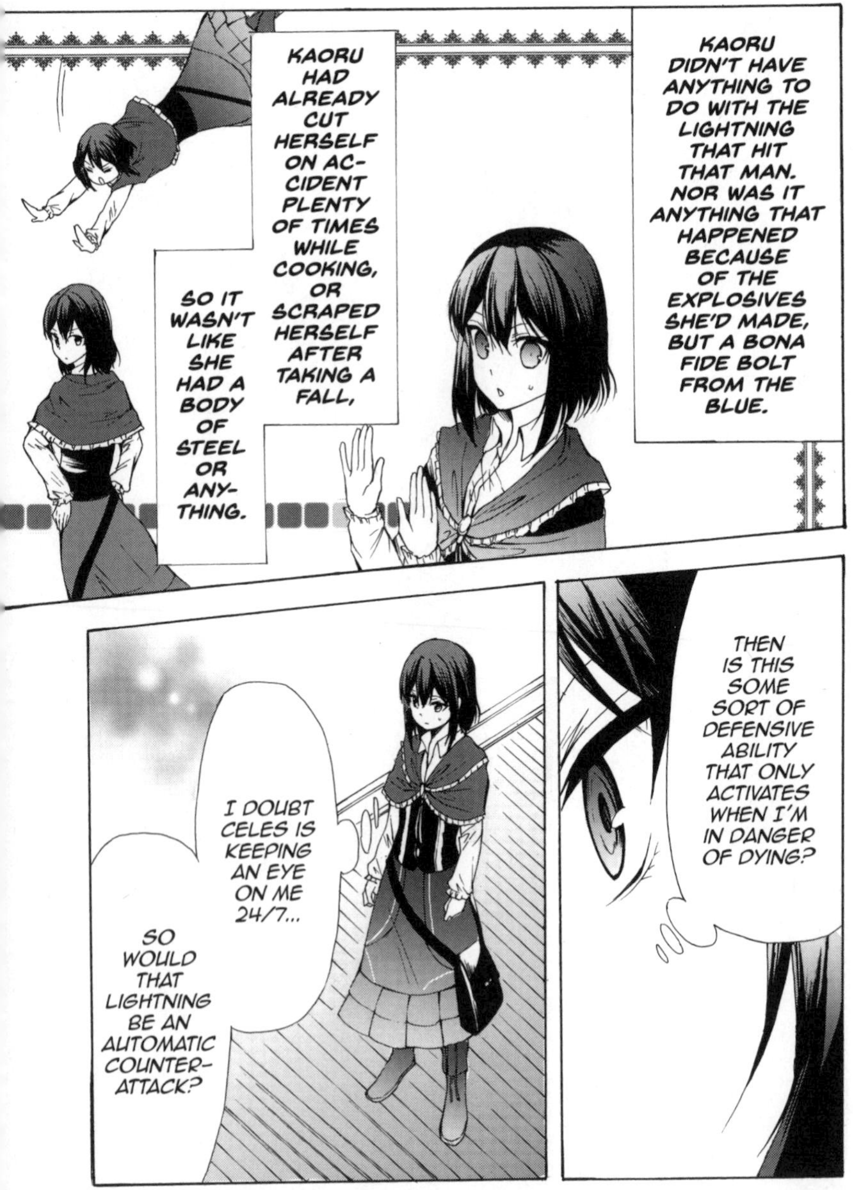
KAORU DIDN'T HAVE ANYTHING TO DO WITH THE LIGHTNING THAT HIT THAT MAN. NOR WAS IT ANYTHING THAT HAPPENED BECAUSE OF THE EXPLOSIVES SHE'D MADE, BUT A BONA FIDE BOLT FROM THE BLUE.
KAORU HAD ALREADY CUT HERSELF ON AC-CIDENT PLENTY OF TIMES WHILE COOKING, OR SCRAPED HERSELF AFTER TAKING A FALL,
SO IT WASN'T LIKE SHE HAD A BODY OF STEEL OR ANY-THING.
THEN IS THIS SOME SORT OF DEFENSIVE ABILITY THAT ONLY ACTIVATES WHEN I'M IN DANGER OF DYING?
I DOUBT CELES IS KEEPING AN EYE ON ME 24/7...
SO WOULD THAT LIGHTNING BE AN AUTOMATIC COUNTER-ATTACK?

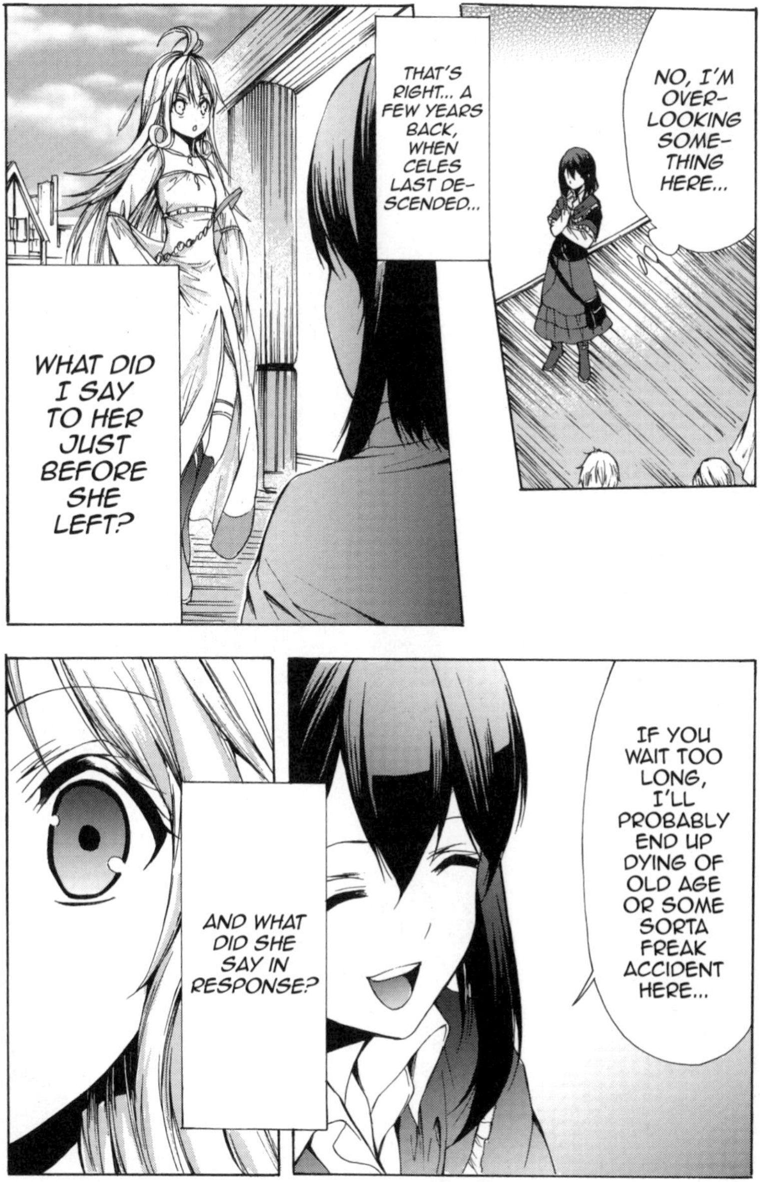
NO, I'M OVER-LOOKING SOME-THING HERE...
THAT'S RIGHT... A FEW YEARS BACK, WHEN CELES LAST DE-SCENDED...
WHAT DID I SAY TO HER JUST BEFORE SHE LEFT?
IF YOU WAIT TOO LONG, I'LL PROBABLY END UP DYING OF OLD AGE OR SOME SORTA FREAK ACCIDENT HERE...
AND WHAT DID SHE SAY IN RESPONSE?

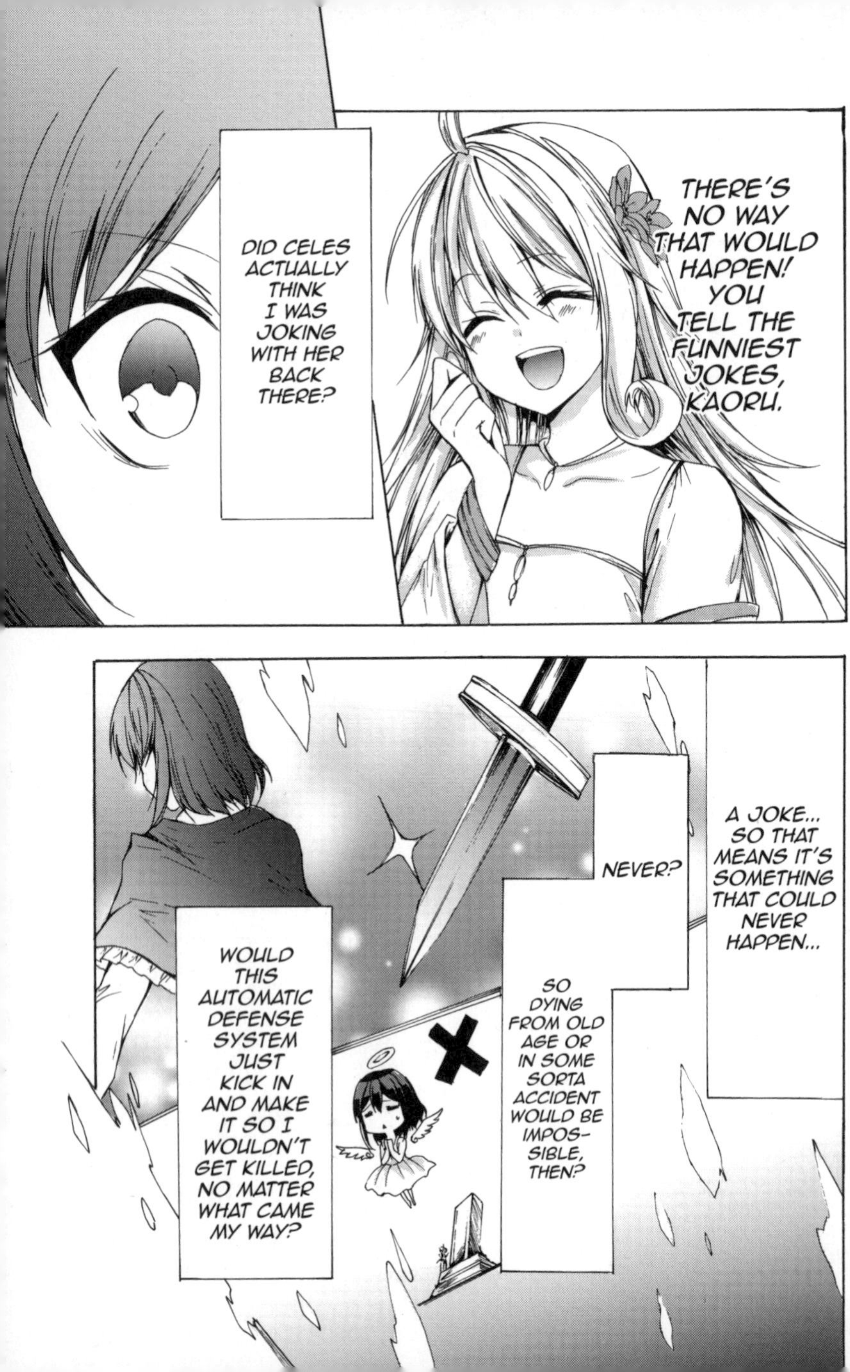
THERE'S NO WAY THAT WOULD HAPPEN! YOU TELL THE FUNNIEST JOKES, KAORU.
DID CELES ACTUALLY THINK I WAS JOKING WITH HER BACK THERE?
A JOKE... SO THAT MEANS IT'S SOMETHING THAT COULD NEVER HAPPEN...
NEVER?
SO DYING FROM OLD AGE OR IN SOME SORTA ACCIDENT WOULD BE IMPOS-SIBLE, THEN?
WOULD THIS AUTOMATIC DEFENSE SYSTEM JUST KICK IN AND MAKE IT SO I WOULDN'T GET KILLED, NO MATTER WHAT CAME MY WAY?

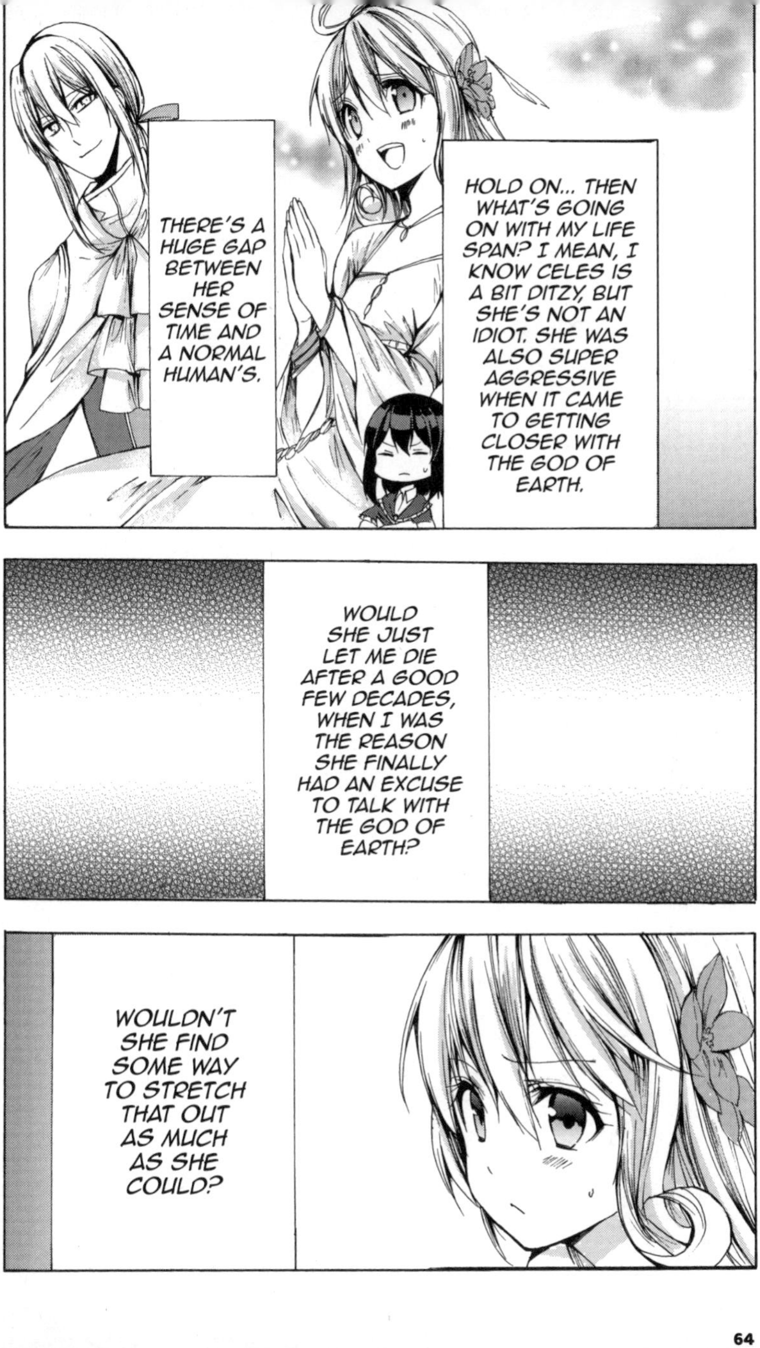
HOLD ON... THEN WHAT'S GOING ON WITH MY LIFE SPAN? I MEAN, I KNOW CELES IS A BIT DITZY, BUT SHE'S NOT AN IDIOT. SHE WAS ALSO SUPER AGGRESSIVE WHEN IT CAME TO GETTING CLOSER WITH THE GOD OF EARTH.
THERE'S A HUGE GAP BETWEEN HER SENSE OF TIME AND A NORMAL HUMAN'S.
WOULD SHE JUST LET ME DIE AFTER A GOOD FEW DECADES, WHEN I WAS THE REASON SHE FINALLY HAD AN EXCUSE TO TALK WITH THE GOD OF EARTH?
WOULDN'T SHE FIND SOME WAY TO STRETCH THAT OUT AS MUCH AS SHE COULD?

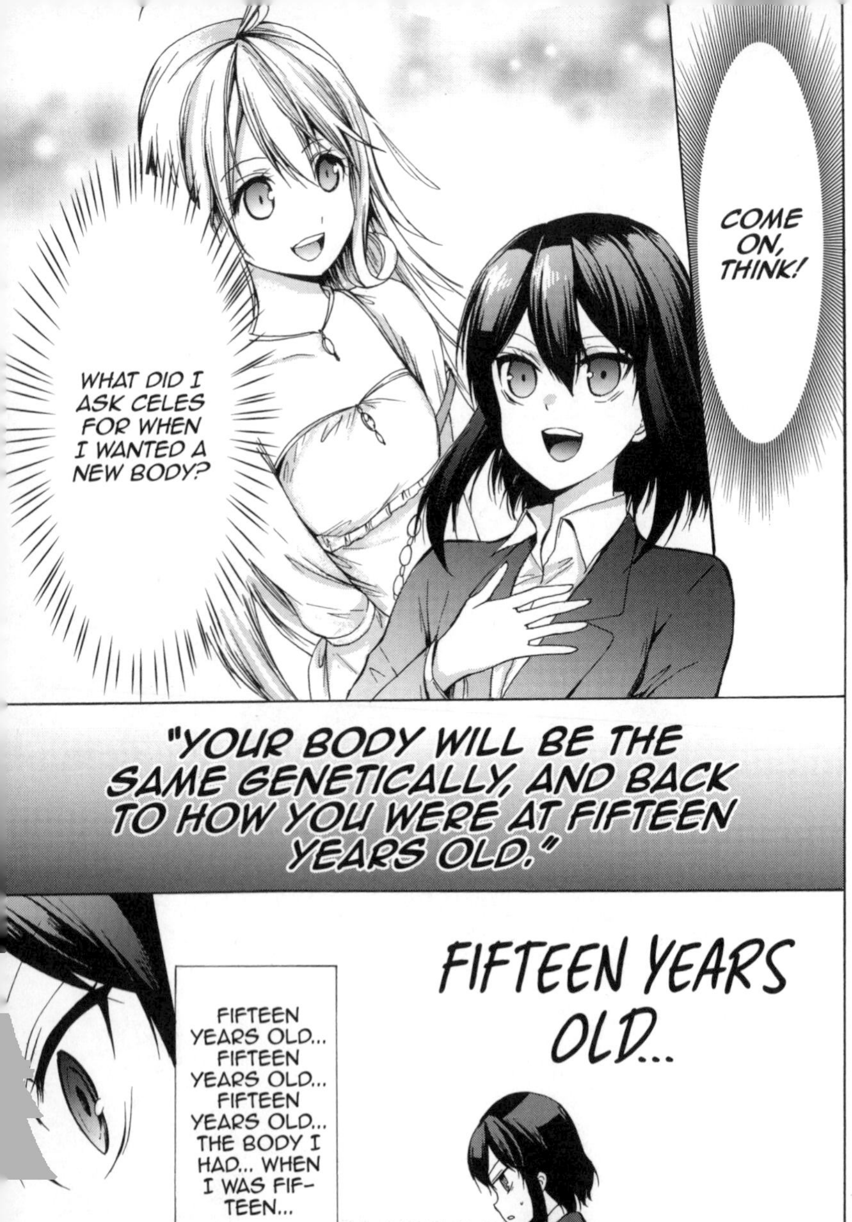
COME ON, THINK!
WHAT DID I ASK CELES FOR WHEN I WANTED A NEW BODY?
"YOUR BODY WILL BE THE SAME GENETICALLY, AND BACK TO HOW YOU WERE AT FIFTEEN YEARS OLD."
FIFTEEN YEARS OLD...
FIFTEEN YEARS OLD... FIFTEEN YEARS OLD... FIFTEEN YEARS OLD... THE BODY I HAD... WHEN I WAS FIF-TEEN...

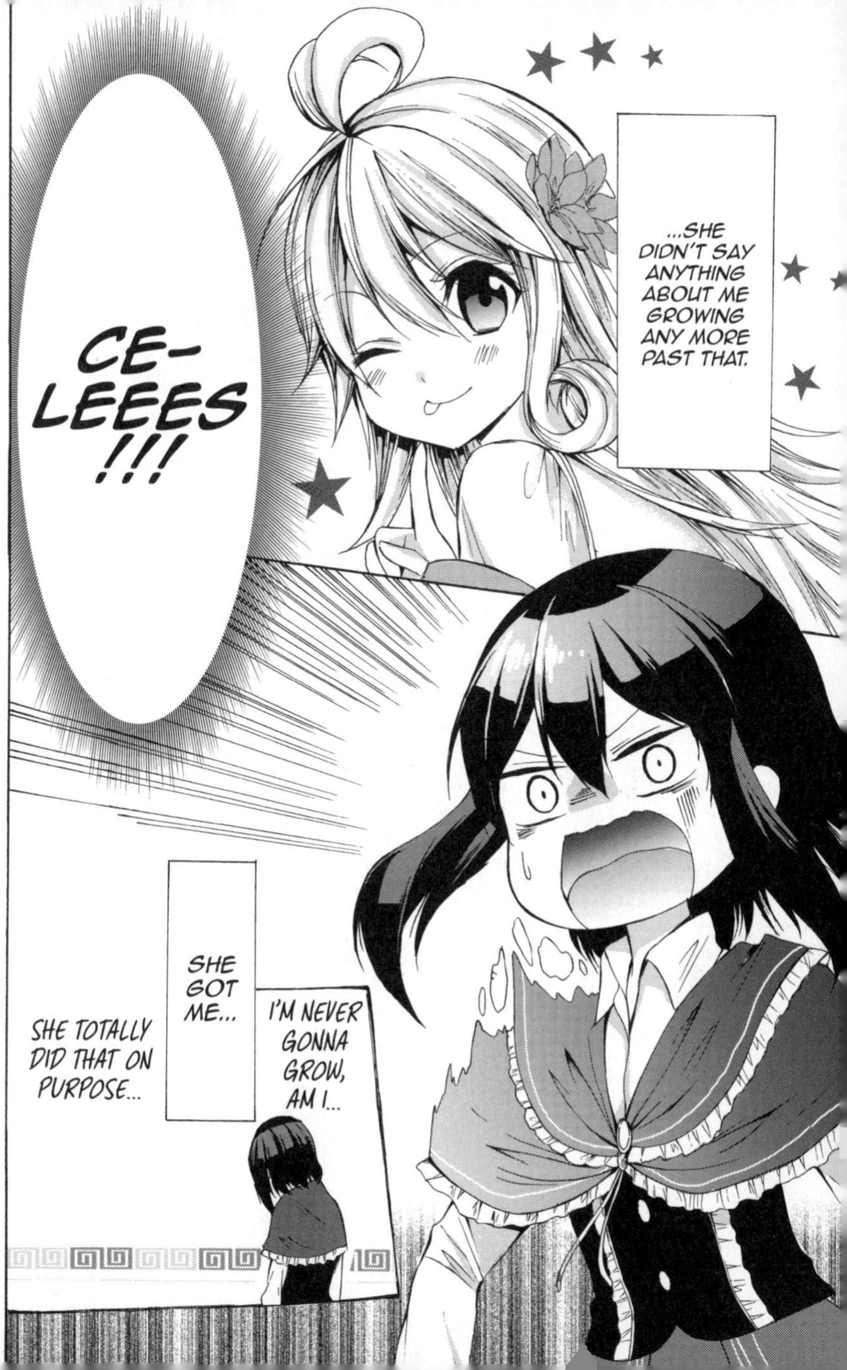
...SHE DIDN'T SAY ANYTHING ABOUT ME GROWING ANY MORE PAST THAT.
CE-LEEES!!!
SHE GOT ME...
I'M NEVER GONNA GROW, AM I...
SHE TOTALLY DID THAT ON PURPOSE...

CHAPTER 25 END

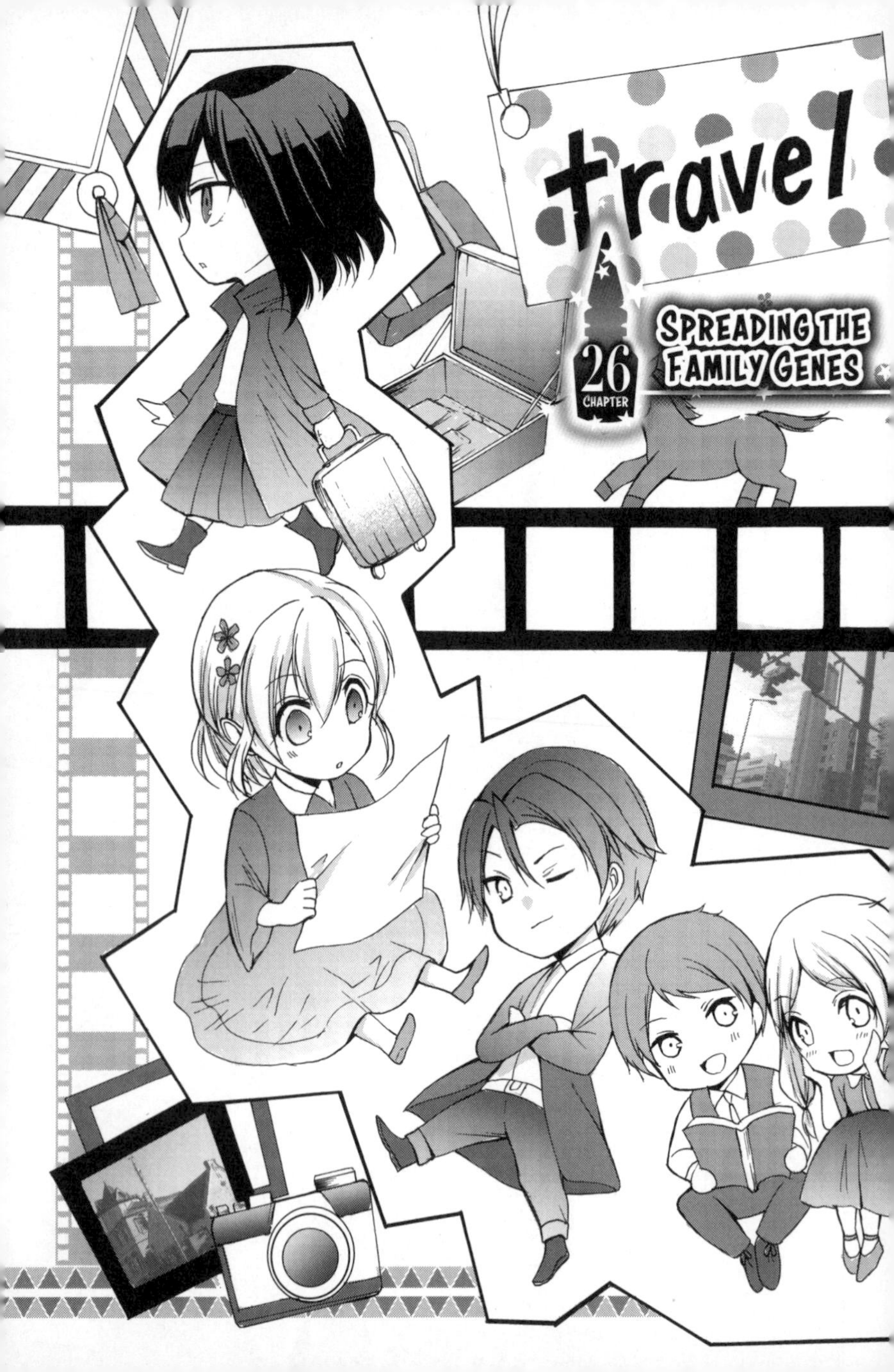
travel
26
CHAPTER
SPREADING THE FAMILY GENES

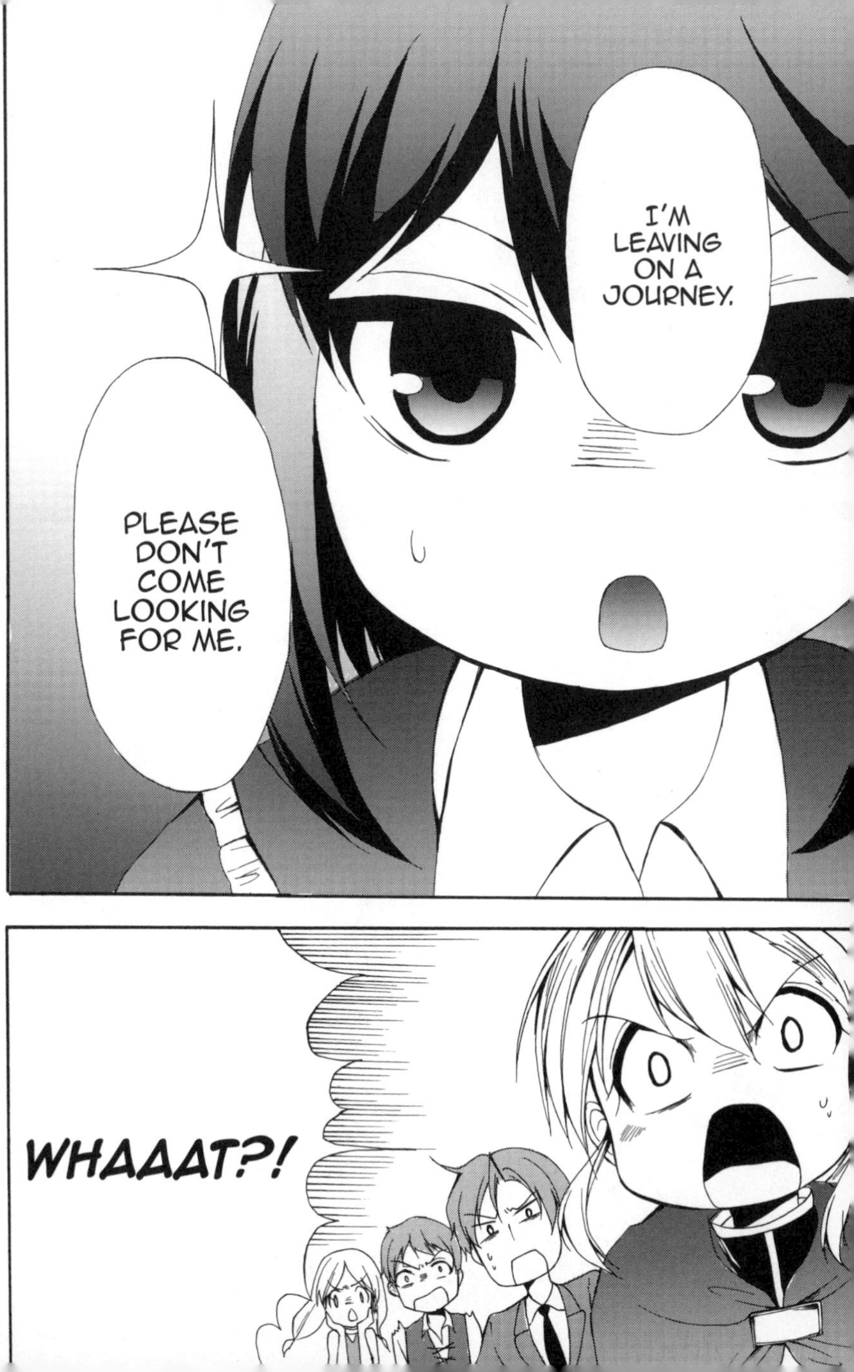
I'M LEAVING ON A JOURNEY.
PLEASE DON'T COME LOOKING FOR ME.
WHAAAT?!

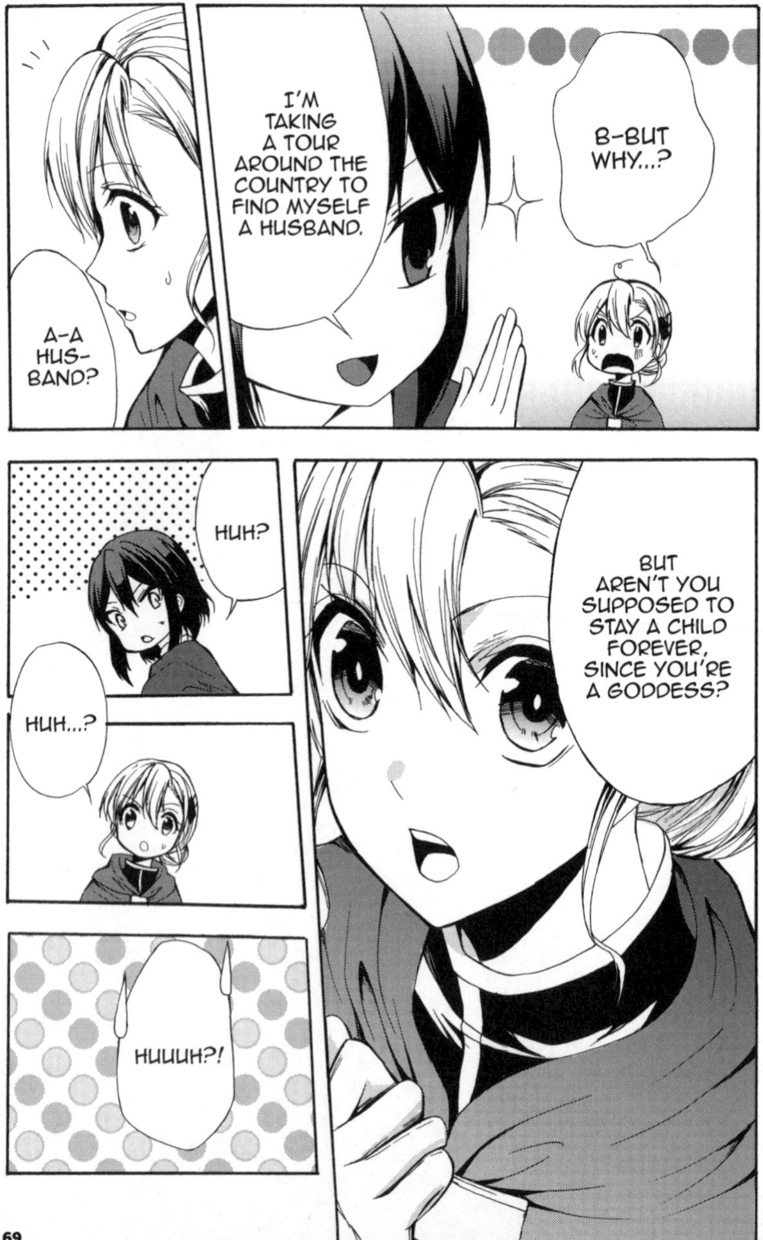
B-BUT WHY...?
I'M TAKING A TOUR AROUND THE COUNTRY TO FIND MYSELF A HUSBAND.
A-A HUS-BAND?
BUT AREN'T YOU SUPPOSED TO STAY A CHILD FOREVER, SINCE YOU'RE A GODDESS?
HUH?
HUH...?
HUUUH?!

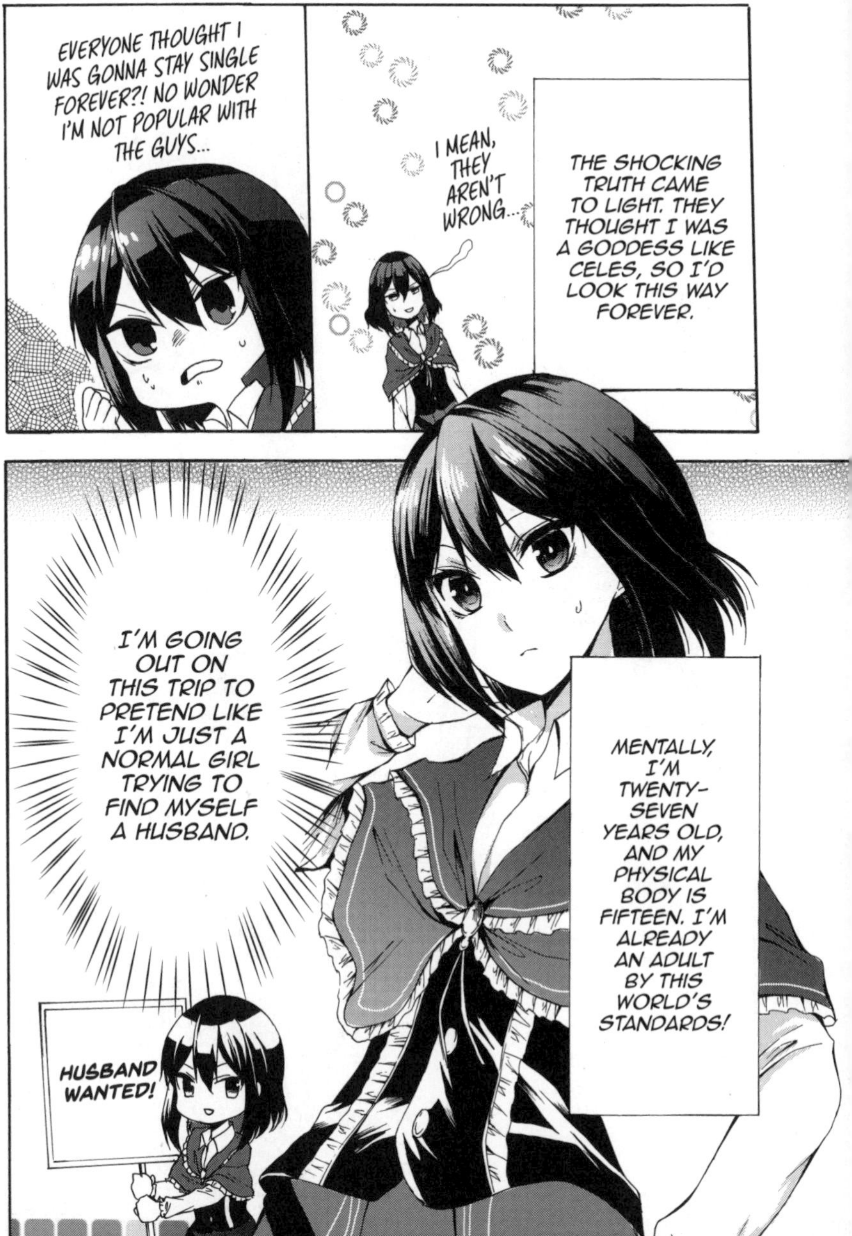
THE SHOCKING TRUTH CAME TO LIGHT. THEY THOUGHT I WAS A GODDESS LIKE CELES, SO I'D LOOK THIS WAY FOREVER.
I MEAN, THEY AREN'T WRONG...
EVERYONE THOUGHT I WAS GONNA STAY SINGLE FOREVER?! NO WONDER I'M NOT POPULAR WITH THE GUYS...
MENTALLY, I'M TWENTY-SEVEN YEARS OLD, AND MY PHYSICAL BODY IS FIFTEEN. I'M ALREADY AN ADULT BY THIS WORLD'S STANDARDS!
I'M GOING OUT ON THIS TRIP TO PRETEND LIKE I'M JUST A NORMAL GIRL TRYING TO FIND MYSELF A HUSBAND.
HUSBAND WANTED!

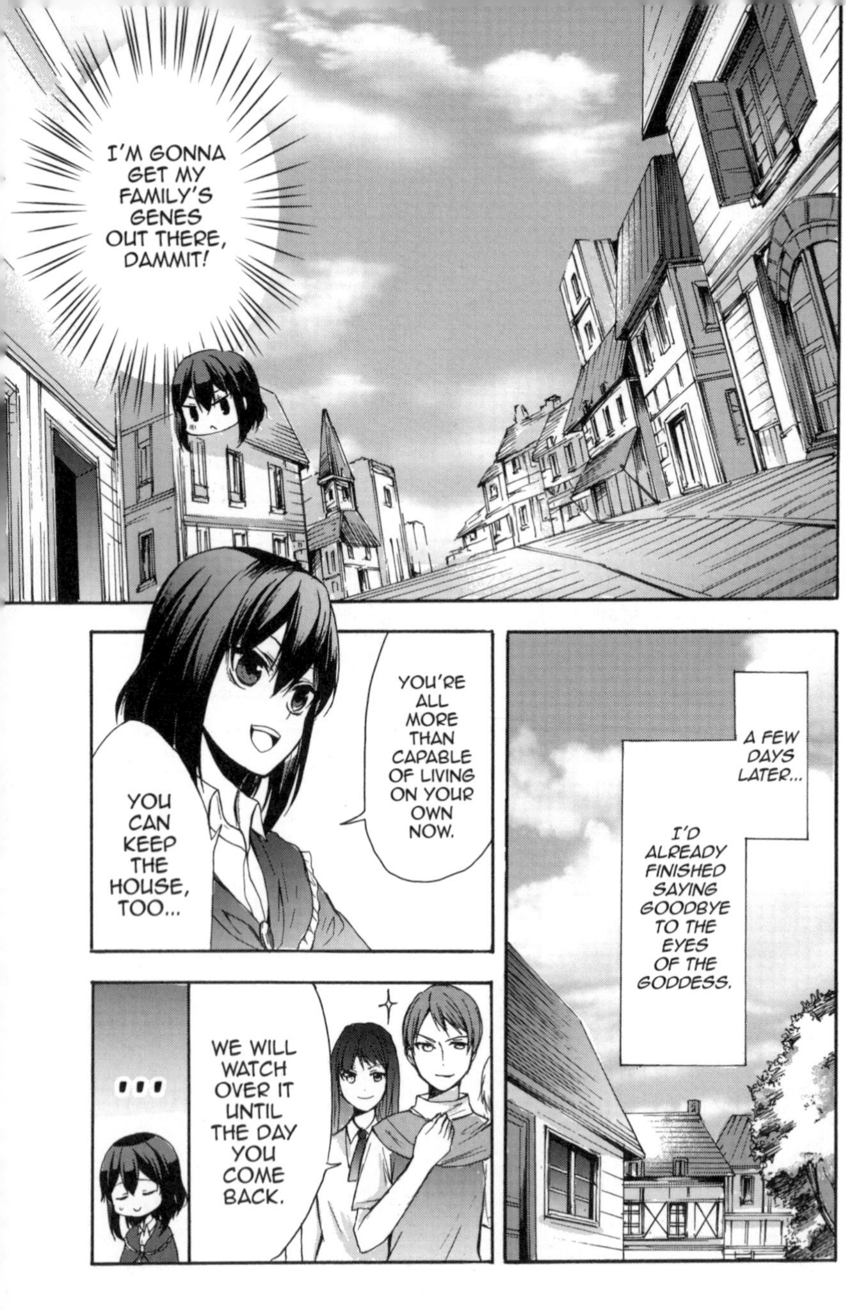
I'M GONNA GET MY FAMILY'S GENES OUT THERE, DAMMIT!
A FEW DAYS LATER...
I'D ALREADY FINISHED SAYING GOODBYE TO THE EYES OF THE GODDESS.
YOU'RE ALL MORE THAN CAPABLE OF LIVING ON YOUR OWN NOW.
YOU CAN KEEP THE HOUSE, TOO...
WE WILL WATCH OVER IT UNTIL THE DAY YOU COME BACK.
...

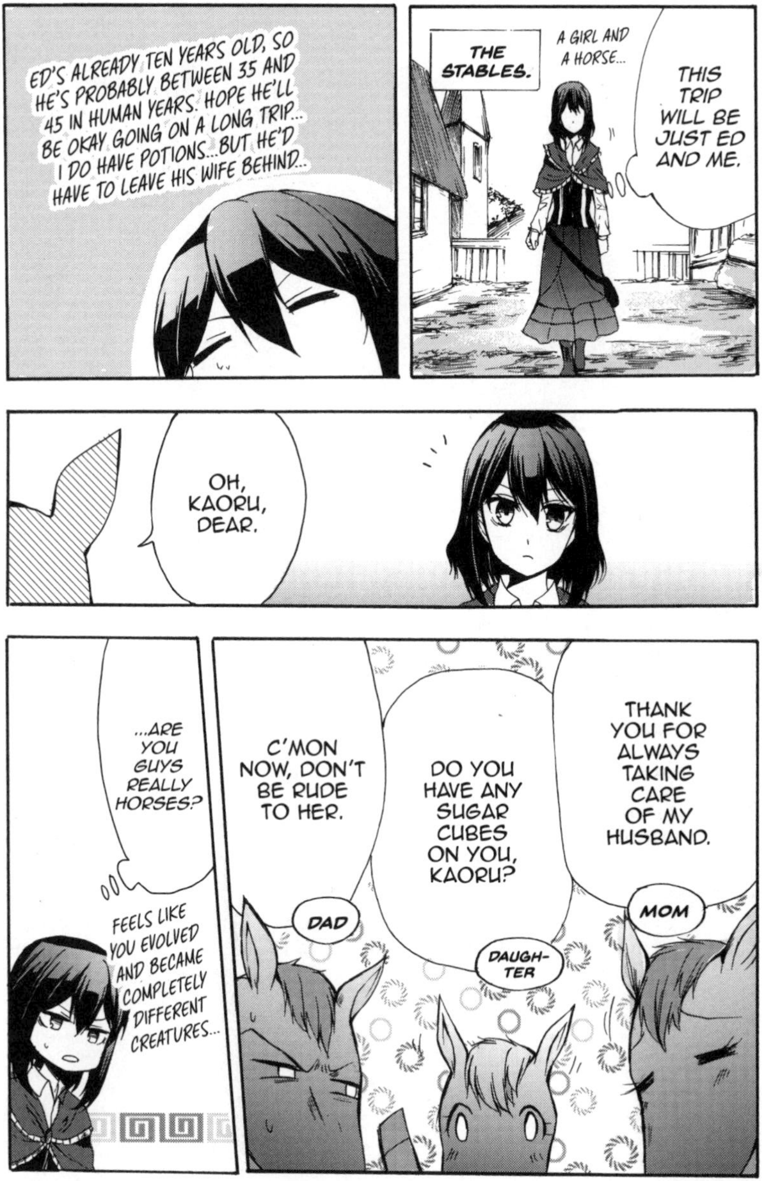
THE STABLES.
A GIRL AND A HORSE...
THIS TRIP WILL BE JUST ED AND ME.
ED'S ALREADY TEN YEARS OLD, SO HE'S PROBABLY BETWEEN 35 AND 45 IN HUMAN YEARS. HOPE HE'LL BE OKAY GOING ON A LONG TRIP... I DO HAVE POTIONS...BUT HE'D HAVE TO LEAVE HIS WIFE BEHIND...
OH, KAORU, DEAR.
THANK YOU FOR ALWAYS TAKING CARE OF MY HUSBAND.
MOM
DO YOU HAVE ANY SUGAR CUBES ON YOU, KAORU?
DAUGHTER
C'MON NOW, DON'T BE RUDE TO HER.
DAD
...ARE YOU GUYS REALLY HORSES?
FEELS LIKE YOU EVOLVED AND BECAME COMPLETELY DIFFERENT CREATURES...

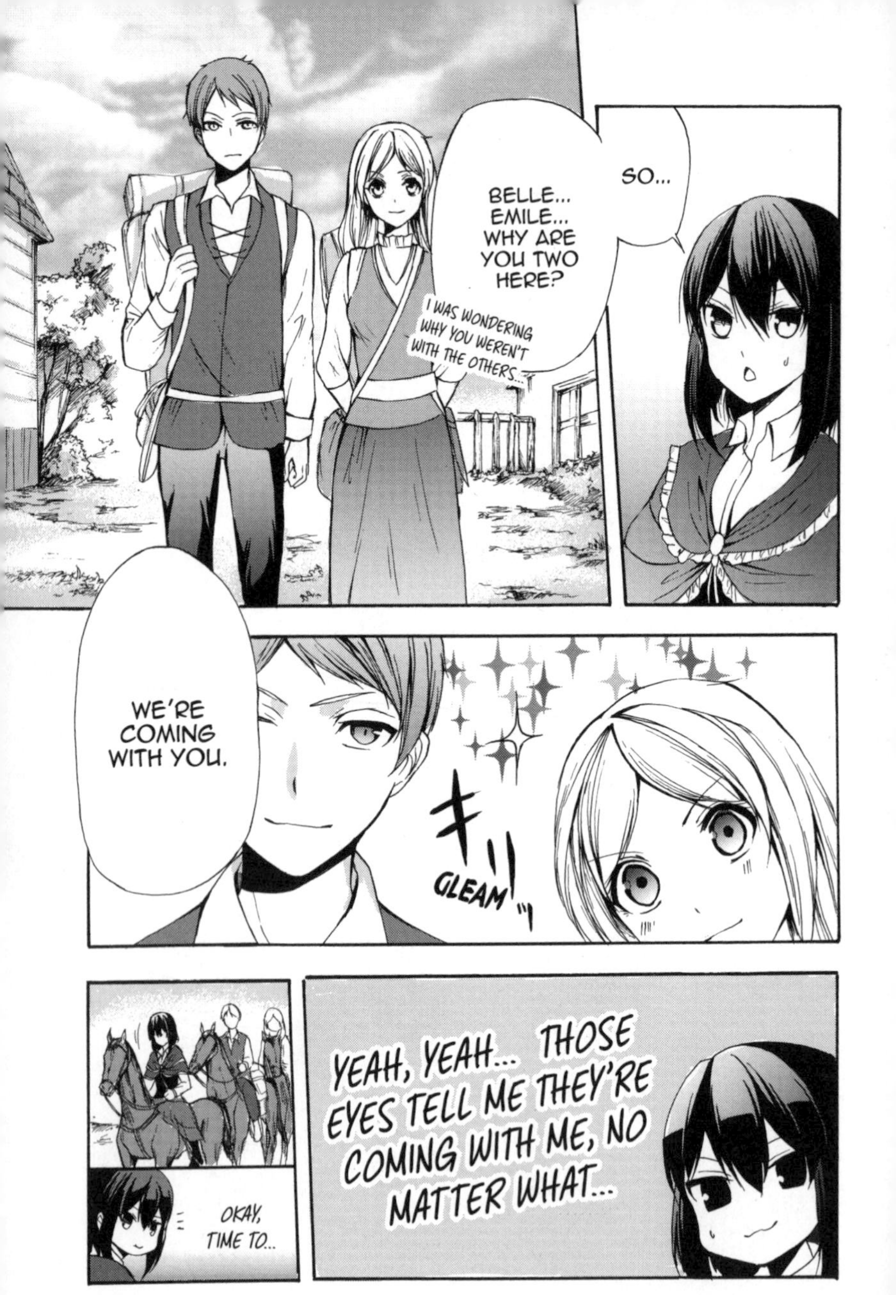
SO...
BELLE... EMILE... WHY ARE YOU TWO HERE?
I WAS WONDERING WHY YOU WEREN'T WITH THE OTHERS...
WE'RE COMING WITH YOU.
GLEAM
YEAH, YEAH... THOSE EYES TELL ME THEY'RE COMING WITH ME, NO MATTER WHAT...
OKAY, TIME TO...

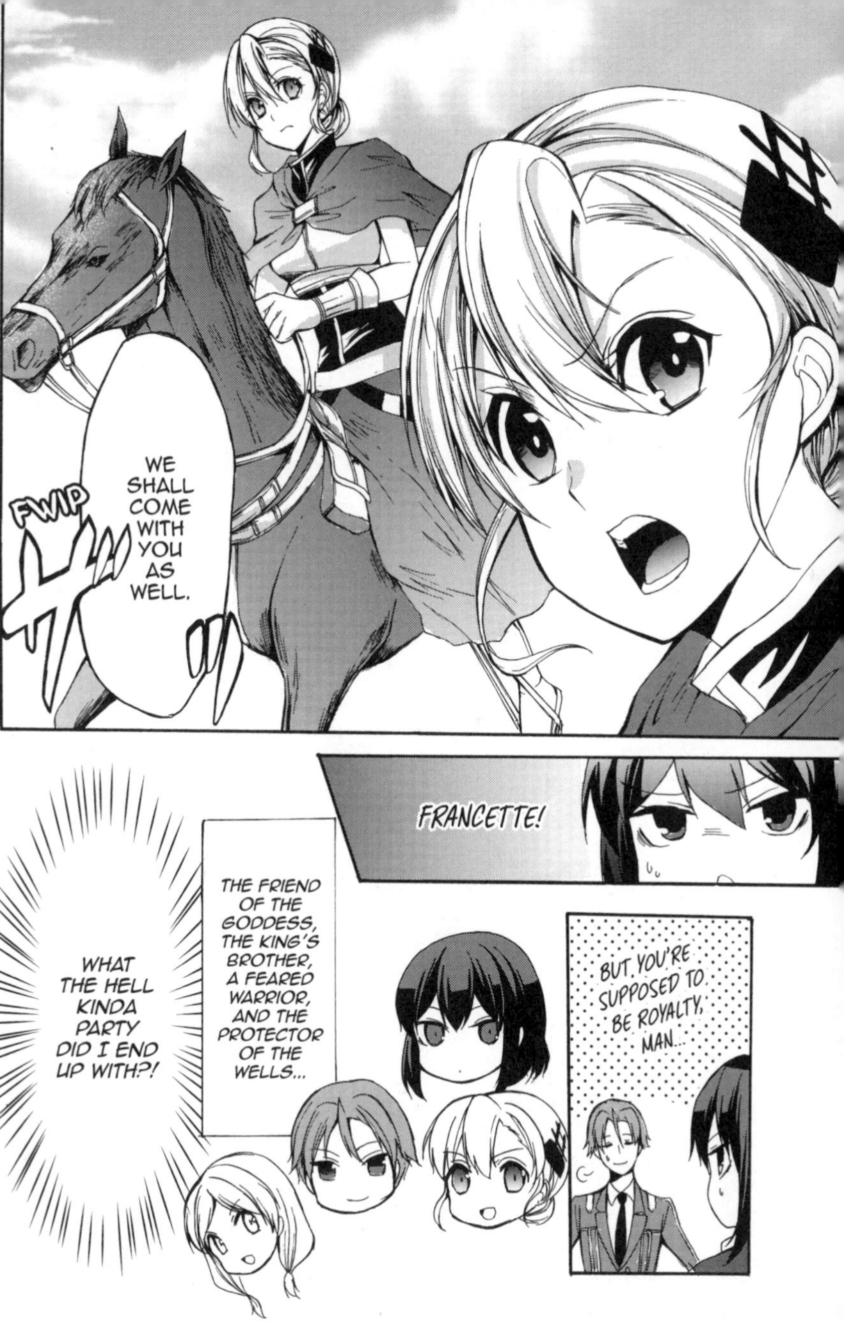
WE SHALL COME WITH YOU AS WELL.
FWIP
FRANCETTE!
THE FRIEND OF THE GODDESS, THE KING'S BROTHER, A FEARED WARRIOR, AND THE PROTECTOR OF THE WELLS...
WHAT THE HELL KINDA PARTY DID I END UP WITH?!
BUT, YOU'RE SUPPOSED TO BE ROYALTY, MAN...

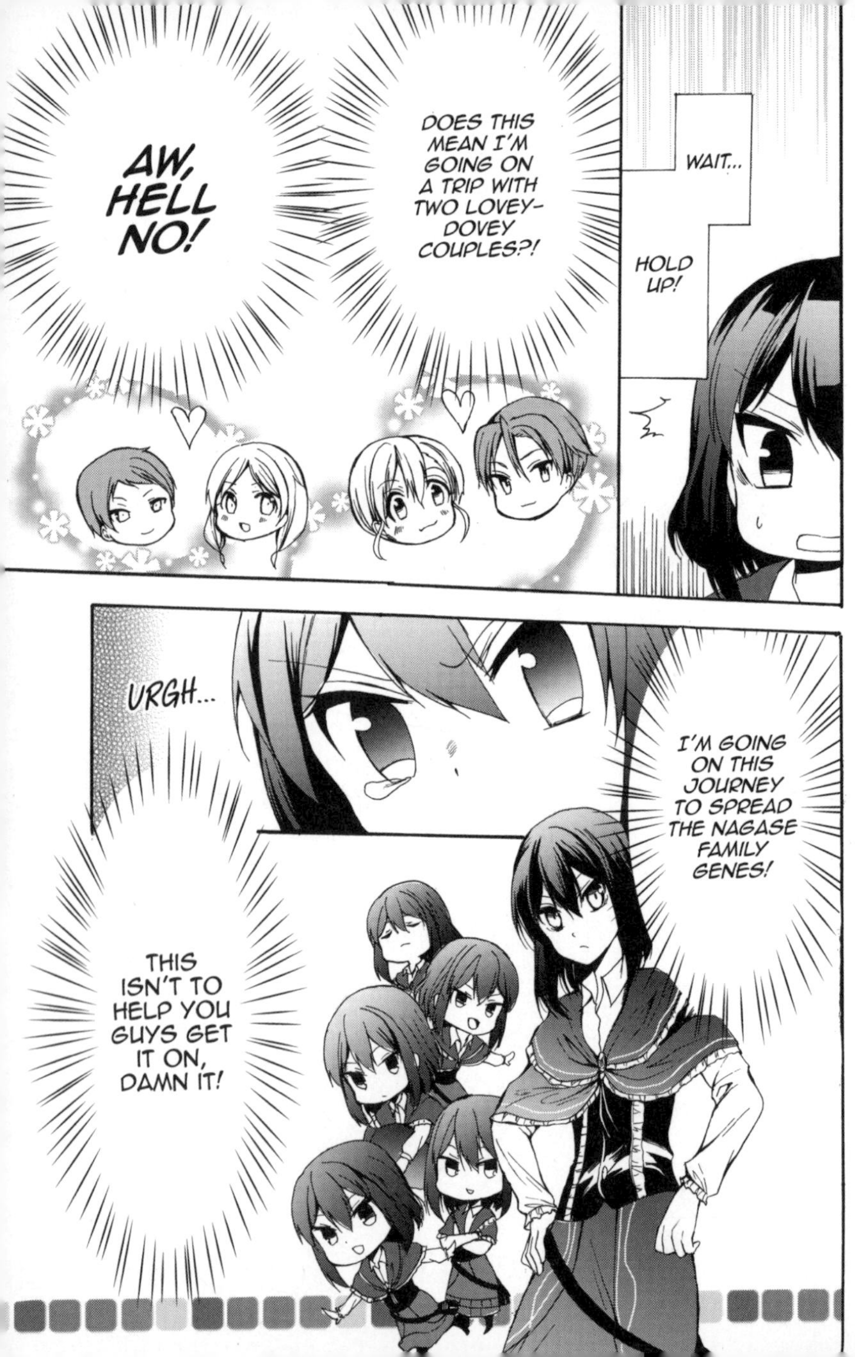
WAIT...
HOLD UP!
DOES THIS MEAN I'M GOING ON A TRIP WITH TWO LOVEY-DOVEY COUPLES?!
AW, HELL NO!
URGH...
I'M GOING ON THIS JOURNEY TO SPREAD THE NAGASE FAMILY GENES!
THIS ISN'T TO HELP YOU GUYS GET IT ON, DAMN IT!

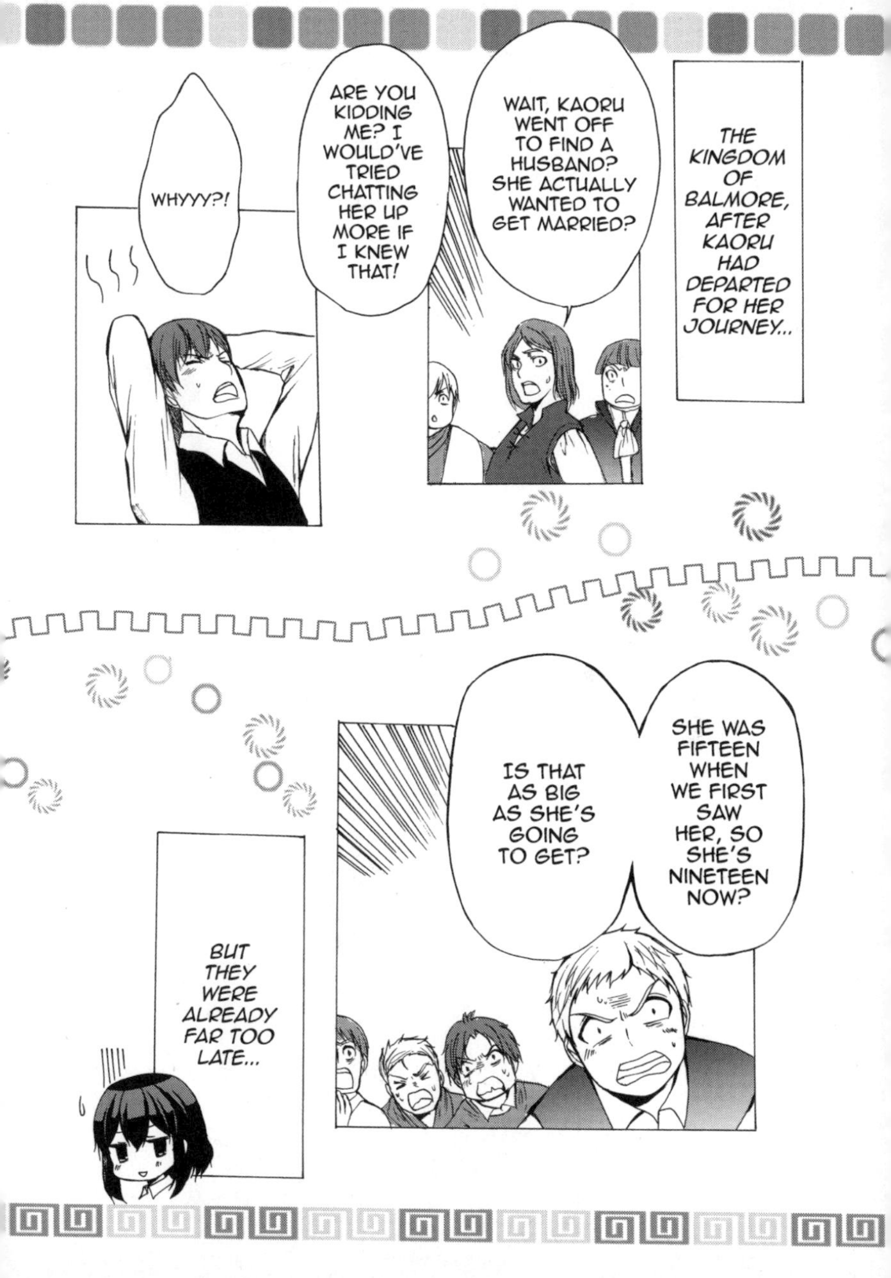
THE KINGDOM OF BALMORE, AFTER KAORU HAD DEPARTED FOR HER JOURNEY...
WAIT, KAORU WENT OFF TO FIND A HUSBAND? SHE ACTUALLY WANTED TO GET MARRIED?
ARE YOU KIDDING ME? I WOULD'VE TRIED CHATTING HER UP MORE IF I KNEW THAT!
WHYYY?!
SHE WAS FIFTEEN WHEN WE FIRST SAW HER, SO SHE'S NINETEEN NOW?
IS THAT AS BIG AS SHE'S GOING TO GET?
BUT THEY WERE ALREADY FAR TOO LATE...

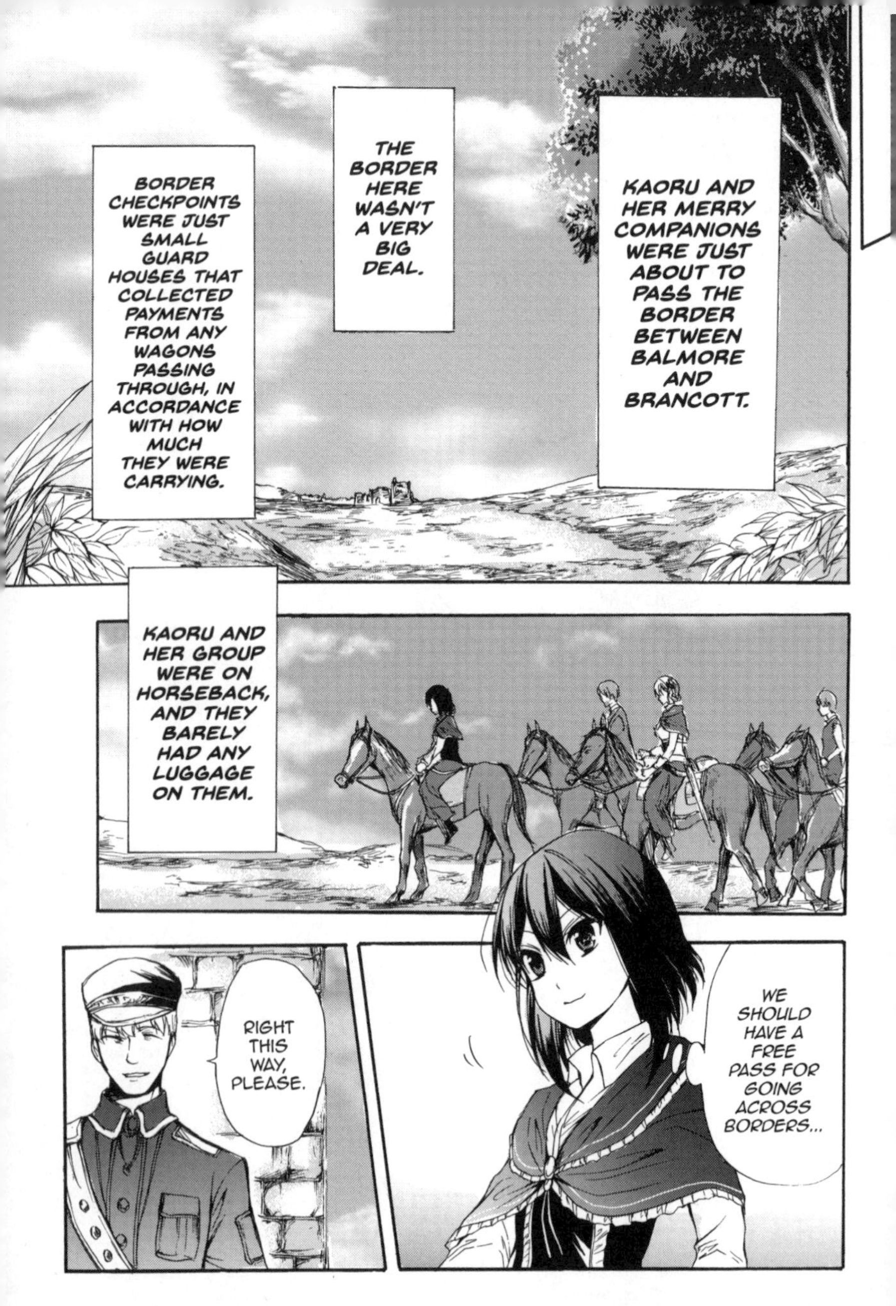
KAORU AND HER MERRY COMPANIONS WERE JUST ABOUT TO PASS THE BORDER BETWEEN BALMORE AND BRANCOTT.
THE BORDER HERE WASN'T A VERY BIG DEAL.
BORDER CHECKPOINTS WERE JUST SMALL GUARD HOUSES THAT COLLECTED PAYMENTS FROM ANY WAGONS PASSING THROUGH, IN ACCORDANCE WITH HOW MUCH THEY WERE CARRYING.
KAORU AND HER GROUP WERE ON HORSEBACK, AND THEY BARELY HAD ANY LUGGAGE ON THEM.
WE SHOULD HAVE A FREE PASS FOR GOING ACROSS BORDERS...
RIGHT THIS WAY, PLEASE.

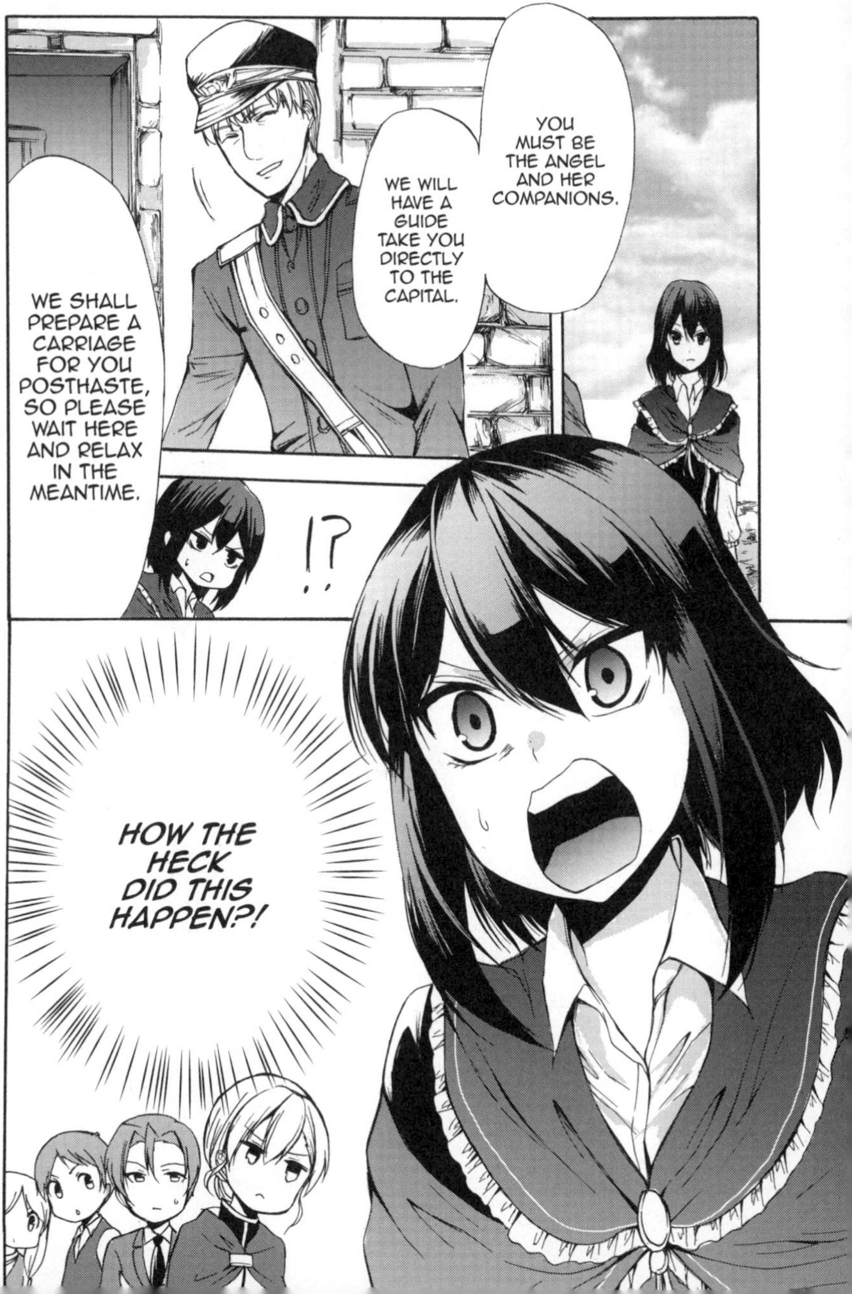
YOU MUST BE THE ANGEL AND HER COMPANIONS.
WE WILL HAVE A GUIDE TAKE YOU DIRECTLY TO THE CAPITAL.
WE SHALL PREPARE A CARRIAGE FOR YOU POSTHASTE, SO PLEASE WAIT HERE AND RELAX IN THE MEANTIME.
!?
HOW THE HECK DID THIS HAPPEN?!

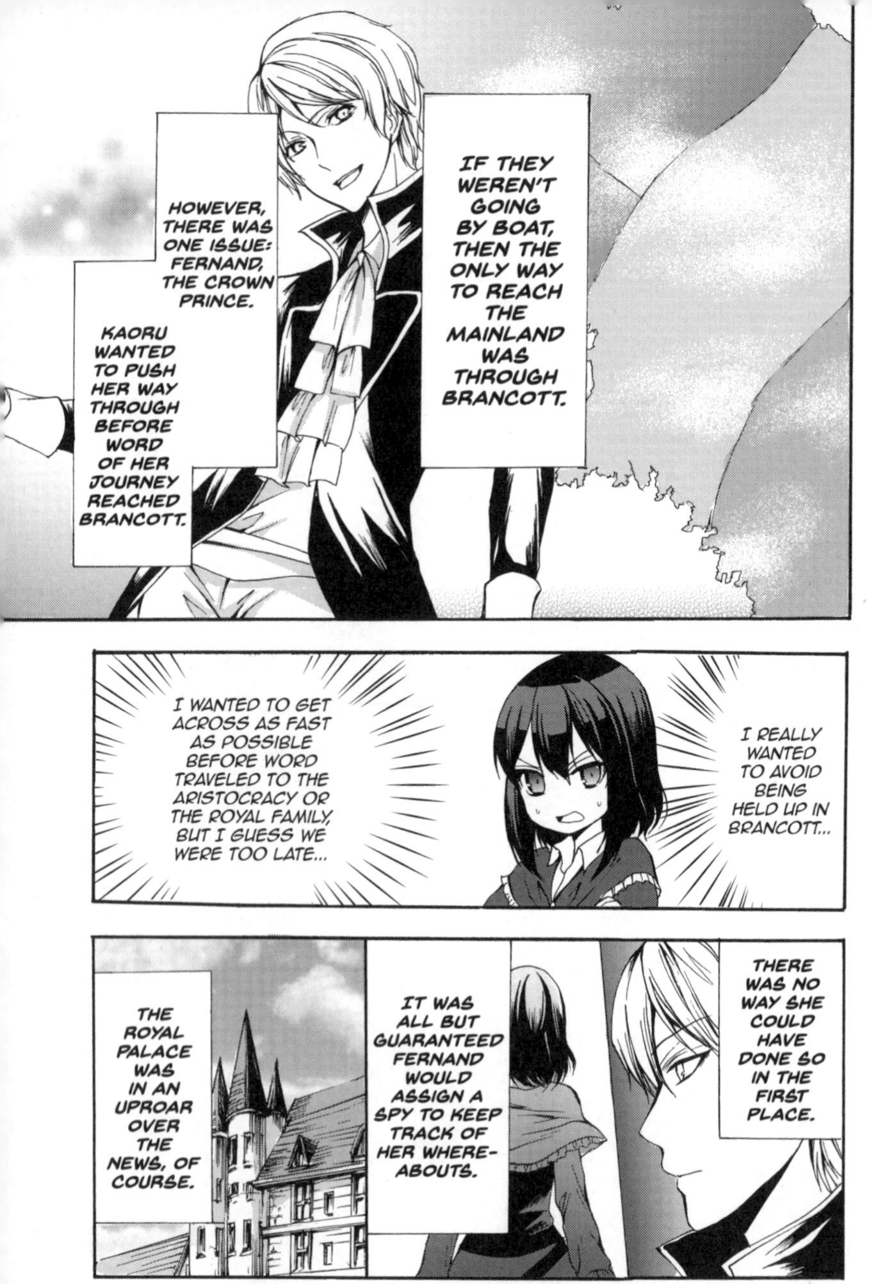
IF THEY WEREN'T GOING BY BOAT, THEN THE ONLY WAY TO REACH THE MAINLAND WAS THROUGH BRANCOTT.
HOWEVER, THERE WAS ONE ISSUE: FERNAND, THE CROWN PRINCE.
KAORU WANTED TO PUSH HER WAY THROUGH BEFORE WORD OF HER JOURNEY REACHED BRANCOTT.
I REALLY WANTED TO AVOID BEING HELD UP IN BRANCOTT...
I WANTED TO GET ACROSS AS FAST AS POSSIBLE BEFORE WORD TRAVELED TO THE ARISTOCRACY OR THE ROYAL FAMILY, BUT I GUESS WE WERE TOO LATE...
THERE WAS NO WAY SHE COULD HAVE DONE SO IN THE FIRST PLACE.
IT WAS ALL BUT GUARANTEED FERNAND WOULD ASSIGN A SPY TO KEEP TRACK OF HER WHERE-ABOUTS.
THE ROYAL PALACE WAS IN AN UPROAR OVER THE NEWS, OF COURSE.

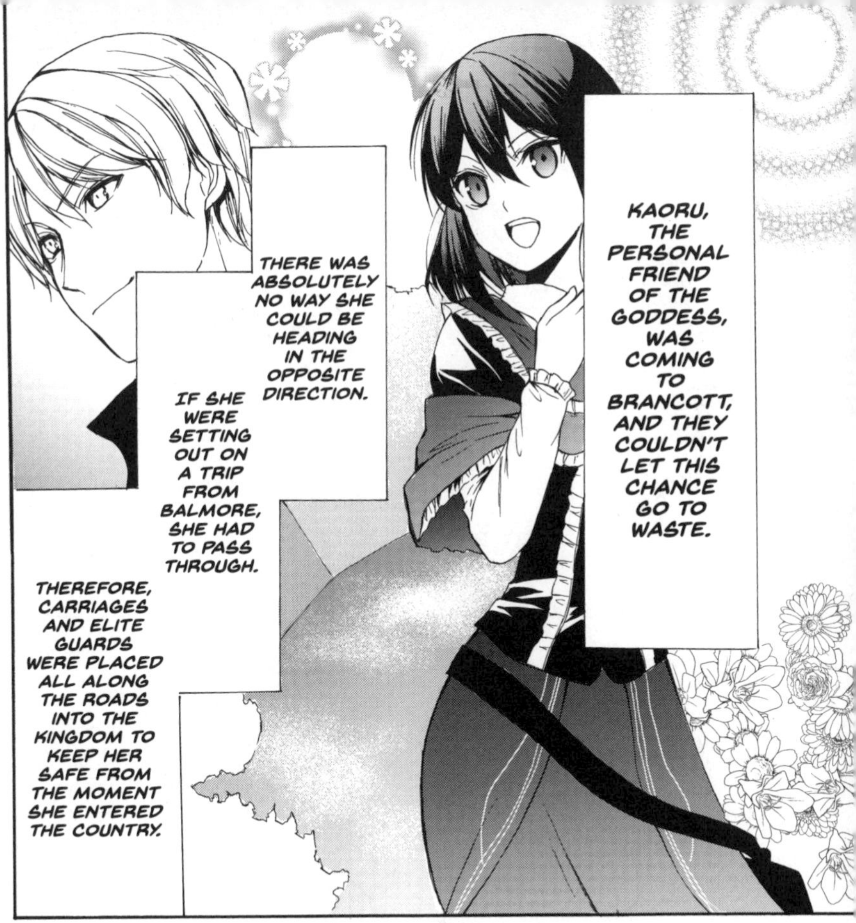
KAORU, THE PERSONAL FRIEND OF THE GODDESS, WAS COMING TO BRANCOTT, AND THEY COULDN'T LET THIS CHANCE GO TO WASTE.
THERE WAS ABSOLUTELY NO WAY SHE COULD BE HEADING IN THE OPPOSITE DIRECTION.
IF SHE WERE SETTING OUT ON A TRIP FROM BALMORE, SHE HAD TO PASS THROUGH.
THEREFORE, CARRIAGES AND ELITE GUARDS WERE PLACED ALL ALONG THE ROADS INTO THE KINGDOM TO KEEP HER SAFE FROM THE MOMENT SHE ENTERED THE COUNTRY.
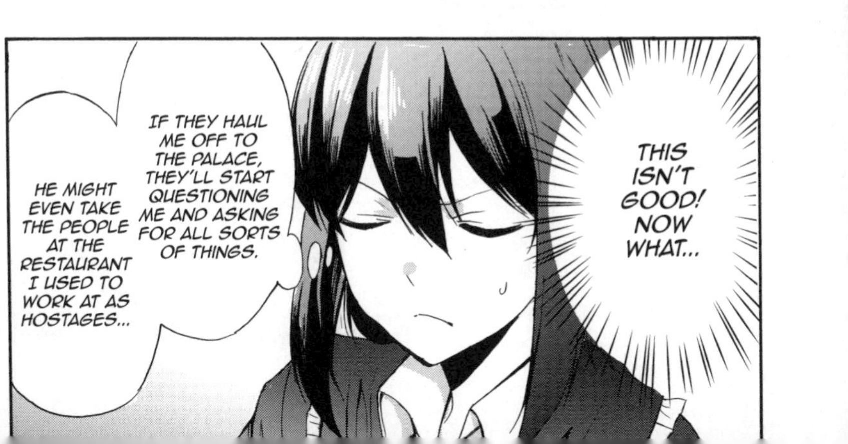
THIS ISN'T GOOD! NOW WHAT...
IF THEY HAUL ME OFF TO THE PALACE, THEY'LL START QUESTIONING ME AND ASKING FOR ALL SORTS OF THINGS.
HE MIGHT EVEN TAKE THE PEOPLE AT THE RESTAURANT I USED TO WORK AT AS HOSTAGES...

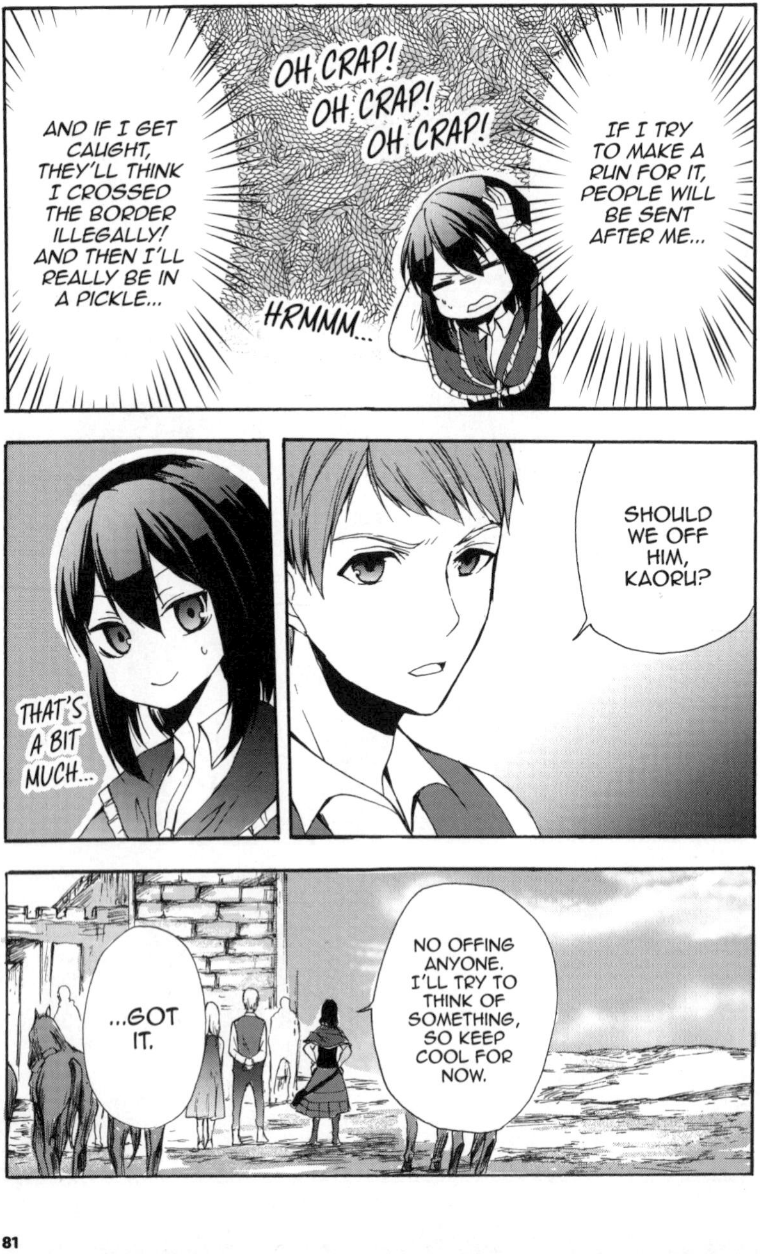
IF I TRY TO MAKE A RUN FOR IT, PEOPLE WILL BE SENT AFTER ME...
OH CRAP! OH CRAP! OH CRAP!
AND IF I GET CAUGHT, THEY'LL THINK I CROSSED THE BORDER ILLEGALLY! AND THEN I'LL REALLY BE IN A PICKLE...
HRMMM...
SHOULD WE OFF HIM, KAORU?
THAT'S A BIT MUCH...
NO OFFING ANYONE. I'LL TRY TO THINK OF SOMETHING, SO KEEP COOL FOR NOW.
...GOT IT.

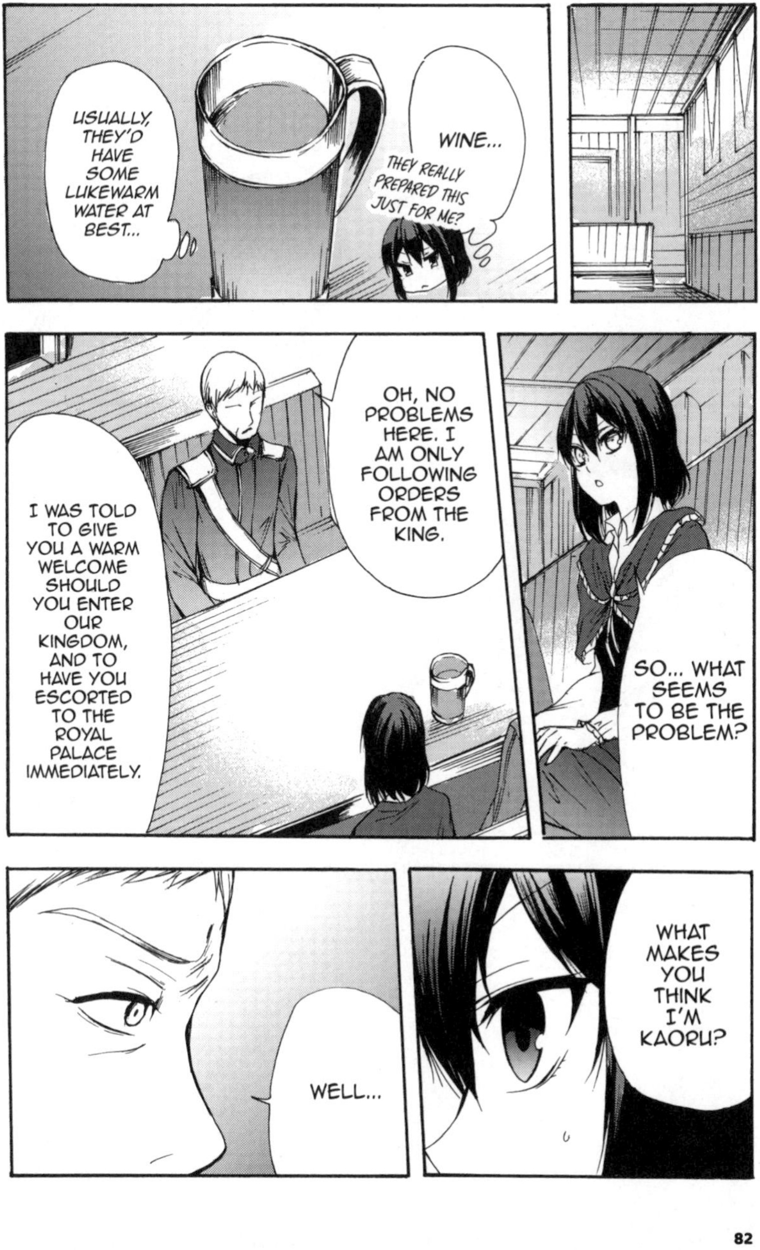
WINE...
THEY REALLY PREPARED THIS JUST FOR ME?
USUALLY, THEY'D HAVE SOME LUKEWARM WATER AT BEST...
SO... WHAT SEEMS TO BE THE PROBLEM?
OH, NO PROBLEMS HERE. I AM ONLY FOLLOWING ORDERS FROM THE KING.
I WAS TOLD TO GIVE YOU A WARM WELCOME SHOULD YOU ENTER OUR KINGDOM, AND TO HAVE YOU ESCORTED TO THE ROYAL PALACE IMMEDIATELY.
WHAT MAKES YOU THINK I'M KAORU?
WELL...

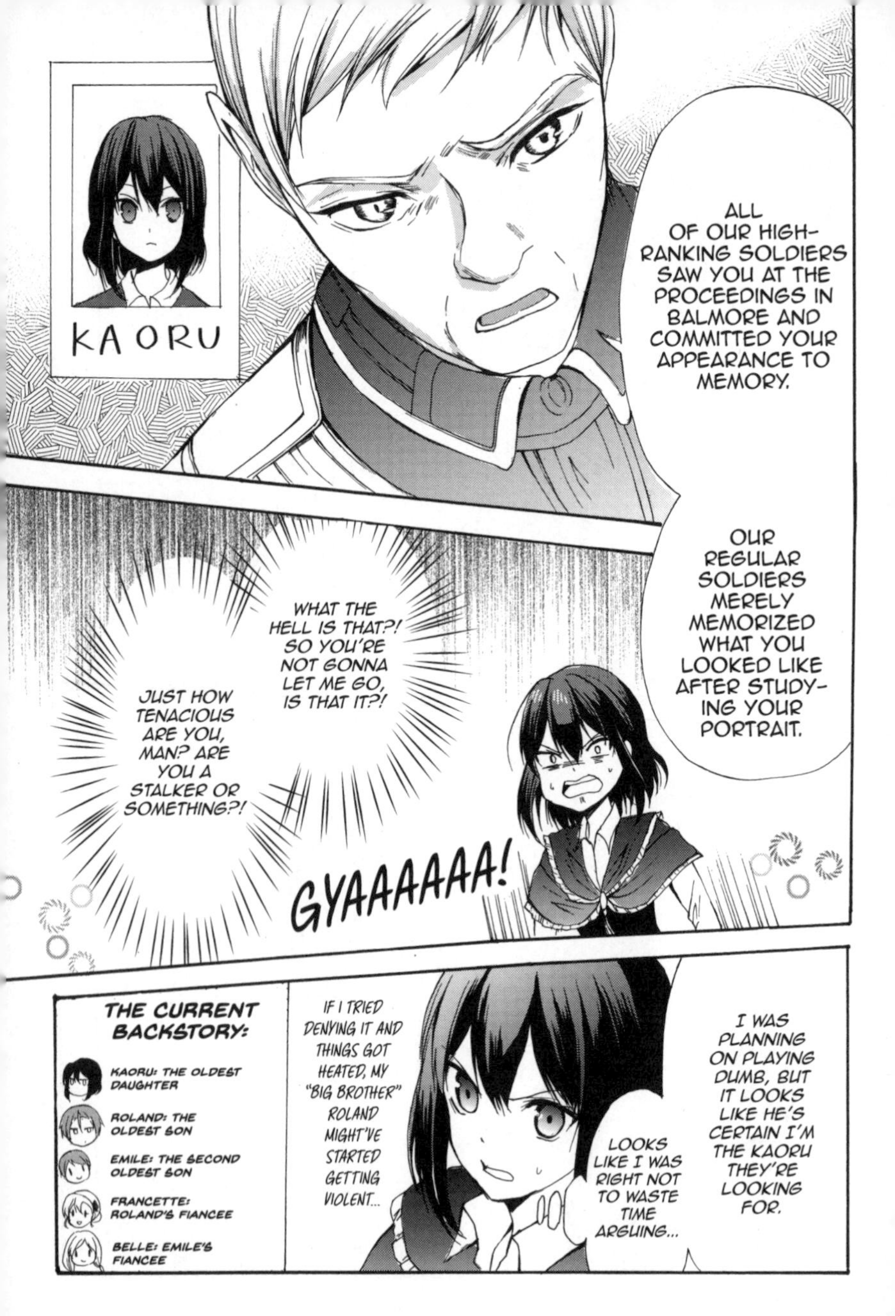
ALL OF OUR HIGH-RANKING SOLDIERS SAW YOU AT THE PROCEEDINGS IN BALMORE AND COMMITTED YOUR APPEARANCE TO MEMORY.
KAORU
OUR REGULAR SOLDIERS MERELY MEMORIZED WHAT YOU LOOKED LIKE AFTER STUDYING YOUR PORTRAIT.
WHAT THE HELL IS THAT?! SO YOU'RE NOT GONNA LET ME GO, IS THAT IT?!
JUST HOW TENACIOUS ARE YOU, MAN? ARE YOU A STALKER OR SOMETHING?!
GYAAAAAAA!
I WAS PLANNING ON PLAYING DUMB, BUT IT LOOKS LIKE HE'S CERTAIN I'M THE KAORU THEY'RE LOOKING FOR.
LOOKS LIKE I WAS RIGHT NOT TO WASTE TIME ARGUING...
IF I TRIED DENYING IT AND THINGS GOT HEATED, MY "BIG BROTHER" ROLAND MIGHT'VE STARTED GETTING VIOLENT...
THE CURRENT BACKSTORY:
KAORU: THE OLDEST DAUGHTER
ROLAND: THE OLDEST SON
EMILE: THE SECOND OLDEST SON
FRANCETTE: ROLAND'S FIANCEE
BELLE: EMILE'S FIANCEE

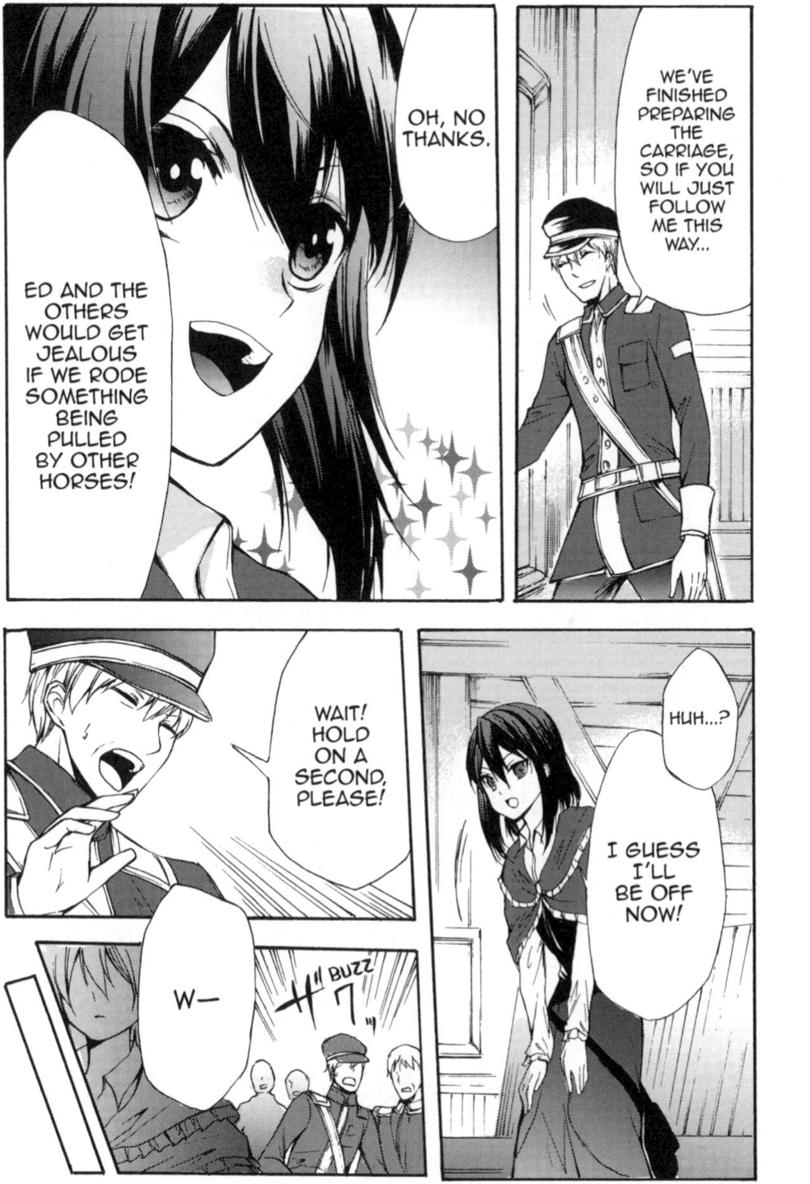
WE'VE FINISHED PREPARING THE CARRIAGE, SO IF YOU WILL JUST FOLLOW ME THIS WAY...
OH, NO THANKS.
ED AND THE OTHERS WOULD GET JEALOUS IF WE RODE SOMETHING BEING PULLED BY OTHER HORSES!
HUH...?
I GUESS I'LL BE OFF NOW!
WAIT! HOLD ON A SECOND, PLEASE!
BUZZ
W—

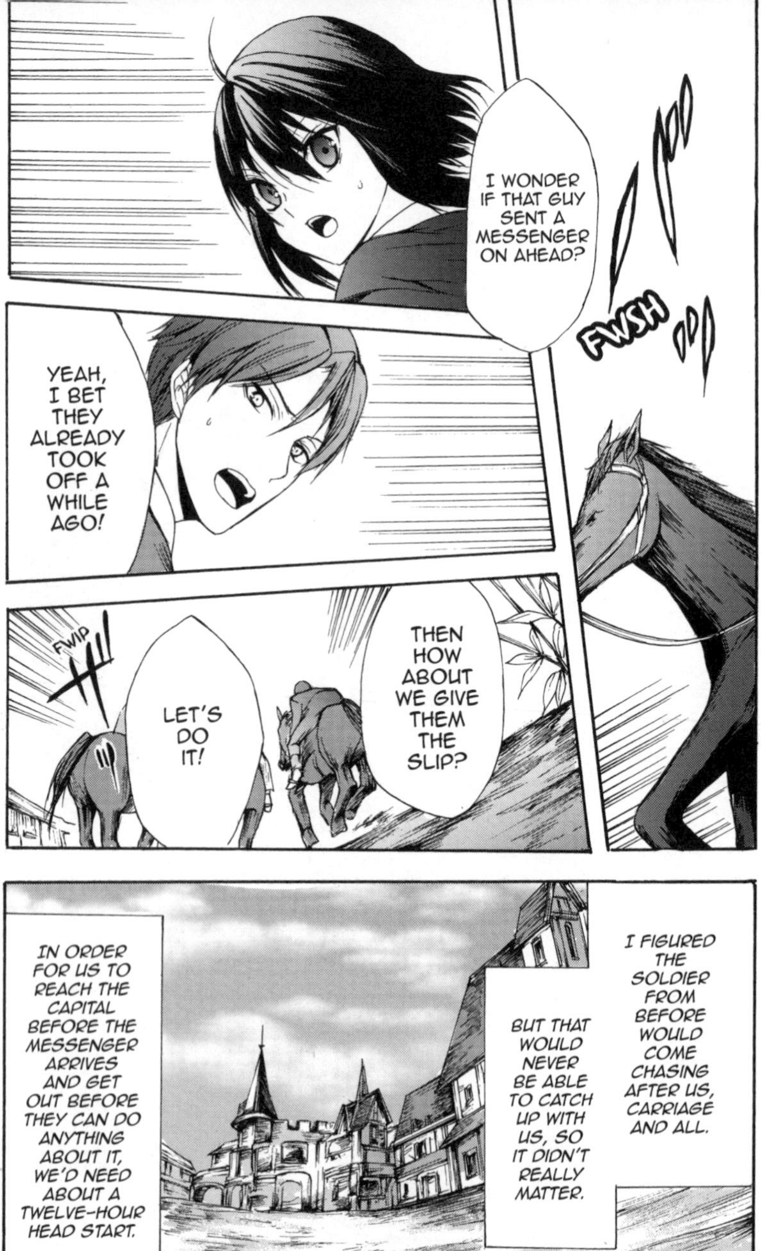
FWSH
I WONDER IF THAT GUY SENT A MESSENGER ON AHEAD?
YEAH, I BET THEY ALREADY TOOK OFF A WHILE AGO!
THEN HOW ABOUT WE GIVE THEM THE SLIP?
LET'S DO IT!
FWIP
I FIGURED THE SOLDIER FROM BEFORE WOULD COME CHASING AFTER US, CARRIAGE AND ALL.
BUT THAT WOULD NEVER BE ABLE TO CATCH UP WITH US, SO IT DIDN'T REALLY MATTER.
IN ORDER FOR US TO REACH THE CAPITAL BEFORE THE MESSENGER ARRIVES AND GET OUT BEFORE THEY CAN DO ANYTHING ABOUT IT, WE'D NEED ABOUT A TWELVE-HOUR HEAD START.

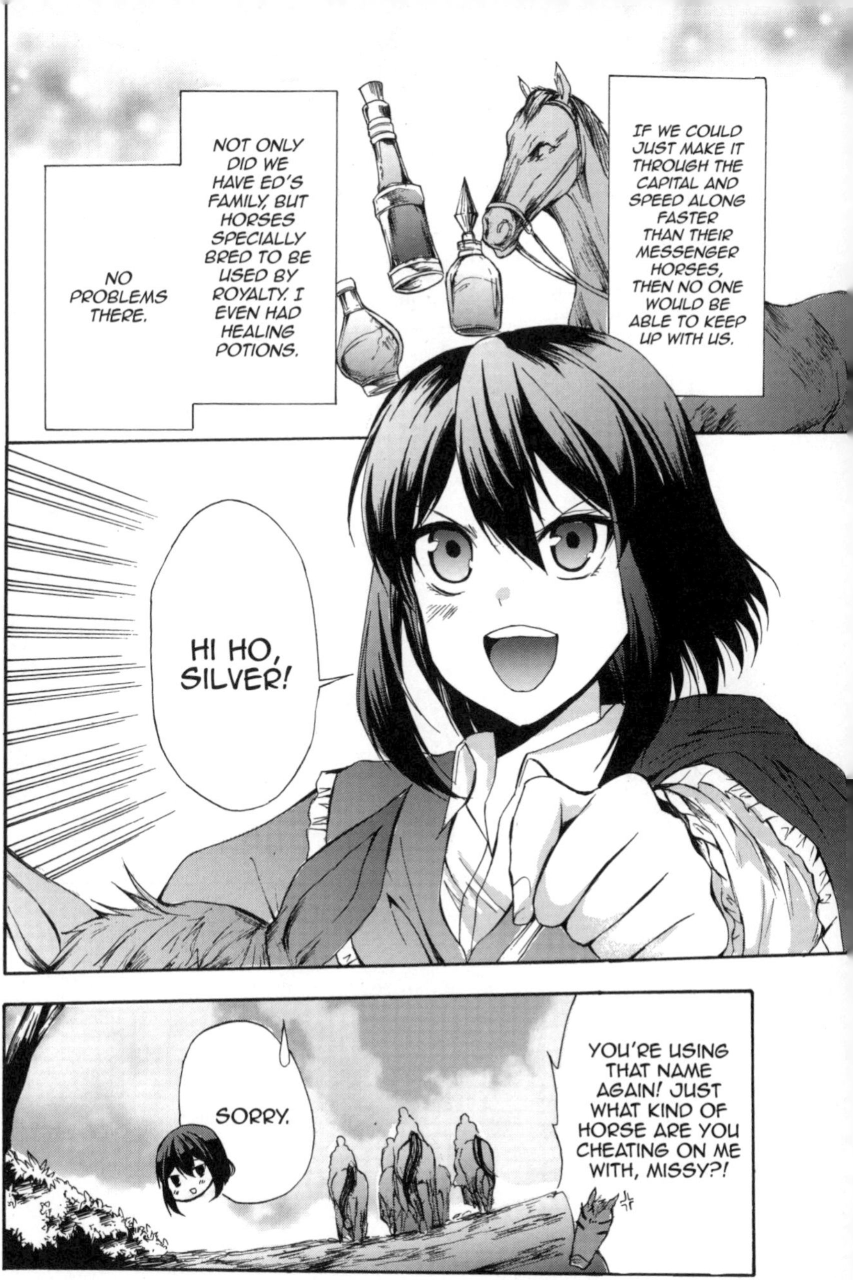
IF WE COULD JUST MAKE IT THROUGH THE CAPITAL AND SPEED ALONG FASTER THAN THEIR MESSENGER HORSES, THEN NO ONE WOULD BE ABLE TO KEEP UP WITH US.
NOT ONLY DID WE HAVE ED'S FAMILY, BUT HORSES SPECIALLY BRED TO BE USED BY ROYALTY. I EVEN HAD HEALING POTIONS.
NO PROBLEMS THERE.
HI HO, SILVER!
YOU'RE USING THAT NAME AGAIN! JUST WHAT KIND OF HORSE ARE YOU CHEATING ON ME WITH, MISSY?!
SORRY.

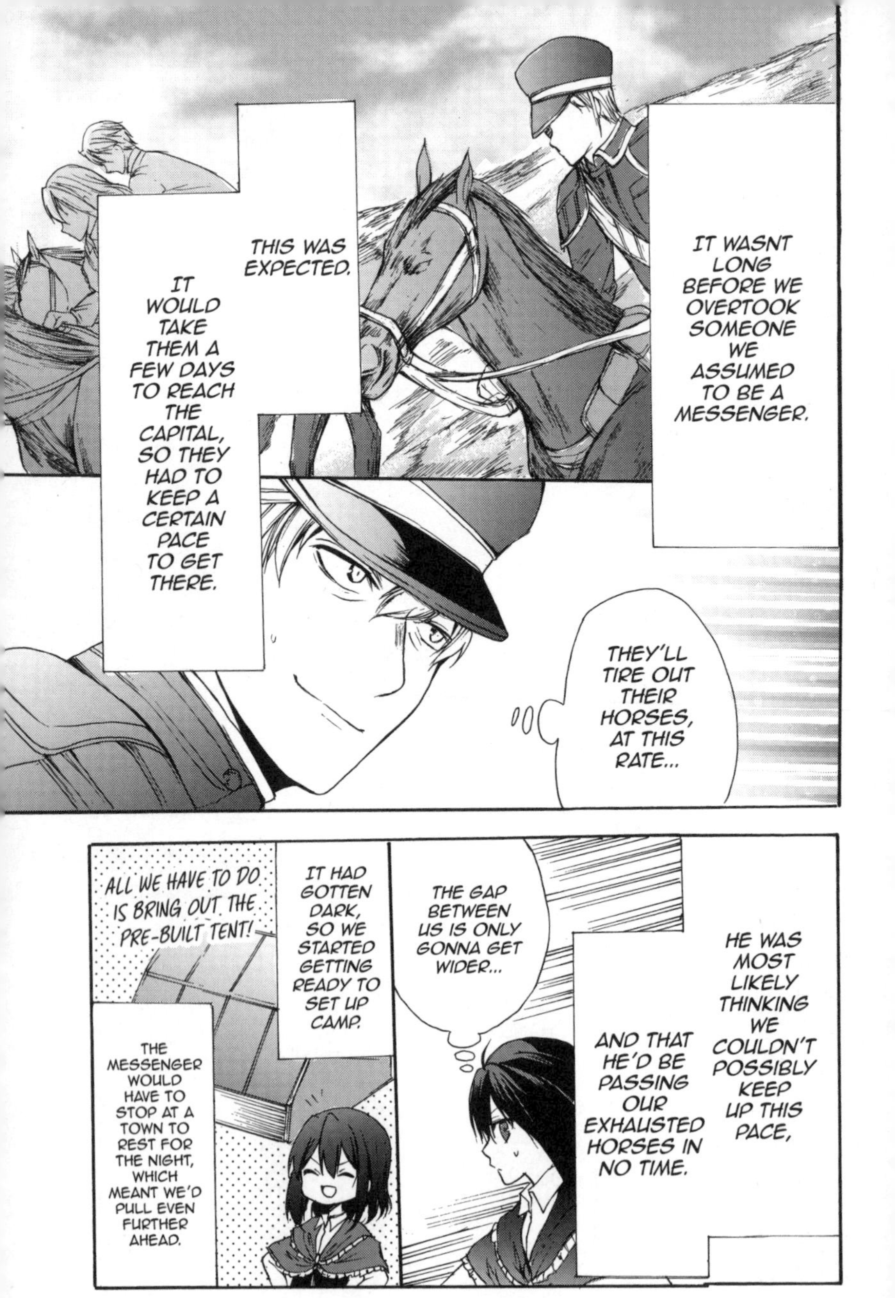
IT WASNT LONG BEFORE WE OVERTOOK SOMEONE WE ASSUMED TO BE A MESSENGER.
THIS WAS EXPECTED.
IT WOULD TAKE THEM A FEW DAYS TO REACH THE CAPITAL, SO THEY HAD TO KEEP A CERTAIN PACE TO GET THERE.
THEY'LL TIRE OUT THEIR HORSES, AT THIS RATE...
HE WAS MOST LIKELY THINKING WE COULDN'T POSSIBLY KEEP UP THIS PACE,
AND THAT HE'D BE PASSING OUR EXHAUSTED HORSES IN NO TIME.
THE GAP BETWEEN US IS ONLY GONNA GET WIDER...
IT HAD GOTTEN DARK, SO WE STARTED GETTING READY TO SET UP CAMP.
ALL WE HAVE TO DO IS BRING OUT THE PRE-BUILT TENT!
THE MESSENGER WOULD HAVE TO STOP AT A TOWN TO REST FOR THE NIGHT, WHICH MEANT WE'D PULL EVEN FURTHER AHEAD.

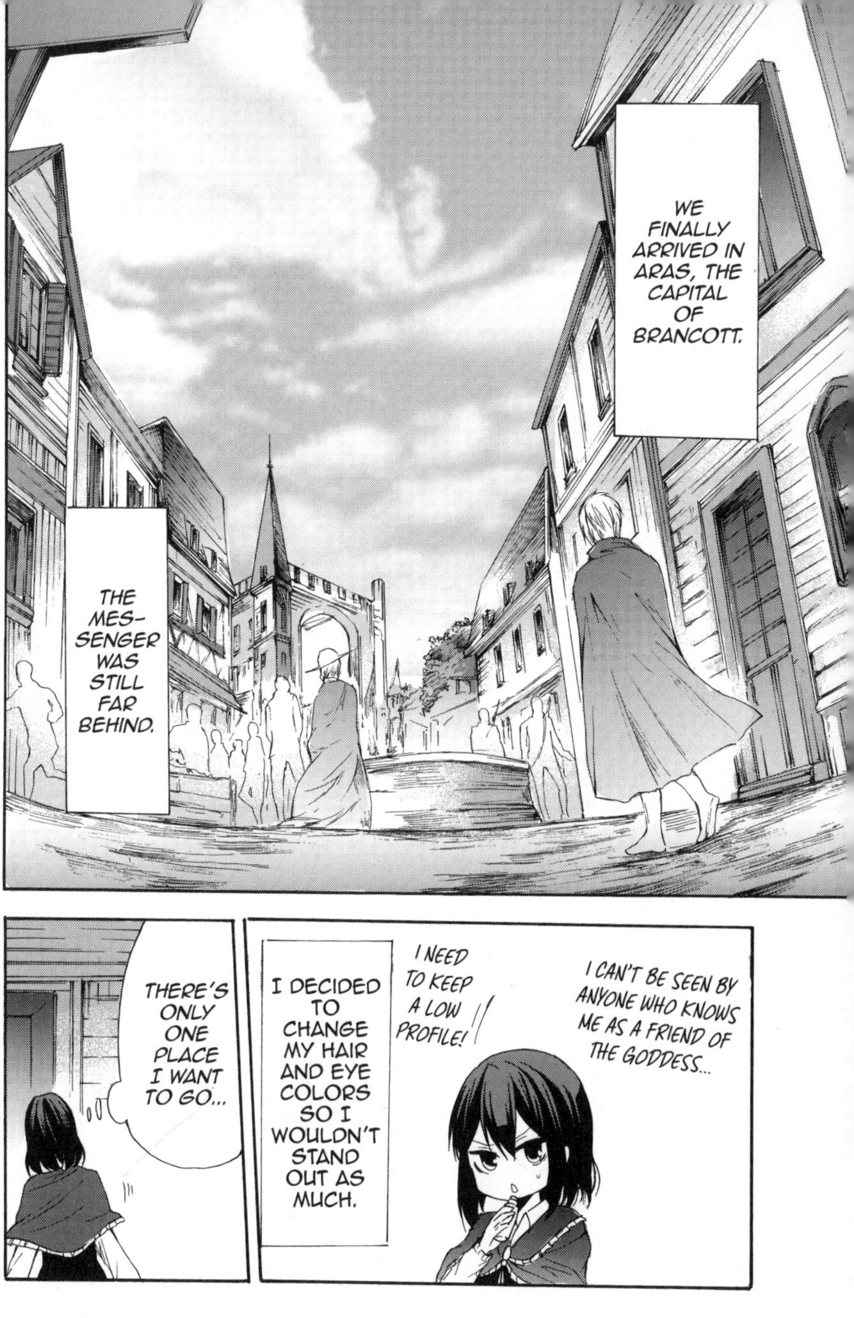
WE FINALLY ARRIVED IN ARAS, THE CAPITAL OF BRANCOTT.
THE MES-SENGER WAS STILL FAR BEHIND.
I CAN'T BE SEEN BY ANYONE WHO KNOWS ME AS A FRIEND OF THE GODDESS...
I NEED TO KEEP A LOW PROFILE!
I DECIDED TO CHANGE MY HAIR AND EYE COLORS SO I WOULDN'T STAND OUT AS MUCH.
THERE'S ONLY ONE PLACE I WANT TO GO...

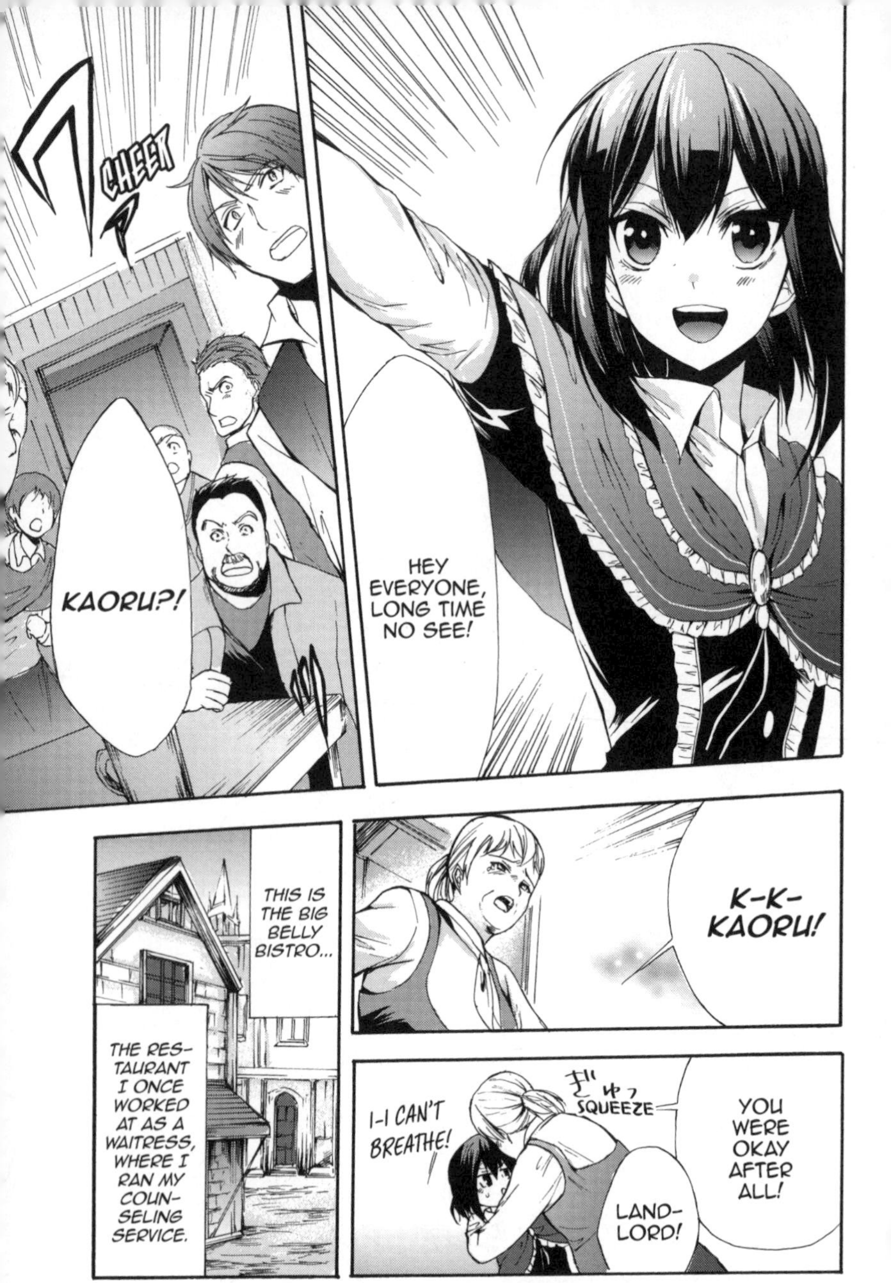
HEY EVERYONE, LONG TIME NO SEE!
CHEER
KAORU?!
K-K-KAORU!
YOU WERE OKAY AFTER ALL!
ぎゅっ SQUEEZE
LAND-LORD!
I-I CAN'T BREATHE!
THIS IS THE BIG BELLY BISTRO...
THE RES-TAURANT I ONCE WORKED AT AS A WAITRESS, WHERE I RAN MY COUN-SELING SERVICE.

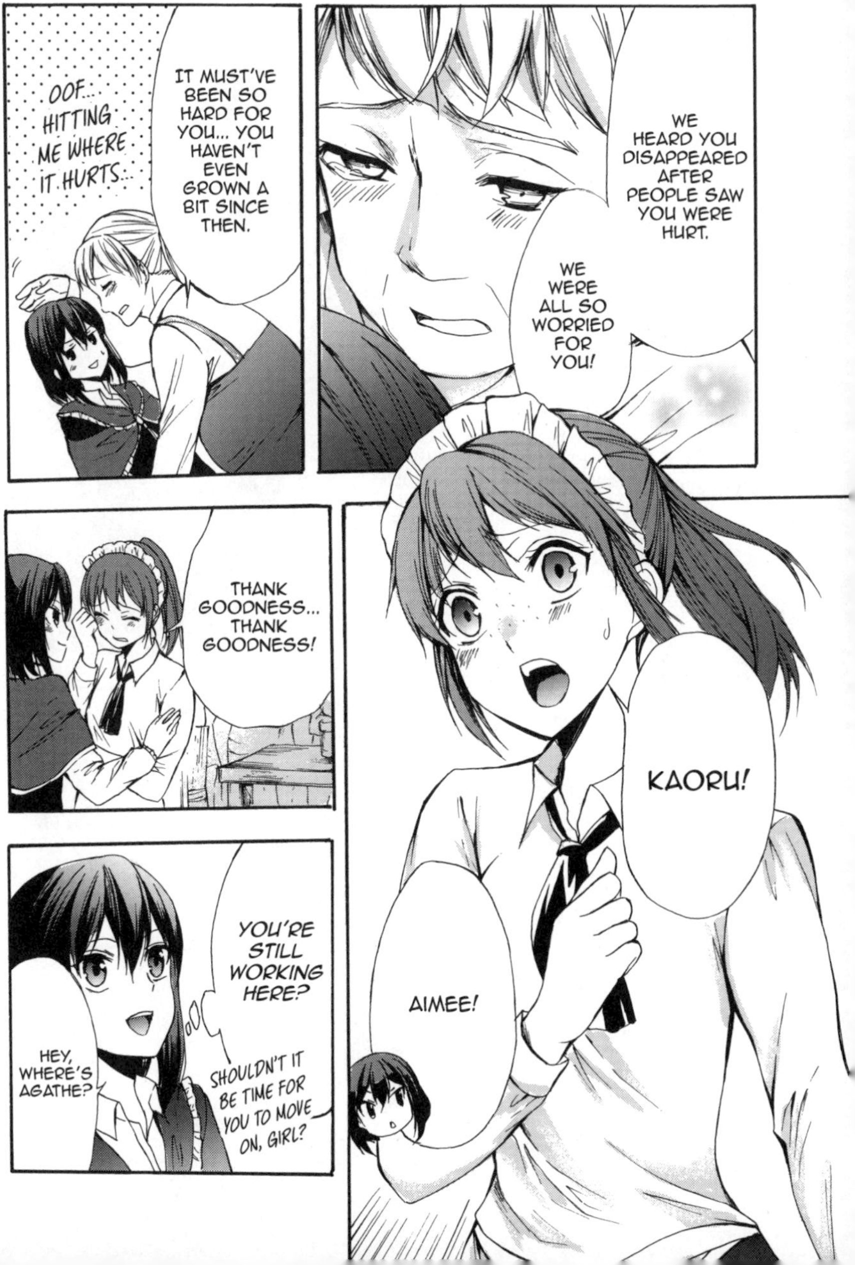
WE HEARD YOU DISAPPEARED AFTER PEOPLE SAW YOU WERE HURT.
WE WERE ALL SO WORRIED FOR YOU!
IT MUST'VE BEEN SO HARD FOR YOU... YOU HAVEN'T EVEN GROWN A BIT SINCE THEN.
OOF... HITTING ME WHERE IT HURTS...
KAORU!
AIMEE!
THANK GOODNESS... THANK GOODNESS!
YOU'RE STILL WORKING HERE?
SHOULDN'T IT BE TIME FOR YOU TO MOVE ON, GIRL?
HEY, WHERE'S AGATHE?

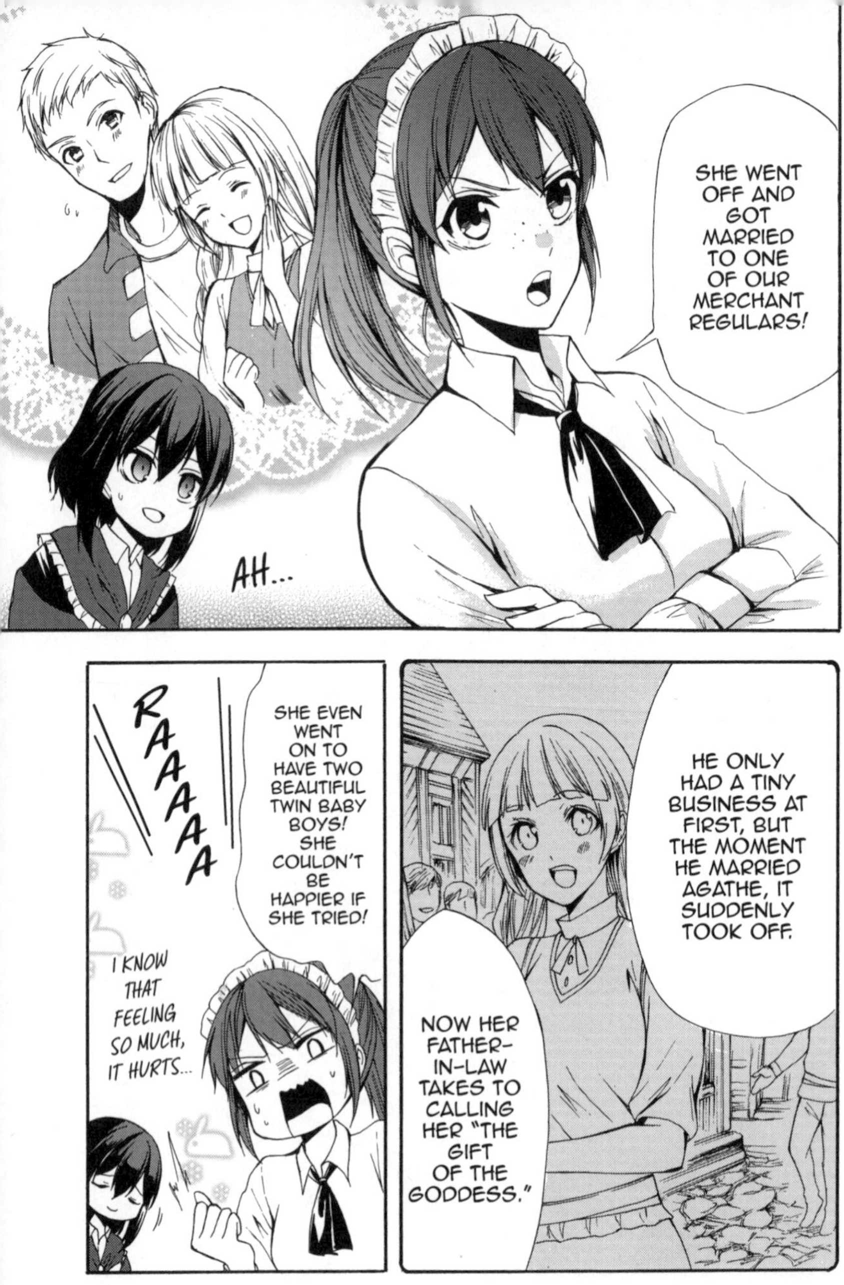
SHE WENT OFF AND GOT MARRIED TO ONE OF OUR MERCHANT REGULARS!
AH...
HE ONLY HAD A TINY BUSINESS AT FIRST, BUT THE MOMENT HE MARRIED AGATHE, IT SUDDENLY TOOK OFF.
NOW HER FATHER-IN-LAW TAKES TO CALLING HER "THE GIFT OF THE GODDESS."
SHE EVEN WENT ON TO HAVE TWO BEAUTIFUL TWIN BABY BOYS! SHE COULDN'T BE HAPPIER IF SHE TRIED!
RAAAAAA
I KNOW THAT FEELING SO MUCH, IT HURTS...

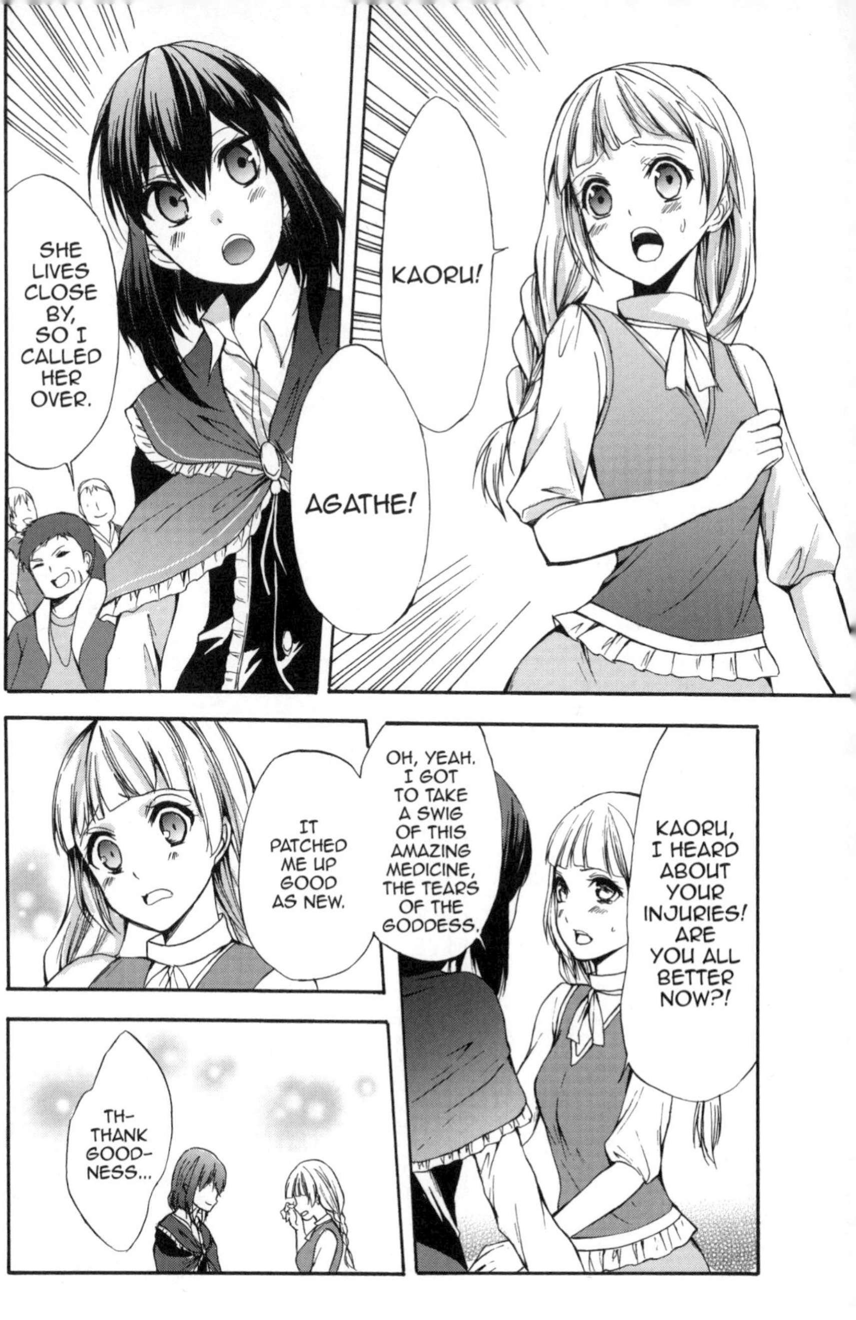
KAORU!
AGATHE!
SHE LIVES CLOSE BY, SO I CALLED HER OVER.
KAORU, I HEARD ABOUT YOUR INJURIES! ARE YOU ALL BETTER NOW?!
OH, YEAH. I GOT TO TAKE A SWIG OF THIS AMAZING MEDICINE, THE TEARS OF THE GODDESS.
IT PATCHED ME UP GOOD AS NEW.
TH-THANK GOODNESS...

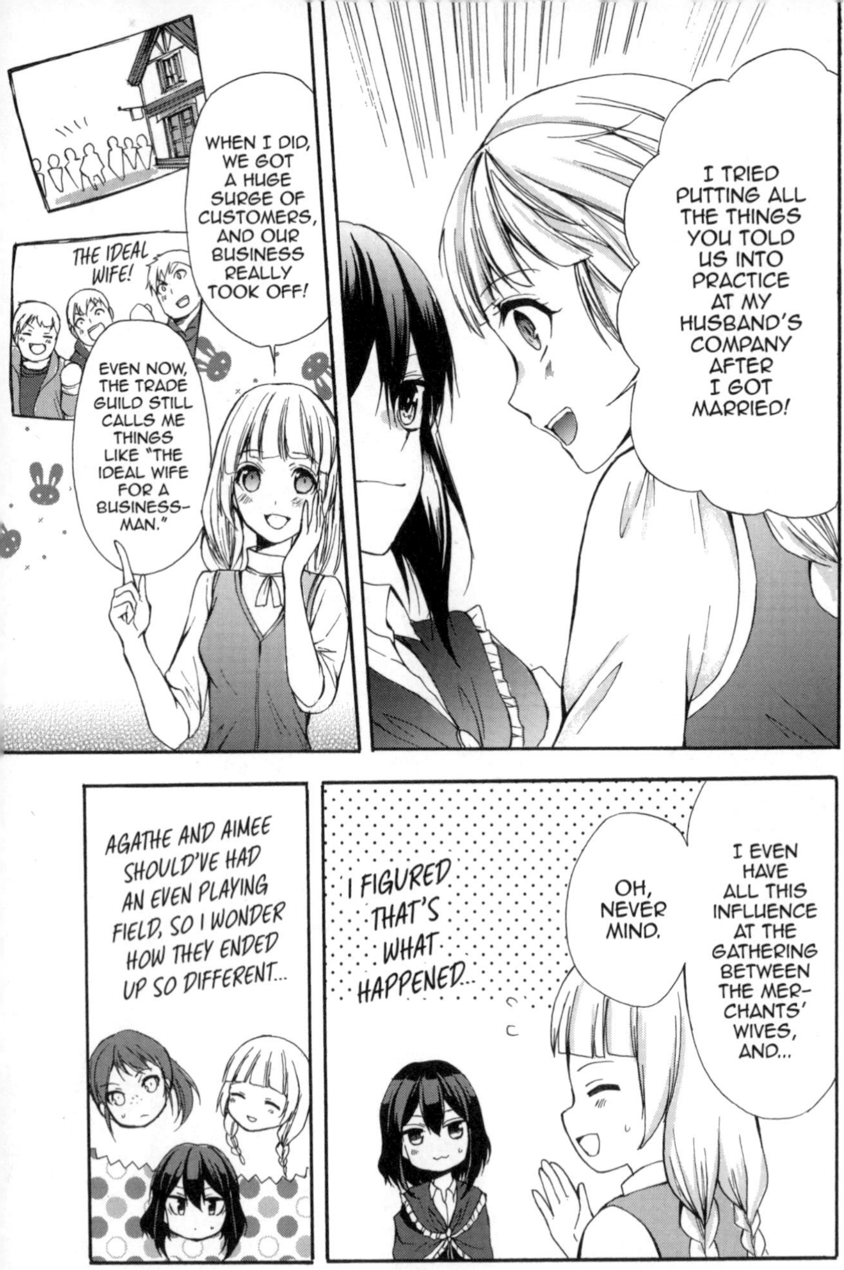
I TRIED PUTTING ALL THE THINGS YOU TOLD US INTO PRACTICE AT MY HUSBAND'S COMPANY AFTER I GOT MARRIED!
WHEN I DID, WE GOT A HUGE SURGE OF CUSTOMERS, AND OUR BUSINESS REALLY TOOK OFF!
THE IDEAL WIFE!
EVEN NOW, THE TRADE GUILD STILL CALLS ME THINGS LIKE "THE IDEAL WIFE FOR A BUSINESS-MAN."
I EVEN HAVE ALL THIS INFLUENCE AT THE GATHERING BETWEEN THE MER-CHANTS' WIVES, AND...
OH, NEVER MIND.
I FIGURED THAT'S WHAT HAPPENED...
AGATHE AND AIMEE SHOULD'VE HAD AN EVEN PLAYING FIELD, SO I WONDER HOW THEY ENDED UP SO DIFFERENT...

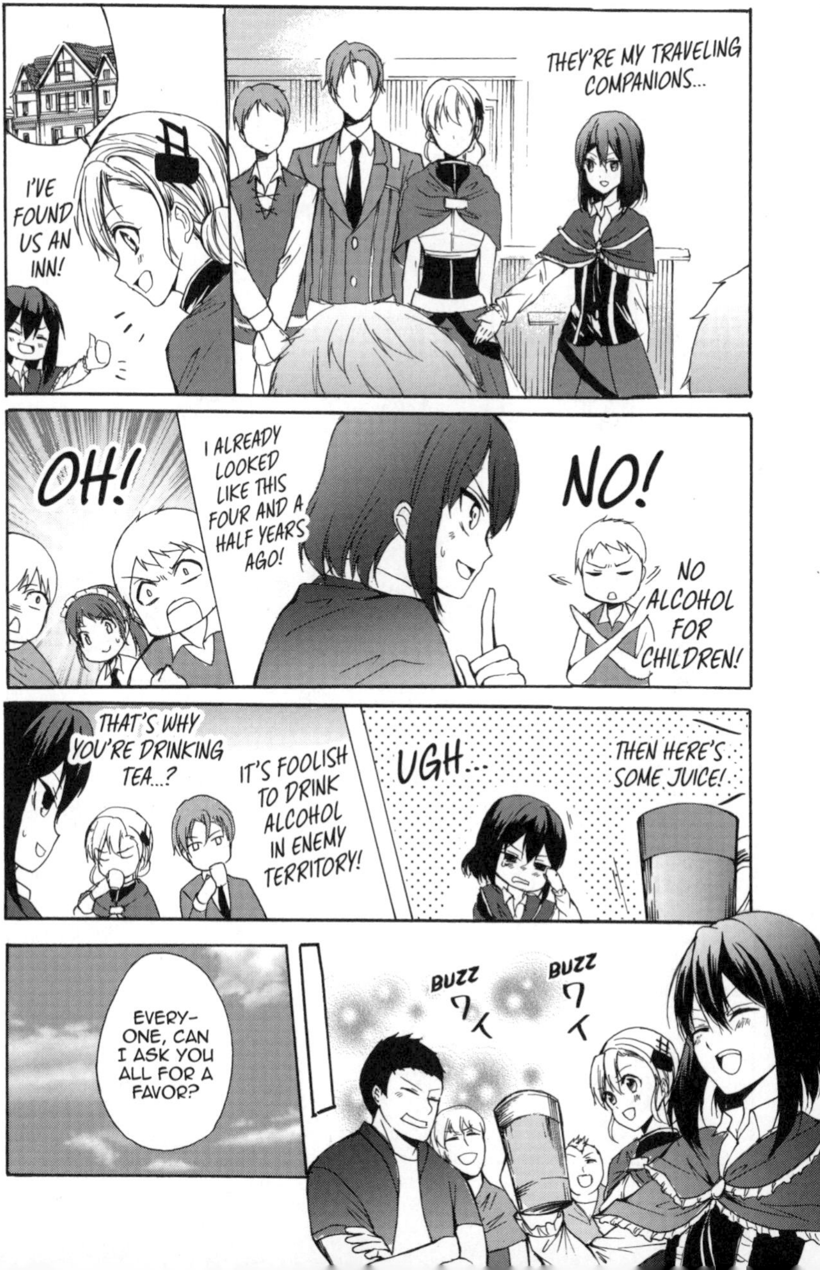
THEY'RE MY TRAVELING COMPANIONS...
I'VE FOUND US AN INN!
NO!
NO ALCOHOL FOR CHILDREN!
I ALREADY LOOKED LIKE THIS FOUR AND A HALF YEARS AGO!
OH!
THEN HERE'S SOME JUICE!
UGH...
THAT'S WHY YOU'RE DRINKING TEA...?
IT'S FOOLISH TO DRINK ALCOHOL IN ENEMY TERRITORY!
BUZZ ワイ
BUZZ ワイ
EVERY-ONE, CAN I ASK YOU ALL FOR A FAVOR?

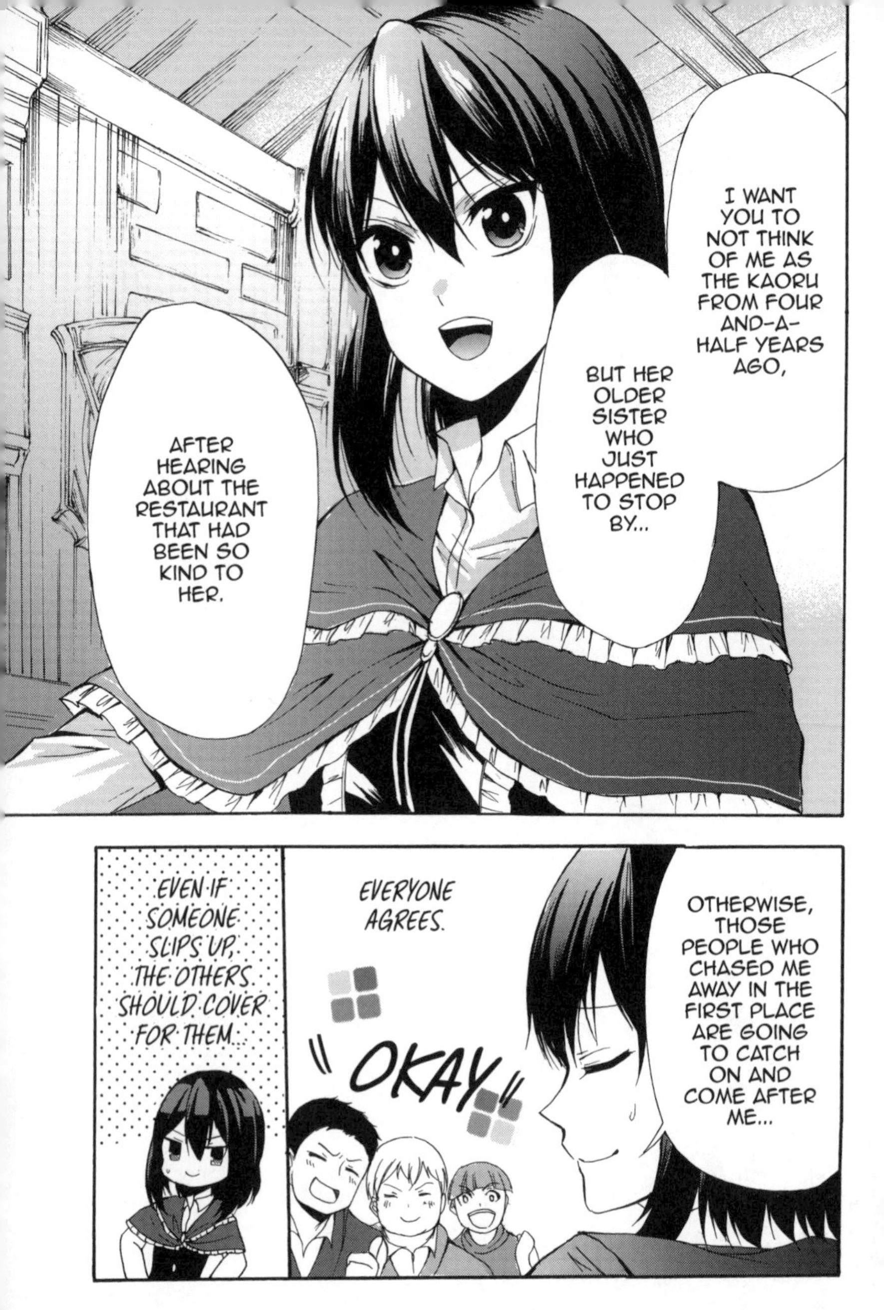
I WANT YOU TO NOT THINK OF ME AS THE KAORU FROM FOUR AND-A-HALF YEARS AGO,
BUT HER OLDER SISTER WHO JUST HAPPENED TO STOP BY...
AFTER HEARING ABOUT THE RESTAURANT THAT HAD BEEN SO KIND TO HER.
OTHERWISE, THOSE PEOPLE WHO CHASED ME AWAY IN THE FIRST PLACE ARE GOING TO CATCH ON AND COME AFTER ME...
EVERYONE AGREES.
OKAY
EVEN IF SOMEONE SLIPS UP, THE OTHERS SHOULD COVER FOR THEM...

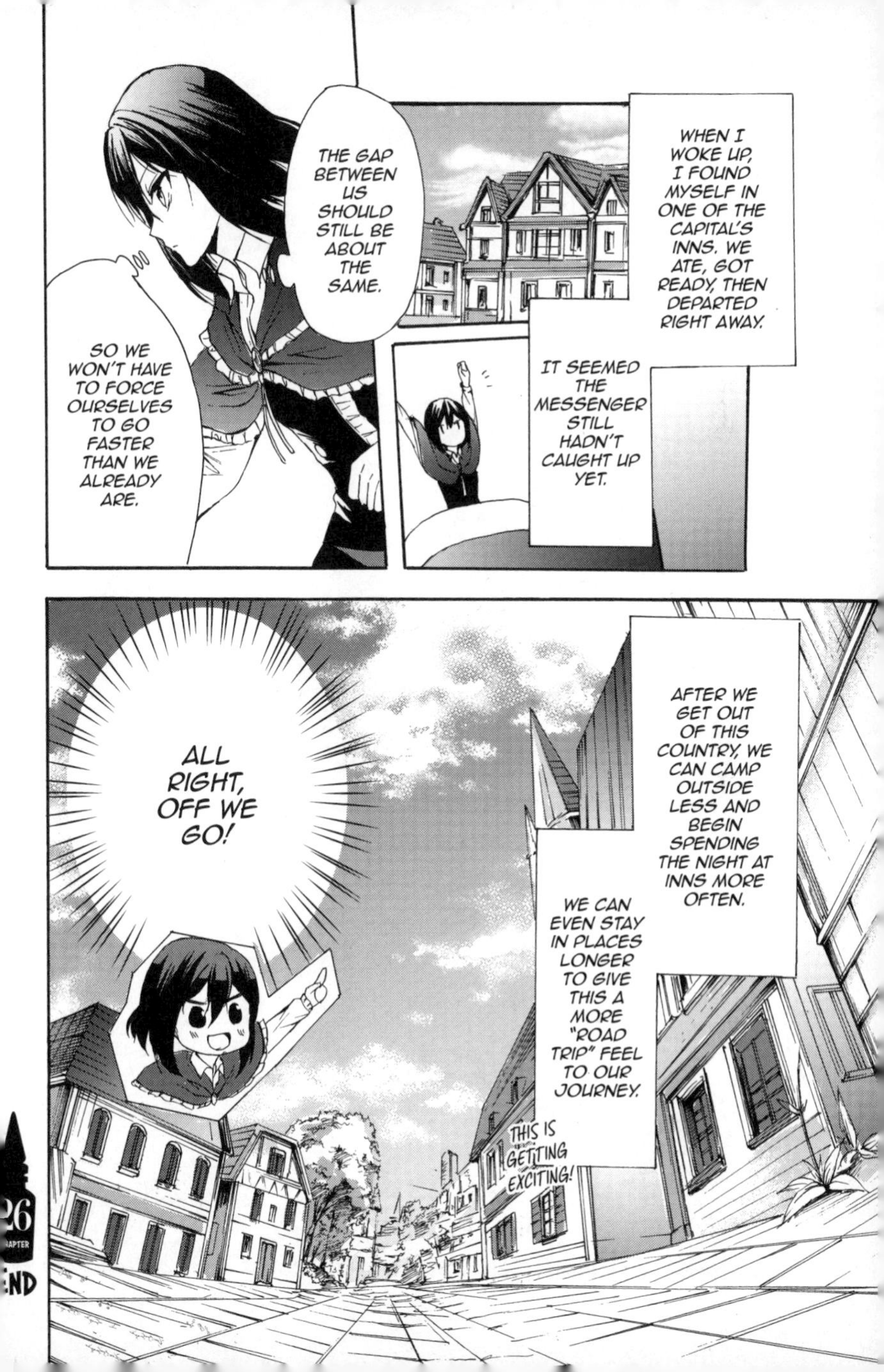
WHEN I WOKE UP, I FOUND MYSELF IN ONE OF THE CAPITAL'S INNS. WE ATE, GOT READY, THEN DEPARTED RIGHT AWAY.
IT SEEMED THE MESSENGER STILL HADN'T CAUGHT UP YET.
THE GAP BETWEEN US SHOULD STILL BE ABOUT THE SAME.
SO WE WON'T HAVE TO FORCE OURSELVES TO GO FASTER THAN WE ALREADY ARE.
AFTER WE GET OUT OF THIS COUNTRY, WE CAN CAMP OUTSIDE LESS AND BEGIN SPENDING THE NIGHT AT INNS MORE OFTEN.
WE CAN EVEN STAY IN PLACES LONGER TO GIVE THIS A MORE "ROAD TRIP" FEEL TO OUR JOURNEY.
ALL RIGHT, OFF WE GO!
THIS IS GETTING EXCITING!

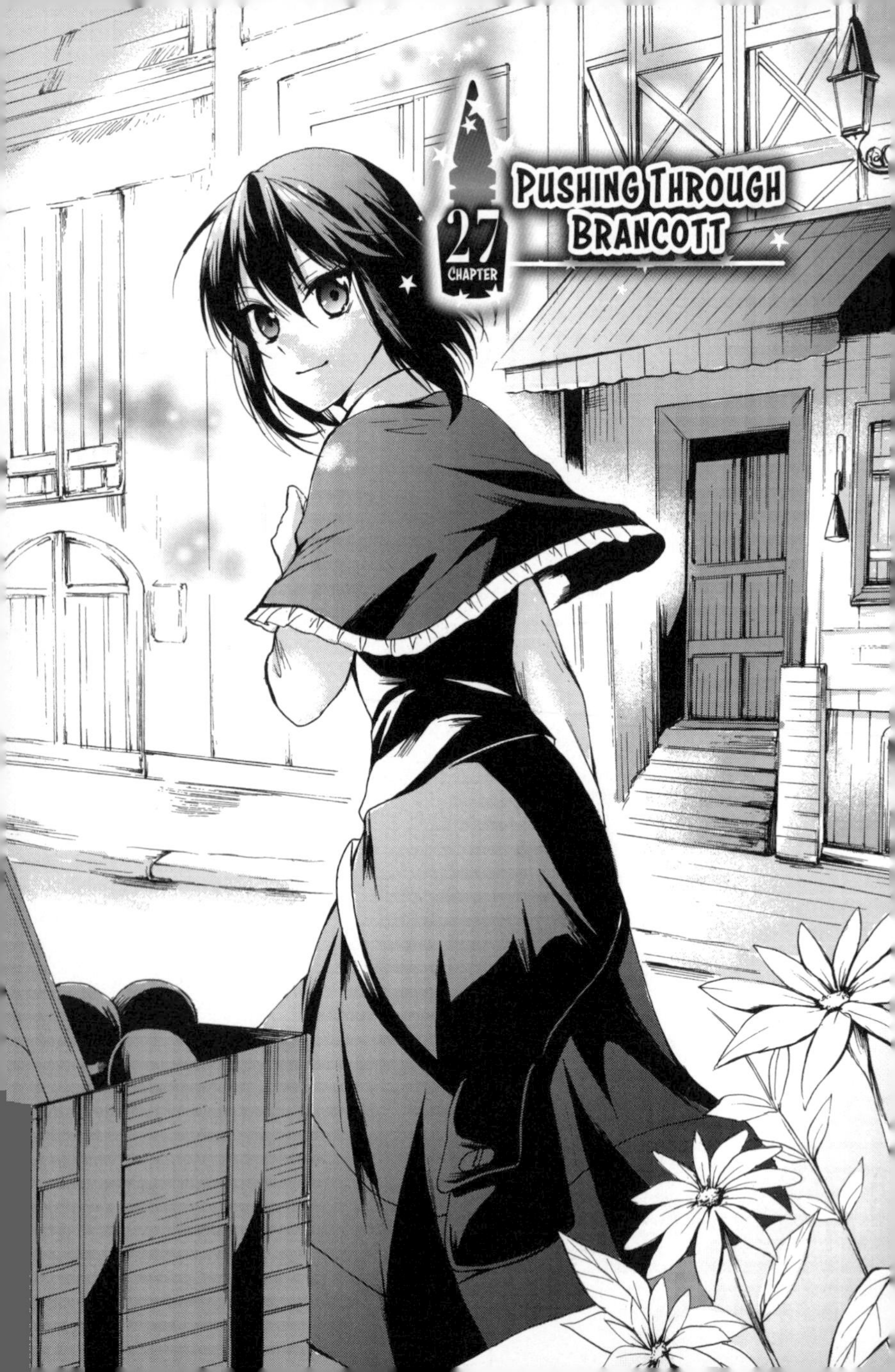
27
CHAPTER
PUSHING THROUGH
BRANCOTT

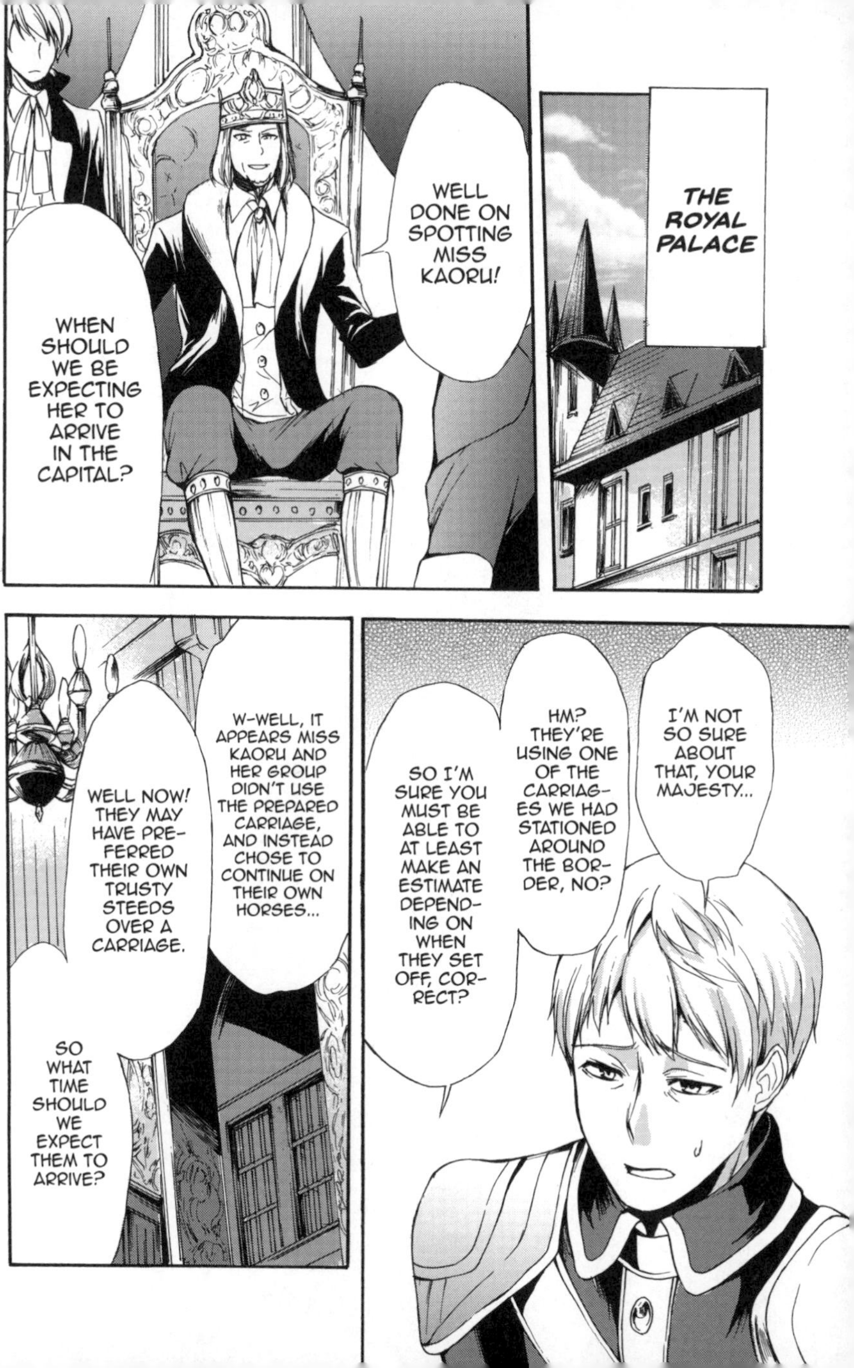
THE ROYAL PALACE
WELL DONE ON SPOTTING MISS KAORU!
WHEN SHOULD WE BE EXPECTING HER TO ARRIVE IN THE CAPITAL?
I'M NOT SO SURE ABOUT THAT, YOUR MAJESTY...
HM? THEY'RE USING ONE OF THE CARRIAGES WE HAD STATIONED AROUND THE BORDER, NO?
SO I'M SURE YOU MUST BE ABLE TO AT LEAST MAKE AN ESTIMATE DEPENDING ON WHEN THEY SET OFF, CORRECT?
W-WELL, IT APPEARS MISS KAORU AND HER GROUP DIDN'T USE THE PREPARED CARRIAGE, AND INSTEAD CHOSE TO CONTINUE ON THEIR OWN HORSES...
WELL NOW! THEY MAY HAVE PREFERRED THEIR OWN TRUSTY STEEDS OVER A CARRIAGE.
SO WHAT TIME SHOULD WE EXPECT THEM TO ARRIVE?

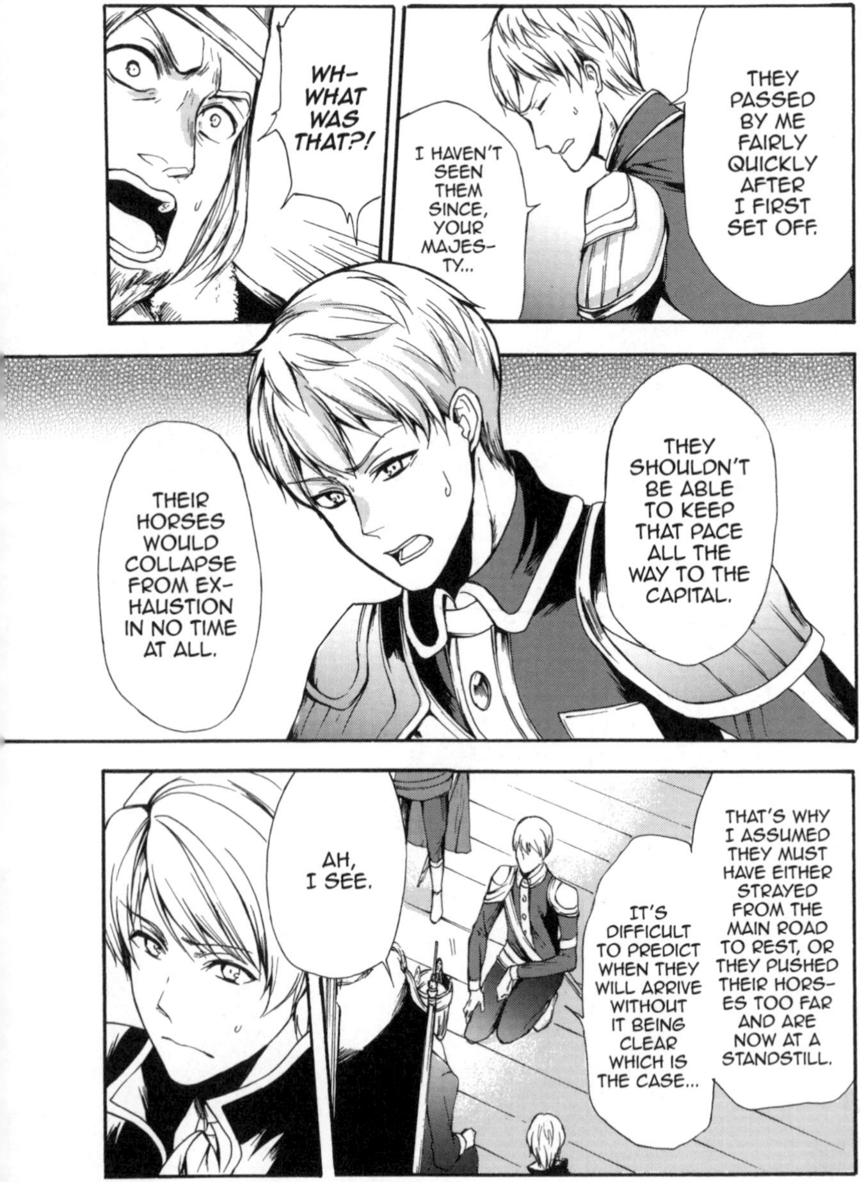
THEY PASSED BY ME FAIRLY QUICKLY AFTER I FIRST SET OFF.
I HAVEN'T SEEN THEM SINCE, YOUR MAJESTY...
WH- WHAT WAS THAT?!
THEY SHOULDN'T BE ABLE TO KEEP THAT PACE ALL THE WAY TO THE CAPITAL.
THEIR HORSES WOULD COLLAPSE FROM EXHAUSTION IN NO TIME AT ALL.
THAT'S WHY I ASSUMED THEY MUST HAVE EITHER STRAYED FROM THE MAIN ROAD TO REST, OR THEY PUSHED THEIR HORSES TOO FAR AND ARE NOW AT A STANDSTILL.
IT'S DIFFICULT TO PREDICT WHEN THEY WILL ARRIVE WITHOUT IT BEING CLEAR WHICH IS THE CASE...
AH, I SEE.

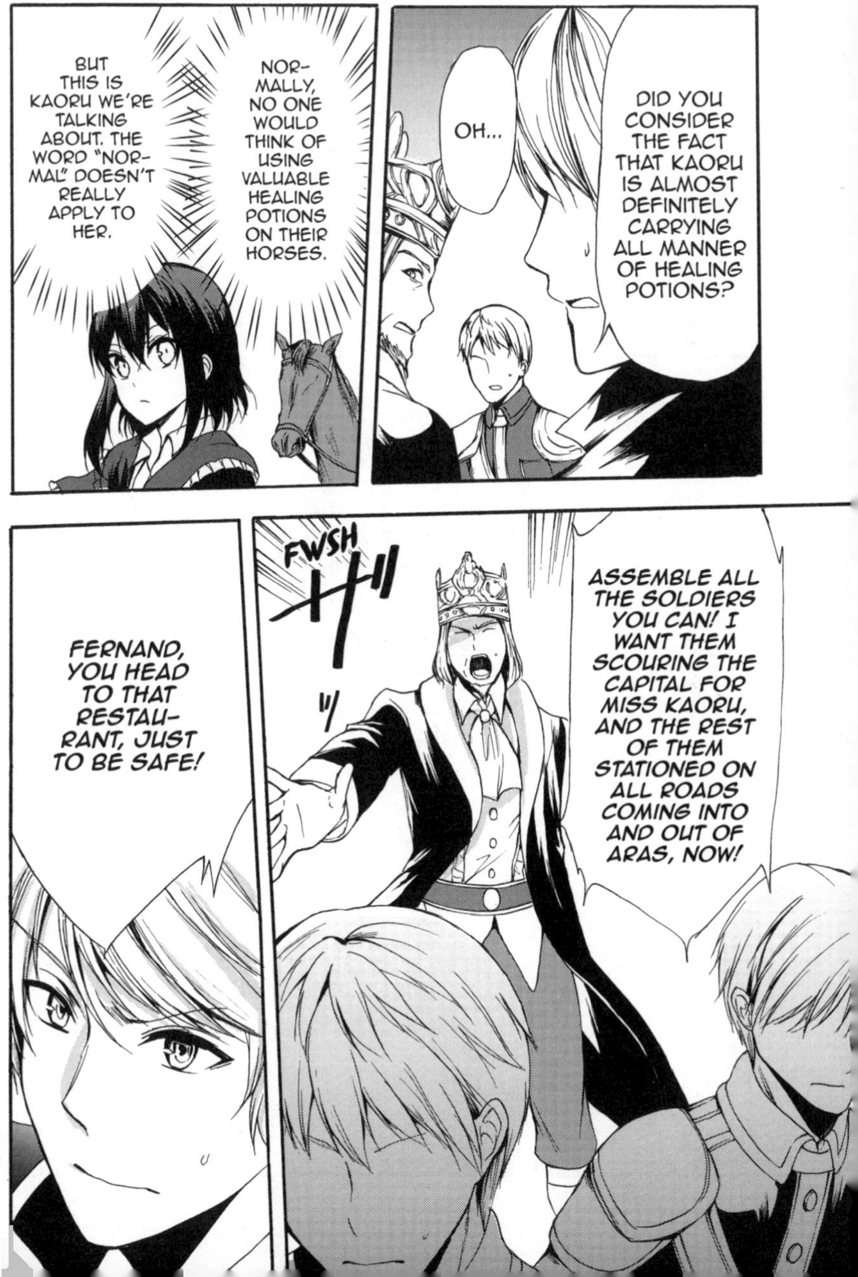
DID YOU CONSIDER THE FACT THAT KAORU IS ALMOST DEFINITELY CARRYING ALL MANNER OF HEALING POTIONS?
OH...
NOR-MALLY, NO ONE WOULD THINK OF USING VALUABLE HEALING POTIONS ON THEIR HORSES.
BUT THIS IS KAORU WE'RE TALKING ABOUT. THE WORD "NOR-MAL" DOESN'T REALLY APPLY TO HER.
ASSEMBLE ALL THE SOLDIERS YOU CAN! I WANT THEM SCOURING THE CAPITAL FOR MISS KAORU, AND THE REST OF THEM STATIONED ON ALL ROADS COMING INTO AND OUT OF ARAS, NOW!
FWSH
FERNAND, YOU HEAD TO THAT RESTAU-RANT, JUST TO BE SAFE!

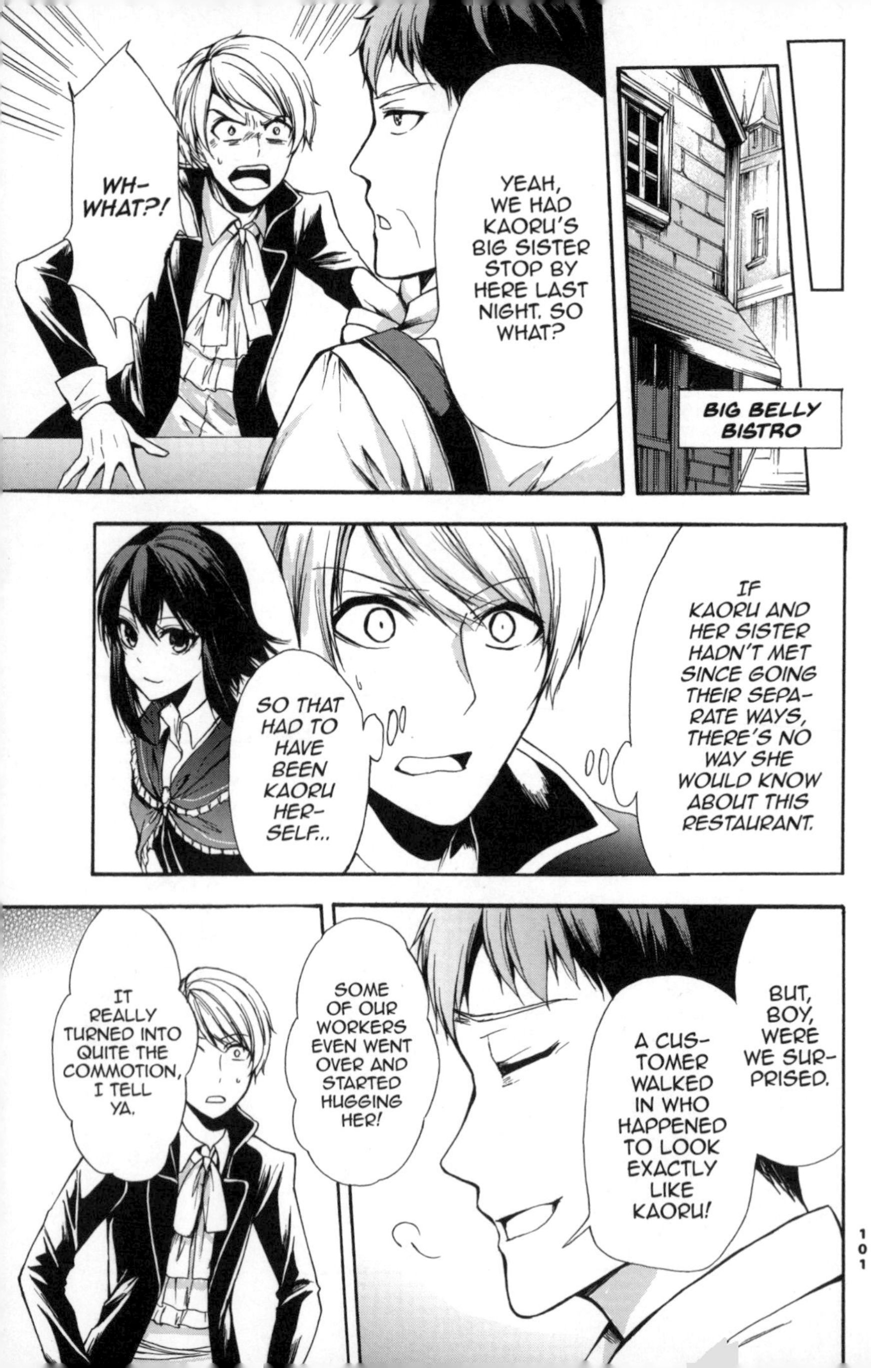
BIG BELLY BISTRO
YEAH, WE HAD KAORU'S BIG SISTER STOP BY HERE LAST NIGHT. SO WHAT?
WH-WHAT?!
IF KAORU AND HER SISTER HADN'T MET SINCE GOING THEIR SEPA-RATE WAYS, THERE'S NO WAY SHE WOULD KNOW ABOUT THIS RESTAURANT.
SO THAT HAD TO HAVE BEEN KAORU HER-SELF...
BUT, BOY, WERE WE SUR-PRISED.
A CUS-TOMER WALKED IN WHO HAPPENED TO LOOK EXACTLY LIKE KAORU!
SOME OF OUR WORKERS EVEN WENT OVER AND STARTED HUGGING HER!
IT REALLY TURNED INTO QUITE THE COMMOTION, I TELL YA.

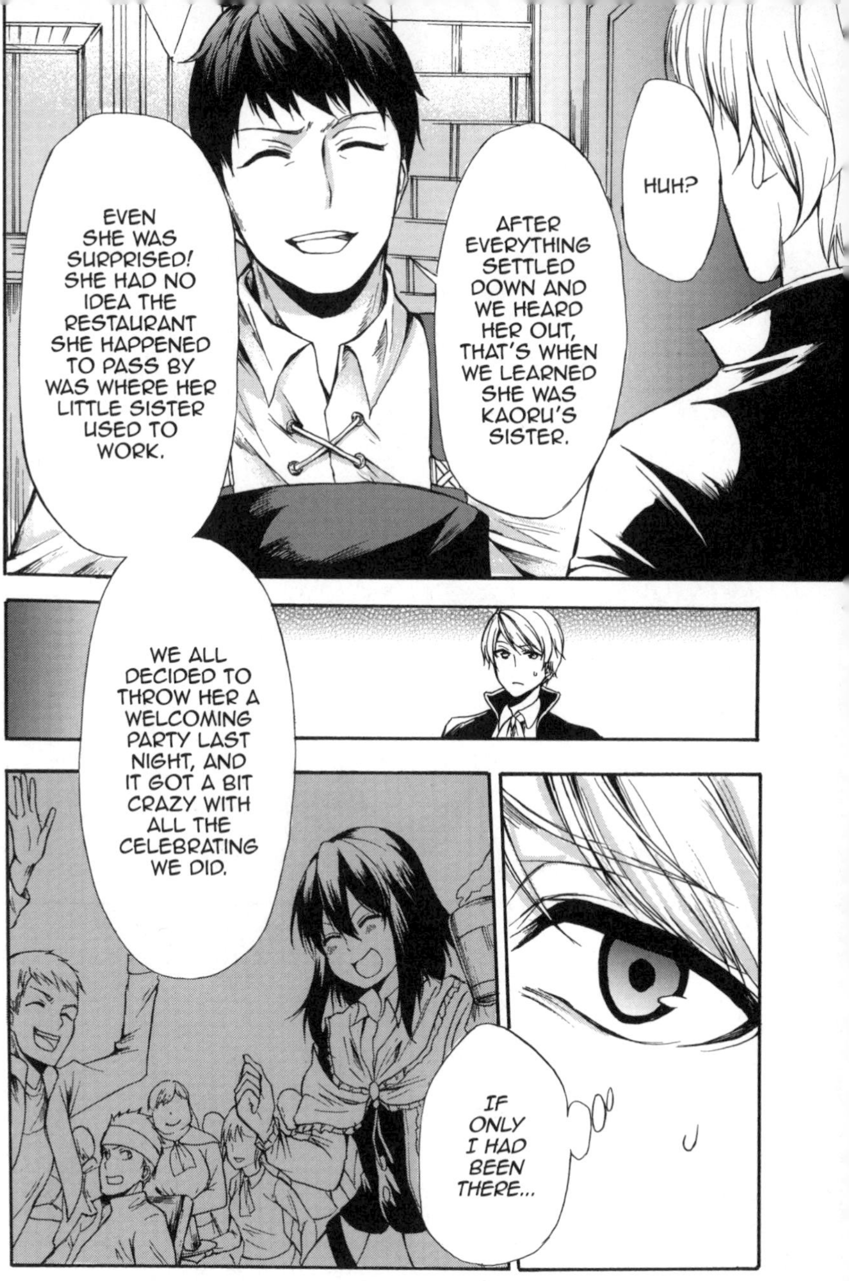
HUH?
AFTER EVERYTHING SETTLED DOWN AND WE HEARD HER OUT, THAT'S WHEN WE LEARNED SHE WAS KAORU'S SISTER.
EVEN SHE WAS SURPRISED! SHE HAD NO IDEA THE RESTAURANT SHE HAPPENED TO PASS BY WAS WHERE HER LITTLE SISTER USED TO WORK.
WE ALL DECIDED TO THROW HER A WELCOMING PARTY LAST NIGHT, AND IT GOT A BIT CRAZY WITH ALL THE CELEBRATING WE DID.
IF ONLY I HAD BEEN THERE...

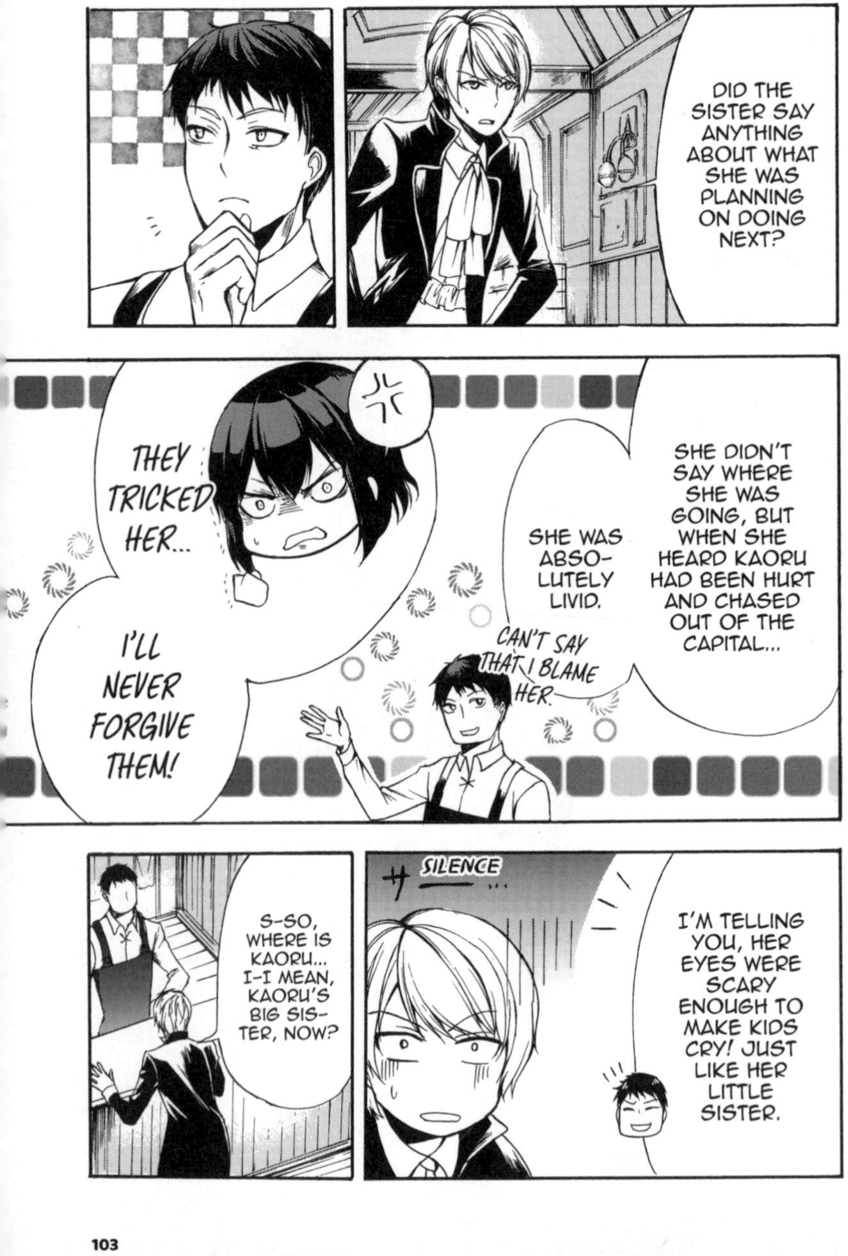
DID THE SISTER SAY ANYTHING ABOUT WHAT SHE WAS PLANNING ON DOING NEXT?
SHE DIDN'T SAY WHERE SHE WAS GOING, BUT WHEN SHE HEARD KAORU HAD BEEN HURT AND CHASED OUT OF THE CAPITAL...
SHE WAS ABSO-LUTELY LIVID.
THEY TRICKED HER...
I'LL NEVER FORGIVE THEM!
CAN'T SAY THAT I BLAME HER.
SILENCE
I'M TELLING YOU, HER EYES WERE SCARY ENOUGH TO MAKE KIDS CRY! JUST LIKE HER LITTLE SISTER.
S-SO, WHERE IS KAORU... I-I MEAN, KAORU'S BIG SIS-TER, NOW?

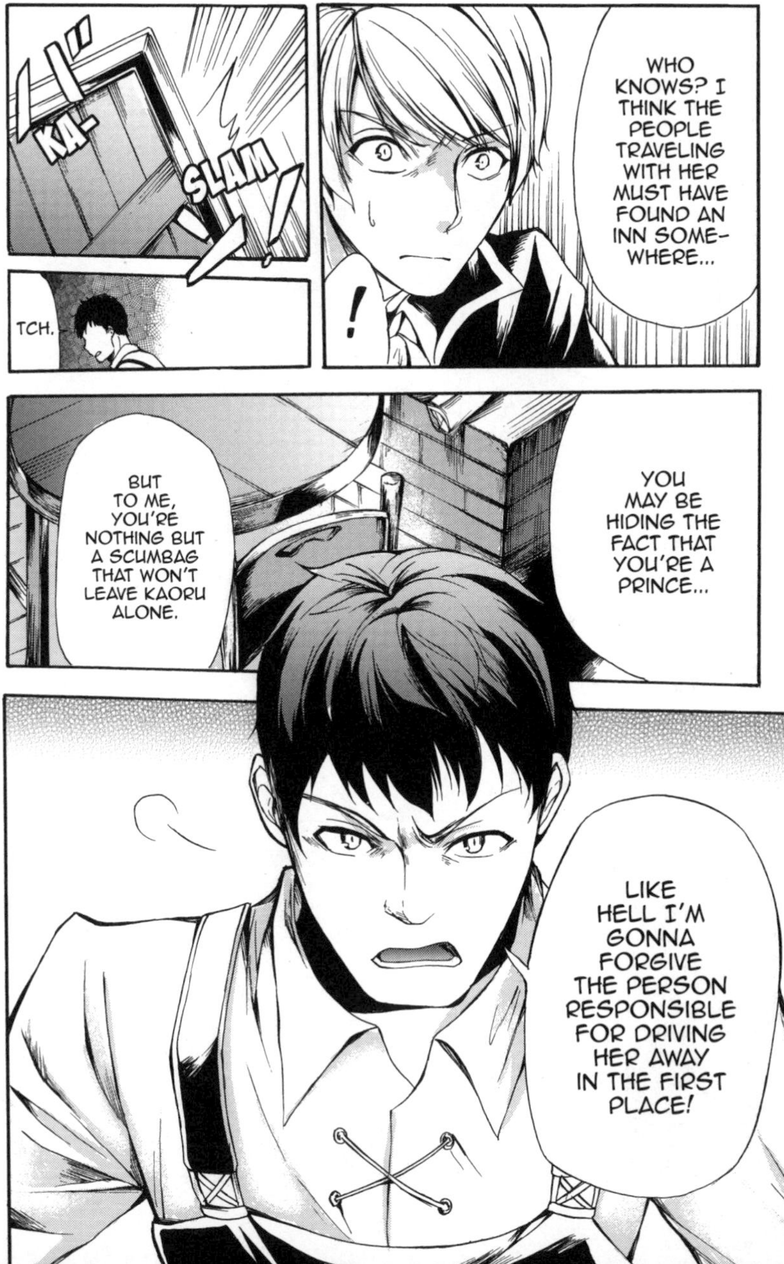
WHO KNOWS? I THINK THE PEOPLE TRAVELING WITH HER MUST HAVE FOUND AN INN SOME-WHERE...
!
KA-
SLAM
TCH.
YOU MAY BE HIDING THE FACT THAT YOU'RE A PRINCE...
BUT TO ME, YOU'RE NOTHING BUT A SCUMBAG THAT WON'T LEAVE KAORU ALONE.
LIKE HELL I'M GONNA FORGIVE THE PERSON RESPONSIBLE FOR DRIVING HER AWAY IN THE FIRST PLACE!

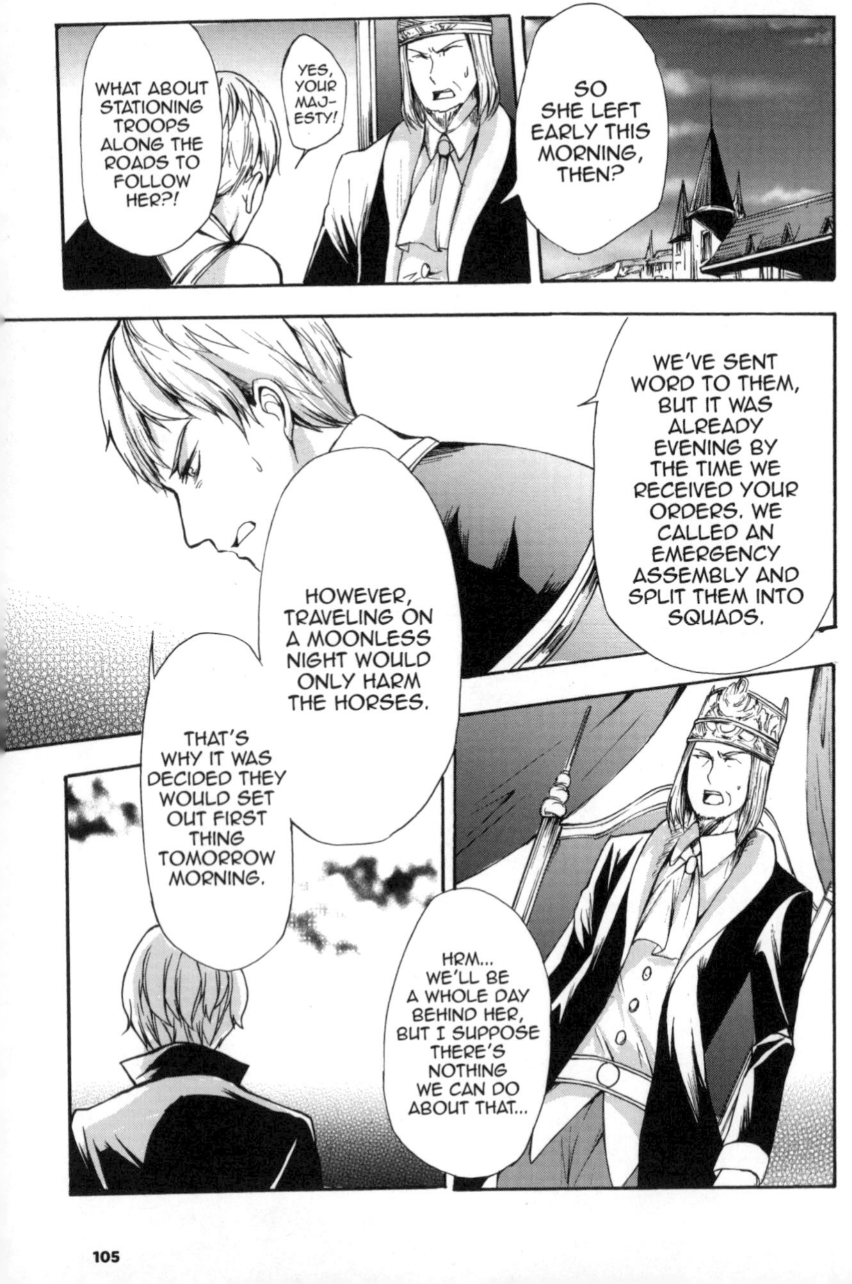
SO SHE LEFT EARLY THIS MORNING, THEN?
YES, YOUR MAJ-ESTY!
WHAT ABOUT STATIONING TROOPS ALONG THE ROADS TO FOLLOW HER?!
WE'VE SENT WORD TO THEM, BUT IT WAS ALREADY EVENING BY THE TIME WE RECEIVED YOUR ORDERS. WE CALLED AN EMERGENCY ASSEMBLY AND SPLIT THEM INTO SQUADS.
HOWEVER, TRAVELING ON A MOONLESS NIGHT WOULD ONLY HARM THE HORSES.
THAT'S WHY IT WAS DECIDED THEY WOULD SET OUT FIRST THING TOMORROW MORNING.
HRM... WE'LL BE A WHOLE DAY BEHIND HER, BUT I SUPPOSE THERE'S NOTHING WE CAN DO ABOUT THAT...

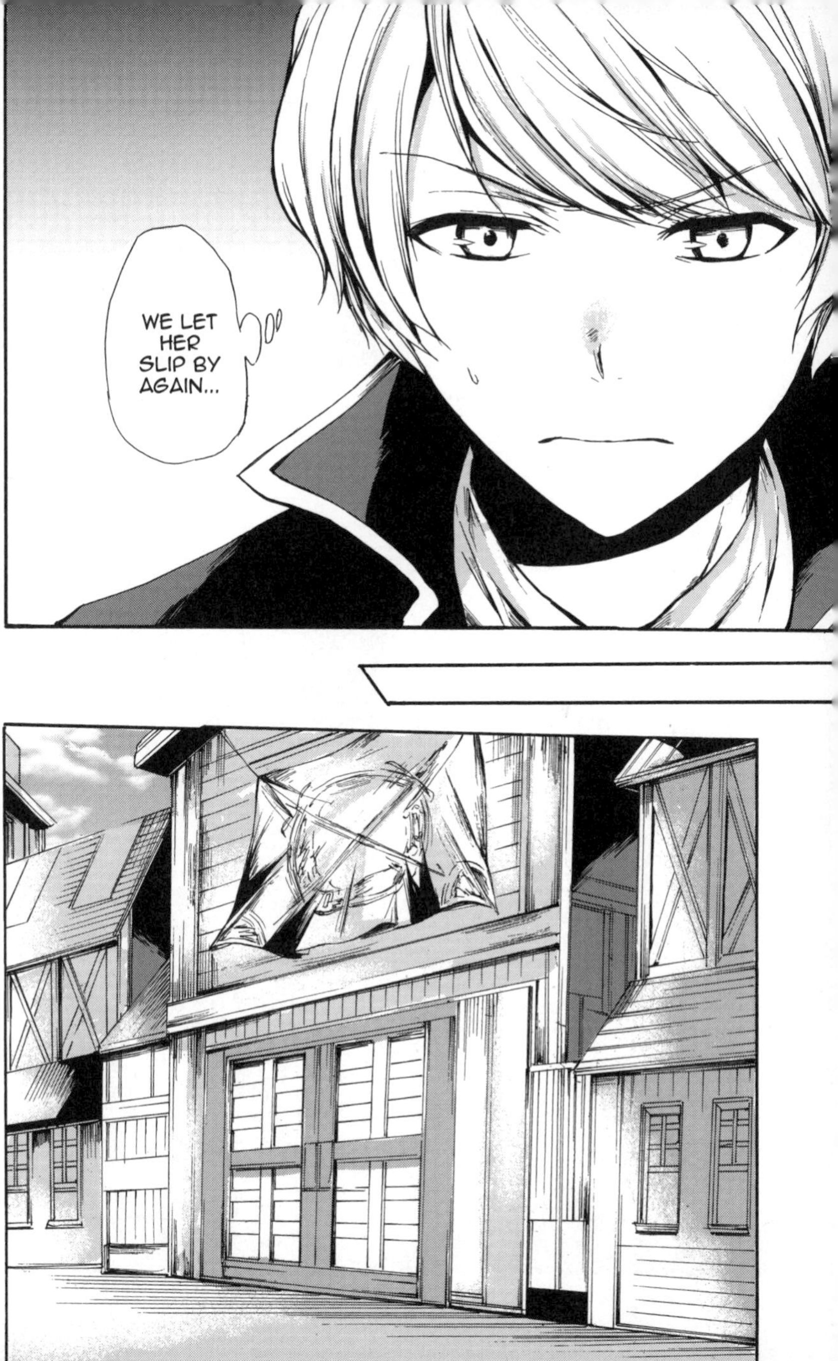
WE LET HER SLIP BY AGAIN...

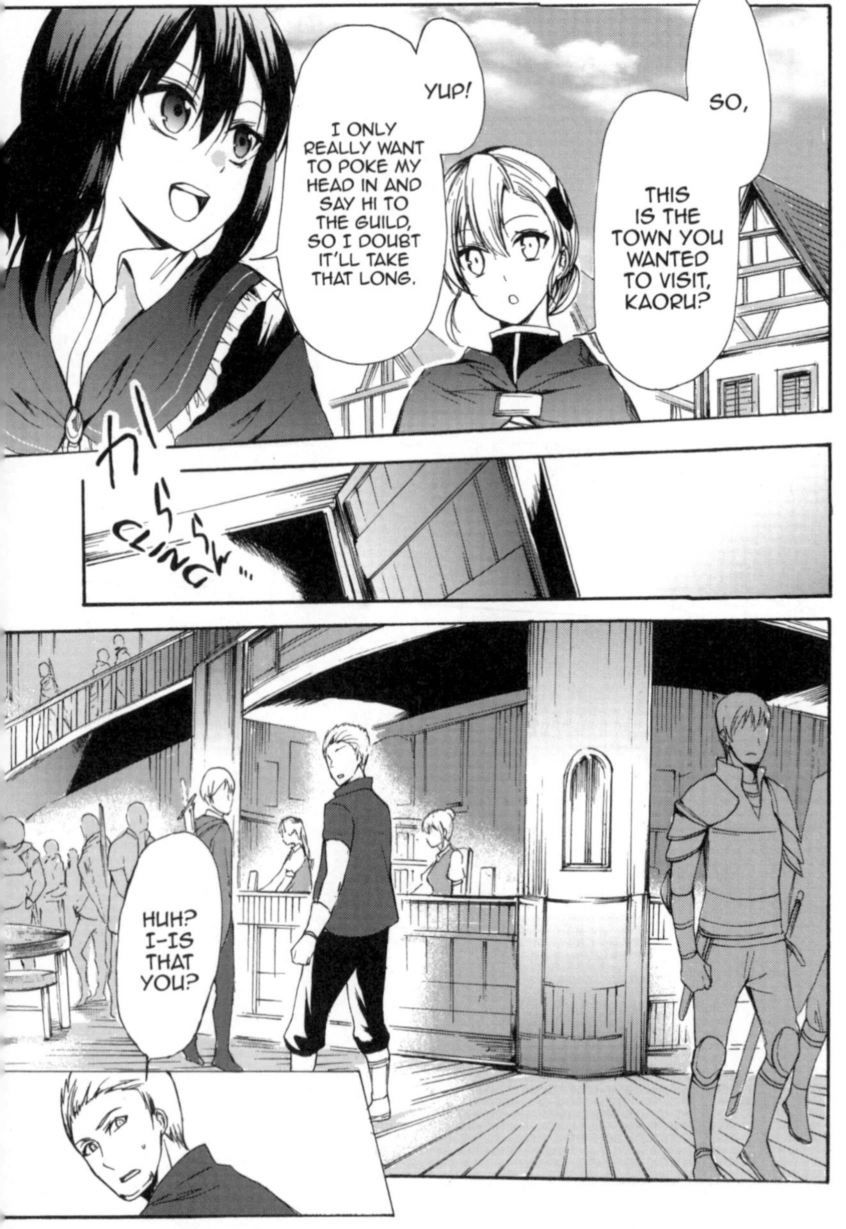
SO,
THIS IS THE TOWN YOU WANTED TO VISIT, KAORU?
YUP!
I ONLY REALLY WANT TO POKE MY HEAD IN AND SAY HI TO THE GUILD, SO I DOUBT IT'LL TAKE THAT LONG.
CLING
HUH? I-IS THAT YOU?

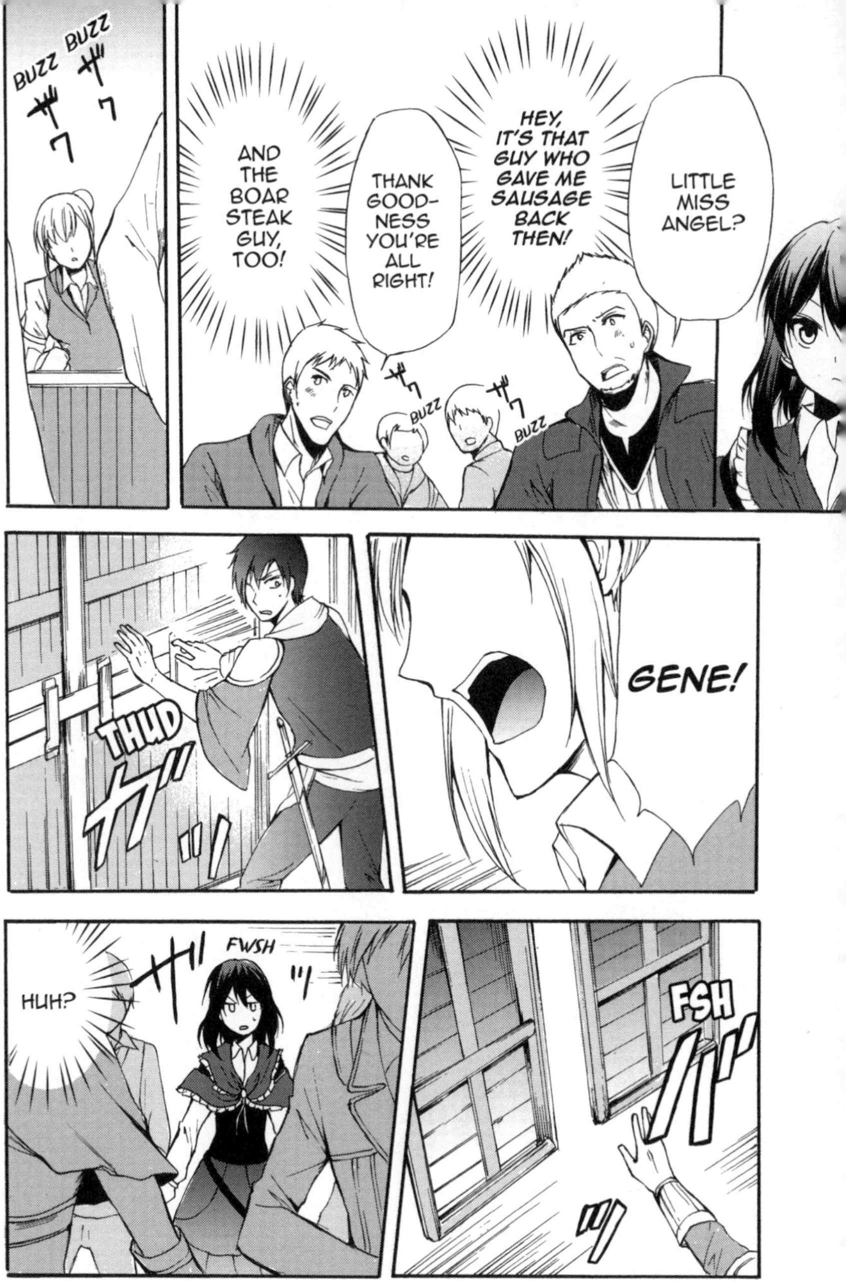
LITTLE MISS ANGEL?
HEY, IT'S THAT GUY WHO GAVE ME SAUSAGE BACK THEN!
THANK GOODNESS YOU'RE ALL RIGHT!
AND THE BOAR STEAK GUY, TOO!
BUZZ
BUZZ
BUZZ BUZZ
GENE!
THUD
FSH
FWSH
HUH?

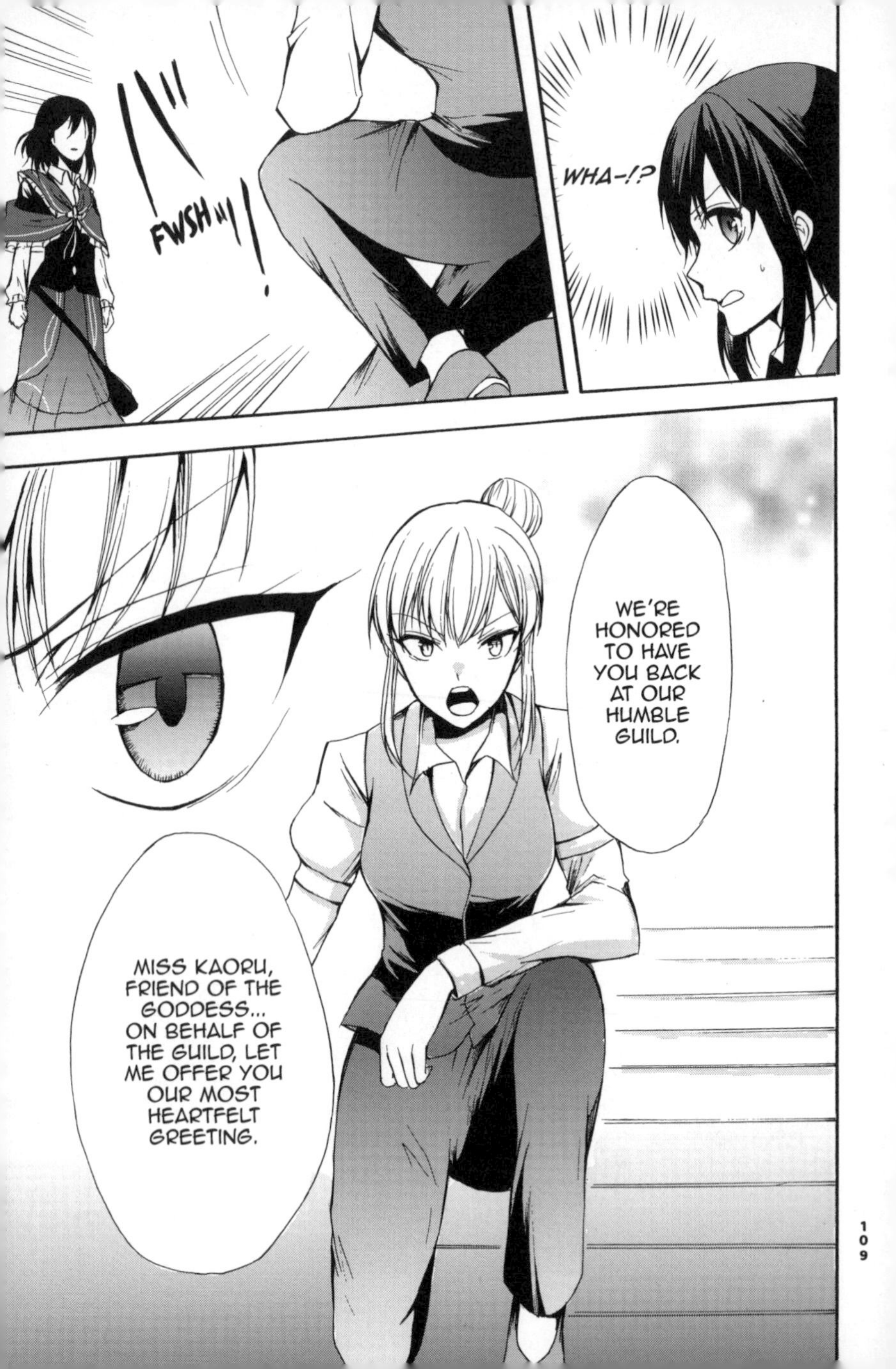
WHA-!?
FWSH
WE'RE HONORED TO HAVE YOU BACK AT OUR HUMBLE GUILD.
MISS KAORU, FRIEND OF THE GODDESS... ON BEHALF OF THE GUILD, LET ME OFFER YOU OUR MOST HEARTFELT GREETING.

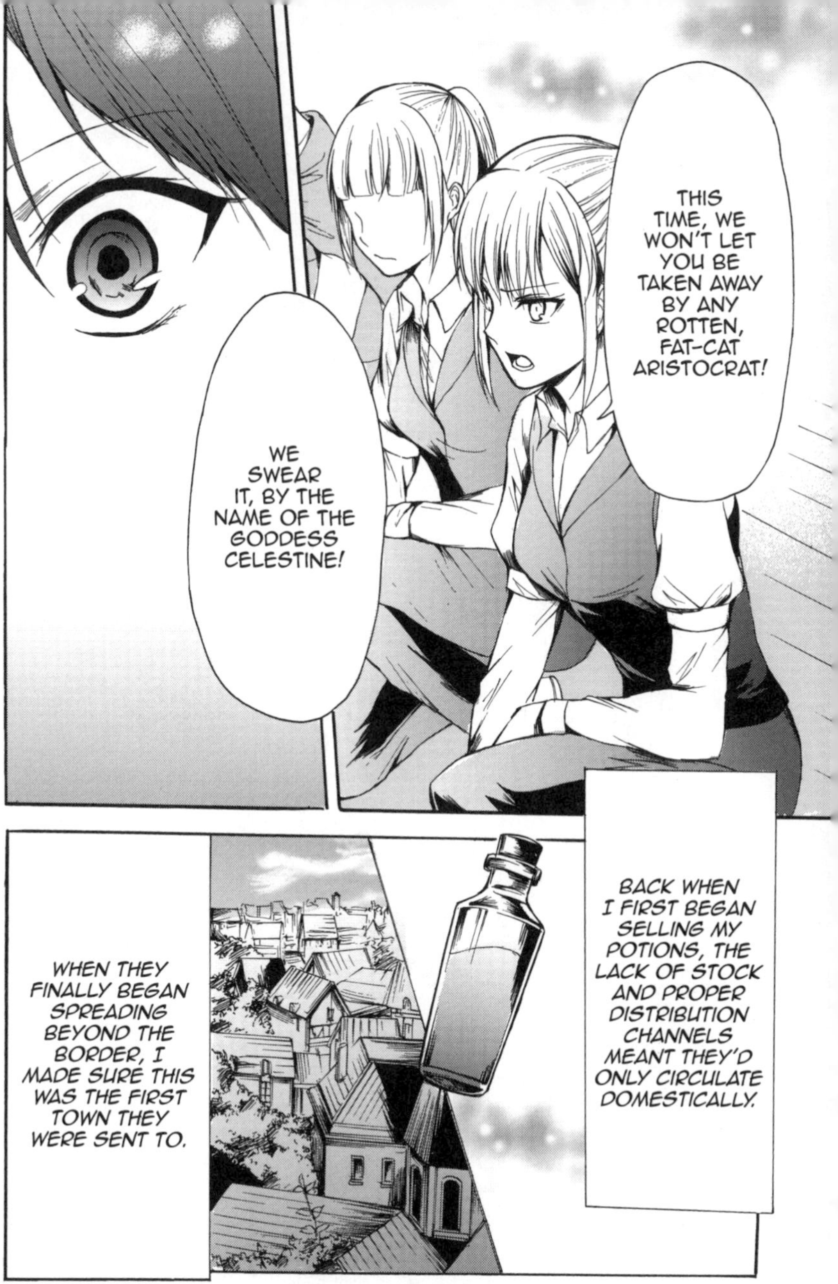
THIS TIME, WE WON'T LET YOU BE TAKEN AWAY BY ANY ROTTEN, FAT-CAT ARISTOCRAT!
WE SWEAR IT, BY THE NAME OF THE GODDESS CELESTINE!
BACK WHEN I FIRST BEGAN SELLING MY POTIONS, THE LACK OF STOCK AND PROPER DISTRIBUTION CHANNELS MEANT THEY'D ONLY CIRCULATE DOMESTICALLY.
WHEN THEY FINALLY BEGAN SPREADING BEYOND THE BORDER, I MADE SURE THIS WAS THE FIRST TOWN THEY WERE SENT TO.

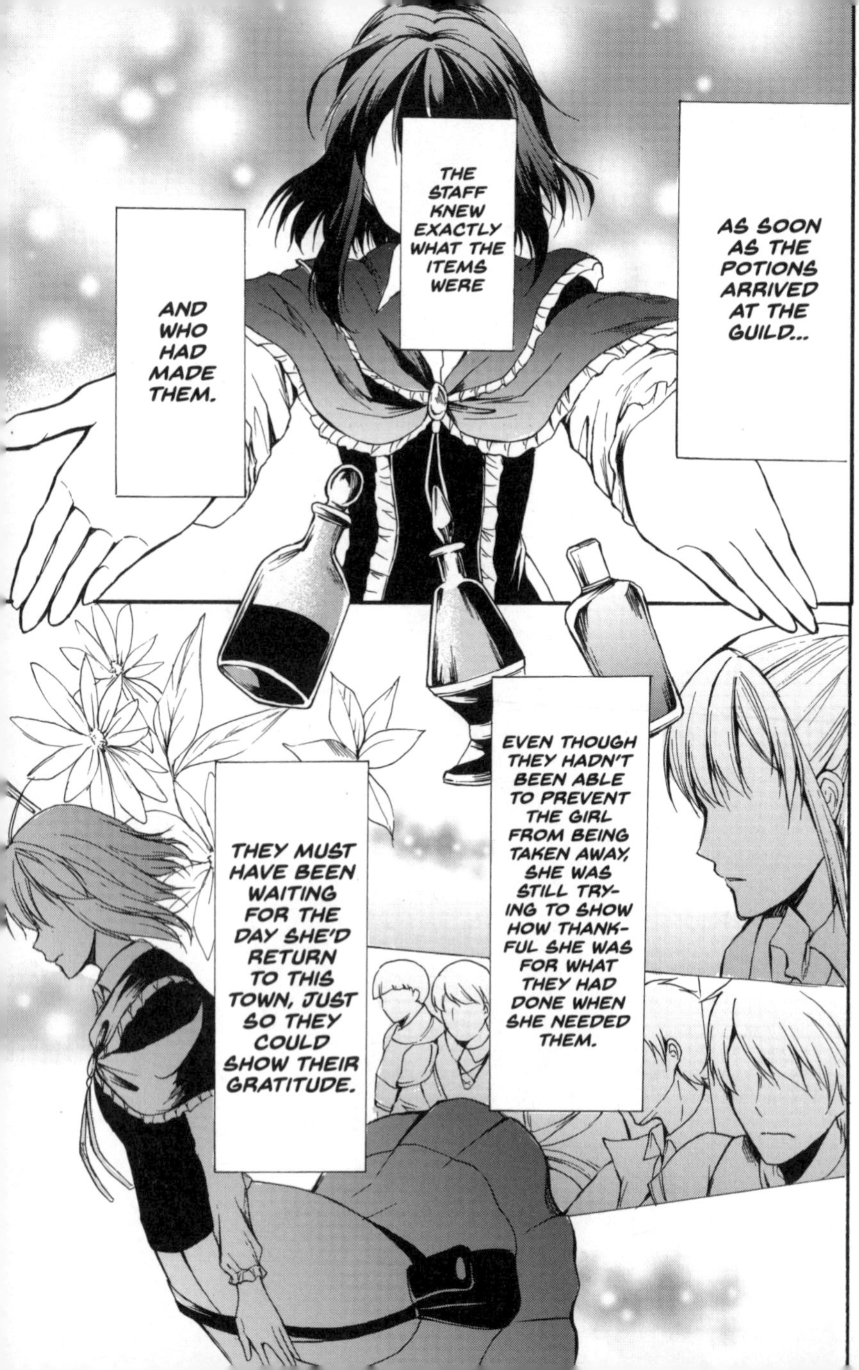
AS SOON AS THE POTIONS ARRIVED AT THE GUILD...
THE STAFF KNEW EXACTLY WHAT THE ITEMS WERE
AND WHO HAD MADE THEM.
EVEN THOUGH THEY HADN'T BEEN ABLE TO PREVENT THE GIRL FROM BEING TAKEN AWAY, SHE WAS STILL TRY-ING TO SHOW HOW THANK-FUL SHE WAS FOR WHAT THEY HAD DONE WHEN SHE NEEDED THEM.
THEY MUST HAVE BEEN WAITING FOR THE DAY SHE'D RETURN TO THIS TOWN, JUST SO THEY COULD SHOW THEIR GRATITUDE.

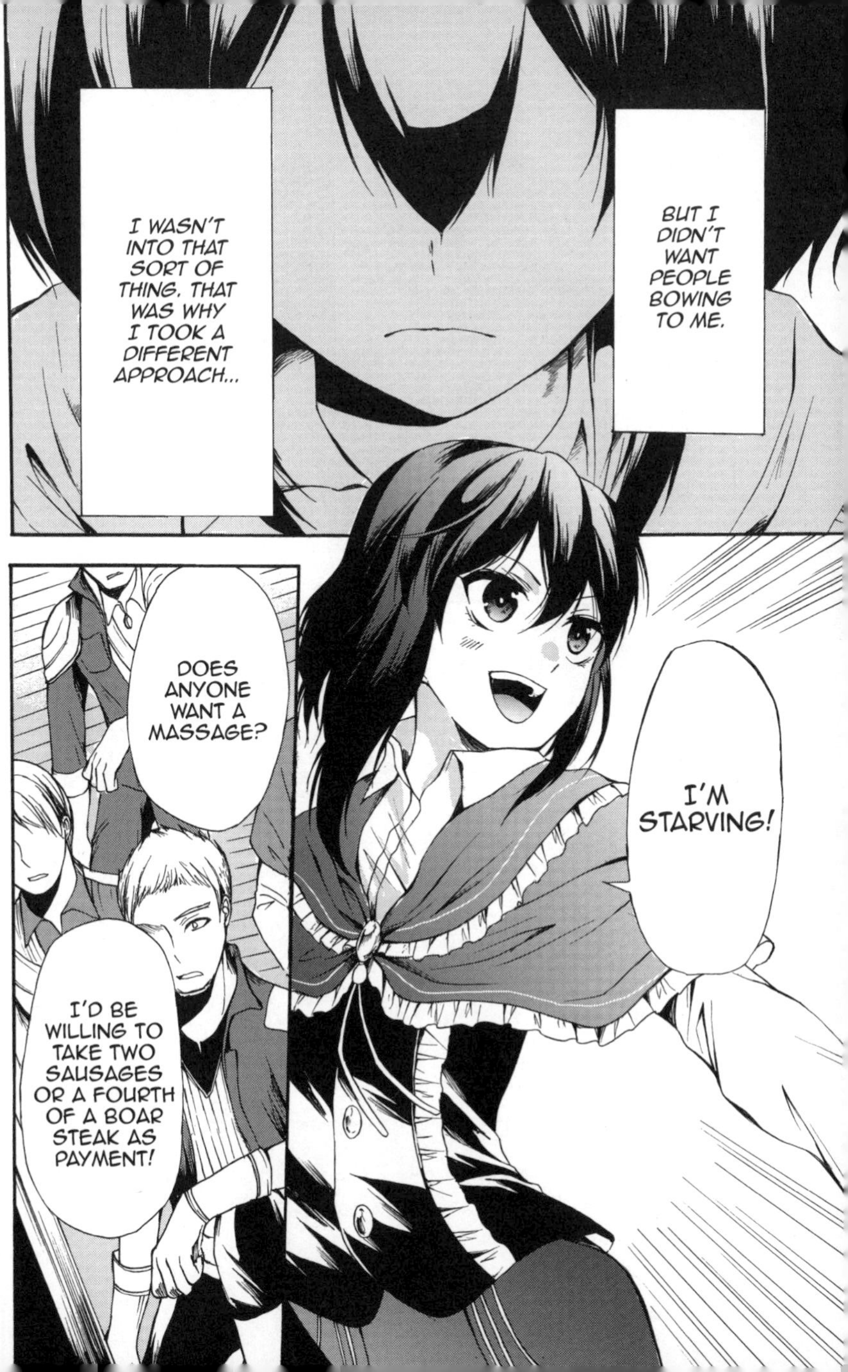
BUT I DIDN'T WANT PEOPLE BOWING TO ME.
I WASN'T INTO THAT SORT OF THING. THAT WAS WHY I TOOK A DIFFERENT APPROACH...
I'M STARVING!
DOES ANYONE WANT A MASSAGE?
I'D BE WILLING TO TAKE TWO SAUSAGES OR A FOURTH OF A BOAR STEAK AS PAYMENT!

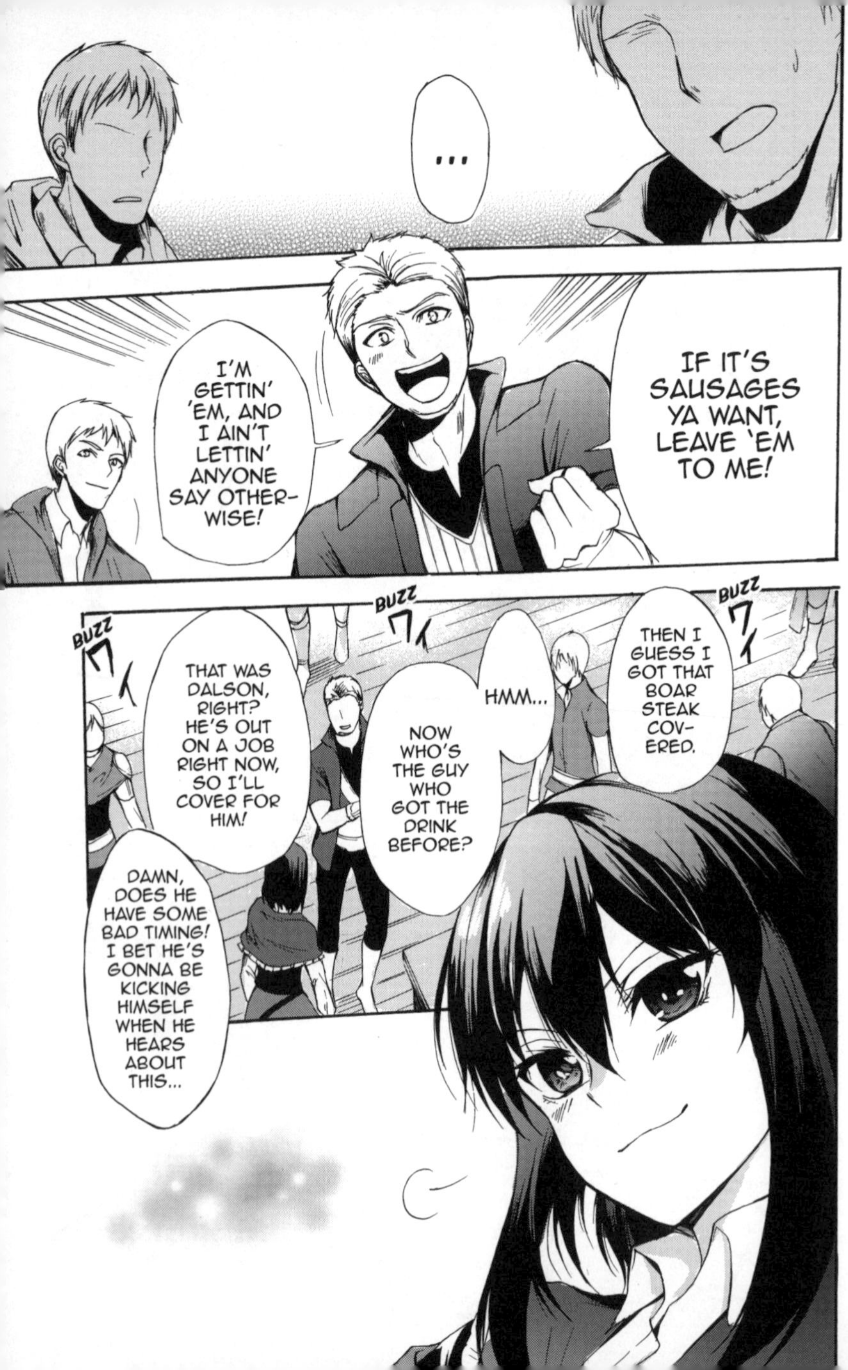
...
IF IT'S SAUSAGES YA WANT, LEAVE 'EM TO ME!
I'M GETTIN' 'EM, AND I AIN'T LETTIN' ANYONE SAY OTHER-WISE!
BUZZ ワイ
THEN I GUESS I GOT THAT BOAR STEAK COV-ERED.
HMM...
BUZZ ワイ
NOW WHO'S THE GUY WHO GOT THE DRINK BEFORE?
THAT WAS DALSON, RIGHT? HE'S OUT ON A JOB RIGHT NOW, SO I'LL COVER FOR HIM!
BUZZ ワイ
DAMN, DOES HE HAVE SOME BAD TIMING! I BET HE'S GONNA BE KICKING HIMSELF WHEN HE HEARS ABOUT THIS...

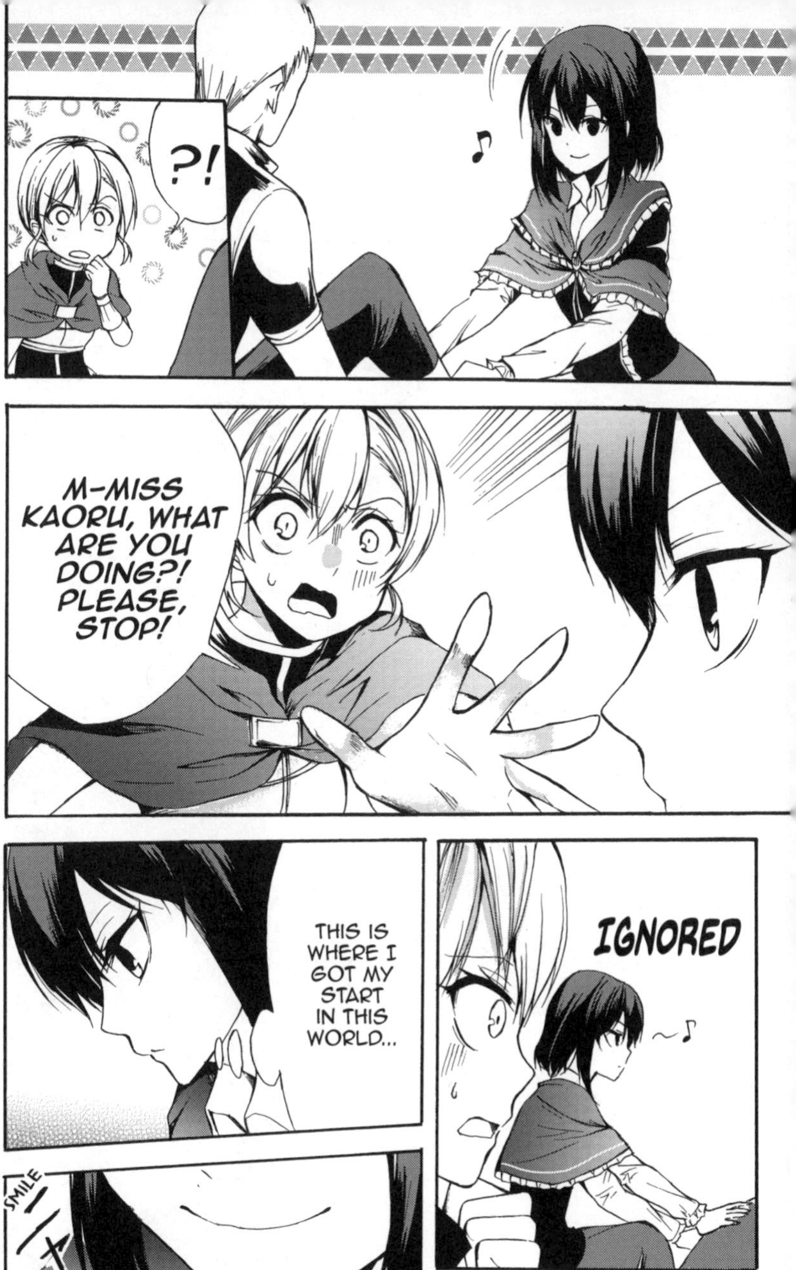
?!
♪
M-MISS KAORU, WHAT ARE YOU DOING?! PLEASE, STOP!
IGNORED
~♪
THIS IS WHERE I GOT MY START IN THIS WORLD...
SMILE

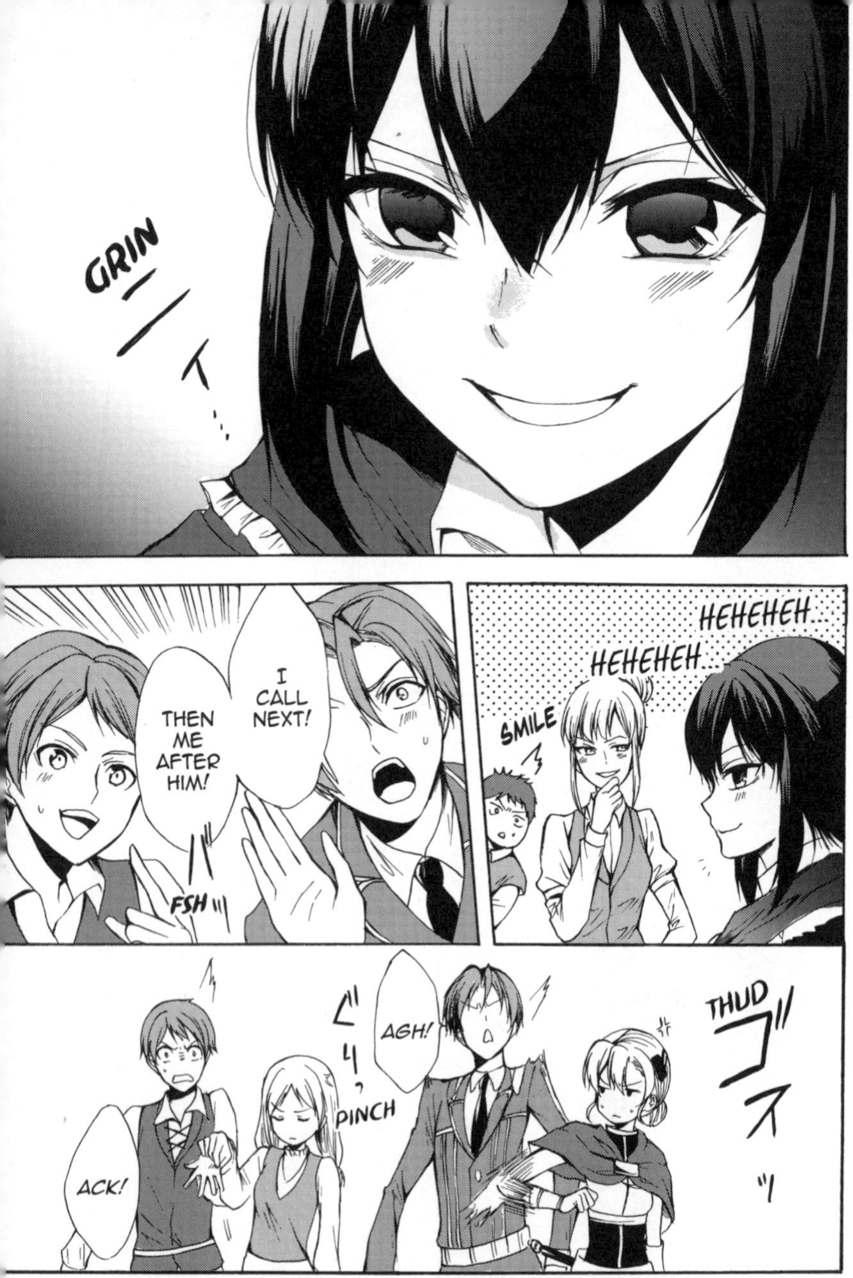
GRIN
HEHEHEH...
HEHEHEH...
SMILE
I CALL NEXT!
THEN ME AFTER HIM!
FSH
THUD
AGH!
PINCH
ACK!

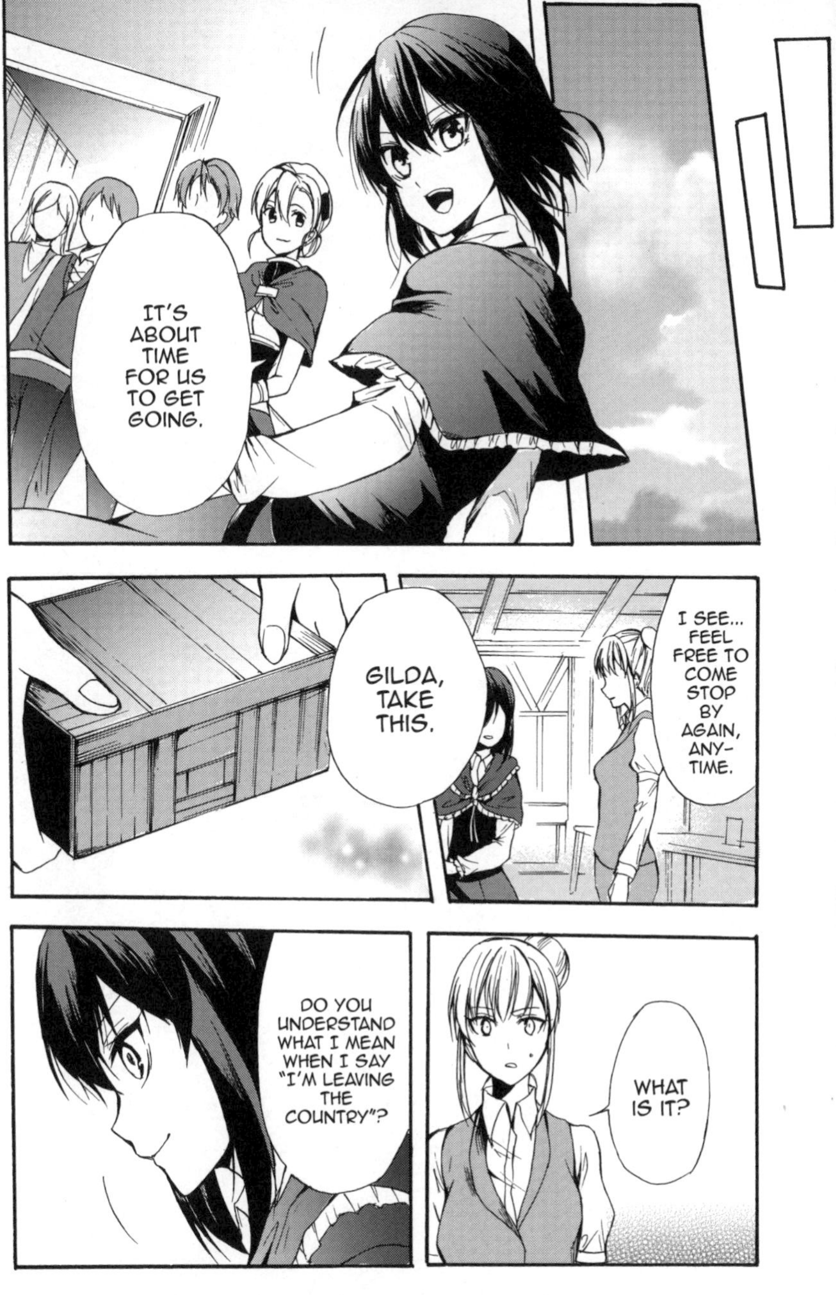
IT'S ABOUT TIME FOR US TO GET GOING.
I SEE... FEEL FREE TO COME STOP BY AGAIN, ANY-TIME.
GILDA, TAKE THIS.
WHAT IS IT?
DO YOU UNDERSTAND WHAT I MEAN WHEN I SAY "I'M LEAVING THE COUNTRY"?

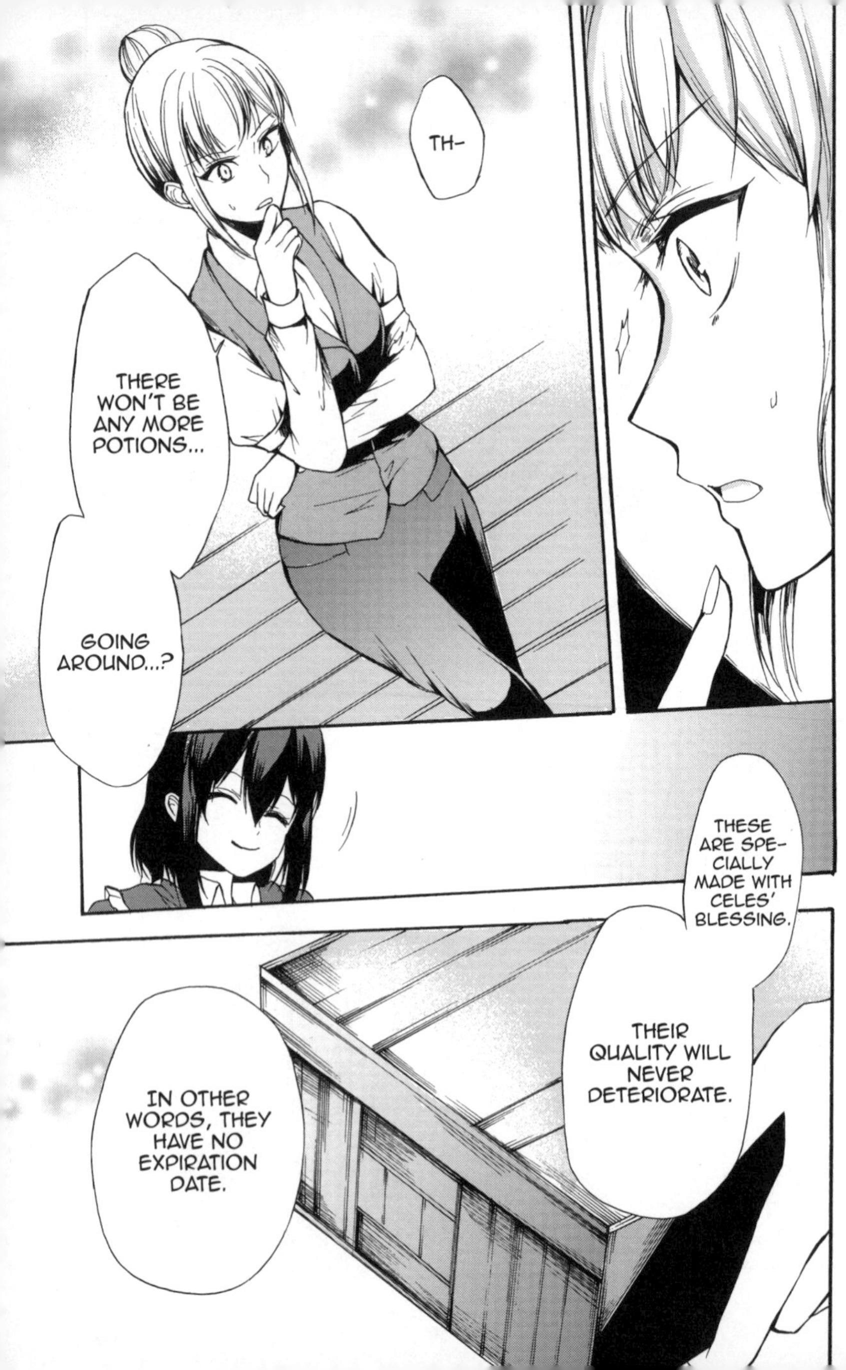
TH-
THERE WON'T BE ANY MORE POTIONS...
GOING AROUND...?
THESE ARE SPE-CIALLY MADE WITH CELES' BLESSING.
THEIR QUALITY WILL NEVER DETERIORATE.
IN OTHER WORDS, THEY HAVE NO EXPIRATION DATE.

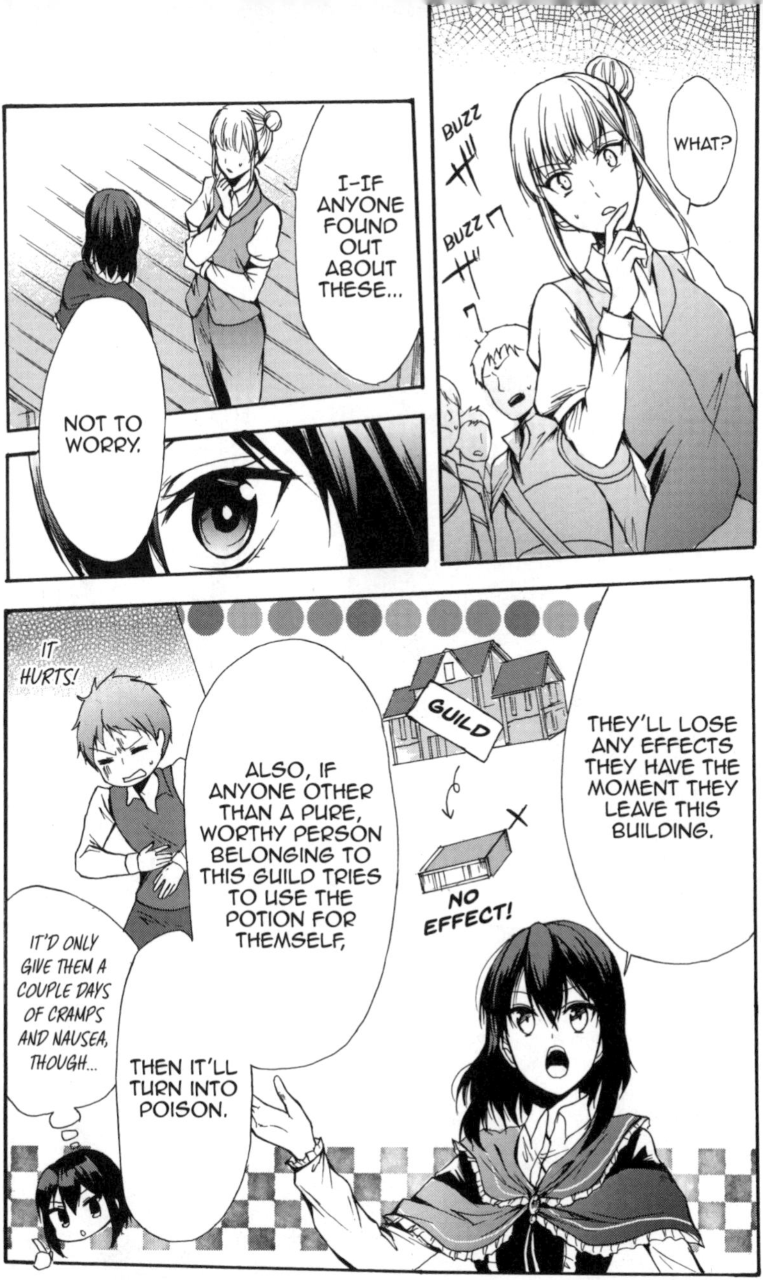
WHAT?
BUZZ
BUZZ
I-IF ANYONE FOUND OUT ABOUT THESE...
NOT TO WORRY.
THEY'LL LOSE ANY EFFECTS THEY HAVE THE MOMENT THEY LEAVE THIS BUILDING.
GUILD
NO EFFECT!
ALSO, IF ANYONE OTHER THAN A PURE, WORTHY PERSON BELONGING TO THIS GUILD TRIES TO USE THE POTION FOR THEMSELF,
THEN IT'LL TURN INTO POISON.
IT HURTS!
IT'D ONLY GIVE THEM A COUPLE DAYS OF CRAMPS AND NAUSEA, THOUGH...

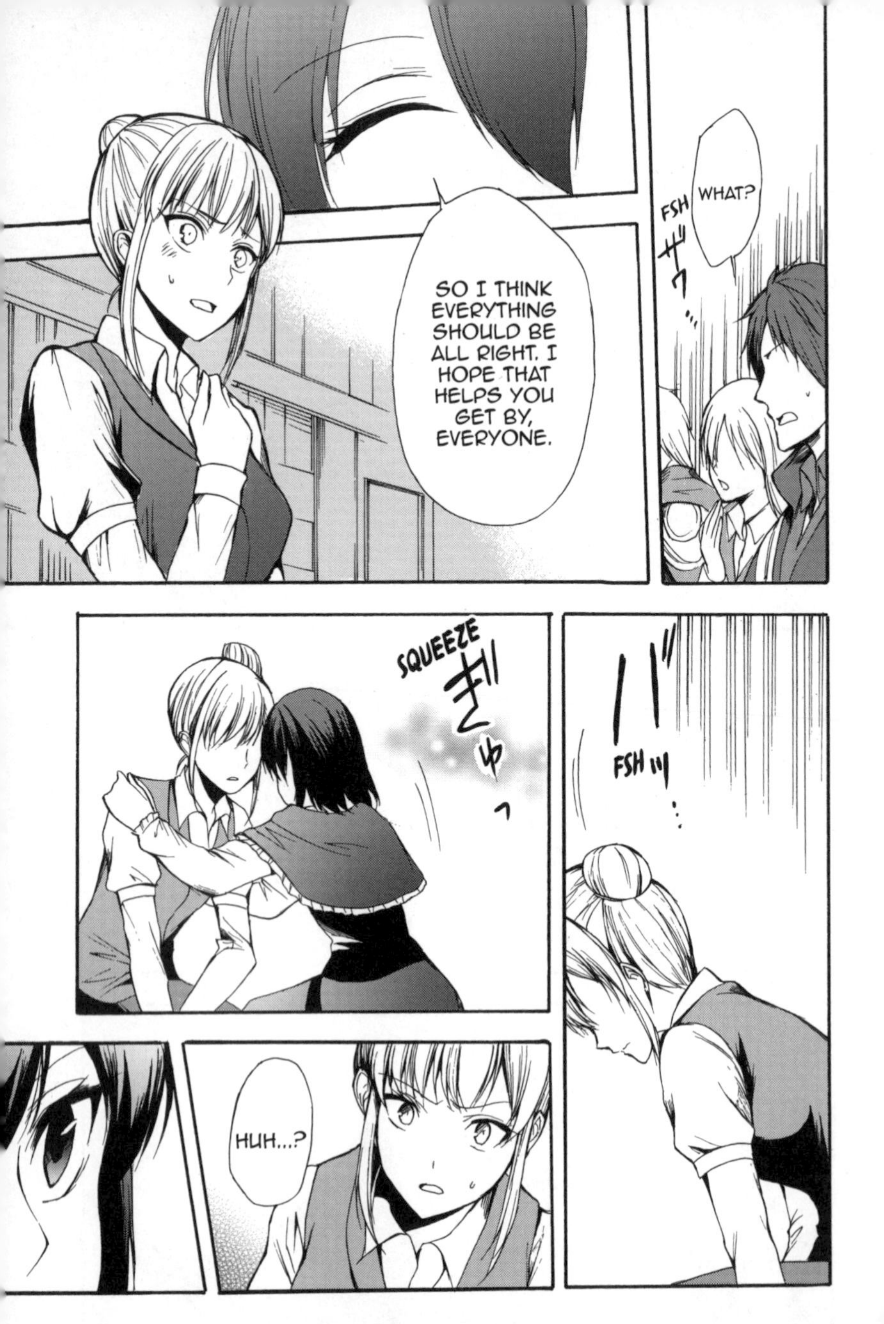
WHAT?
FSH
ザワ…
SO I THINK EVERYTHING SHOULD BE ALL RIGHT. I HOPE THAT HELPS YOU GET BY, EVERYONE.
バッ
FSH
SQUEEZE
ぎゅっ
HUH...?

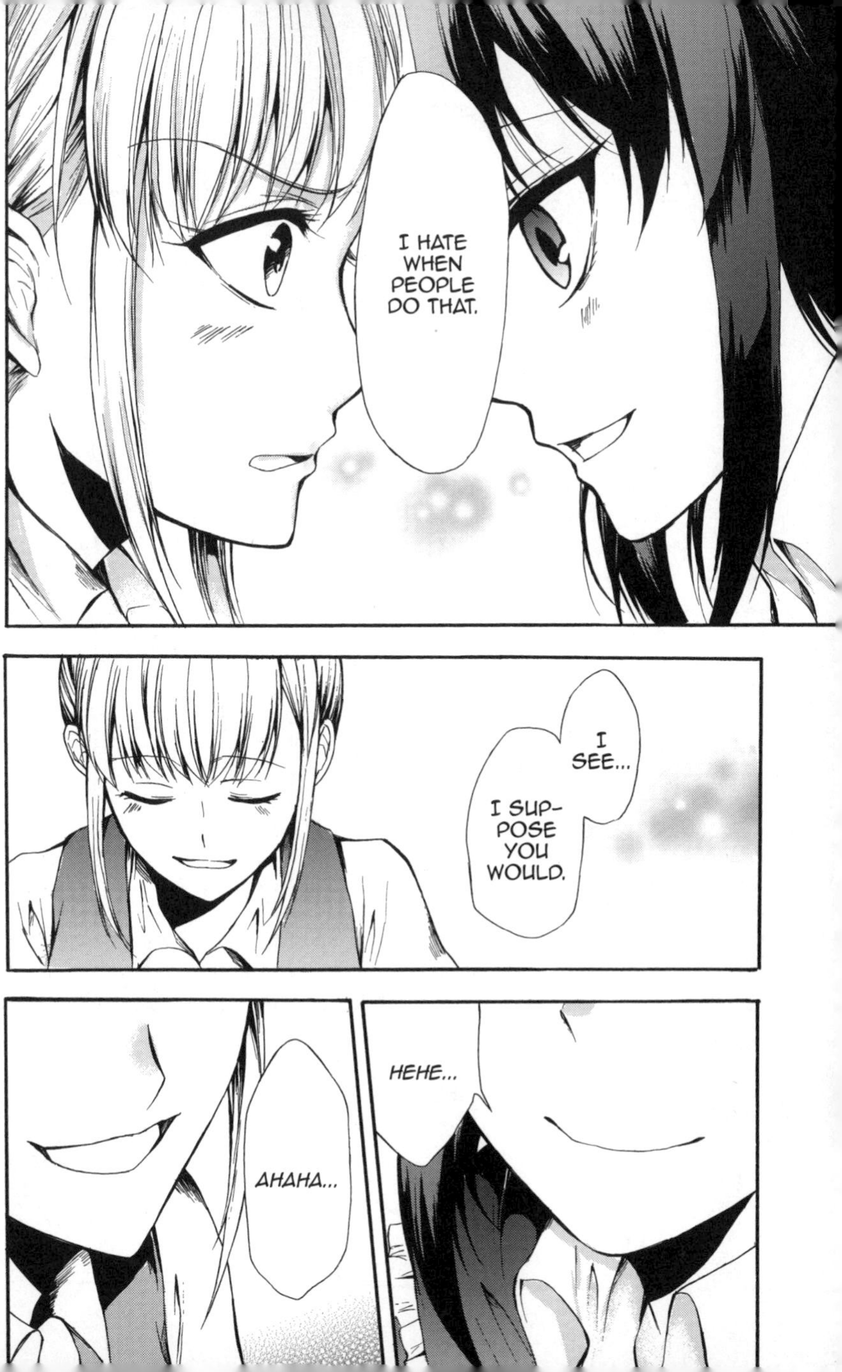
I HATE WHEN PEOPLE DO THAT.
I SEE...
I SUPPOSE YOU WOULD.
HEHE...
AHAHA...

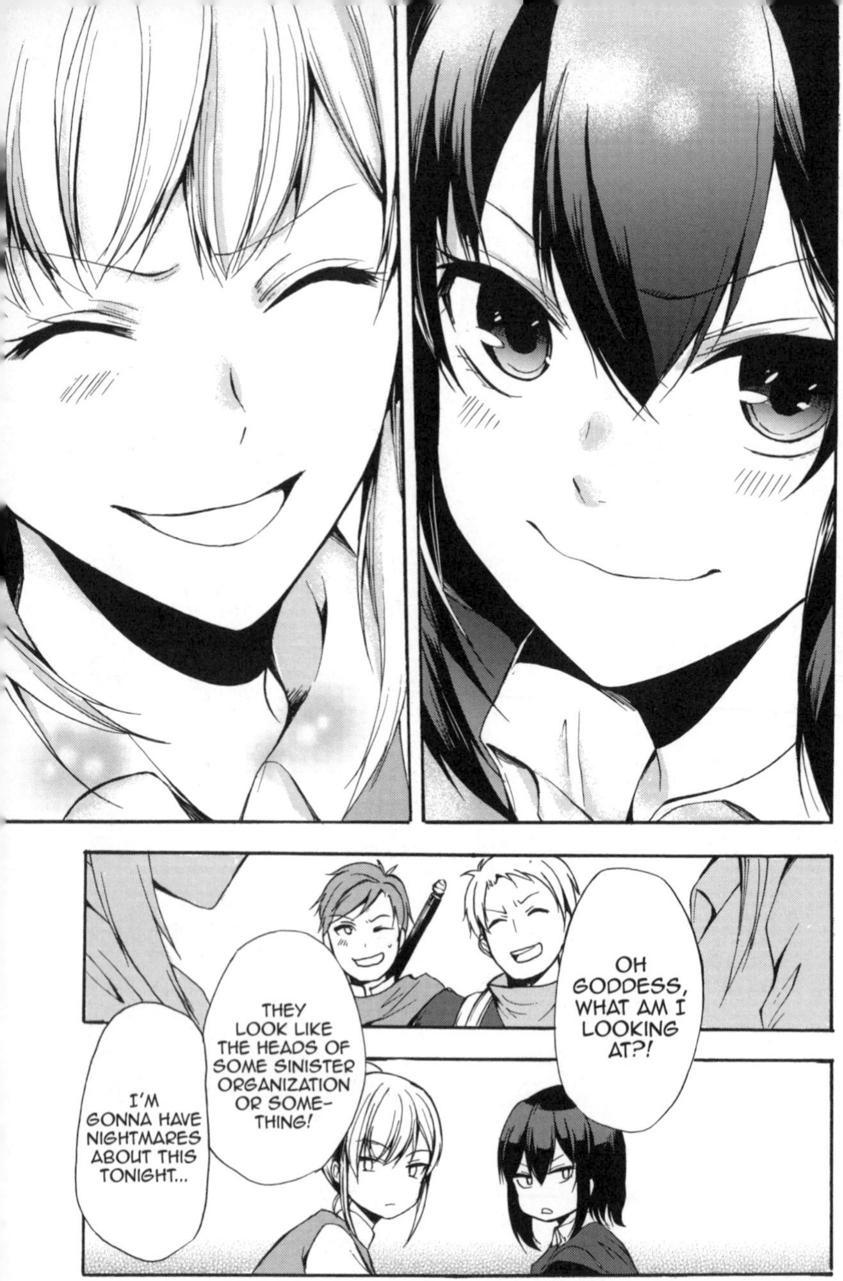
OH GODDESS, WHAT AM I LOOKING AT?!
THEY LOOK LIKE THE HEADS OF SOME SINISTER ORGANIZATION OR SOME-THING!
I'M GONNA HAVE NIGHTMARES ABOUT THIS TONIGHT...

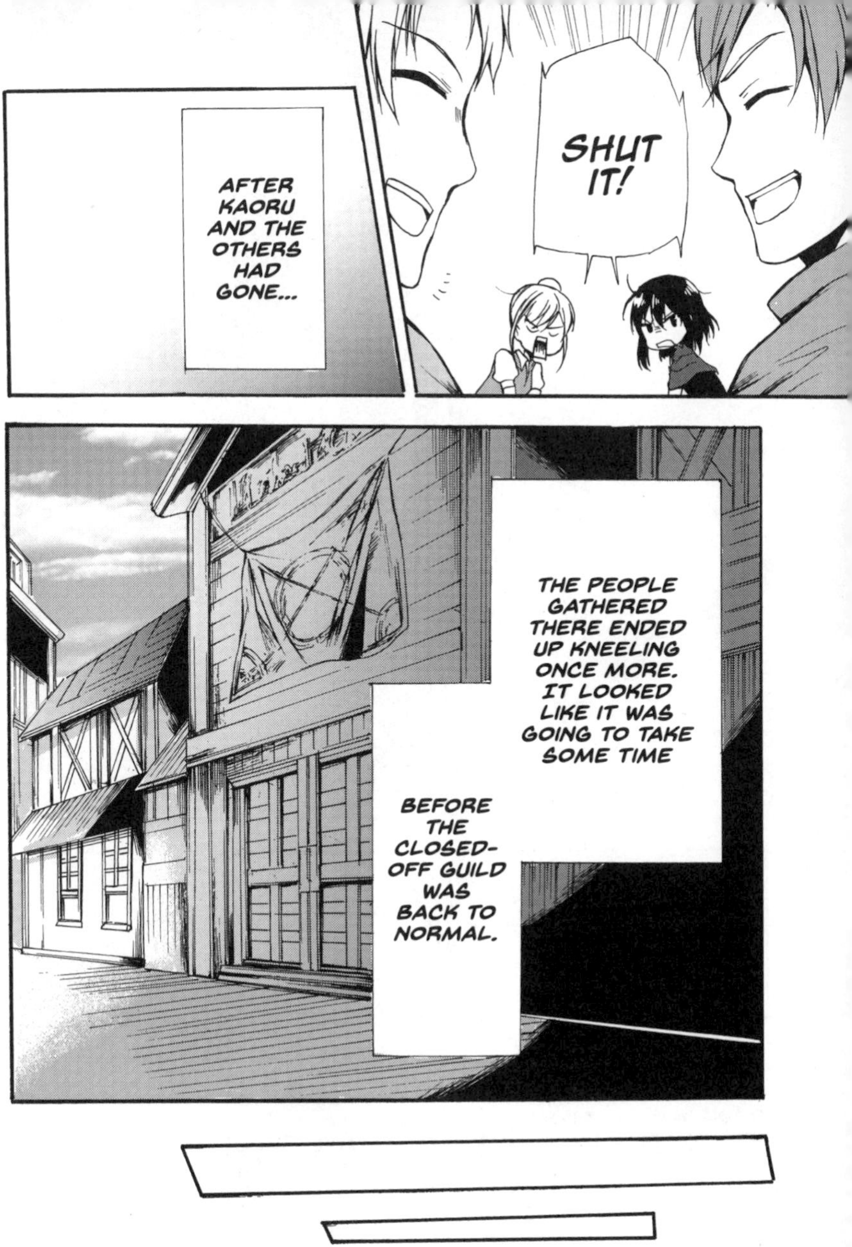
SHUT IT!
AFTER KAORU AND THE OTHERS HAD GONE...
THE PEOPLE GATHERED THERE ENDED UP KNEELING ONCE MORE. IT LOOKED LIKE IT WAS GOING TO TAKE SOME TIME
BEFORE THE CLOSED-OFF GUILD WAS BACK TO NORMAL.

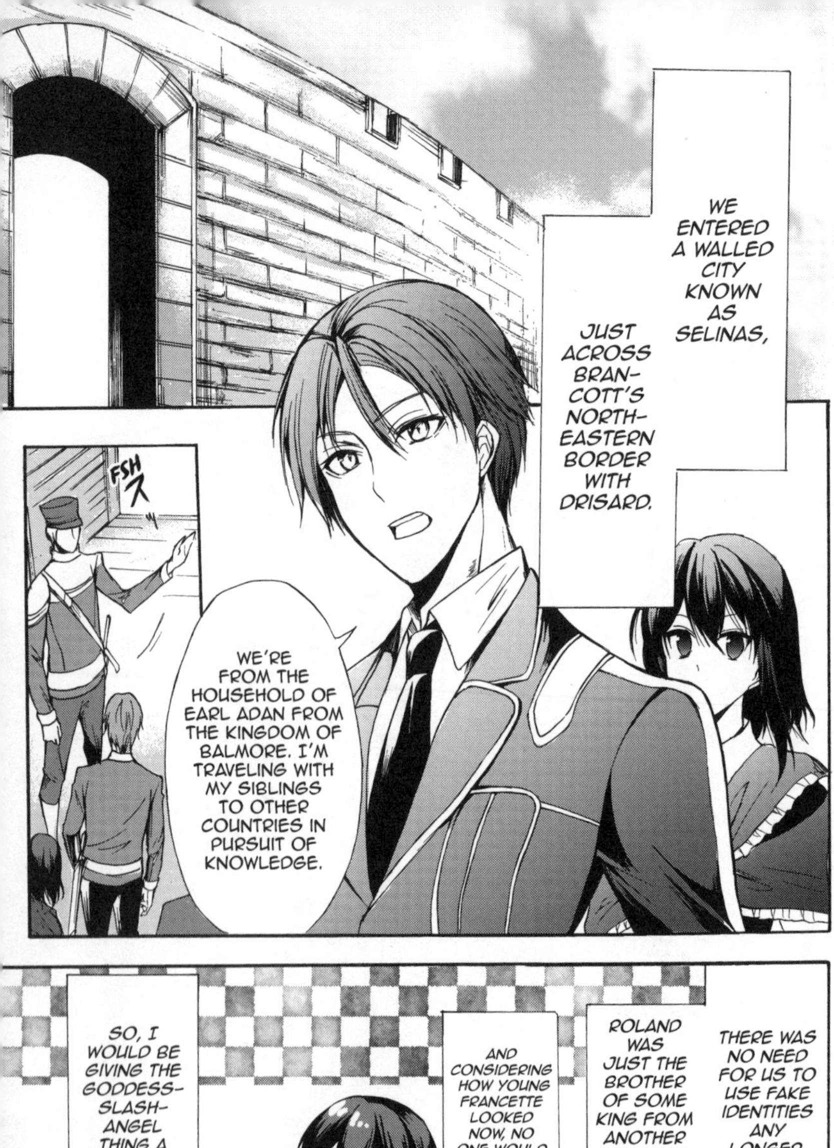
WE ENTERED A WALLED CITY KNOWN AS SELINAS,
JUST ACROSS BRAN-COTT'S NORTH-EASTERN BORDER WITH DRISARD.
WE'RE FROM THE HOUSEHOLD OF EARL ADAN FROM THE KINGDOM OF BALMORE. I'M TRAVELING WITH MY SIBLINGS TO OTHER COUNTRIES IN PURSUIT OF KNOWLEDGE.
FSH ス
THERE WAS NO NEED FOR US TO USE FAKE IDENTITIES ANY LONGER.
ROLAND WAS JUST THE BROTHER OF SOME KING FROM ANOTHER COUNTRY THAT DIDN'T HAVE MUCH TO DO WITH THEM.
AND CONSIDERING HOW YOUNG FRANCETTE LOOKED NOW, NO ONE WOULD THINK SHE WAS THE INFAMOUS "FEARSOME FRAN."
SO, I WOULD BE GIVING THE GODDESS-SLASH-ANGEL THING A REST FOR THE TIME BEING.

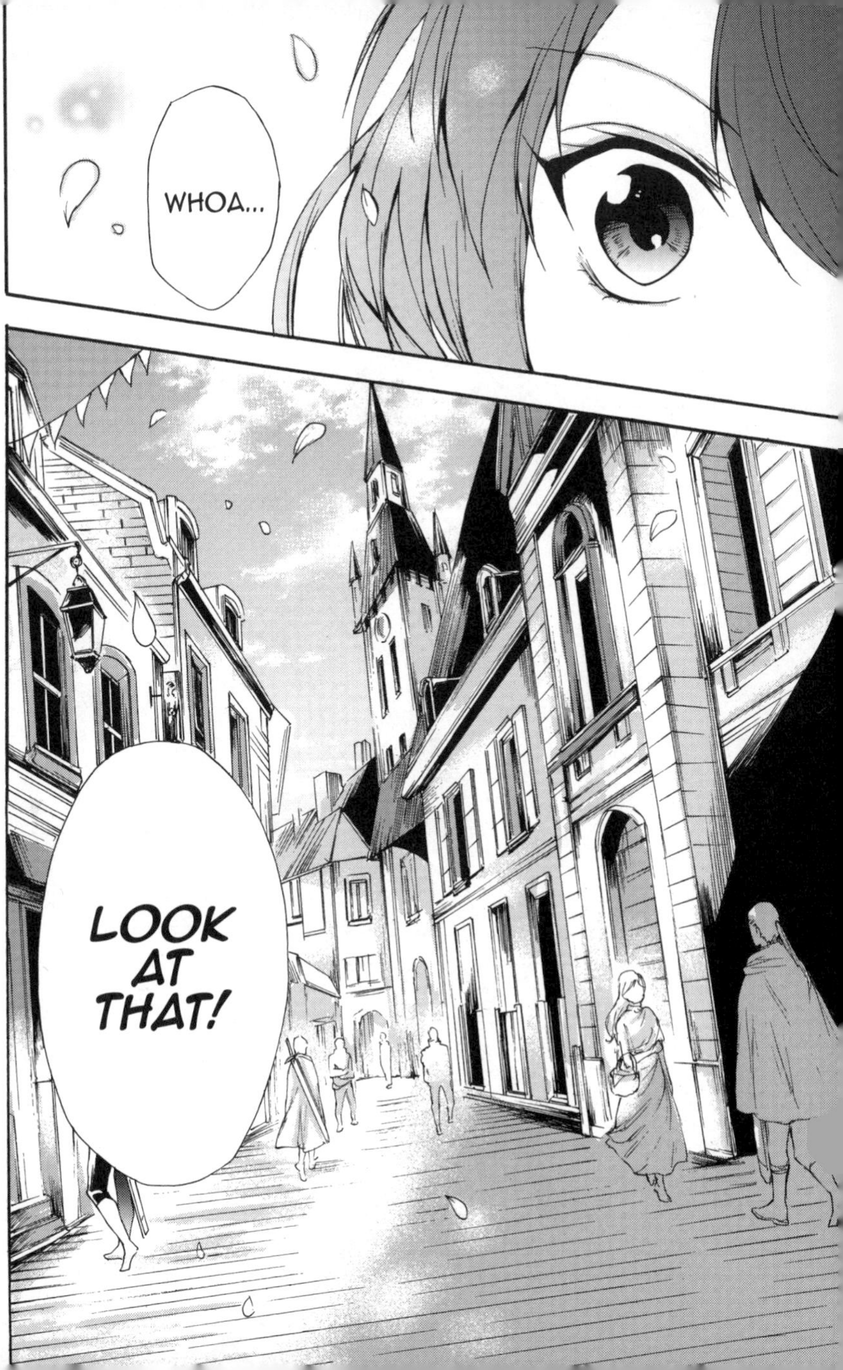
WHOA...
LOOK AT THAT!

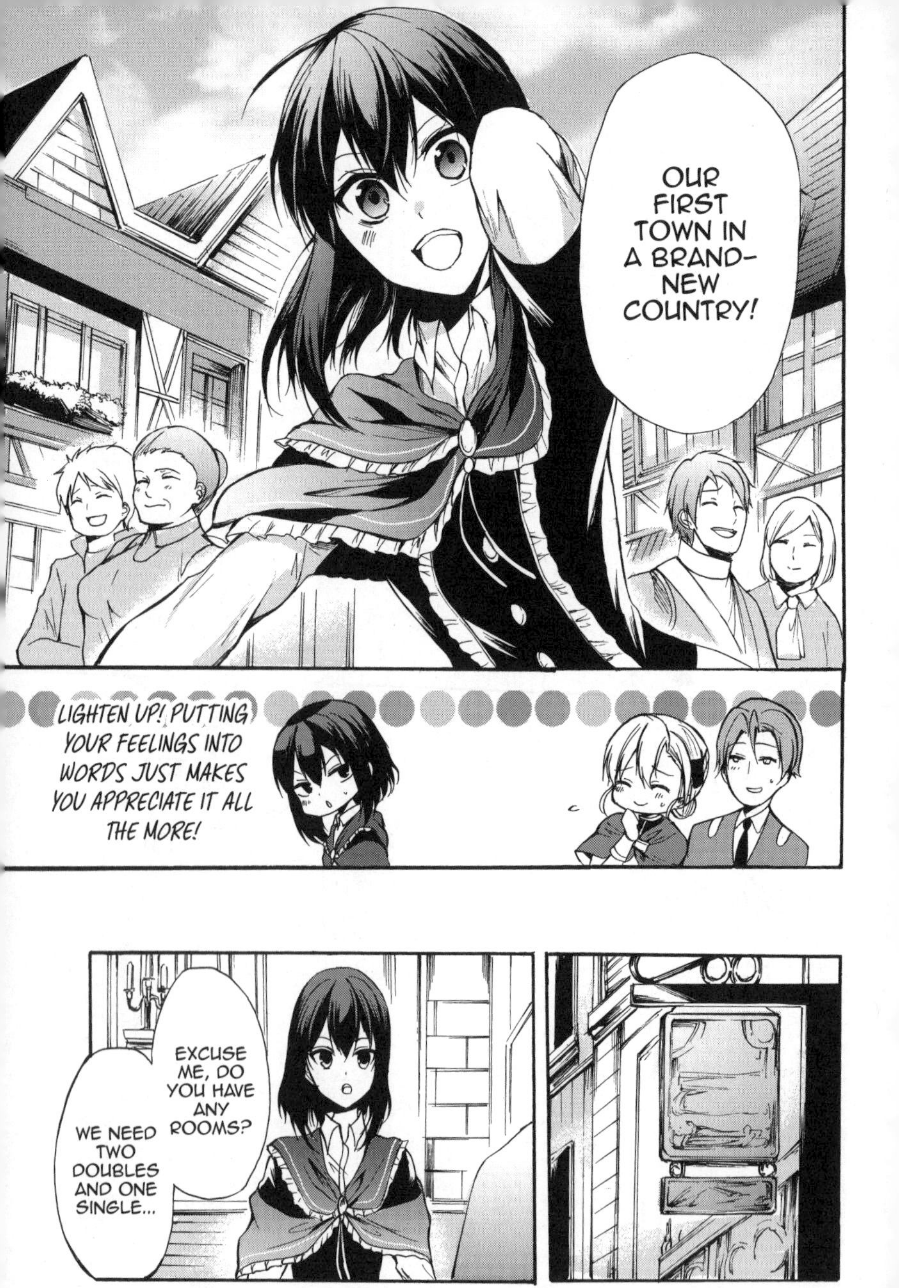
OUR FIRST TOWN IN A BRAND-NEW COUNTRY!
LIGHTEN UP! PUTTING YOUR FEELINGS INTO WORDS JUST MAKES YOU APPRECIATE IT ALL THE MORE!
EXCUSE ME, DO YOU HAVE ANY ROOMS?
WE NEED TWO DOUBLES AND ONE SINGLE...

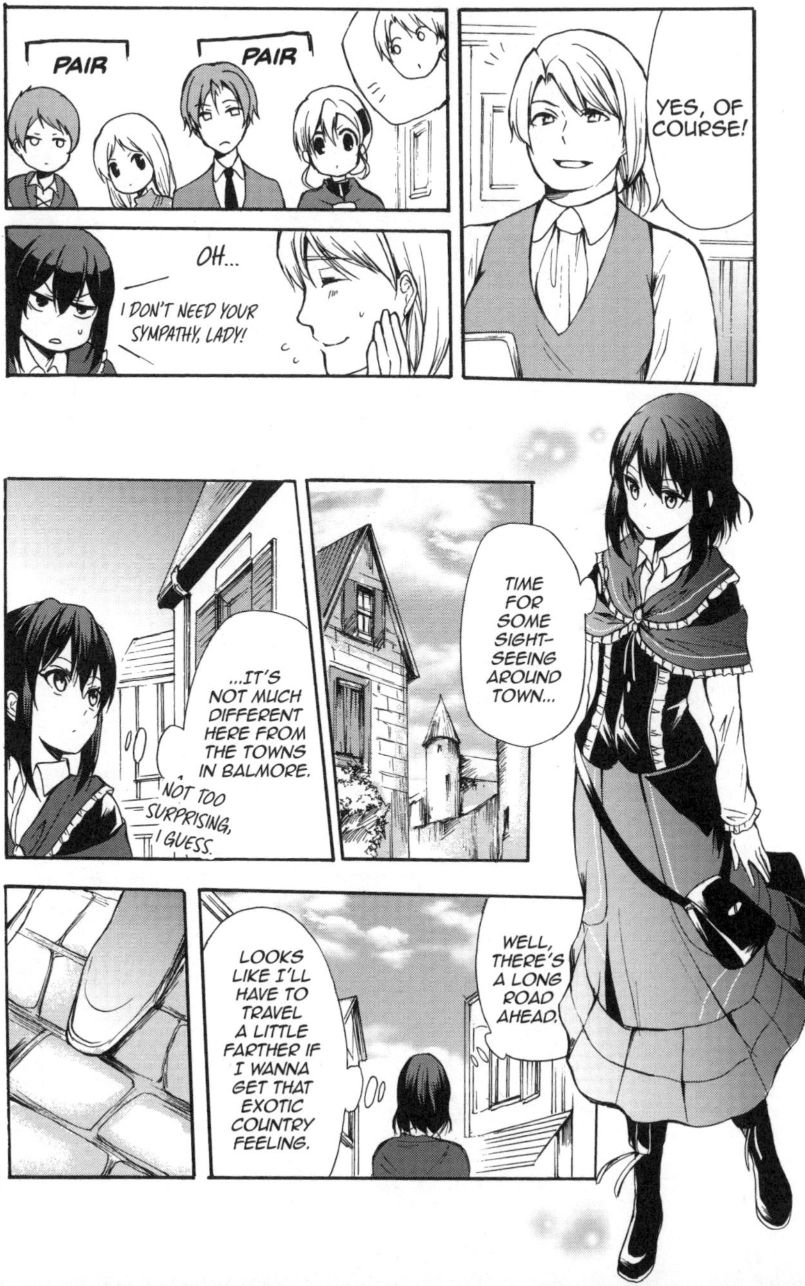
YES, OF COURSE!
PAIR
PAIR
OH...
I DON'T NEED YOUR SYMPATHY, LADY!
TIME FOR SOME SIGHT-SEEING AROUND TOWN...
WELL, THERE'S A LONG ROAD AHEAD.
...IT'S NOT MUCH DIFFERENT HERE FROM THE TOWNS IN BALMORE.
NOT TOO SURPRISING, I GUESS.
LOOKS LIKE I'LL HAVE TO TRAVEL A LITTLE FARTHER IF I WANNA GET THAT EXOTIC COUNTRY FEELING.

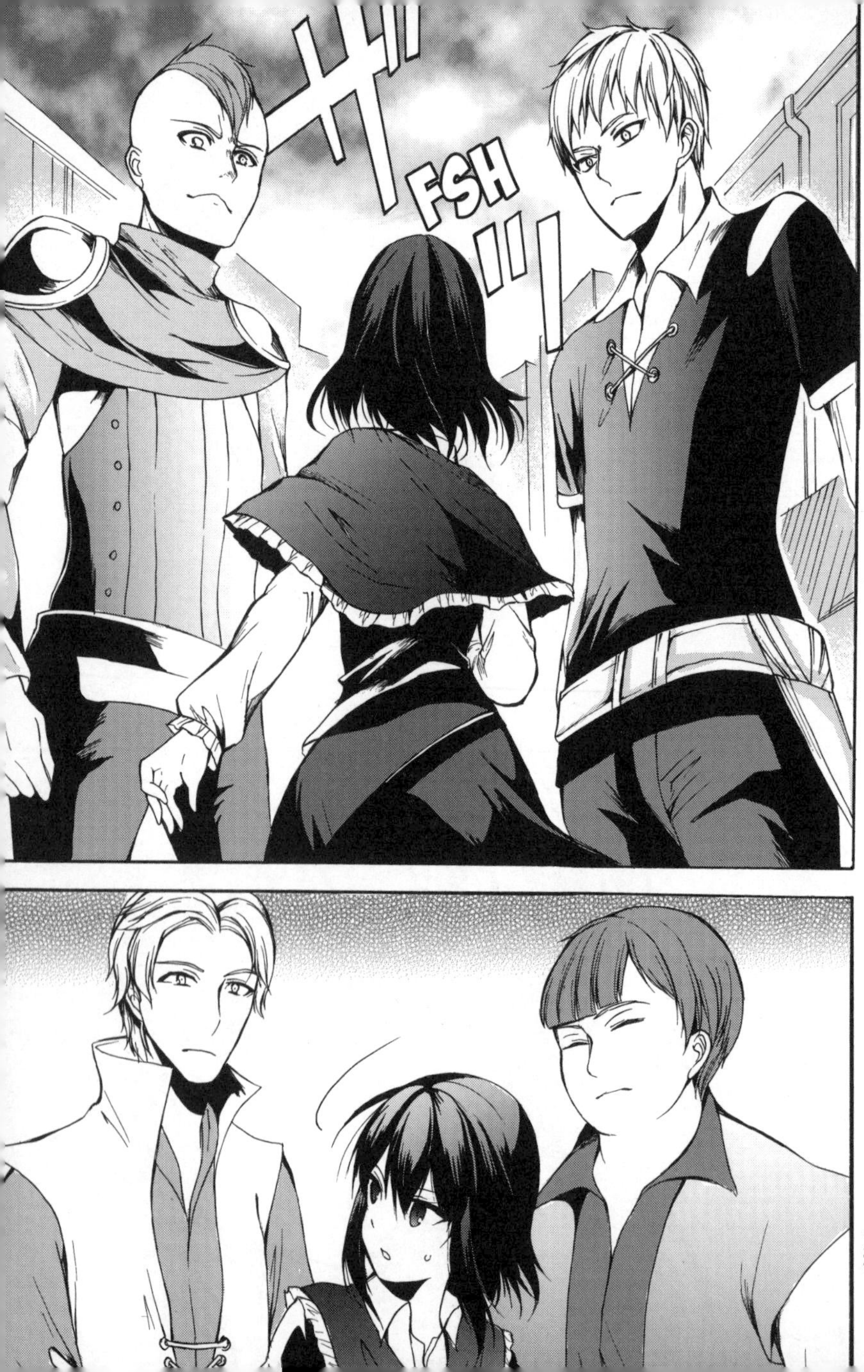
FSH

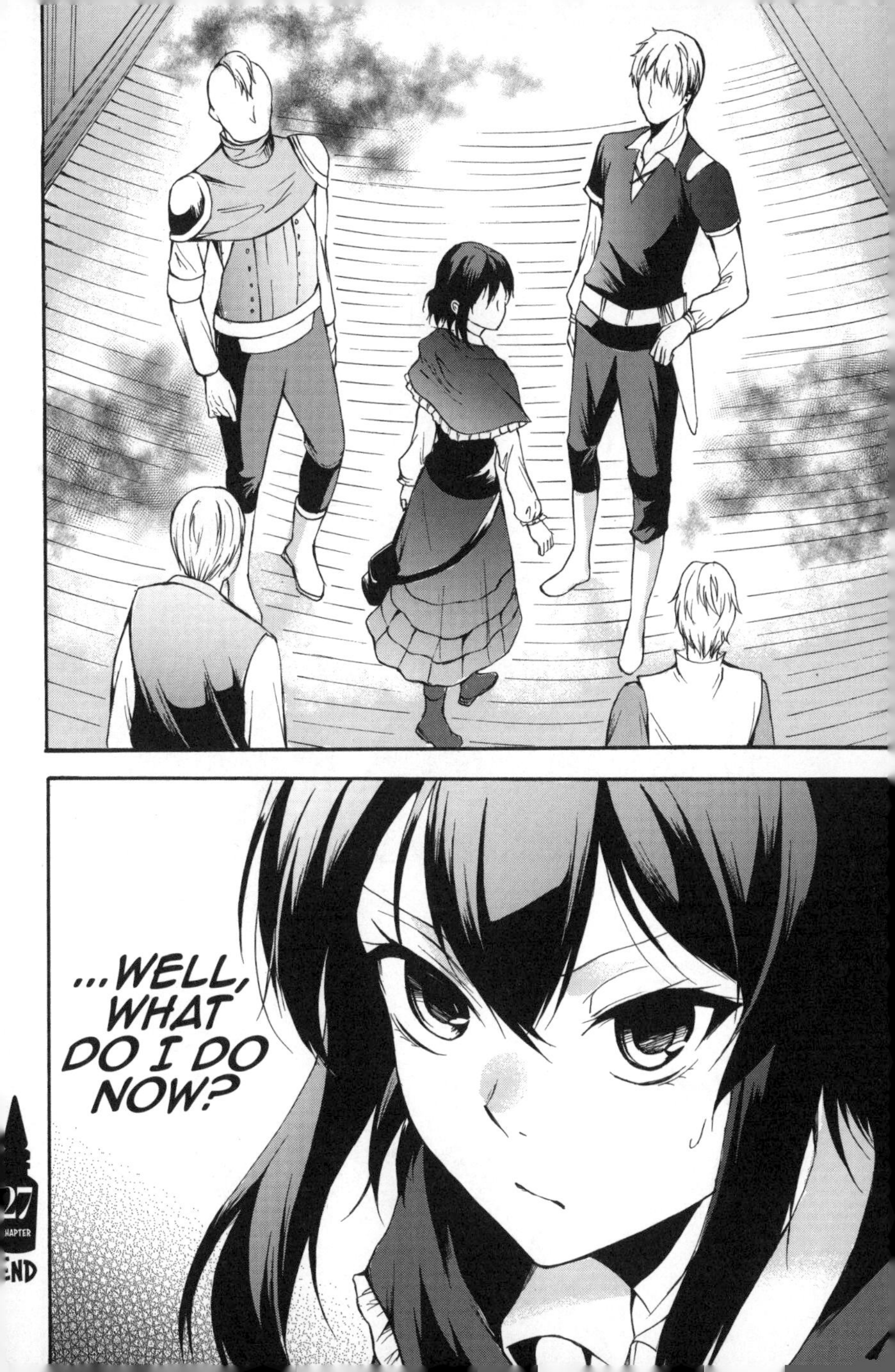
...WELL, WHAT DO I DO NOW?
27 CHAPTER END

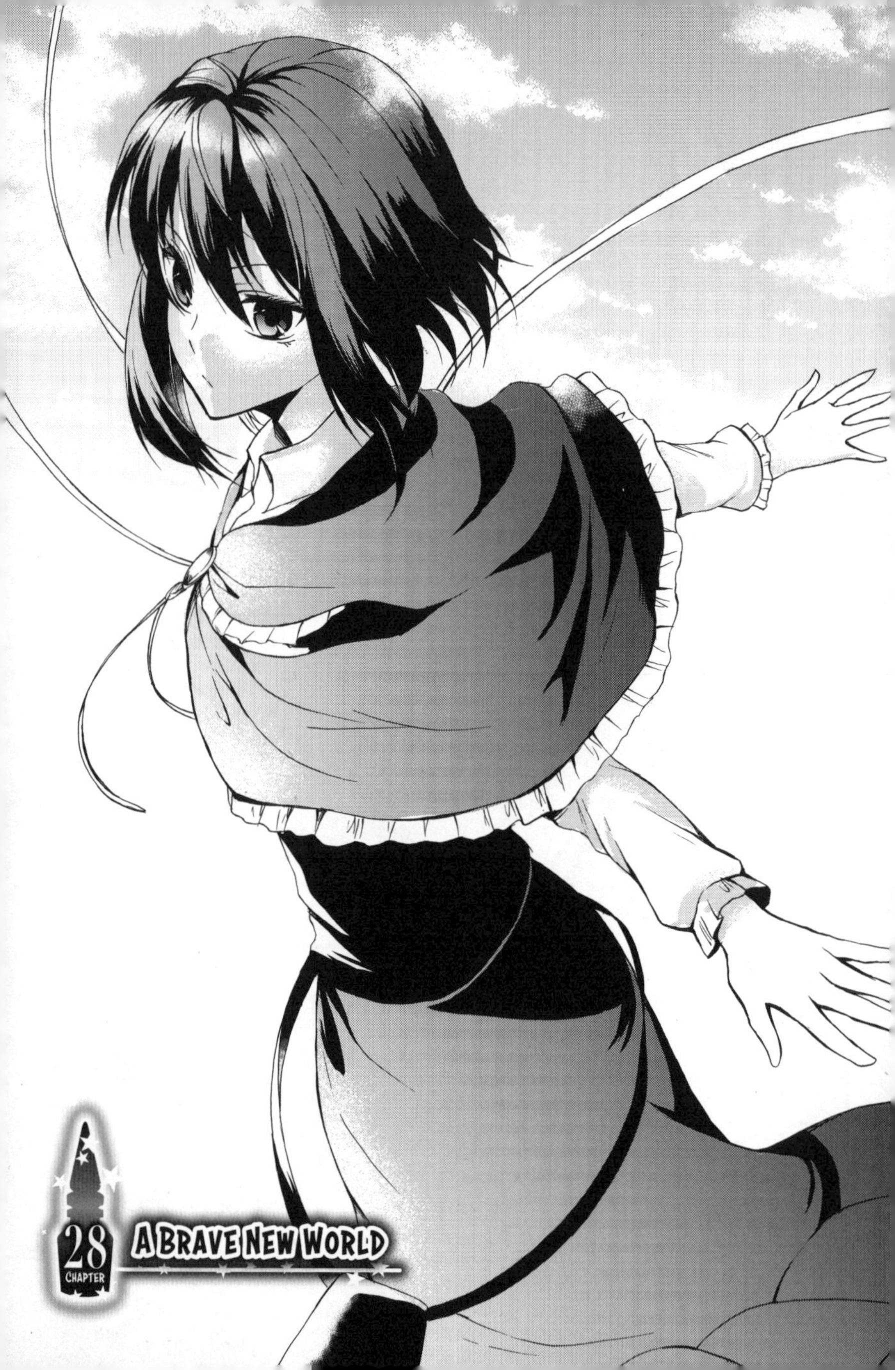
28
CHAPTER
A BRAVE NEW WORLD

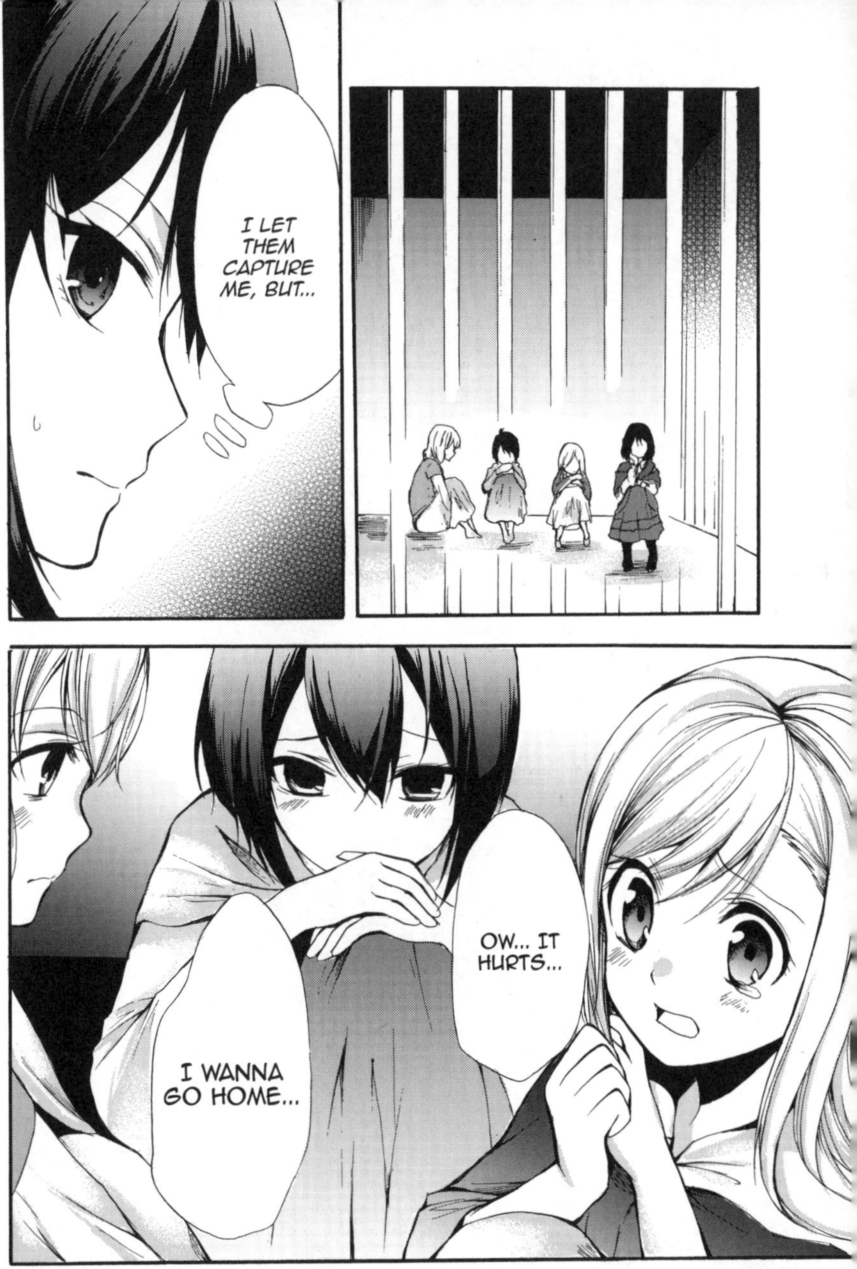
I LET THEM CAPTURE ME, BUT...
OW... IT HURTS...
I WANNA GO HOME...

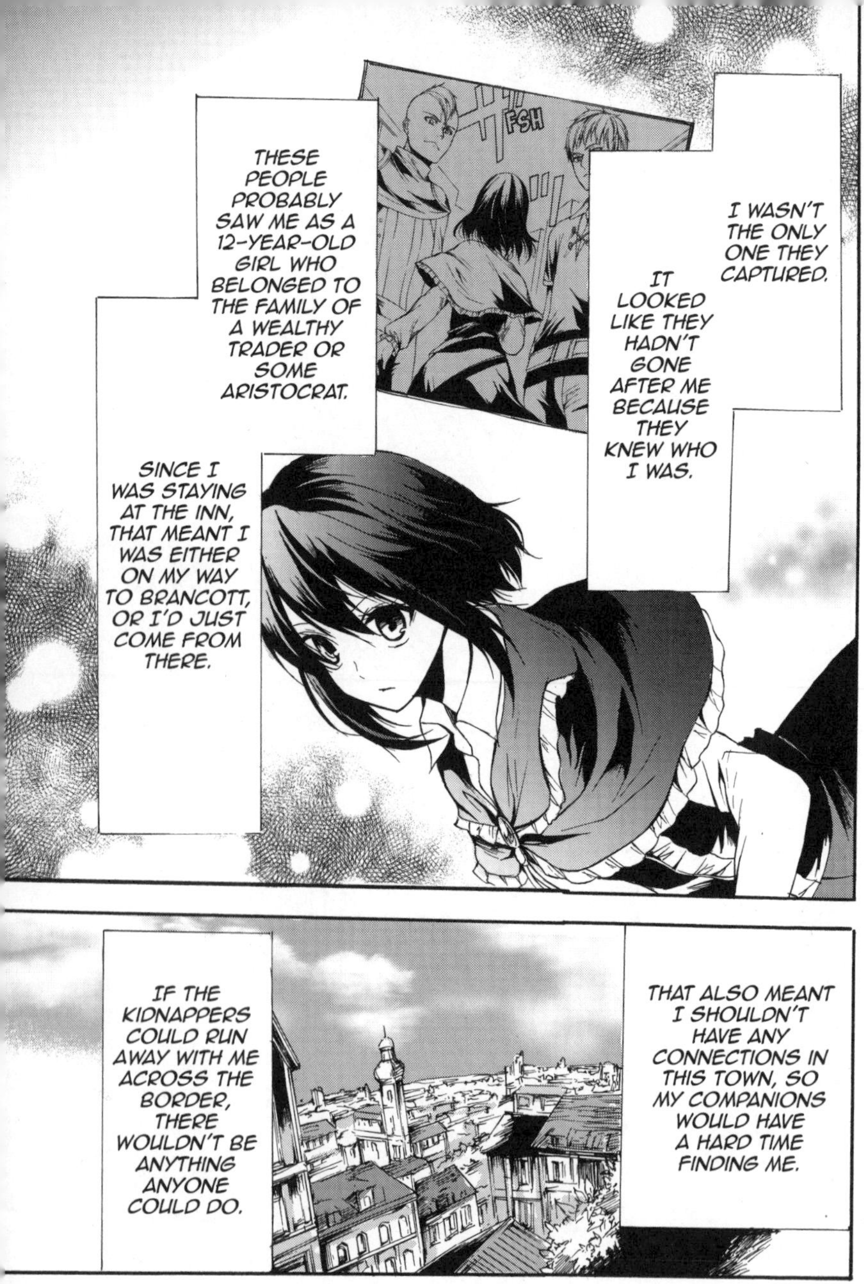
I WASN'T THE ONLY ONE THEY CAPTURED.
IT LOOKED LIKE THEY HADN'T GONE AFTER ME BECAUSE THEY KNEW WHO I WAS.
FSH
THESE PEOPLE PROBABLY SAW ME AS A 12-YEAR-OLD GIRL WHO BELONGED TO THE FAMILY OF A WEALTHY TRADER OR SOME ARISTOCRAT.
SINCE I WAS STAYING AT THE INN, THAT MEANT I WAS EITHER ON MY WAY TO BRANCOTT, OR I'D JUST COME FROM THERE.
THAT ALSO MEANT I SHOULDN'T HAVE ANY CONNECTIONS IN THIS TOWN, SO MY COMPANIONS WOULD HAVE A HARD TIME FINDING ME.
IF THE KIDNAPPERS COULD RUN AWAY WITH ME ACROSS THE BORDER, THERE WOULDN'T BE ANYTHING ANYONE COULD DO.

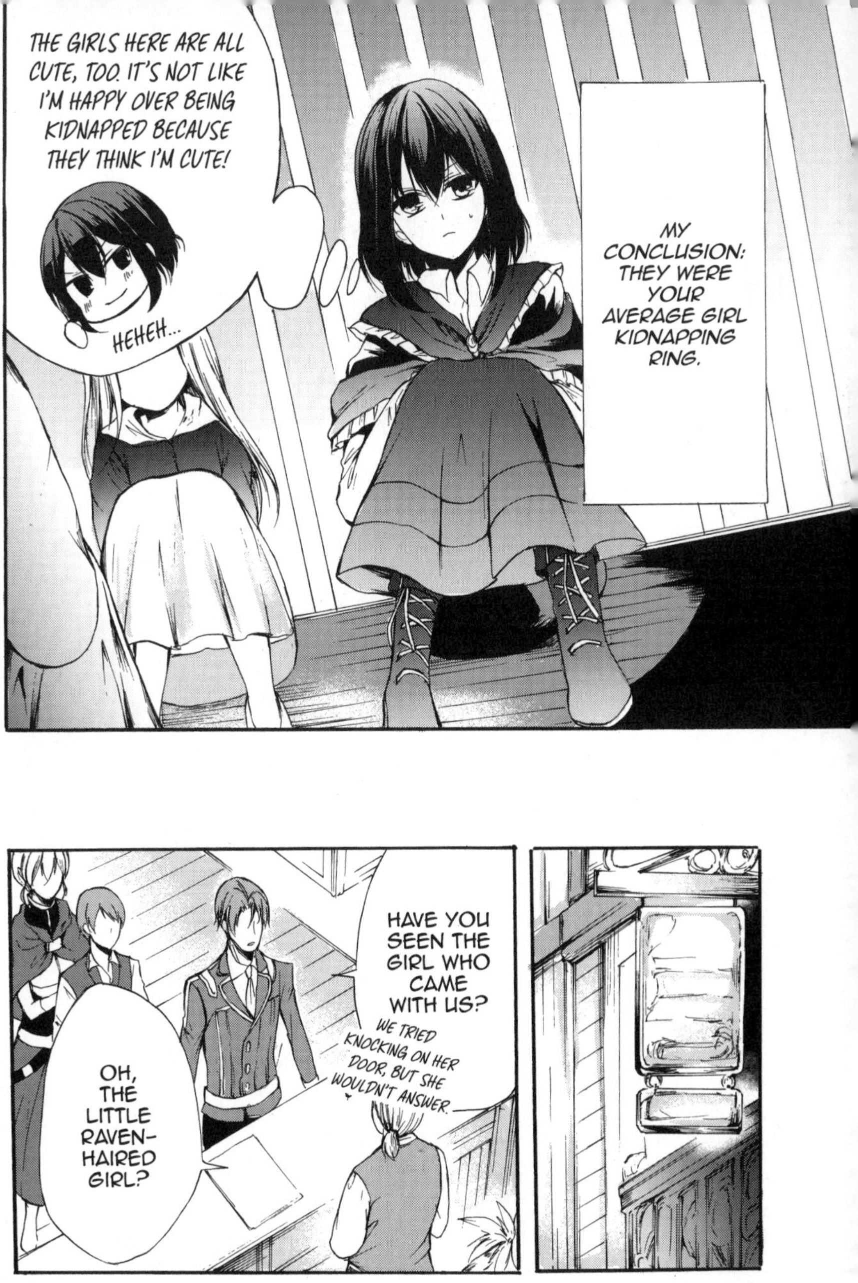
MY CONCLUSION: THEY WERE YOUR AVERAGE GIRL KIDNAPPING RING.
THE GIRLS HERE ARE ALL CUTE, TOO. IT'S NOT LIKE I'M HAPPY OVER BEING KIDNAPPED BECAUSE THEY THINK I'M CUTE!
HEHEH...
HAVE YOU SEEN THE GIRL WHO CAME WITH US?
WE TRIED KNOCKING ON HER DOOR, BUT SHE WOULDN'T ANSWER.
OH, THE LITTLE RAVEN-HAIRED GIRL?

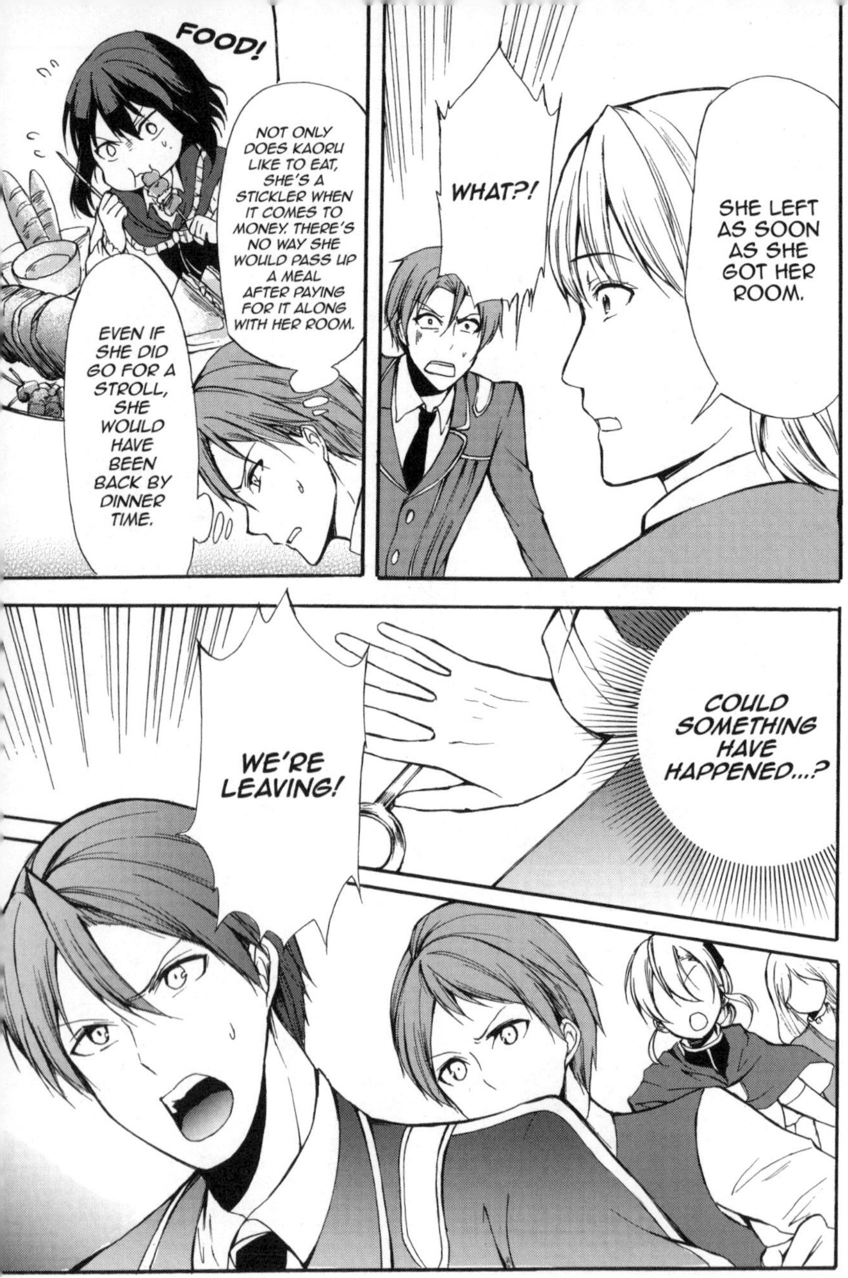
SHE LEFT AS SOON AS SHE GOT HER ROOM.
WHAT?!
NOT ONLY DOES KAORU LIKE TO EAT, SHE'S A STICKLER WHEN IT COMES TO MONEY. THERE'S NO WAY SHE WOULD PASS UP A MEAL AFTER PAYING FOR IT ALONG WITH HER ROOM.
FOOD!
EVEN IF SHE DID GO FOR A STROLL, SHE WOULD HAVE BEEN BACK BY DINNER TIME.
COULD SOMETHING HAVE HAPPENED...?
WE'RE LEAVING!

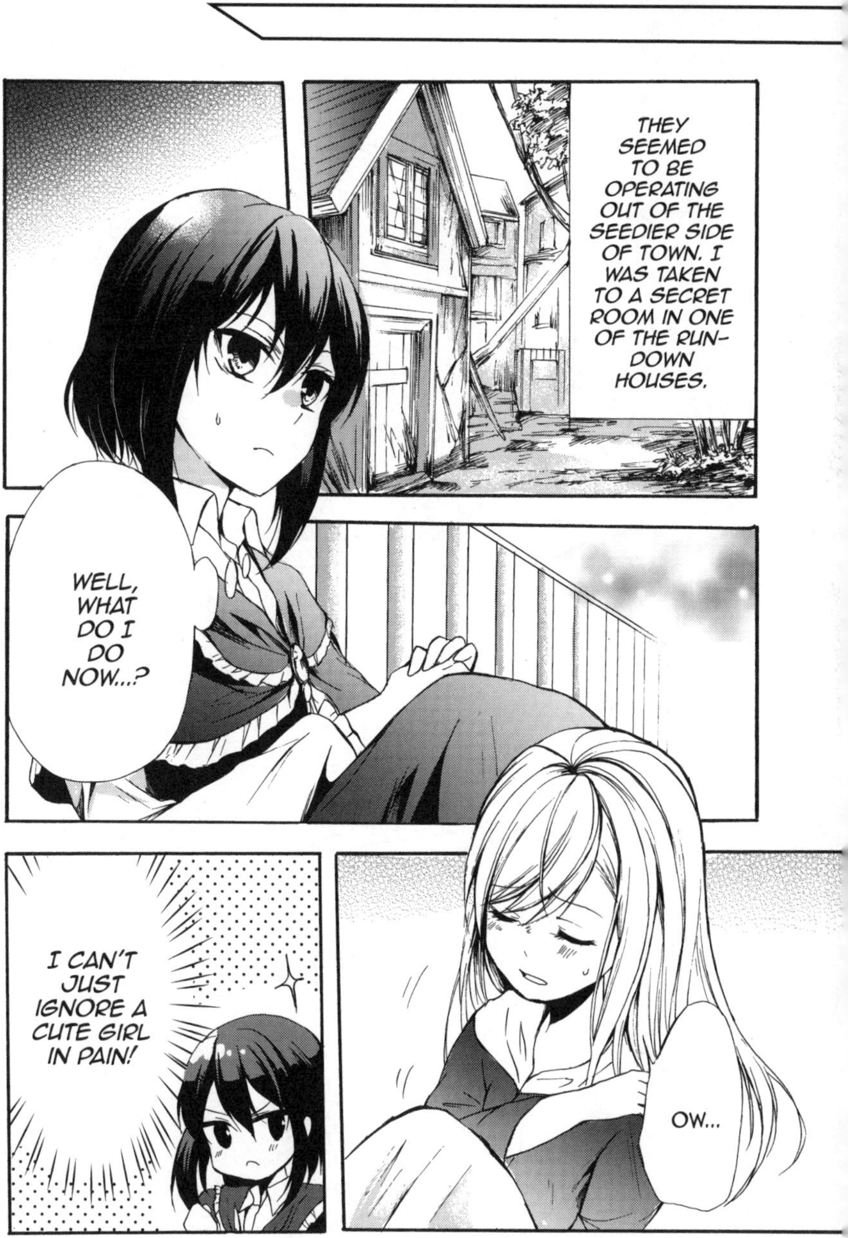
THEY SEEMED TO BE OPERATING OUT OF THE SEEDIER SIDE OF TOWN. I WAS TAKEN TO A SECRET ROOM IN ONE OF THE RUN-DOWN HOUSES.
WELL, WHAT DO I DO NOW...?
OW...
I CAN'T JUST IGNORE A CUTE GIRL IN PAIN!

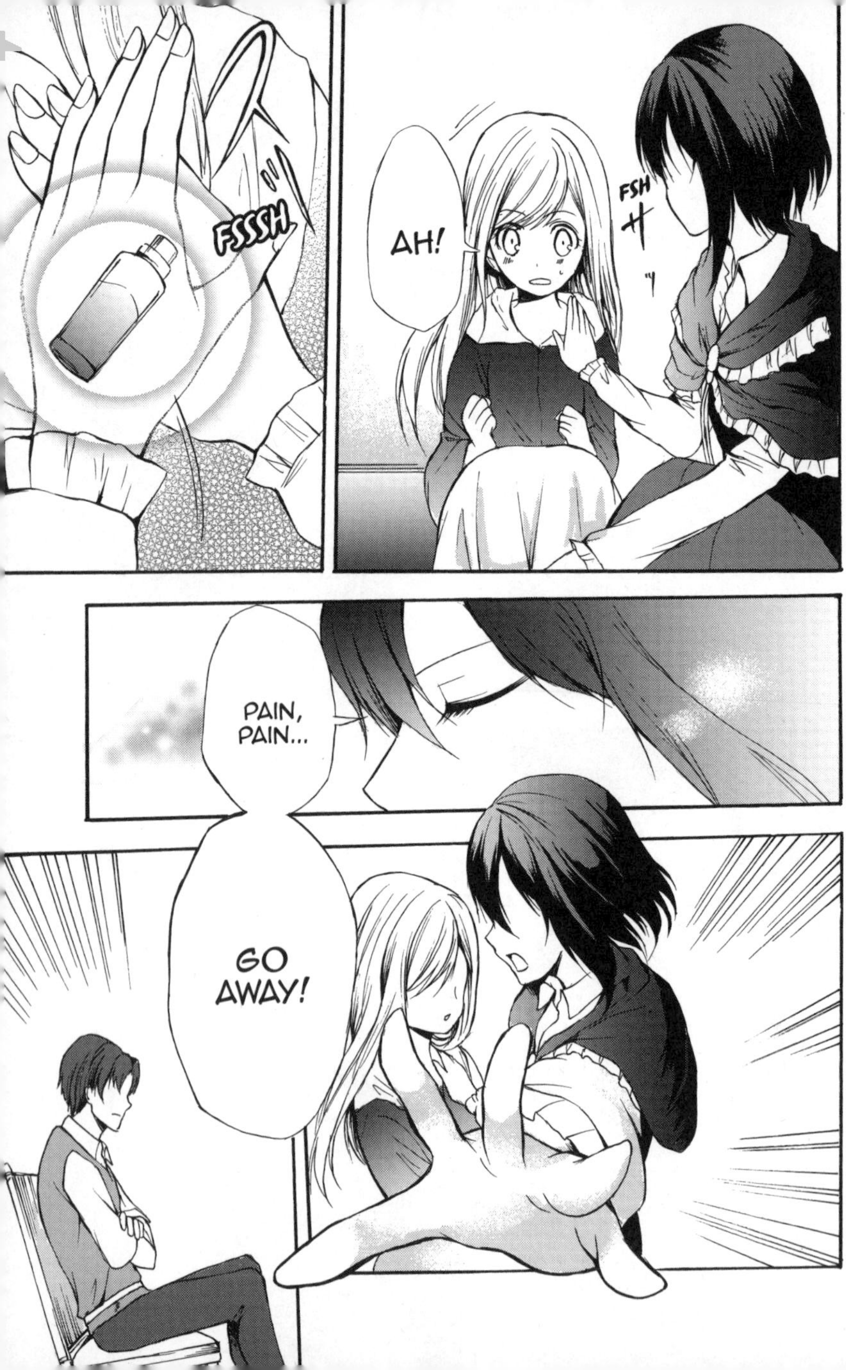
FSH
AH!
FSSSH
PAIN, PAIN...
GO AWAY!

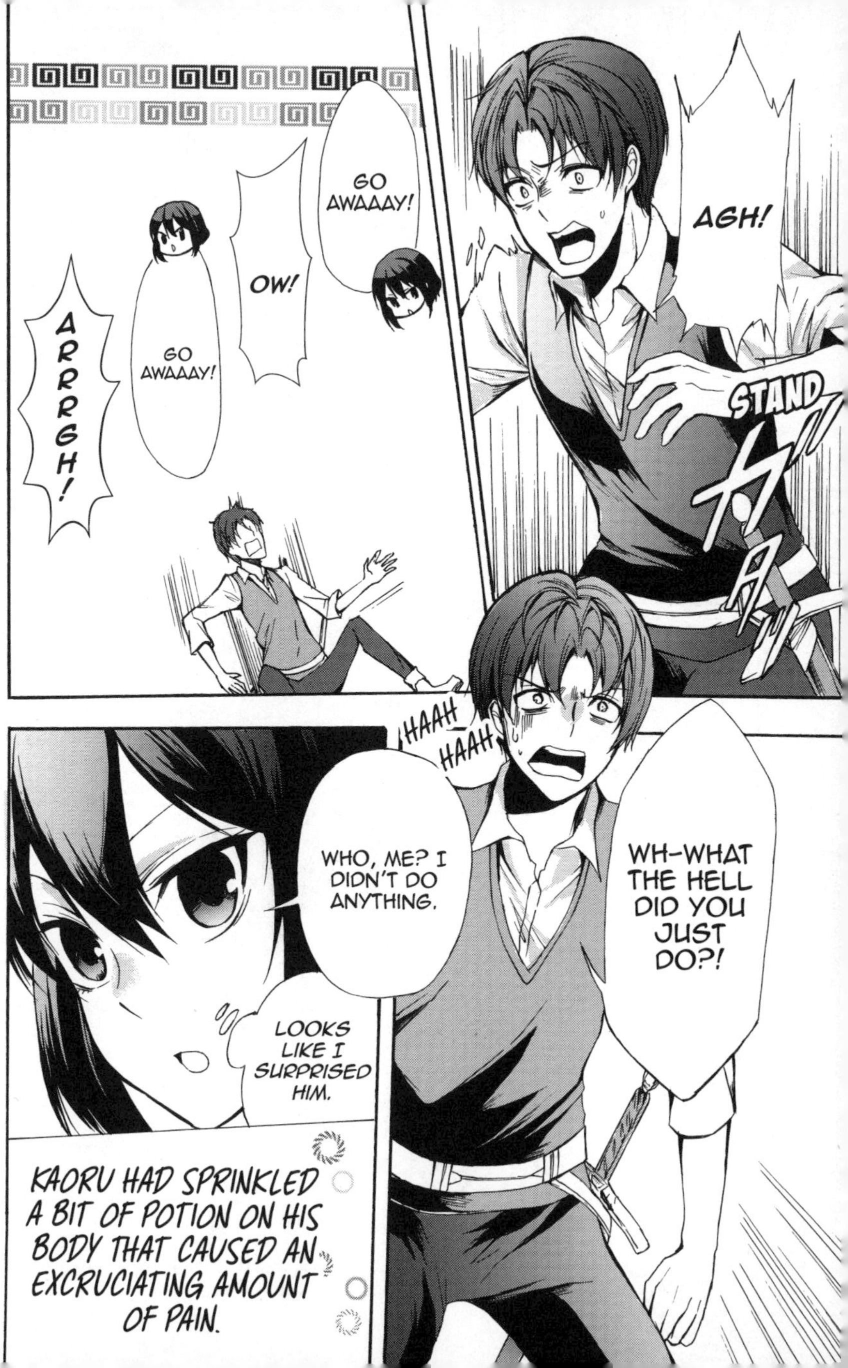
AGH!
STAND
GO AWAAAY!
OW!
GO AWAAAY!
ARRRGH!
HAAH HAAH
WH-WHAT THE HELL DID YOU JUST DO?!
WHO, ME? I DIDN'T DO ANYTHING.
LOOKS LIKE I SURPRISED HIM.
KAORU HAD SPRINKLED A BIT OF POTION ON HIS BODY THAT CAUSED AN EXCRUCIATING AMOUNT OF PAIN.

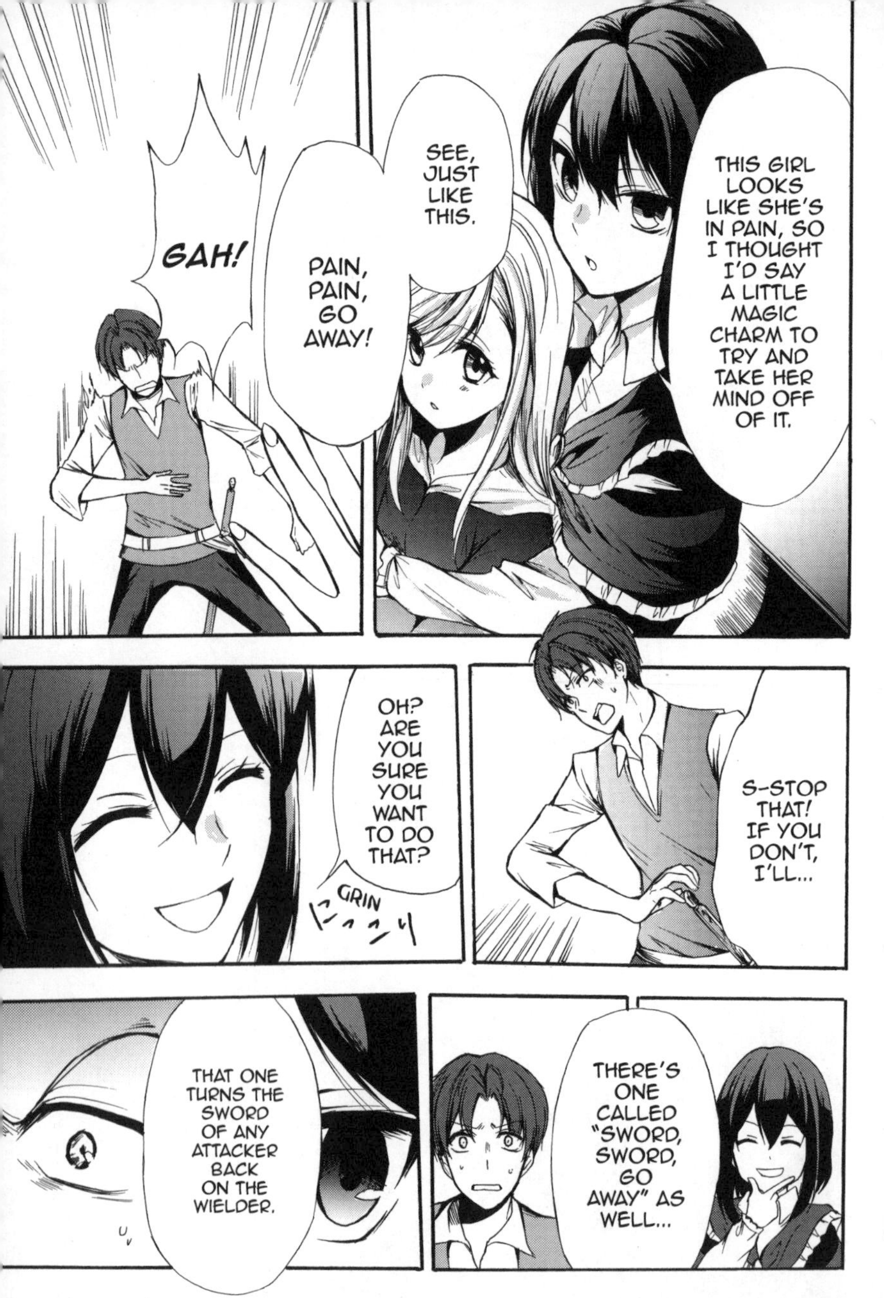
THIS GIRL LOOKS LIKE SHE'S IN PAIN, SO I THOUGHT I'D SAY A LITTLE MAGIC CHARM TO TRY AND TAKE HER MIND OFF OF IT.
SEE, JUST LIKE THIS.
PAIN, PAIN, GO AWAY!
GAH!
S-STOP THAT! IF YOU DON'T, I'LL...
OH? ARE YOU SURE YOU WANT TO DO THAT?
GRIN
THERE'S ONE CALLED "SWORD, SWORD, GO AWAY" AS WELL...
THAT ONE TURNS THE SWORD OF ANY ATTACKER BACK ON THE WIELDER.

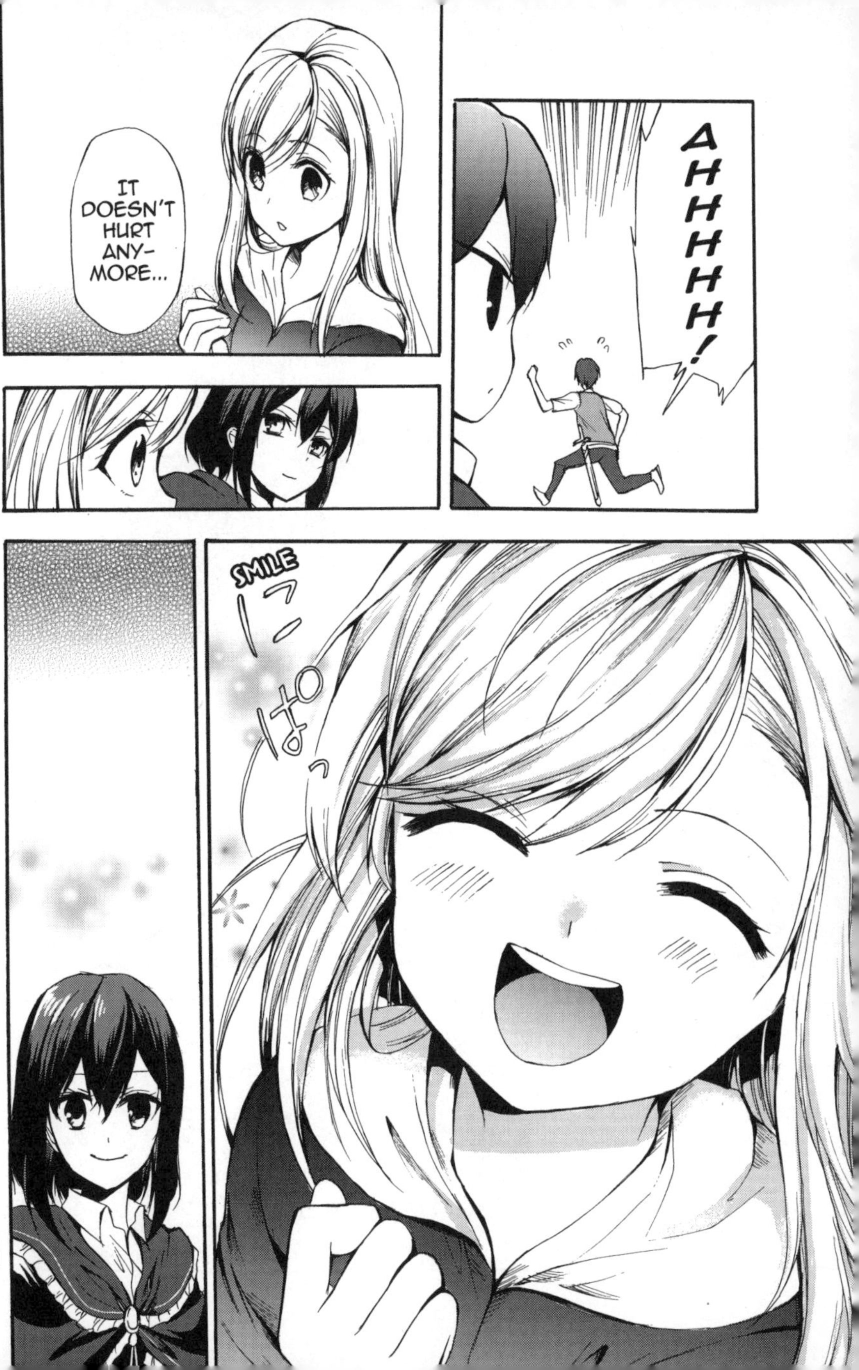
AHHHHHH!
IT DOESN'T HURT ANYMORE...
SMILE
ニコー
ぱっ

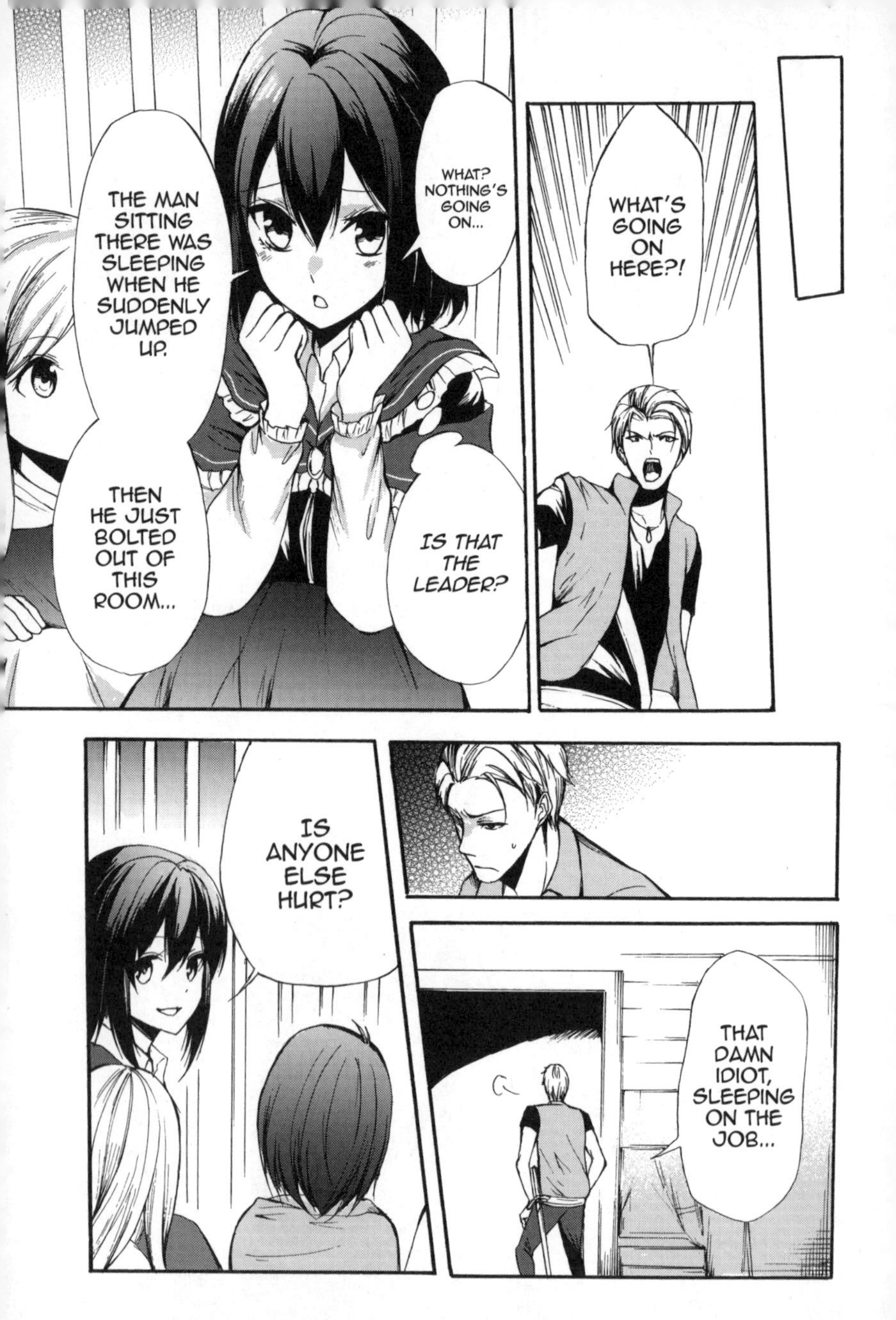
WHAT'S GOING ON HERE?!
WHAT? NOTHING'S GOING ON...
THE MAN SITTING THERE WAS SLEEPING WHEN HE SUDDENLY JUMPED UP.
IS THAT THE LEADER?
THEN HE JUST BOLTED OUT OF THIS ROOM...
THAT DAMN IDIOT, SLEEPING ON THE JOB...
IS ANYONE ELSE HURT?

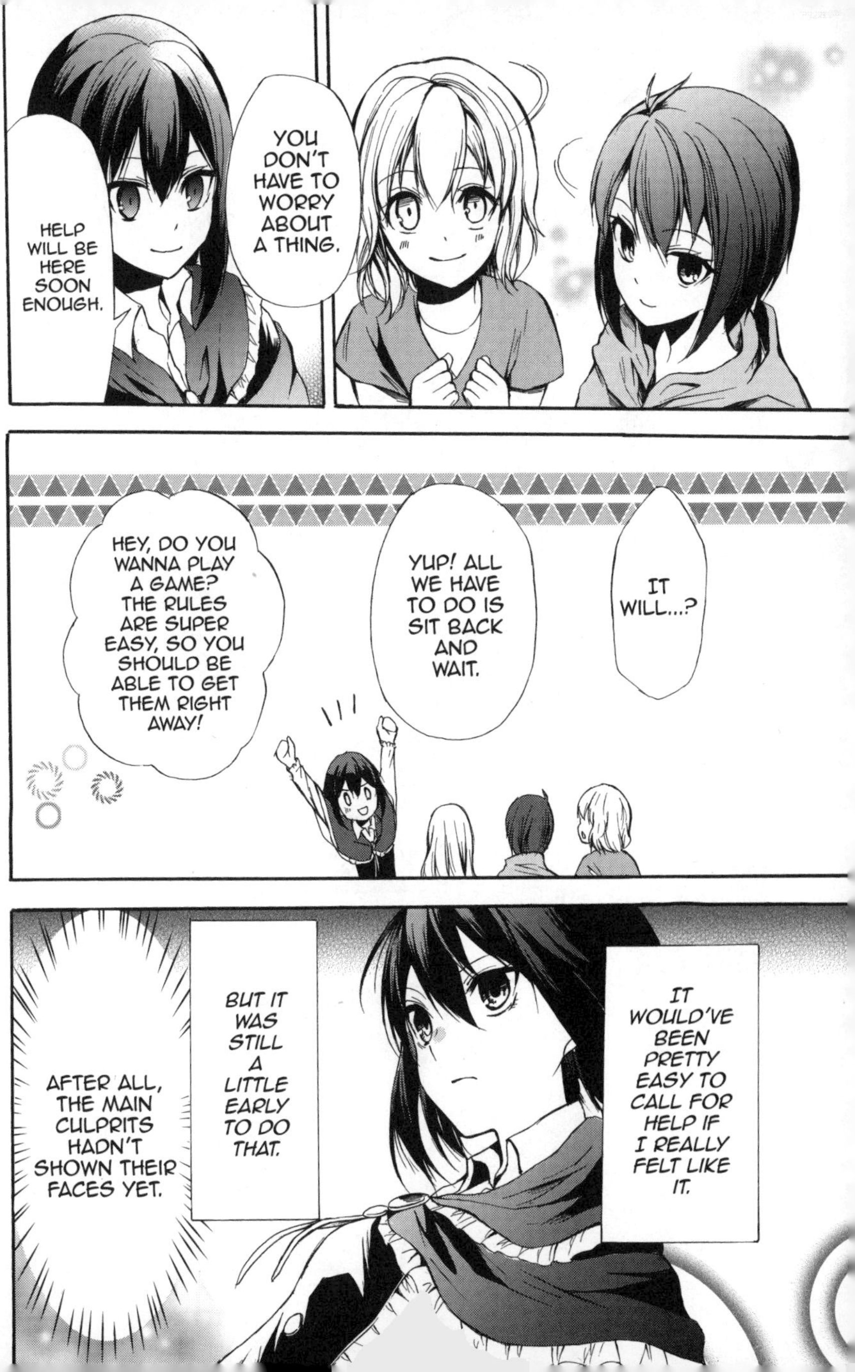
YOU DON'T HAVE TO WORRY ABOUT A THING.
HELP WILL BE HERE SOON ENOUGH.
IT WILL...?
YUP! ALL WE HAVE TO DO IS SIT BACK AND WAIT.
HEY, DO YOU WANNA PLAY A GAME? THE RULES ARE SUPER EASY, SO YOU SHOULD BE ABLE TO GET THEM RIGHT AWAY!
IT WOULD'VE BEEN PRETTY EASY TO CALL FOR HELP IF I REALLY FELT LIKE IT.
BUT IT WAS STILL A LITTLE EARLY TO DO THAT.
AFTER ALL, THE MAIN CULPRITS HADN'T SHOWN THEIR FACES YET.

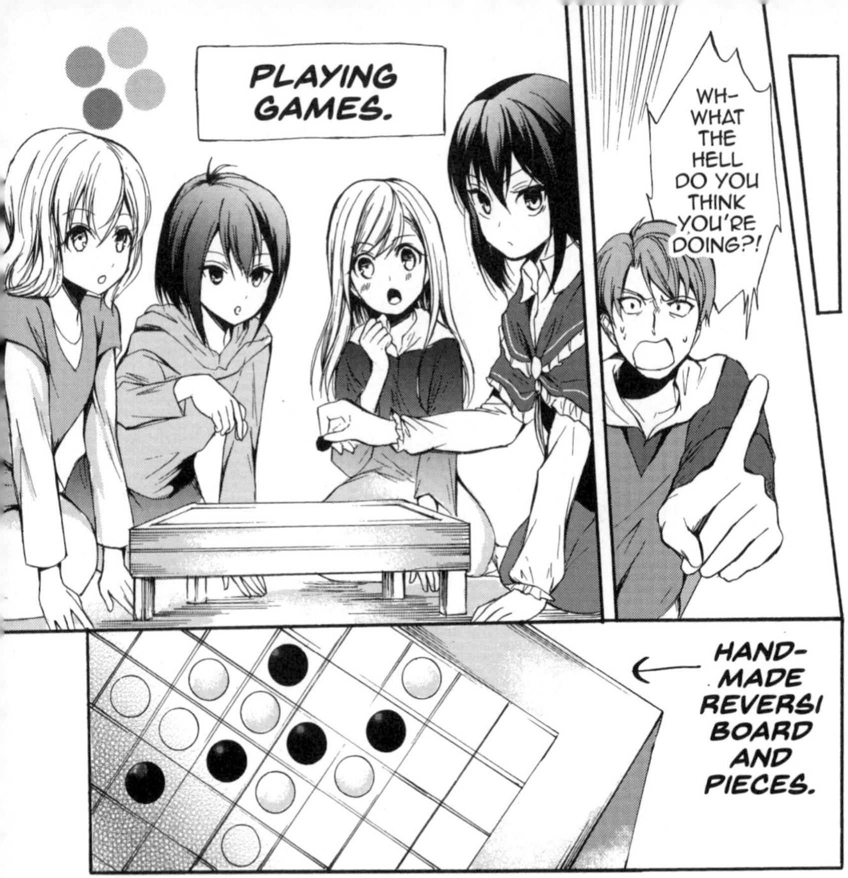
WH-WHAT THE HELL DO YOU THINK YOU'RE DOING?!
PLAYING GAMES.
HAND-MADE REVERSI BOARD AND PIECES.

REVERSI: A GAME THAT'S SIMILAR TO OTHELLO.

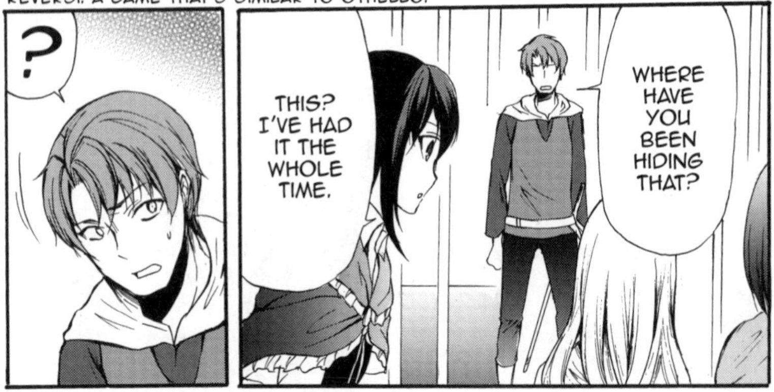
WHERE HAVE YOU BEEN HIDING THAT?
THIS? I'VE HAD IT THE WHOLE TIME.
?

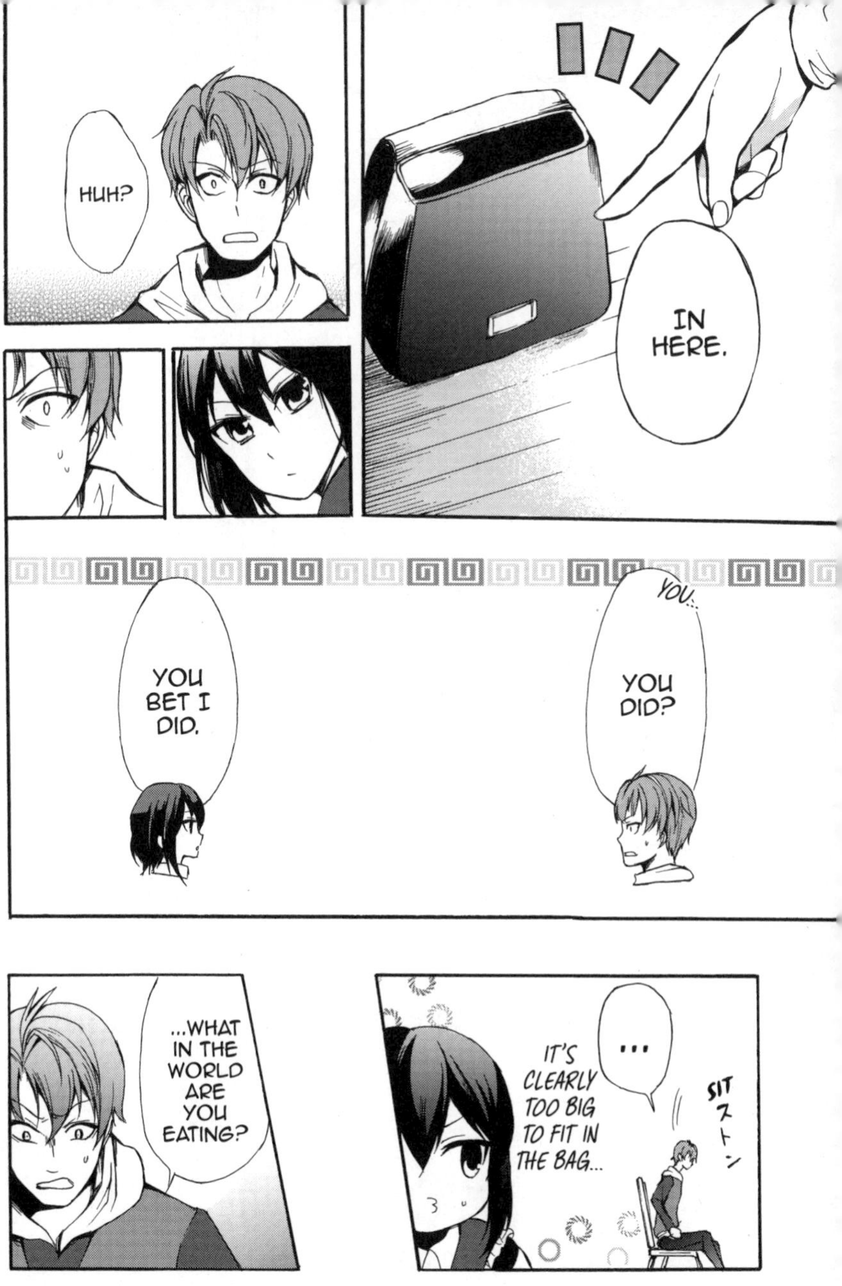
IN HERE.
HUH?
YOU...
YOU DID?
YOU BET I DID.
...
IT'S CLEARLY TOO BIG TO FIT IN THE BAG...
SIT ストン
...WHAT IN THE WORLD ARE YOU EATING?

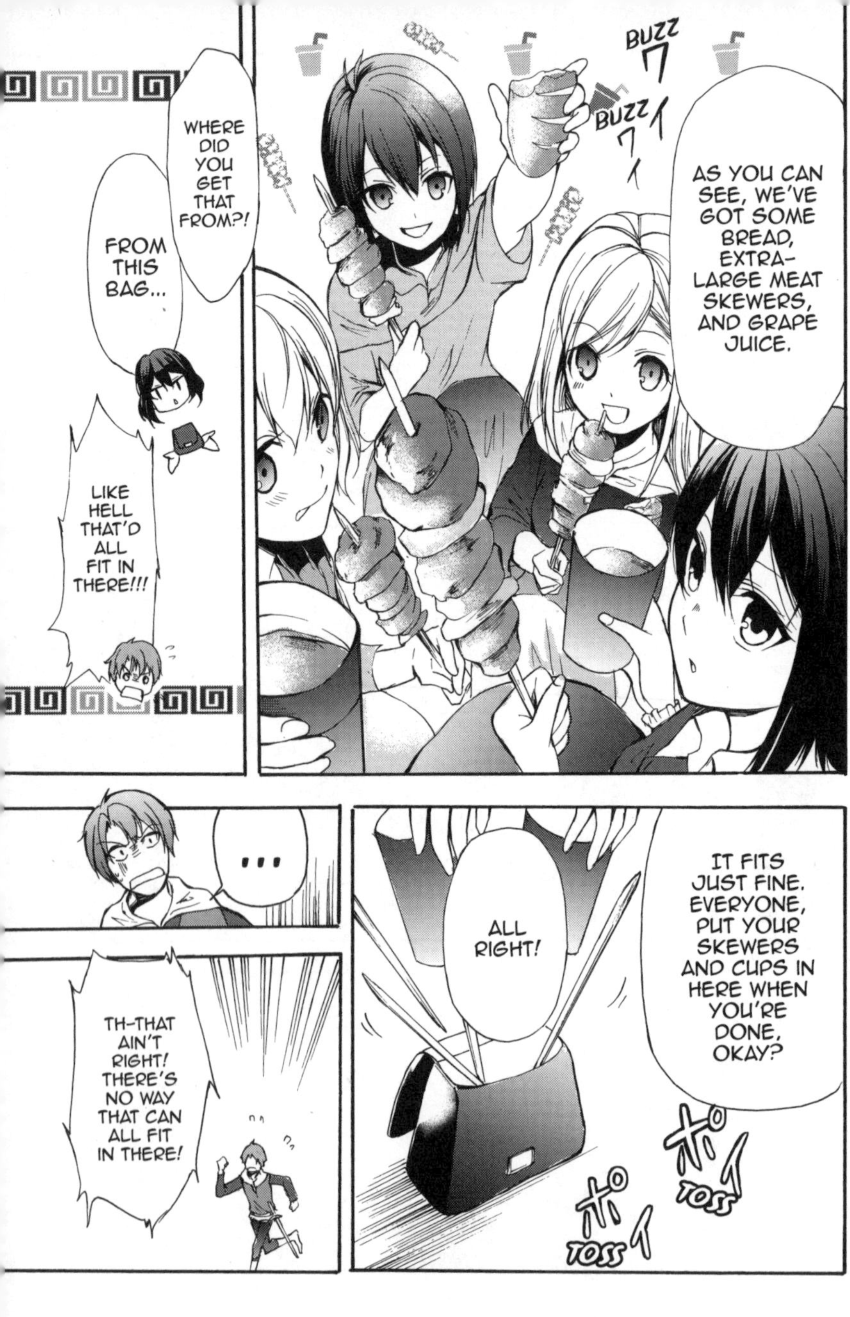

BUZZ ワイ
BUZZ ワイ
AS YOU CAN SEE, WE'VE GOT SOME BREAD, EXTRA-LARGE MEAT SKEWERS, AND GRAPE JUICE.
WHERE DID YOU GET THAT FROM?!
FROM THIS BAG...
LIKE HELL THAT'D ALL FIT IN THERE!!!
IT FITS JUST FINE. EVERYONE, PUT YOUR SKEWERS AND CUPS IN HERE WHEN YOU'RE DONE, OKAY?
ALL RIGHT!
ポイ TOSS
ポイ TOSS
...
TH-THAT AIN'T RIGHT! THERE'S NO WAY THAT CAN ALL FIT IN THERE!

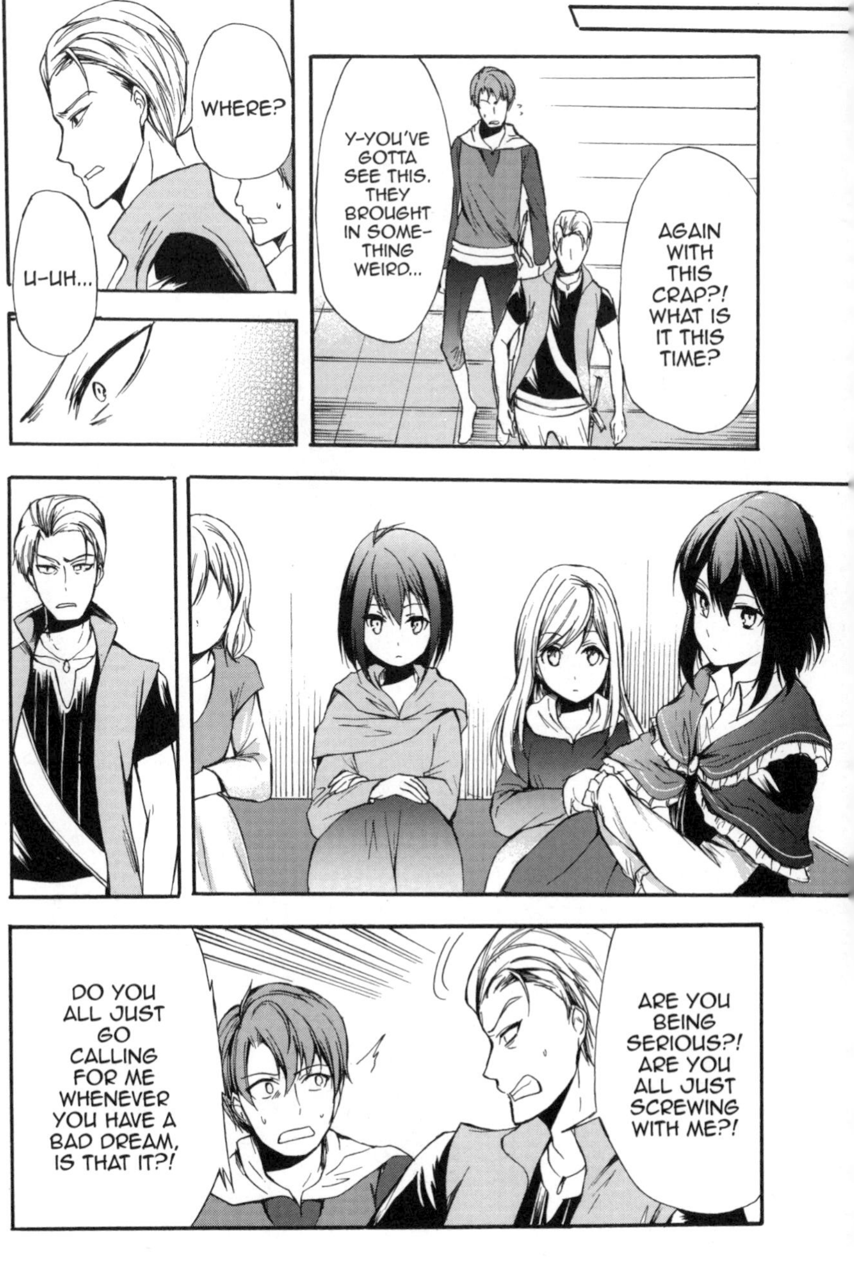
AGAIN WITH THIS CRAP?! WHAT IS IT THIS TIME?
Y-YOU'VE GOTTA SEE THIS. THEY BROUGHT IN SOME-THING WEIRD...
WHERE?
U-UH...
ARE YOU BEING SERIOUS?! ARE YOU ALL JUST SCREWING WITH ME?!
DO YOU ALL JUST GO CALLING FOR ME WHENEVER YOU HAVE A BAD DREAM, IS THAT IT?!

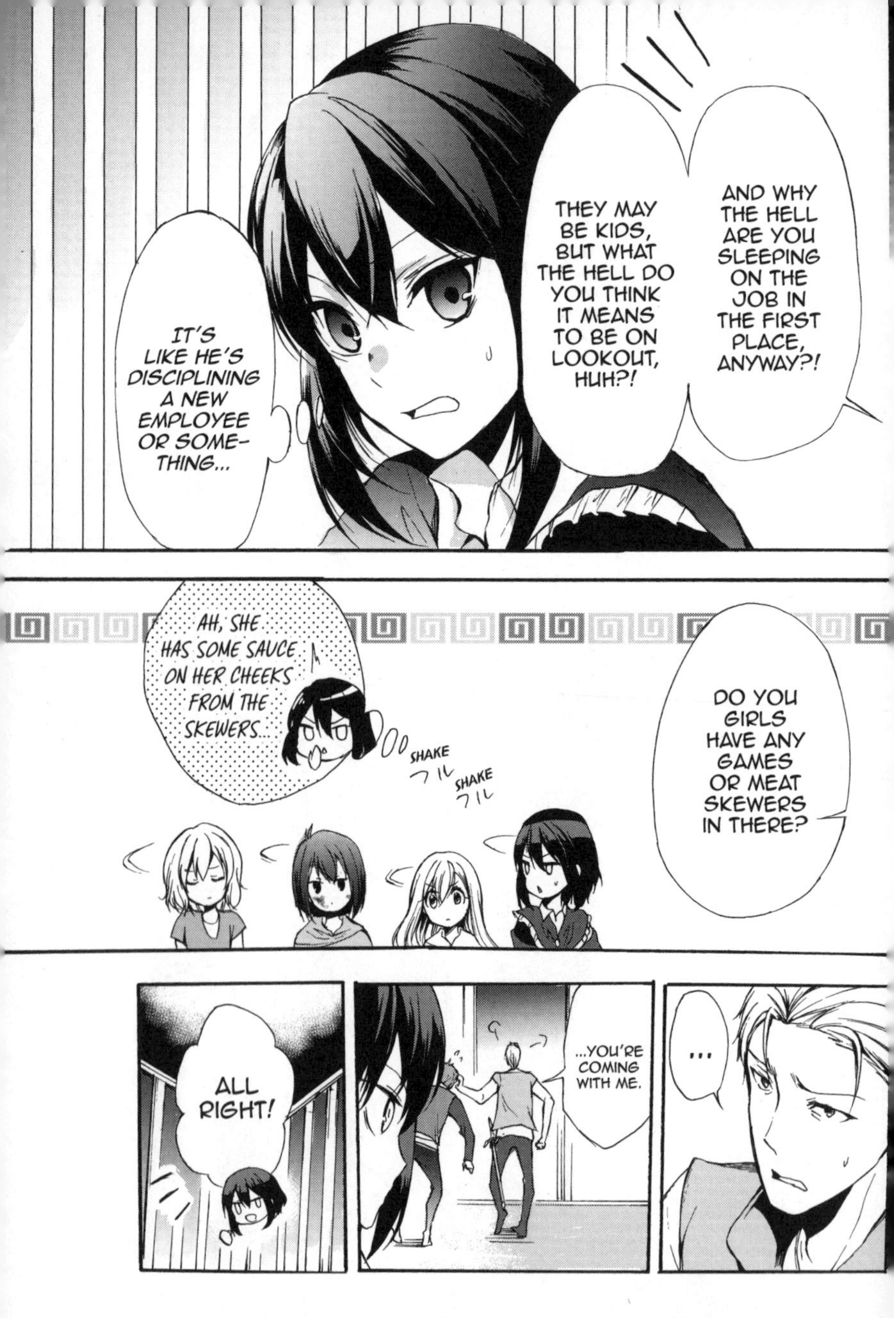
AND WHY THE HELL ARE YOU SLEEPING ON THE JOB IN THE FIRST PLACE, ANYWAY?!
THEY MAY BE KIDS, BUT WHAT THE HELL DO YOU THINK IT MEANS TO BE ON LOOKOUT, HUH?!
IT'S LIKE HE'S DISCIPLINING A NEW EMPLOYEE OR SOME-THING...
DO YOU GIRLS HAVE ANY GAMES OR MEAT SKEWERS IN THERE?
AH, SHE HAS SOME SAUCE ON HER CHEEKS FROM THE SKEWERS...
SHAKE フル
SHAKE フル
...
...YOU'RE COMING WITH ME.
ALL RIGHT!

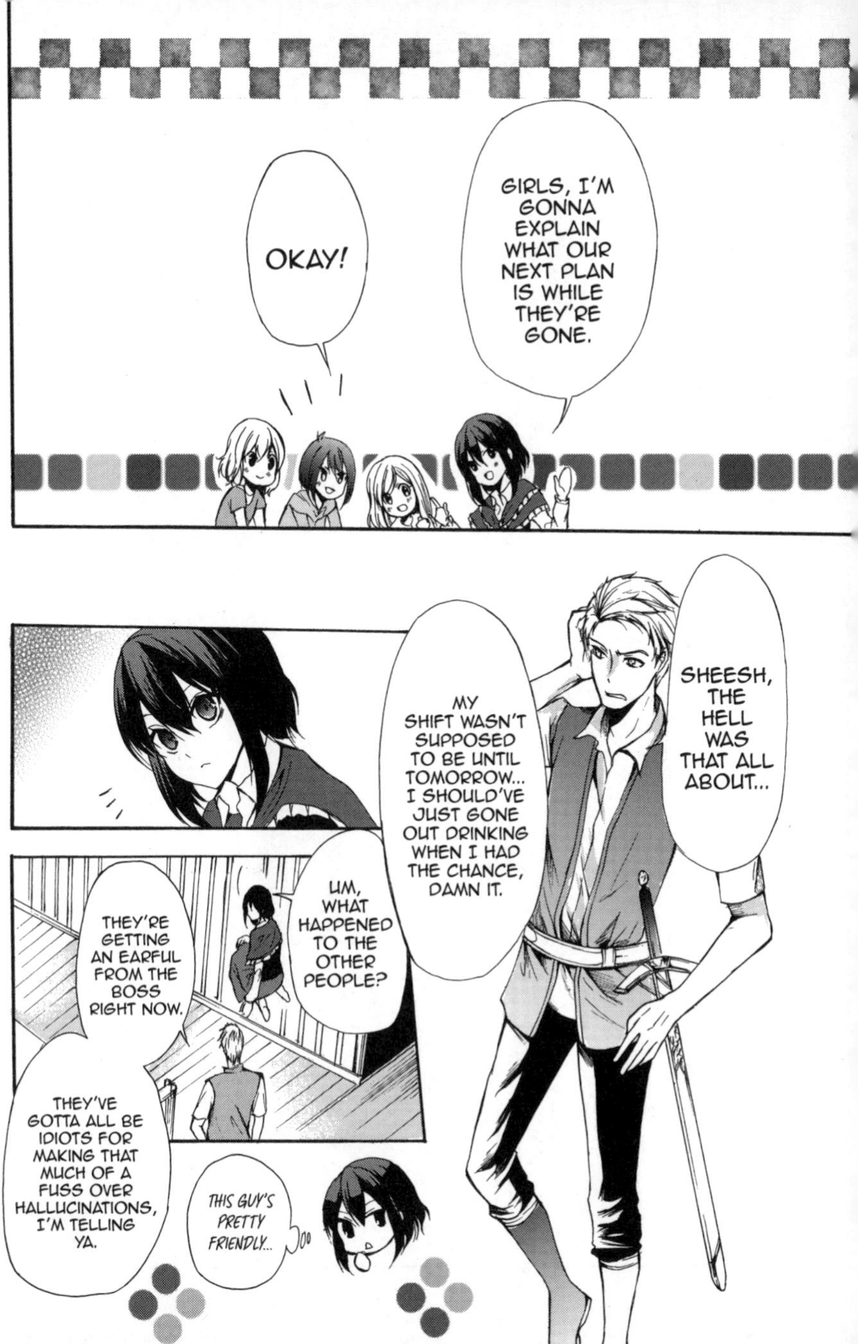
GIRLS, I'M GONNA EXPLAIN WHAT OUR NEXT PLAN IS WHILE THEY'RE GONE.
OKAY!
SHEESH, THE HELL WAS THAT ALL ABOUT...
MY SHIFT WASN'T SUPPOSED TO BE UNTIL TOMORROW... I SHOULD'VE JUST GONE OUT DRINKING WHEN I HAD THE CHANCE, DAMN IT.
UM, WHAT HAPPENED TO THE OTHER PEOPLE?
THEY'RE GETTING AN EARFUL FROM THE BOSS RIGHT NOW.
THEY'VE GOTTA ALL BE IDIOTS FOR MAKING THAT MUCH OF A FUSS OVER HALLUCINATIONS, I'M TELLING YA.
THIS GUY'S PRETTY FRIENDLY...

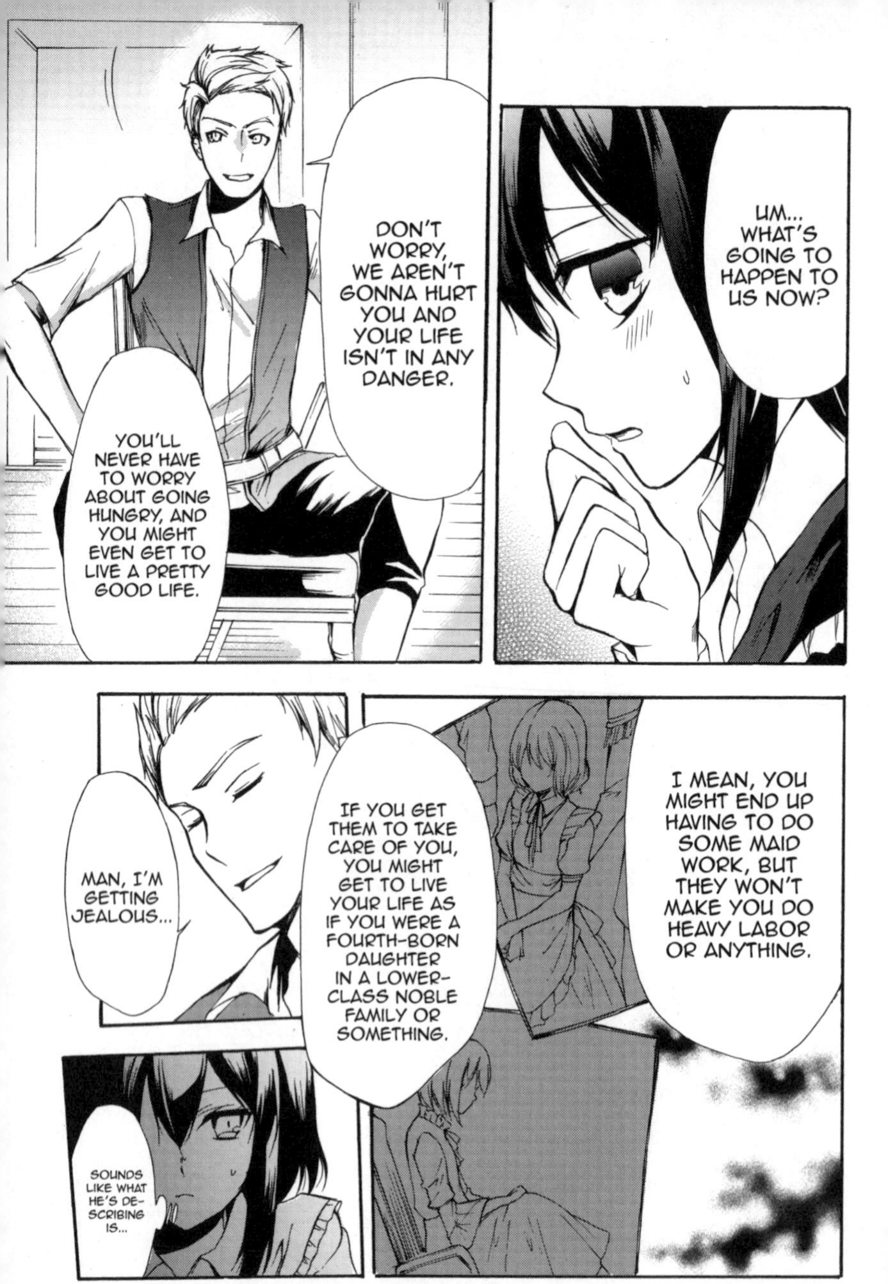

UM... WHAT'S GOING TO HAPPEN TO US NOW?
DON'T WORRY, WE AREN'T GONNA HURT YOU AND YOUR LIFE ISN'T IN ANY DANGER.
YOU'LL NEVER HAVE TO WORRY ABOUT GOING HUNGRY, AND YOU MIGHT EVEN GET TO LIVE A PRETTY GOOD LIFE.
I MEAN, YOU MIGHT END UP HAVING TO DO SOME MAID WORK, BUT THEY WON'T MAKE YOU DO HEAVY LABOR OR ANYTHING.
IF YOU GET THEM TO TAKE CARE OF YOU, YOU MIGHT GET TO LIVE YOUR LIFE AS IF YOU WERE A FOURTH-BORN DAUGHTER IN A LOWER-CLASS NOBLE FAMILY OR SOMETHING.
MAN, I'M GETTING JEALOUS...
SOUNDS LIKE WHAT HE'S DE-SCRIBING IS...

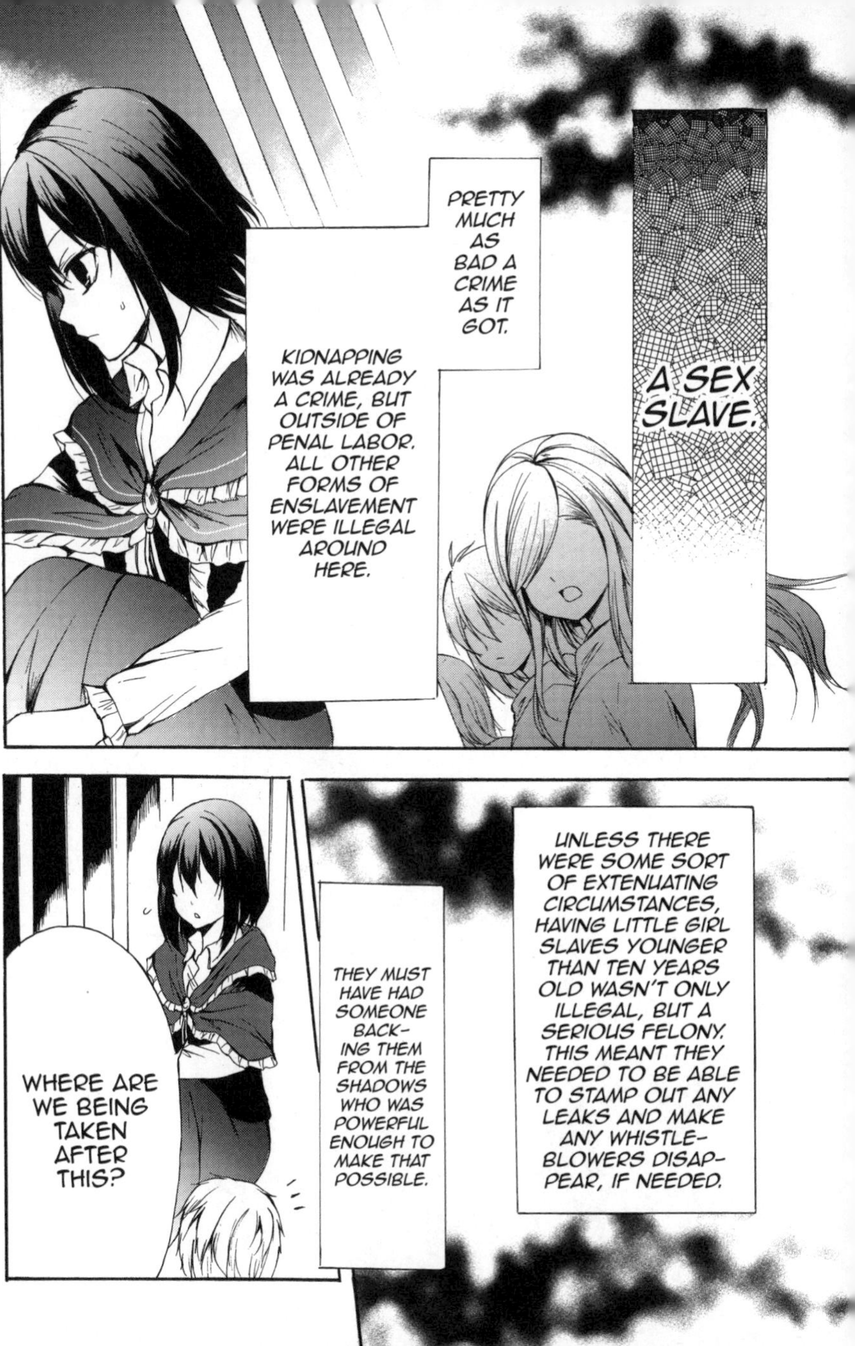
A SEX SLAVE.
PRETTY MUCH AS BAD A CRIME AS IT GOT.
KIDNAPPING WAS ALREADY A CRIME, BUT OUTSIDE OF PENAL LABOR, ALL OTHER FORMS OF ENSLAVEMENT WERE ILLEGAL AROUND HERE.
UNLESS THERE WERE SOME SORT OF EXTENUATING CIRCUMSTANCES, HAVING LITTLE GIRL SLAVES YOUNGER THAN TEN YEARS OLD WASN'T ONLY ILLEGAL, BUT A SERIOUS FELONY. THIS MEANT THEY NEEDED TO BE ABLE TO STAMP OUT ANY LEAKS AND MAKE ANY WHISTLE-BLOWERS DISAPPEAR, IF NEEDED.
THEY MUST HAVE HAD SOMEONE BACKING THEM FROM THE SHADOWS WHO WAS POWERFUL ENOUGH TO MAKE THAT POSSIBLE.
WHERE ARE WE BEING TAKEN AFTER THIS?

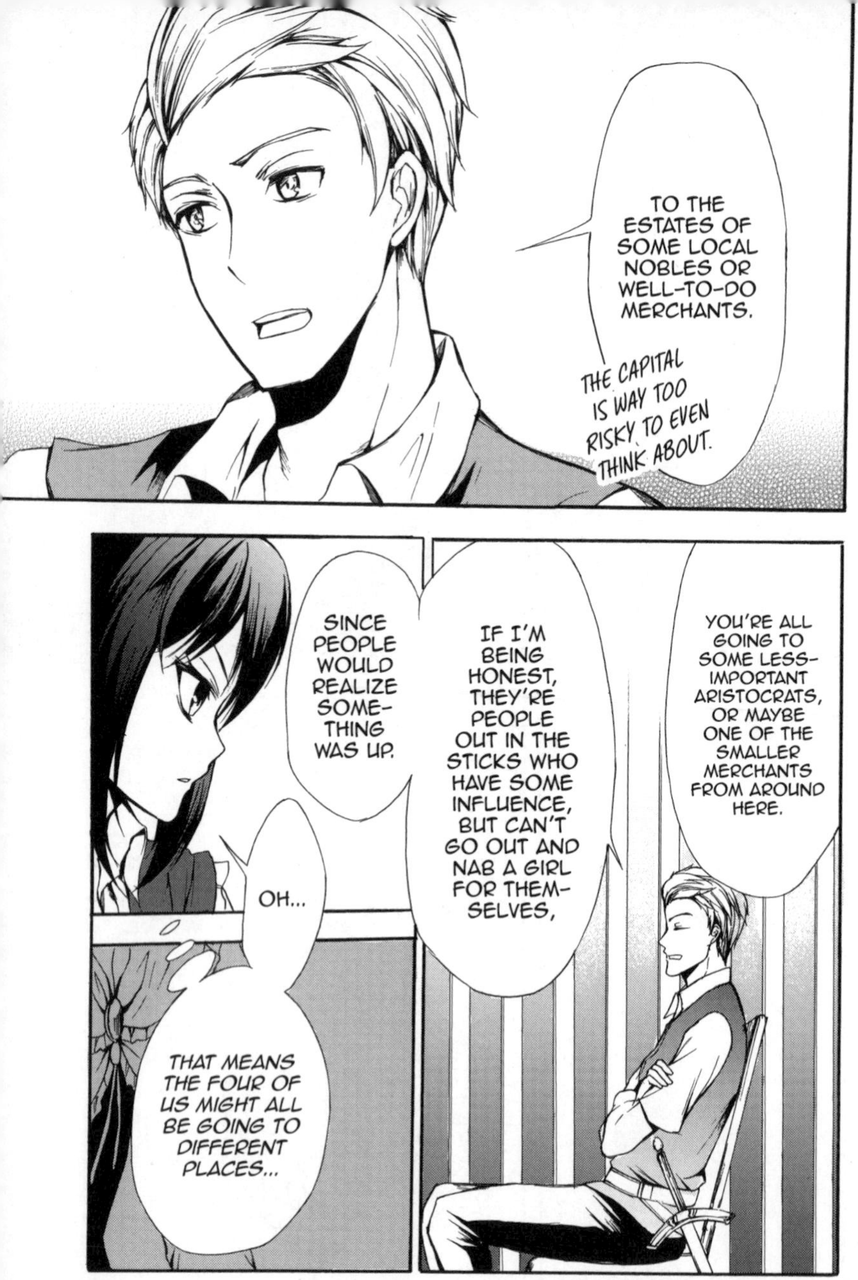
TO THE ESTATES OF SOME LOCAL NOBLES OR WELL-TO-DO MERCHANTS.
THE CAPITAL IS WAY TOO RISKY TO EVEN THINK ABOUT.
YOU'RE ALL GOING TO SOME LESS-IMPORTANT ARISTOCRATS, OR MAYBE ONE OF THE SMALLER MERCHANTS FROM AROUND HERE.
IF I'M BEING HONEST, THEY'RE PEOPLE OUT IN THE STICKS WHO HAVE SOME INFLUENCE, BUT CAN'T GO OUT AND NAB A GIRL FOR THEMSELVES,
SINCE PEOPLE WOULD REALIZE SOMETHING WAS UP.
OH...
THAT MEANS THE FOUR OF US MIGHT ALL BE GOING TO DIFFERENT PLACES...

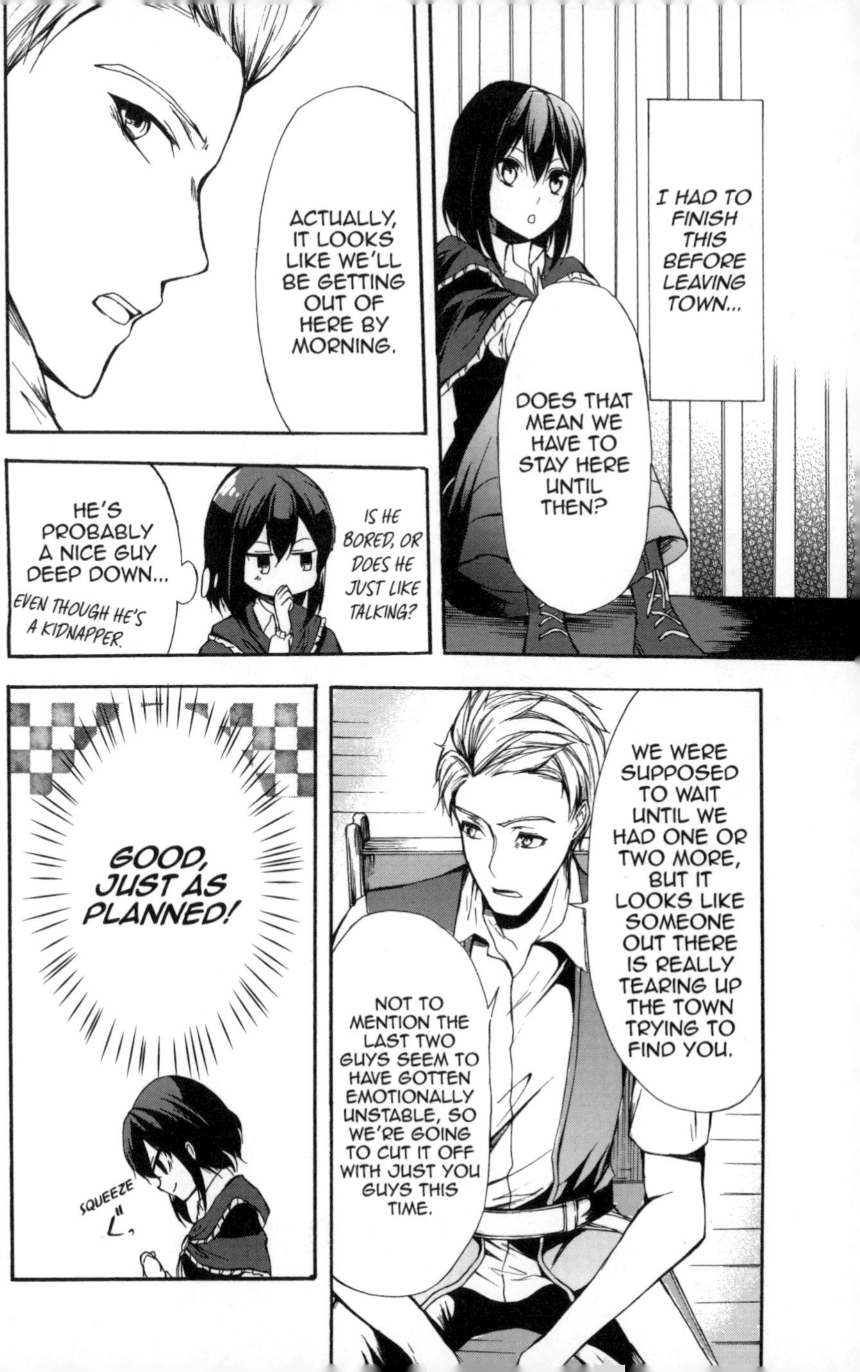
I HAD TO FINISH THIS BEFORE LEAVING TOWN...
DOES THAT MEAN WE HAVE TO STAY HERE UNTIL THEN?
ACTUALLY, IT LOOKS LIKE WE'LL BE GETTING OUT OF HERE BY MORNING.
IS HE BORED, OR DOES HE JUST LIKE TALKING?
HE'S PROBABLY A NICE GUY DEEP DOWN...
EVEN THOUGH HE'S A KIDNAPPER.
WE WERE SUPPOSED TO WAIT UNTIL WE HAD ONE OR TWO MORE, BUT IT LOOKS LIKE SOMEONE OUT THERE IS REALLY TEARING UP THE TOWN TRYING TO FIND YOU.
NOT TO MENTION THE LAST TWO GUYS SEEM TO HAVE GOTTEN EMOTIONALLY UNSTABLE, SO WE'RE GOING TO CUT IT OFF WITH JUST YOU GUYS THIS TIME.
GOOD, JUST AS PLANNED!
SQUEEZE

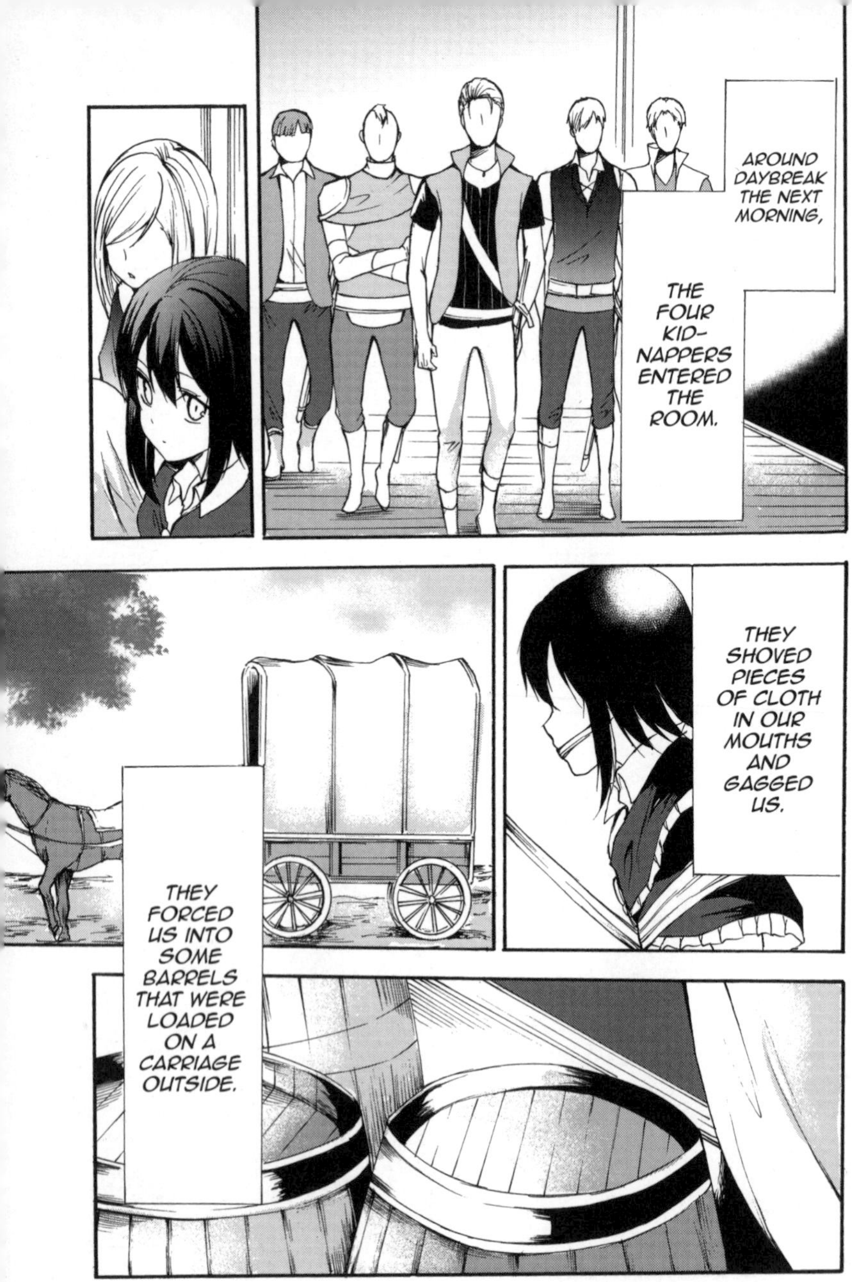
AROUND DAYBREAK THE NEXT MORNING,
THE FOUR KID-NAPPERS ENTERED THE ROOM.
THEY SHOVED PIECES OF CLOTH IN OUR MOUTHS AND GAGGED US.
THEY FORCED US INTO SOME BARRELS THAT WERE LOADED ON A CARRIAGE OUTSIDE.

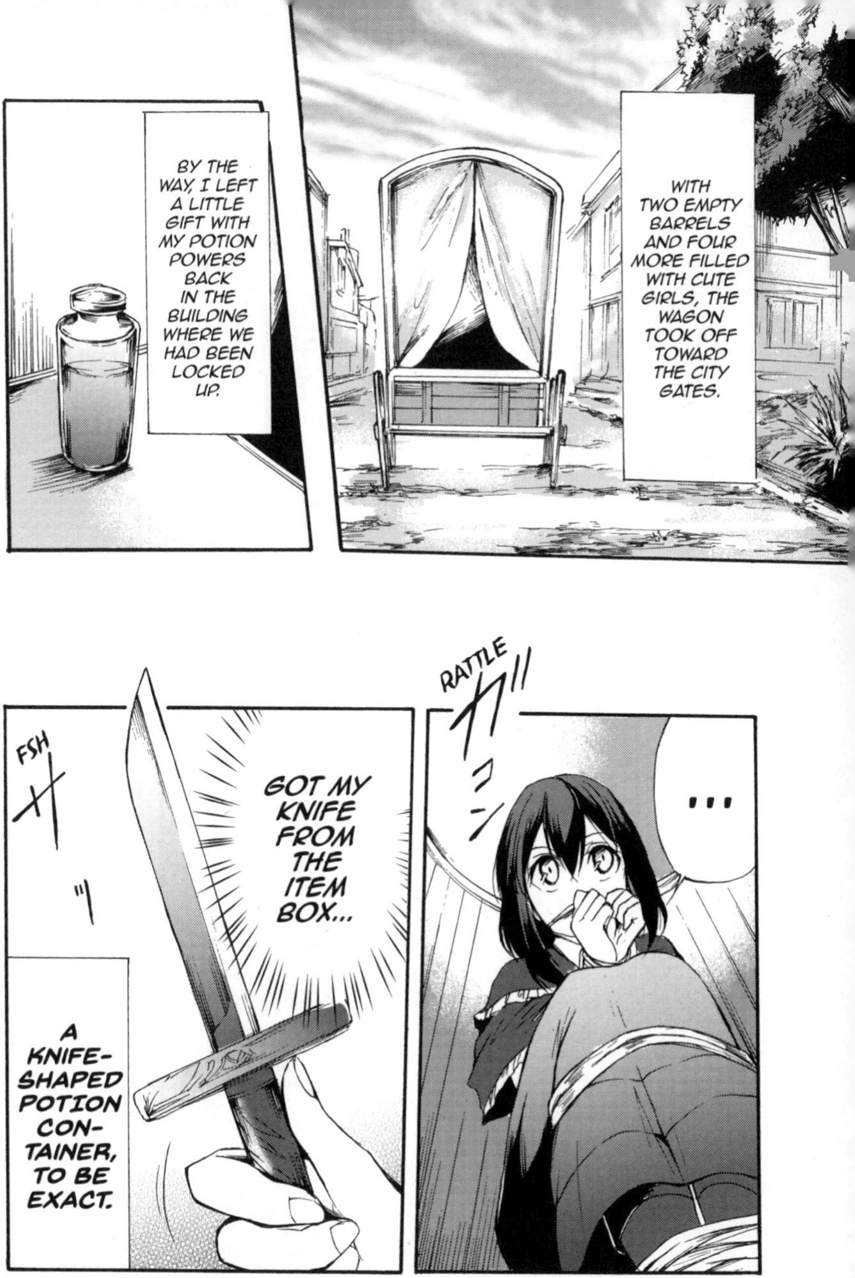
WITH TWO EMPTY BARRELS AND FOUR MORE FILLED WITH CUTE GIRLS, THE WAGON TOOK OFF TOWARD THE CITY GATES.
BY THE WAY, I LEFT A LITTLE GIFT WITH MY POTION POWERS BACK IN THE BUILDING WHERE WE HAD BEEN LOCKED UP.
RATTLE
...
FSH
GOT MY KNIFE FROM THE ITEM BOX...
A KNIFE-SHAPED POTION CON-TAINER, TO BE EXACT.

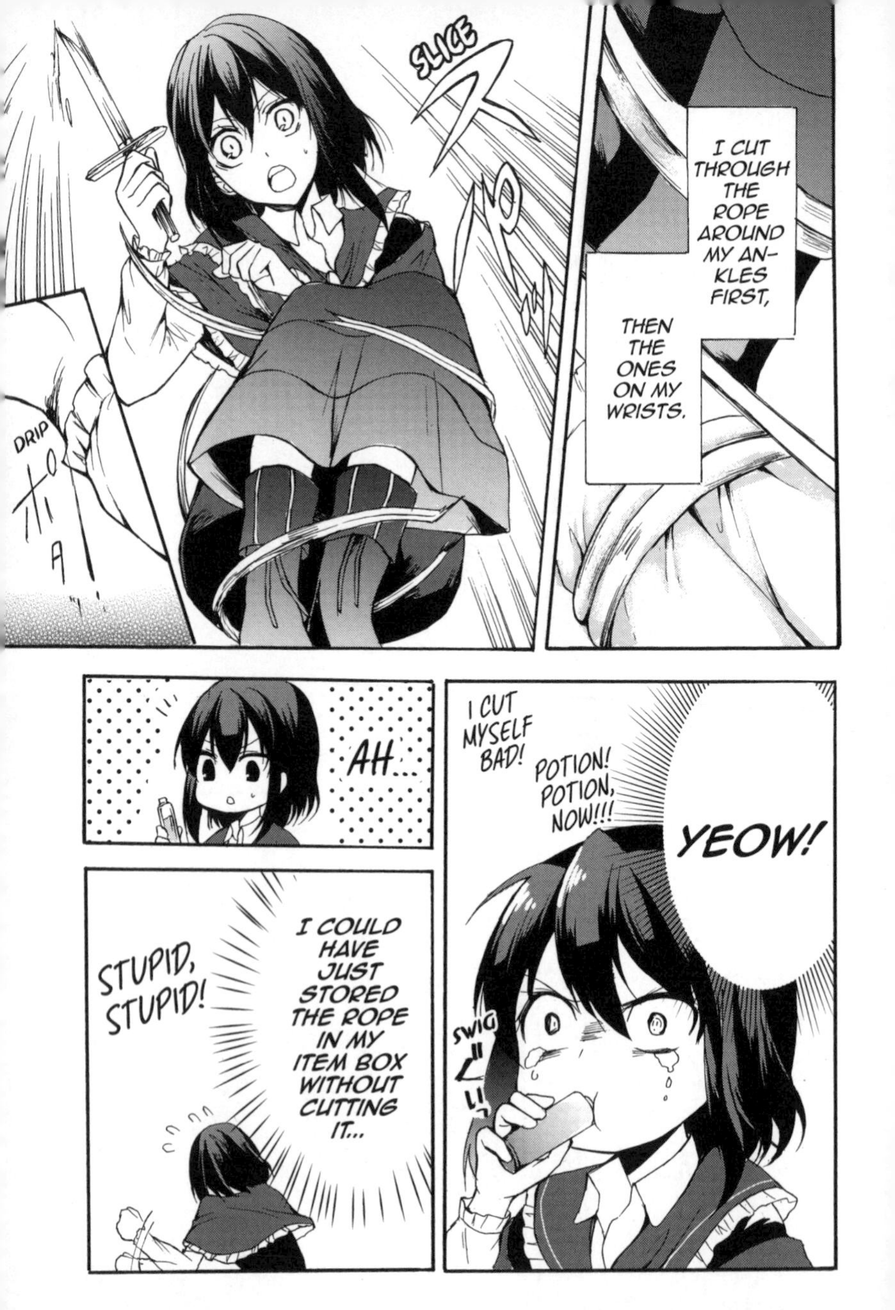
I CUT THROUGH THE ROPE AROUND MY AN-KLES FIRST,
THEN THE ONES ON MY WRISTS.
SLICE
DRIP
I CUT MYSELF BAD!
POTION! POTION, NOW!!!
YEOW!
SWIG
AH...
STUPID, STUPID!
I COULD HAVE JUST STORED THE ROPE IN MY ITEM BOX WITHOUT CUTTING IT...

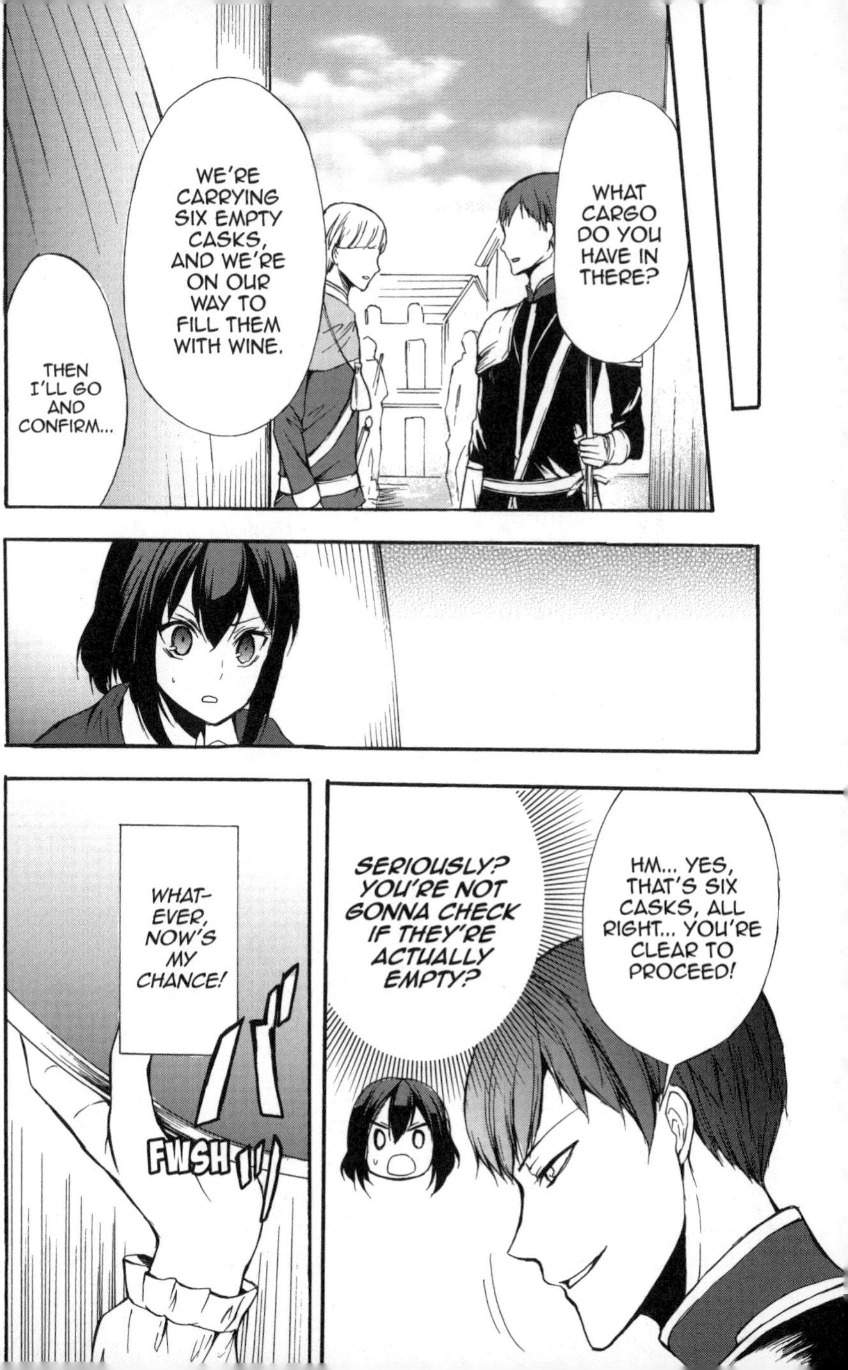
WHAT CARGO DO YOU HAVE IN THERE?
WE'RE CARRYING SIX EMPTY CASKS, AND WE'RE ON OUR WAY TO FILL THEM WITH WINE.
THEN I'LL GO AND CONFIRM...
HM... YES, THAT'S SIX CASKS, ALL RIGHT... YOU'RE CLEAR TO PROCEED!
SERIOUSLY? YOU'RE NOT GONNA CHECK IF THEY'RE ACTUALLY EMPTY?
WHAT-EVER, NOW'S MY CHANCE!
FWSH

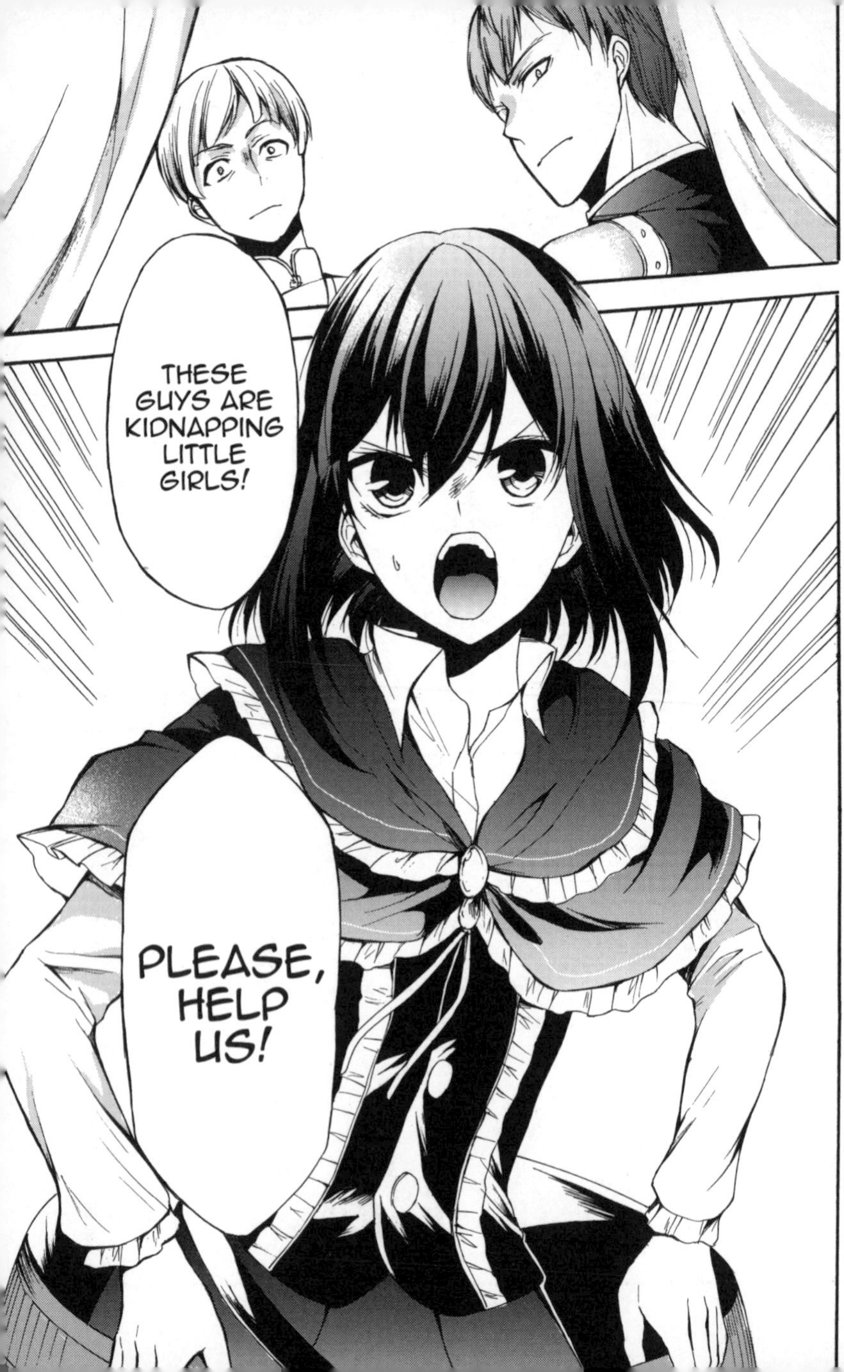
THESE GUYS ARE KIDNAPPING LITTLE GIRLS!
PLEASE, HELP US!

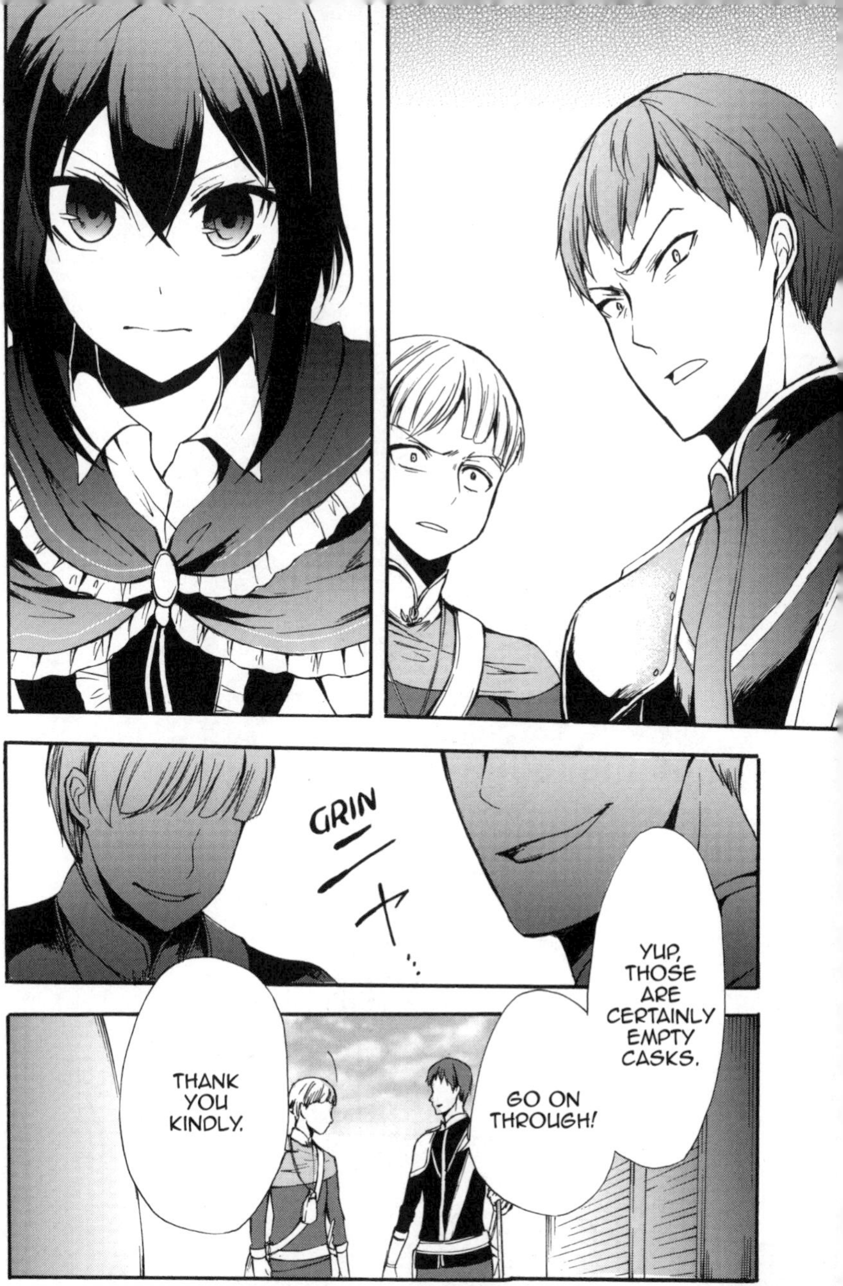
GRIN
ニヤ…
YUP, THOSE ARE CERTAINLY EMPTY CASKS.
GO ON THROUGH!
THANK YOU KINDLY.

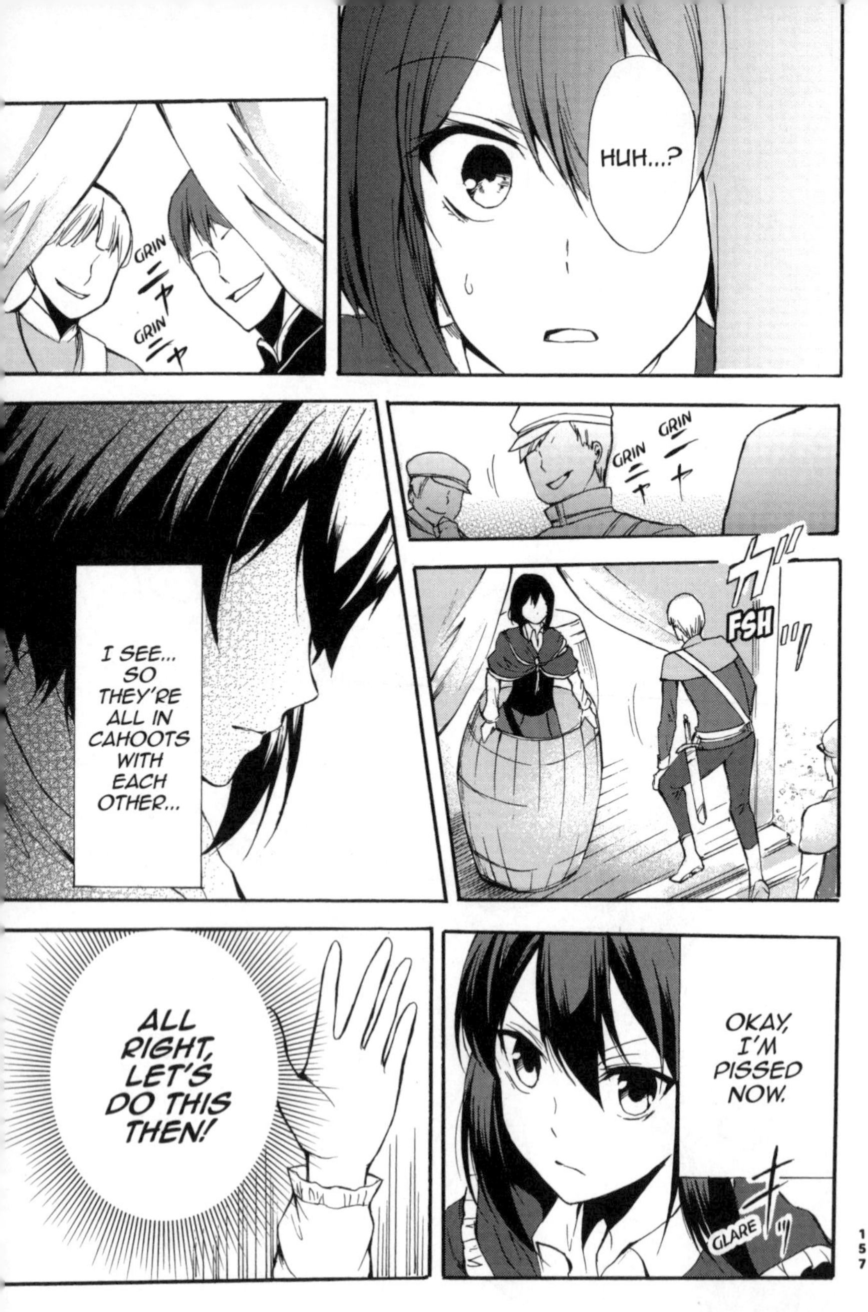
HUH...?
GRIN ニヤ
GRIN ニヤ
GRIN ニヤ
GRIN ニヤ
FSH ガッ
I SEE... SO THEY'RE ALL IN CAHOOTS WITH EACH OTHER...
OKAY, I'M PISSED NOW.
GLARE キッ
ALL RIGHT, LET'S DO THIS THEN!

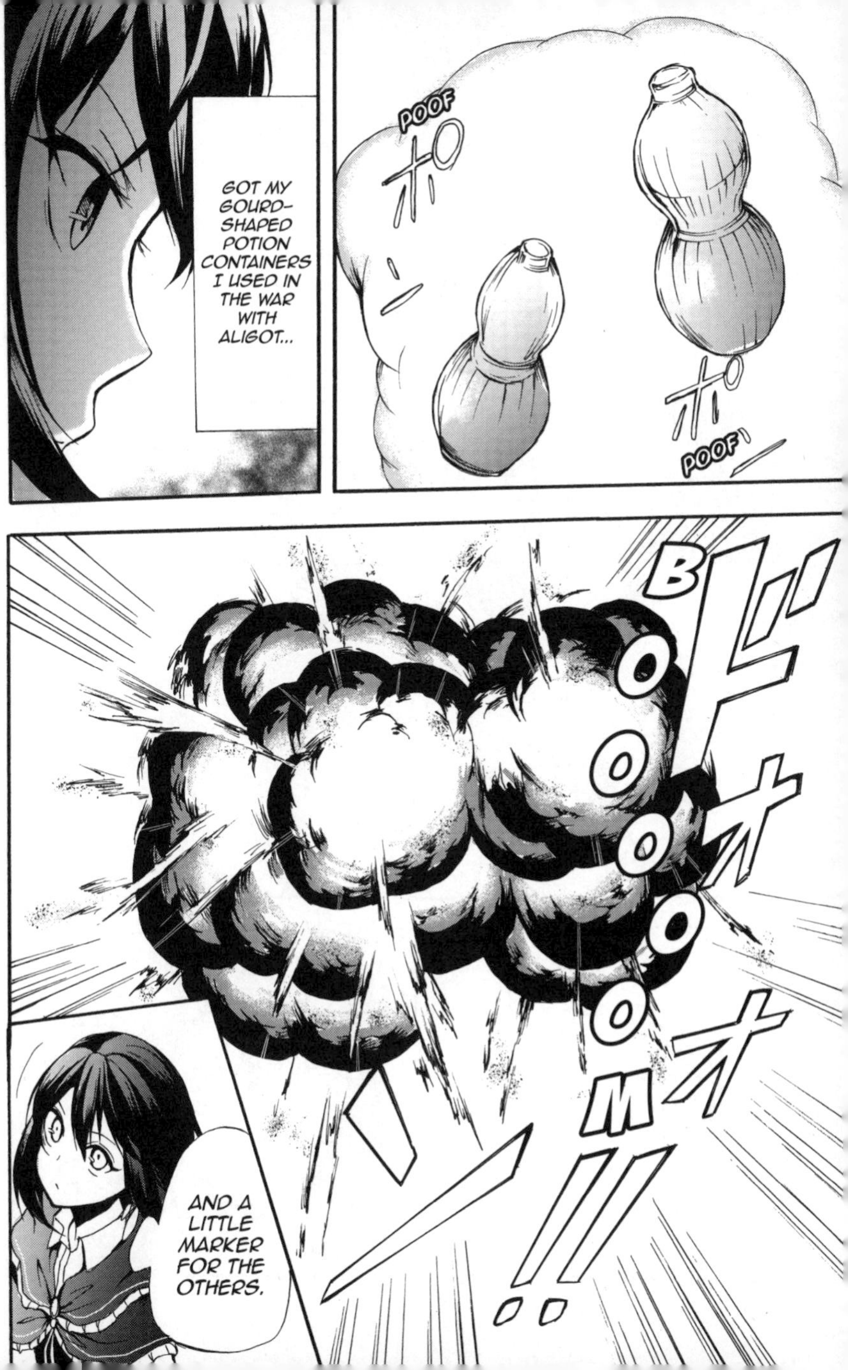
POOF
POOF
GOT MY GOURD-SHAPED POTION CONTAINERS I USED IN THE WAR WITH ALIGOT...
BOOOOOOM!!
AND A LITTLE MARKER FOR THE OTHERS.

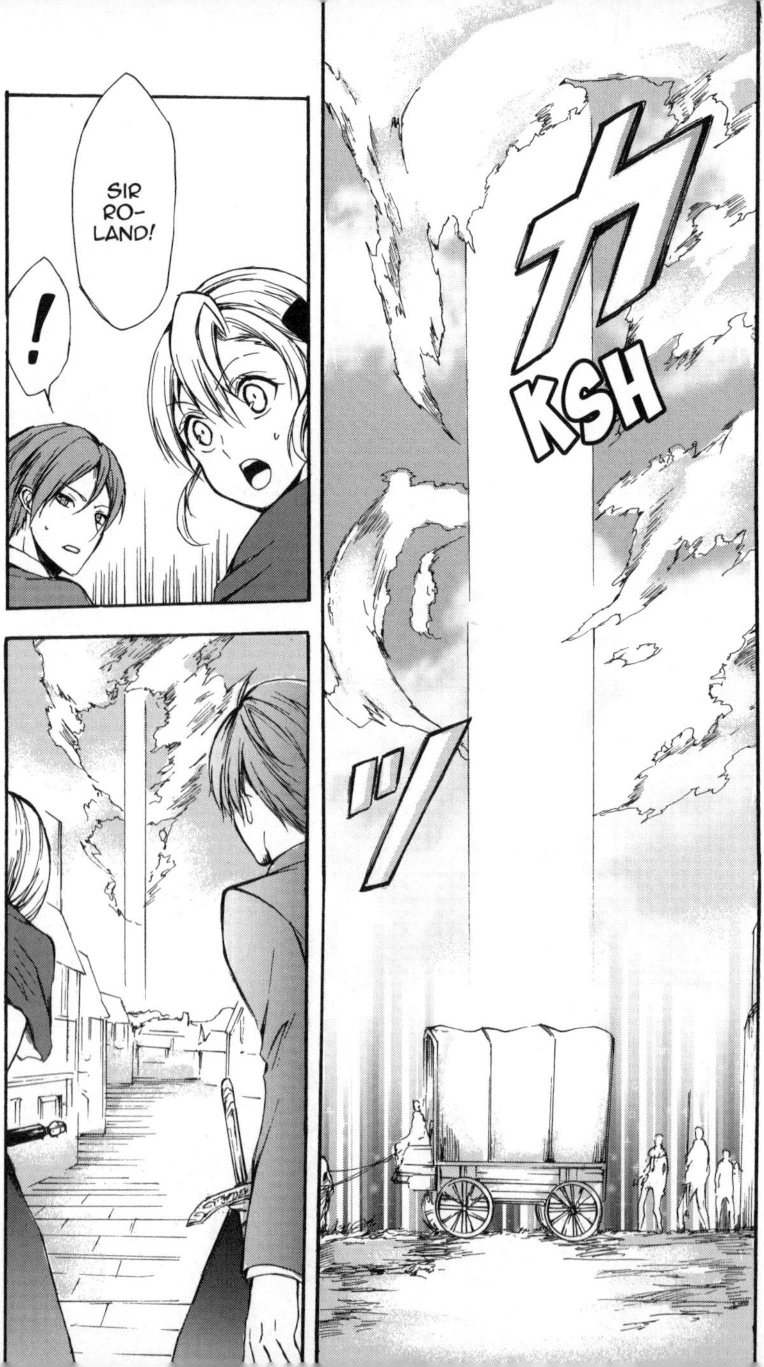
カッ
KSH
SIR RO-LAND!
!

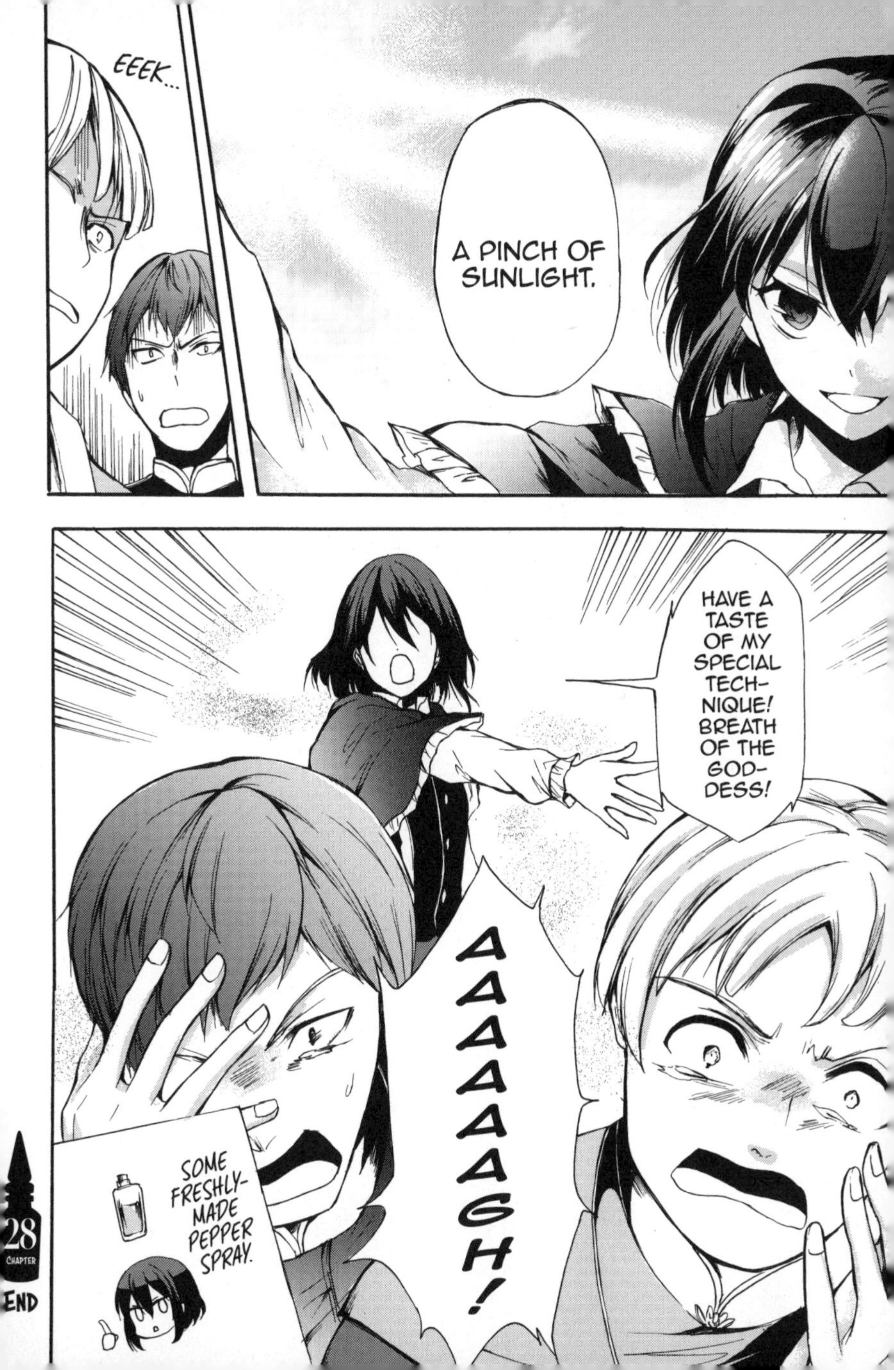
A PINCH OF SUNLIGHT.
EEEK...
HAVE A TASTE OF MY SPECIAL TECH-NIQUE! BREATH OF THE GOD-DESS!
AAAAAAGH!
SOME FRESHLY-MADE PEPPER SPRAY.
28 CHAPTER END

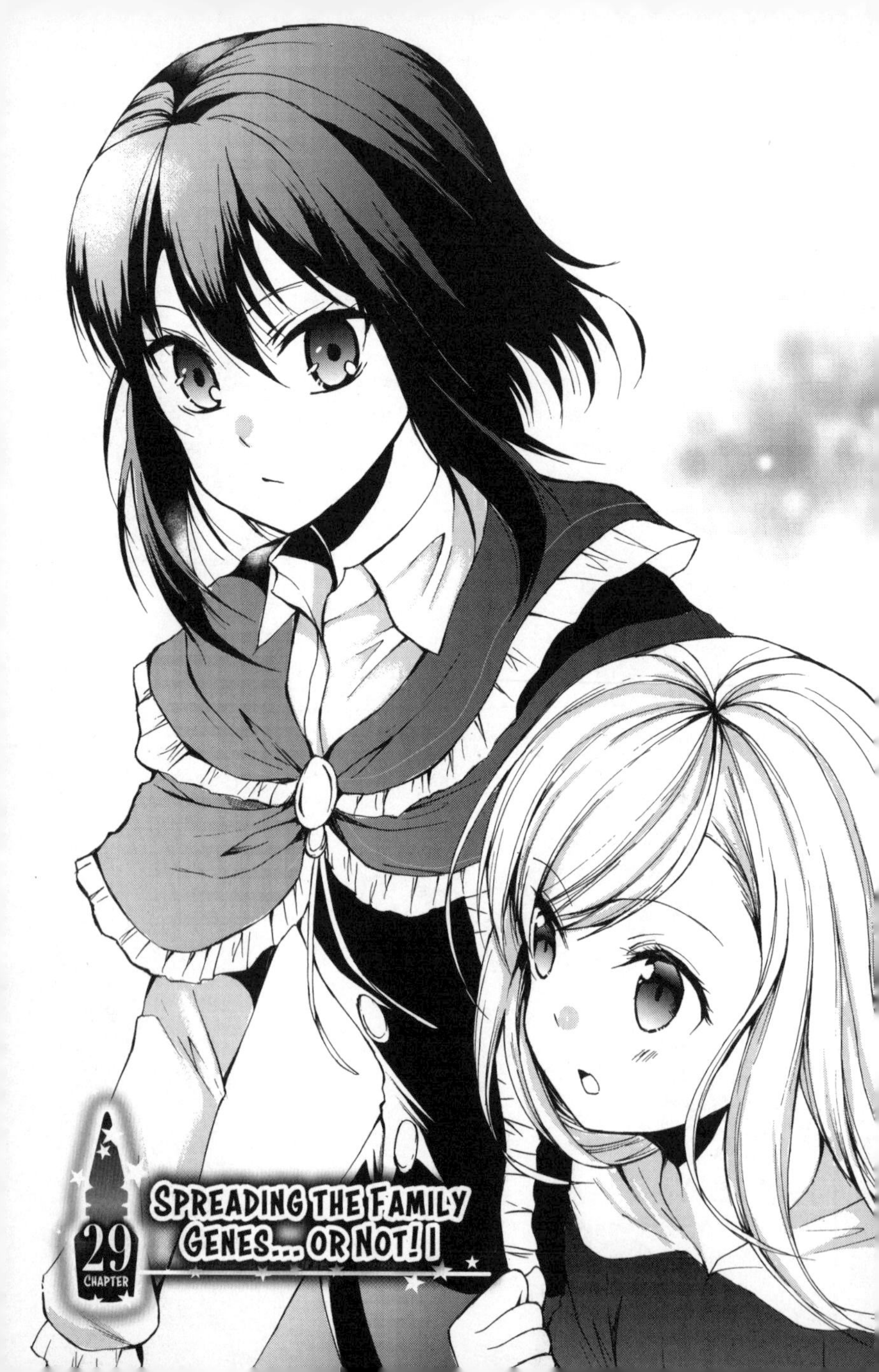
29
CHAPTER
SPREADING THE FAMILY GENES... OR NOT! I

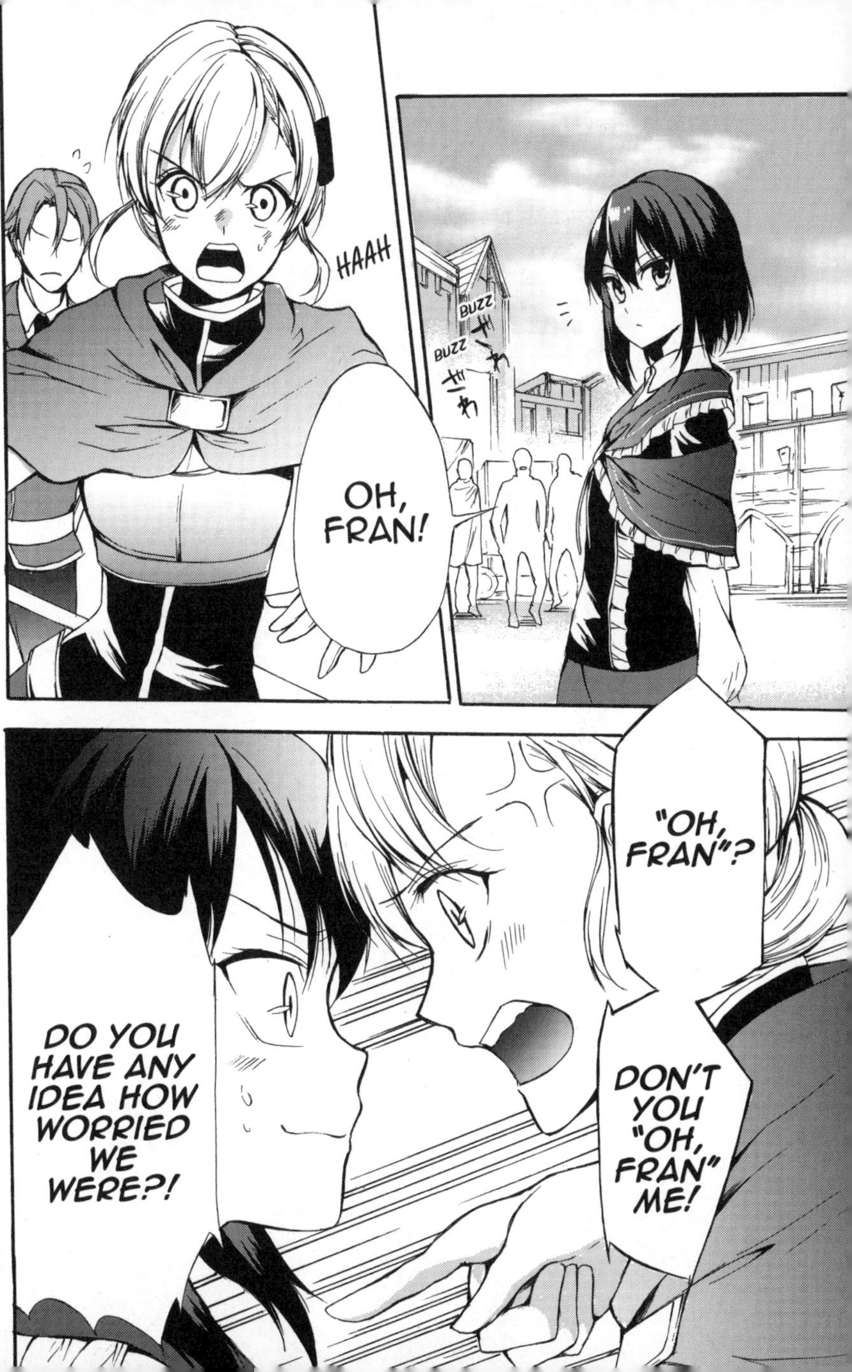
BUZZ
BUZZ
OH, FRAN!
HAAH
"OH, FRAN"?
DON'T YOU "OH, FRAN" ME!
DO YOU HAVE ANY IDEA HOW WORRIED WE WERE?!

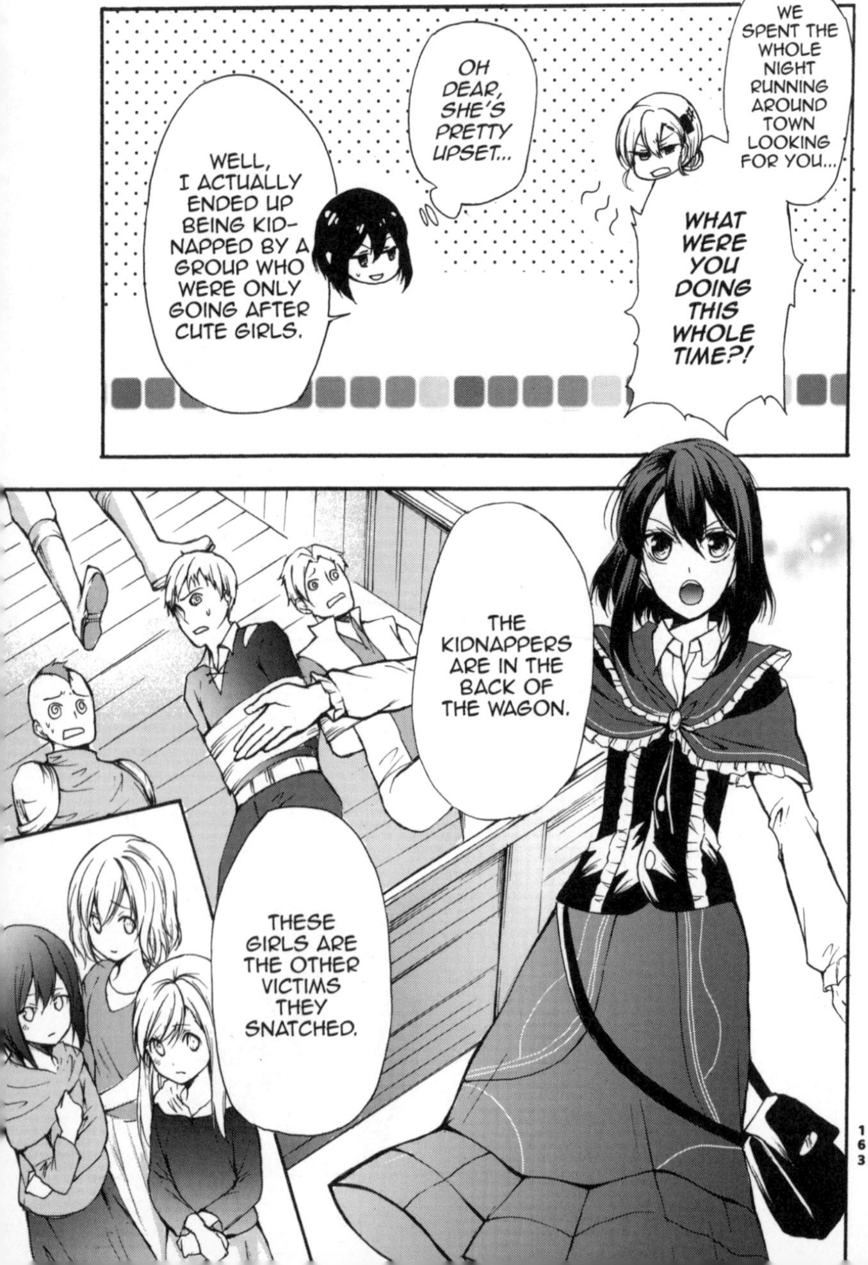
WE SPENT THE WHOLE NIGHT RUNNING AROUND TOWN LOOKING FOR YOU...
WHAT WERE YOU DOING THIS WHOLE TIME?!
OH DEAR, SHE'S PRETTY UPSET...
WELL, I ACTUALLY ENDED UP BEING KID-NAPPED BY A GROUP WHO WERE ONLY GOING AFTER CUTE GIRLS.
THE KIDNAPPERS ARE IN THE BACK OF THE WAGON.
THESE GIRLS ARE THE OTHER VICTIMS THEY SNATCHED.

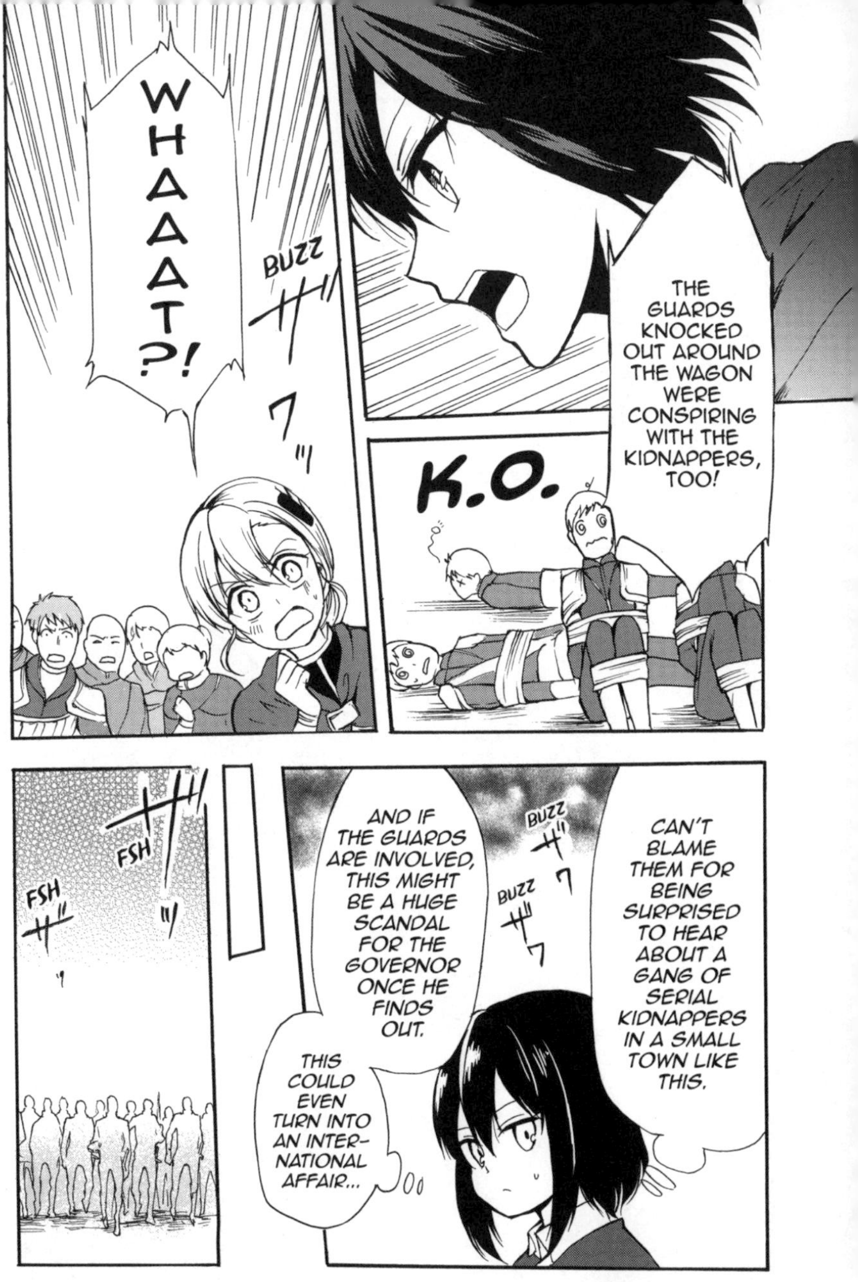
THE GUARDS KNOCKED OUT AROUND THE WAGON WERE CONSPIRING WITH THE KIDNAPPERS, TOO!
K.O.
BUZZ
WHAAAAT?!
CAN'T BLAME THEM FOR BEING SURPRISED TO HEAR ABOUT A GANG OF SERIAL KIDNAPPERS IN A SMALL TOWN LIKE THIS.
AND IF THE GUARDS ARE INVOLVED, THIS MIGHT BE A HUGE SCANDAL FOR THE GOVERNOR ONCE HE FINDS OUT.
BUZZ
BUZZ
THIS COULD EVEN TURN INTO AN INTER-NATIONAL AFFAIR...
FSH
FSH

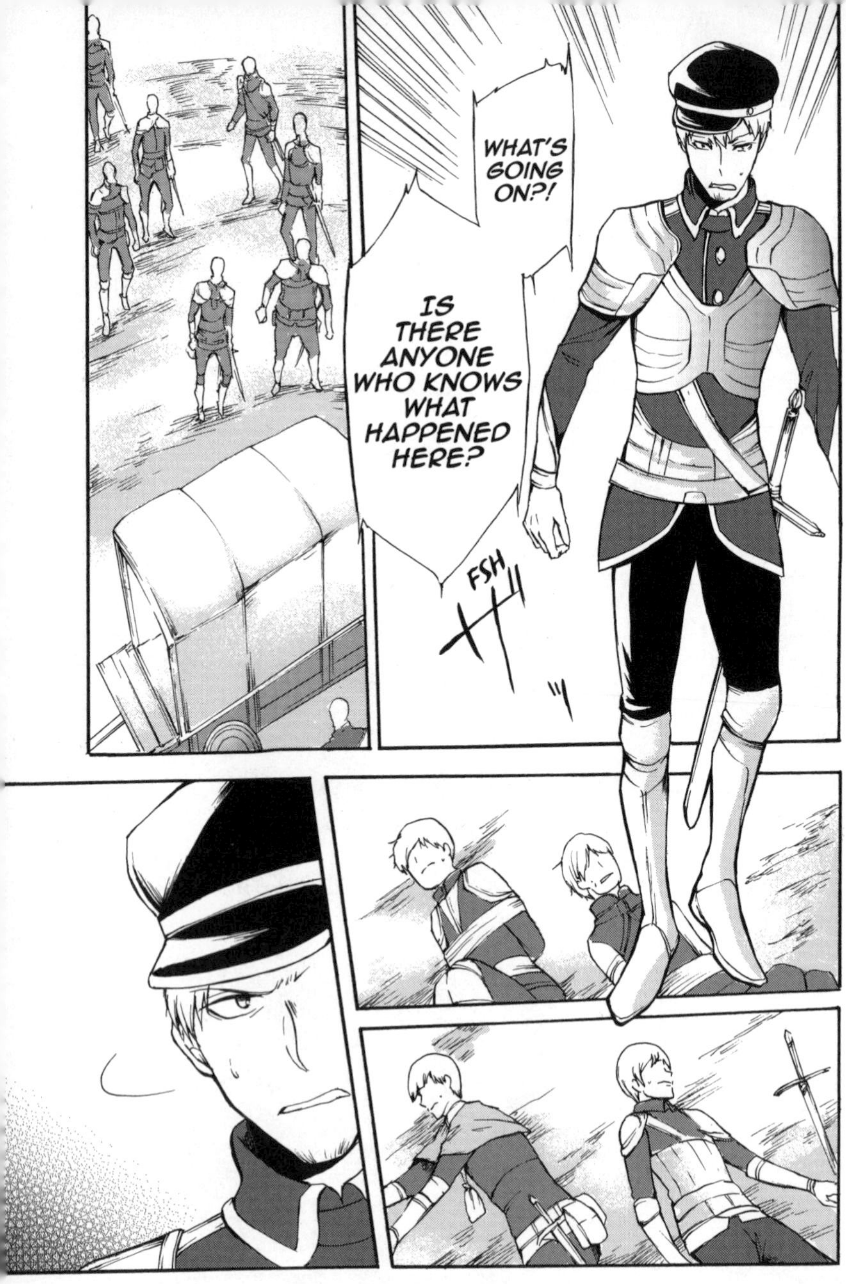
WHAT'S GOING ON?!
IS THERE ANYONE WHO KNOWS WHAT HAPPENED HERE?
FSH

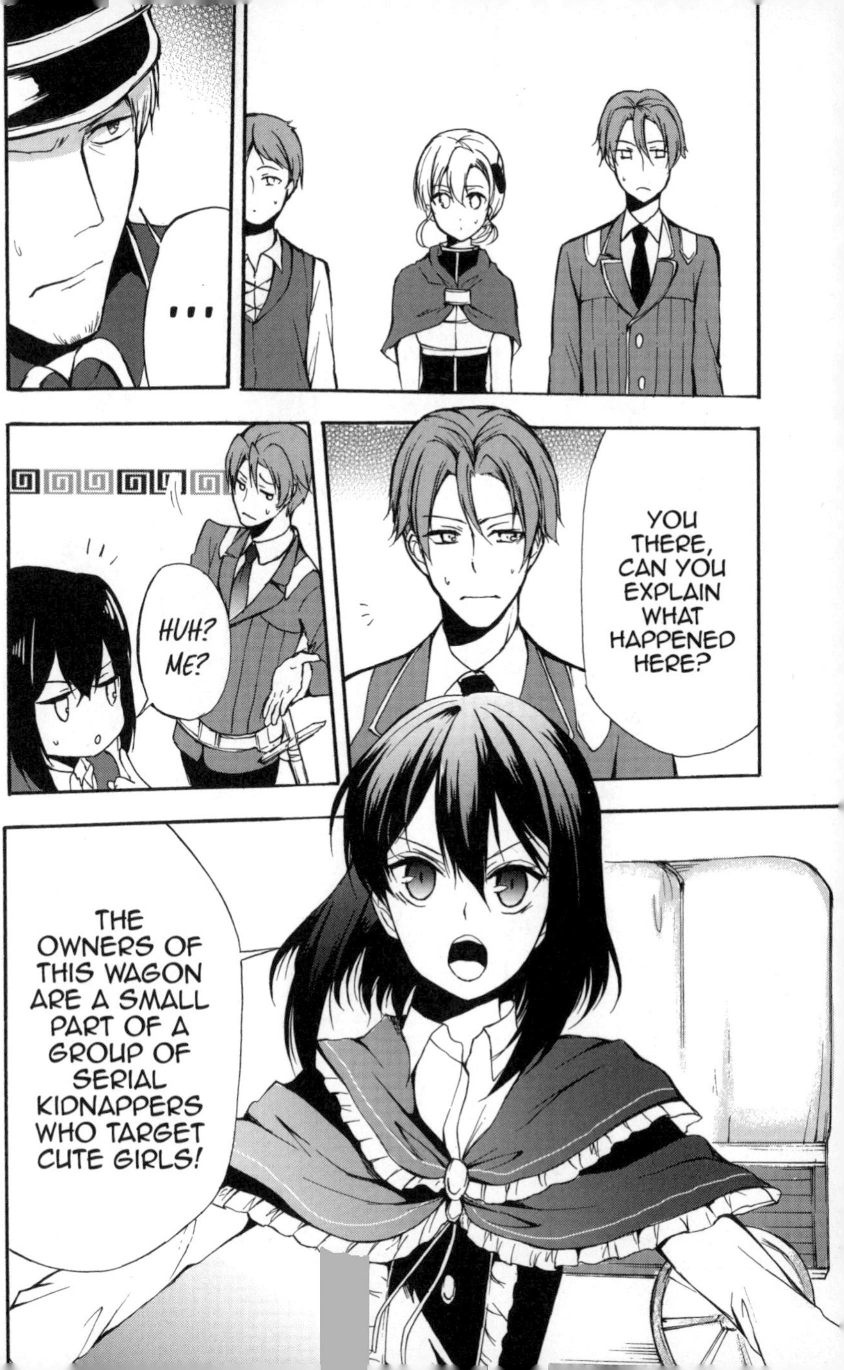
...
YOU THERE, CAN YOU EXPLAIN WHAT HAPPENED HERE?
HUH? ME?
THE OWNERS OF THIS WAGON ARE A SMALL PART OF A GROUP OF SERIAL KIDNAPPERS WHO TARGET CUTE GIRLS!

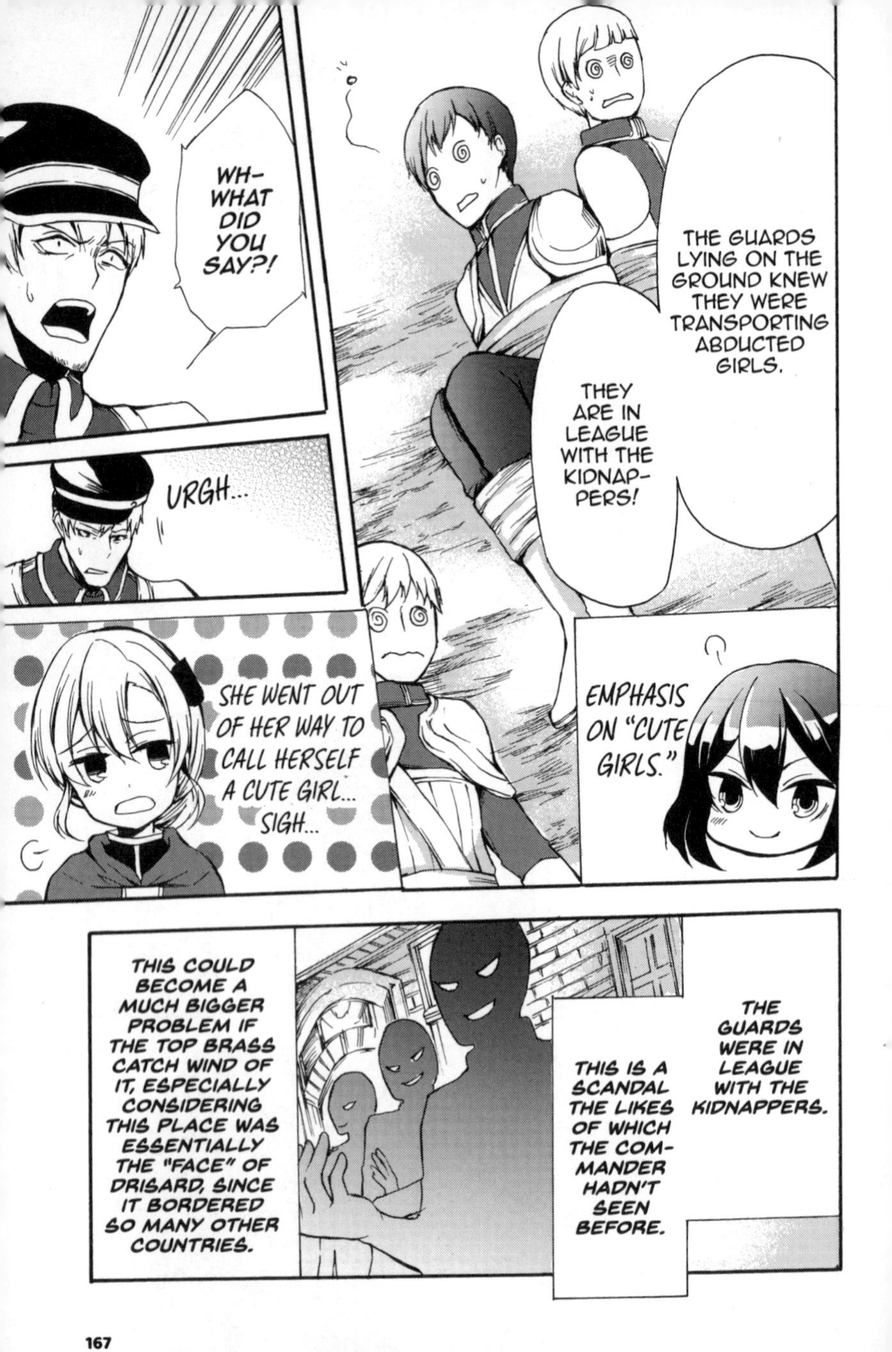
THE GUARDS LYING ON THE GROUND KNEW THEY WERE TRANSPORTING ABDUCTED GIRLS.
THEY ARE IN LEAGUE WITH THE KIDNAPPERS!
EMPHASIS ON "CUTE GIRLS."
WH-WHAT DID YOU SAY?!
URGH...
SHE WENT OUT OF HER WAY TO CALL HERSELF A CUTE GIRL... SIGH...
THE GUARDS WERE IN LEAGUE WITH THE KIDNAPPERS.
THIS IS A SCANDAL THE LIKES OF WHICH THE COMMANDER HADN'T SEEN BEFORE.
THIS COULD BECOME A MUCH BIGGER PROBLEM IF THE TOP BRASS CATCH WIND OF IT, ESPECIALLY CONSIDERING THIS PLACE WAS ESSENTIALLY THE "FACE" OF DRISARD, SINCE IT BORDERED SO MANY OTHER COUNTRIES.

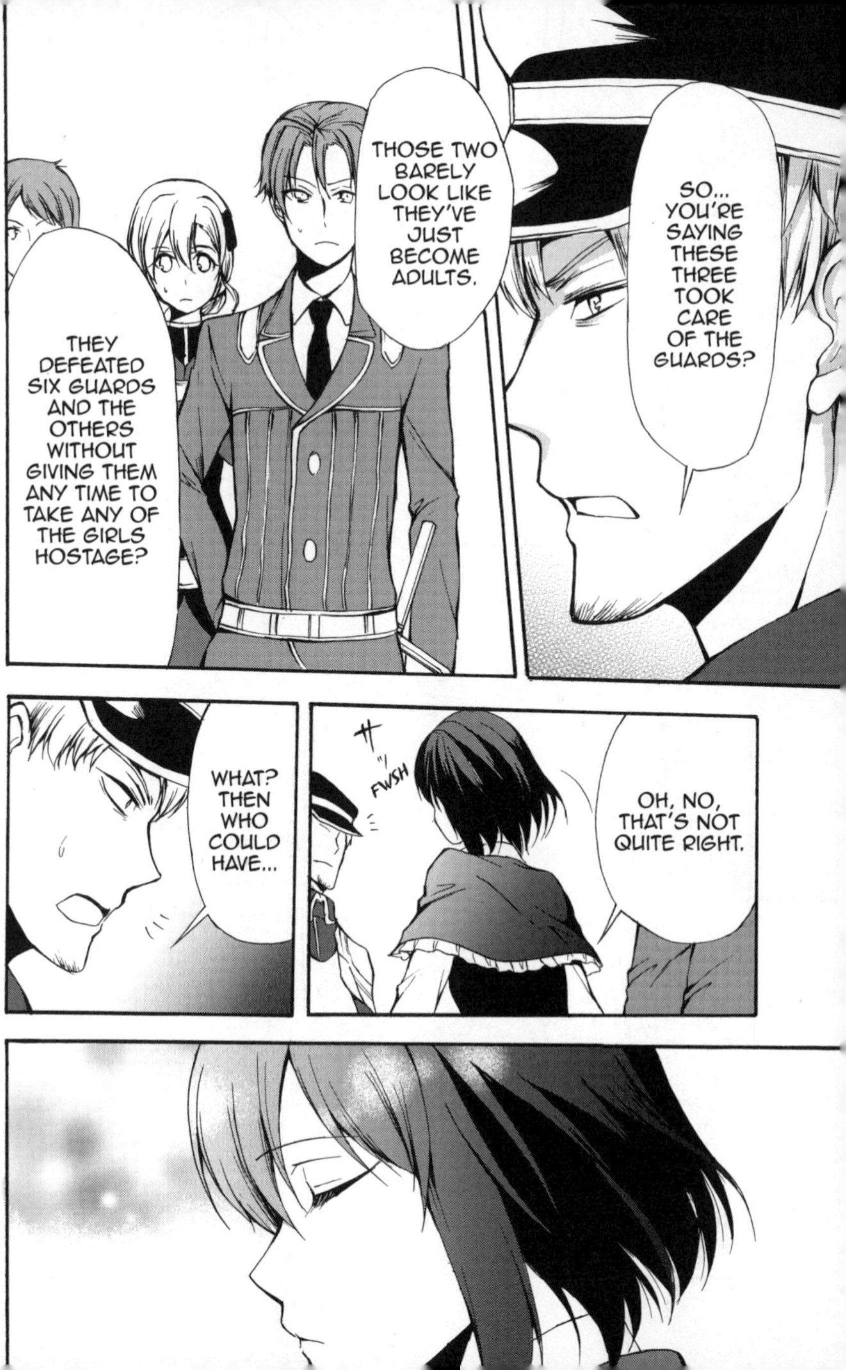
SO... YOU'RE SAYING THESE THREE TOOK CARE OF THE GUARDS?
THOSE TWO BARELY LOOK LIKE THEY'VE JUST BECOME ADULTS.
THEY DEFEATED SIX GUARDS AND THE OTHERS WITHOUT GIVING THEM ANY TIME TO TAKE ANY OF THE GIRLS HOSTAGE?
OH, NO, THAT'S NOT QUITE RIGHT.
FWSH
WHAT? THEN WHO COULD HAVE...

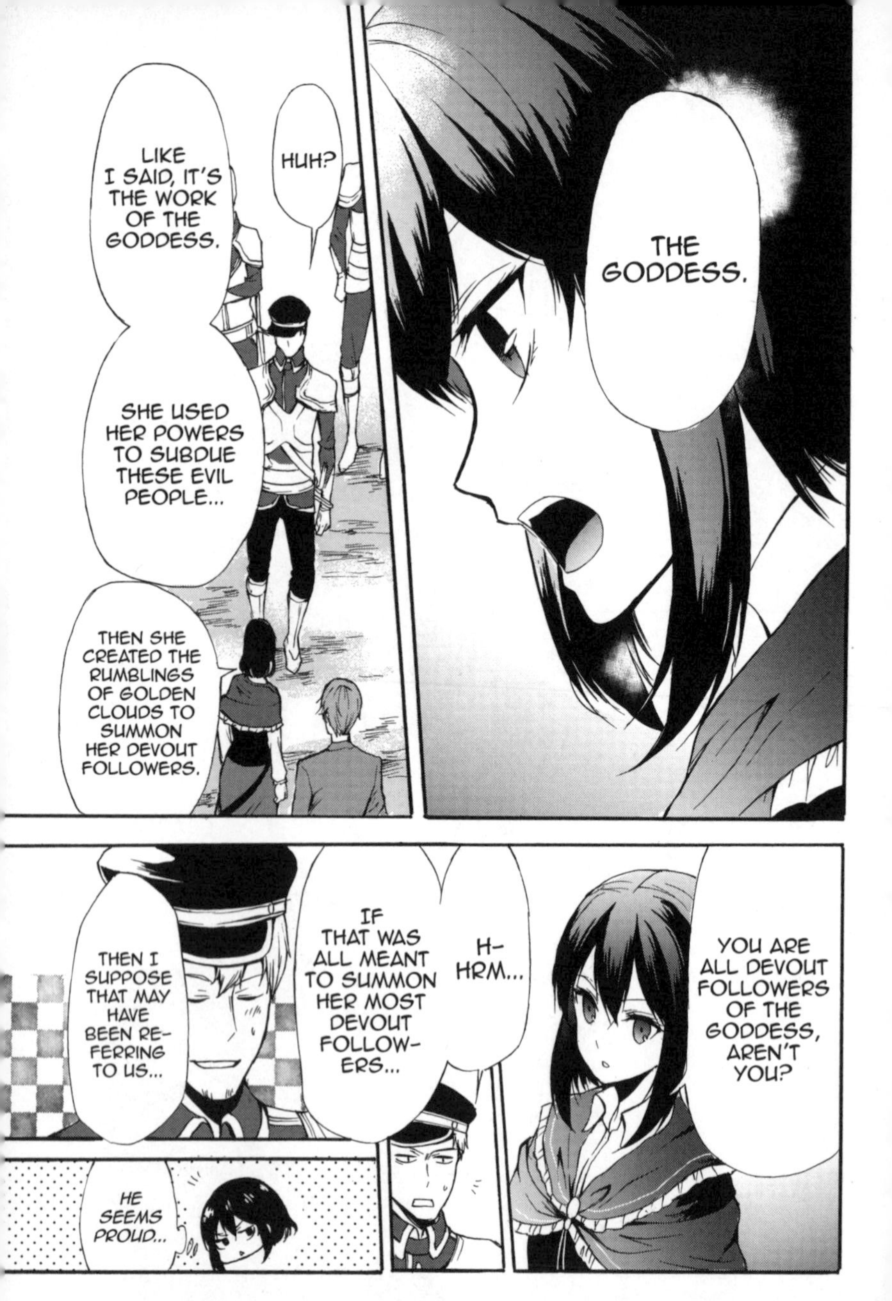
THE GODDESS.
HUH?
LIKE I SAID, IT'S THE WORK OF THE GODDESS.
SHE USED HER POWERS TO SUBDUE THESE EVIL PEOPLE...
THEN SHE CREATED THE RUMBLINGS OF GOLDEN CLOUDS TO SUMMON HER DEVOUT FOLLOWERS.
YOU ARE ALL DEVOUT FOLLOWERS OF THE GODDESS, AREN'T YOU?
H-HRM...
IF THAT WAS ALL MEANT TO SUMMON HER MOST DEVOUT FOLLOW-ERS...
THEN I SUPPOSE THAT MAY HAVE BEEN RE-FERRING TO US...
HE SEEMS PROUD...

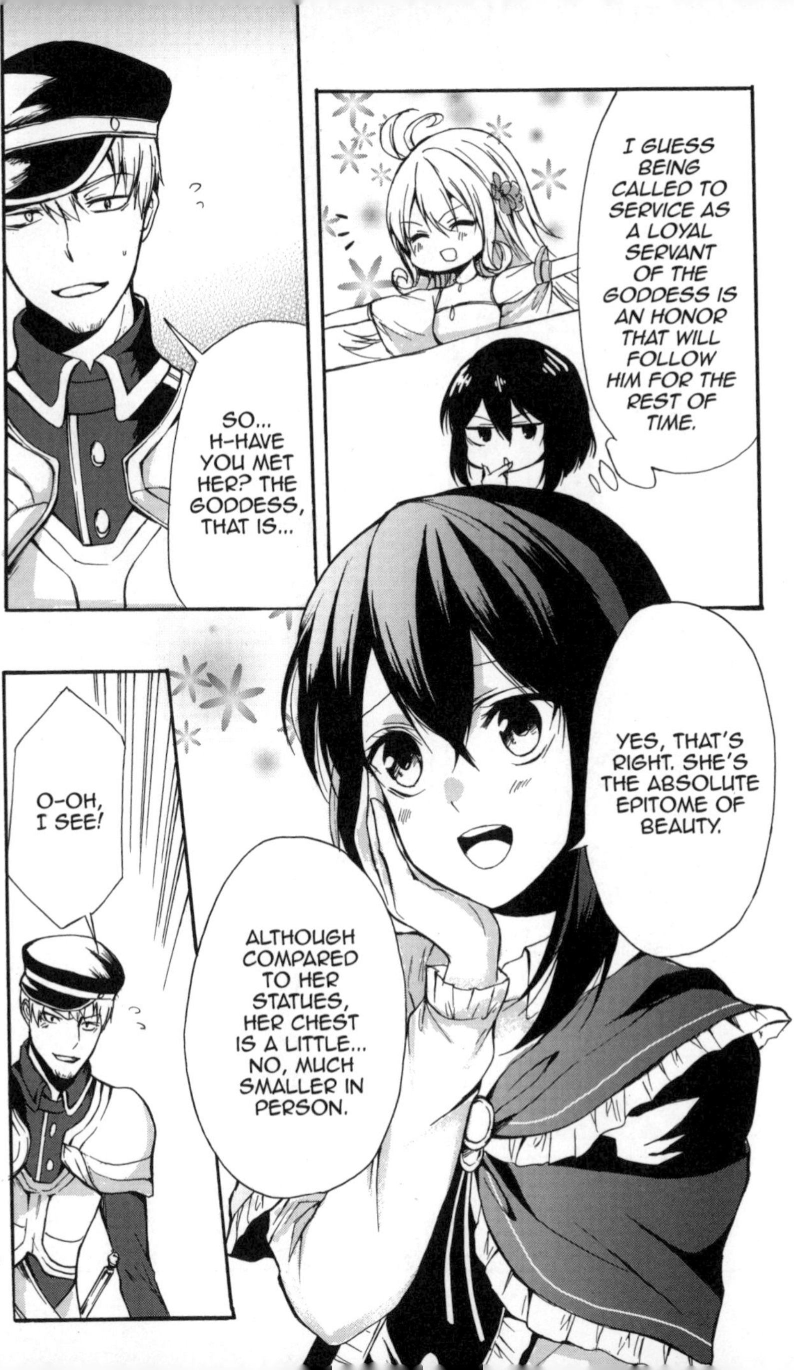

I GUESS BEING CALLED TO SERVICE AS A LOYAL SERVANT OF THE GODDESS IS AN HONOR THAT WILL FOLLOW HIM FOR THE REST OF TIME.
SO... H-HAVE YOU MET HER? THE GODDESS, THAT IS...
YES, THAT'S RIGHT. SHE'S THE ABSOLUTE EPITOME OF BEAUTY.
ALTHOUGH COMPARED TO HER STATUES, HER CHEST IS A LITTLE... NO, MUCH SMALLER IN PERSON.
O-OH, I SEE!

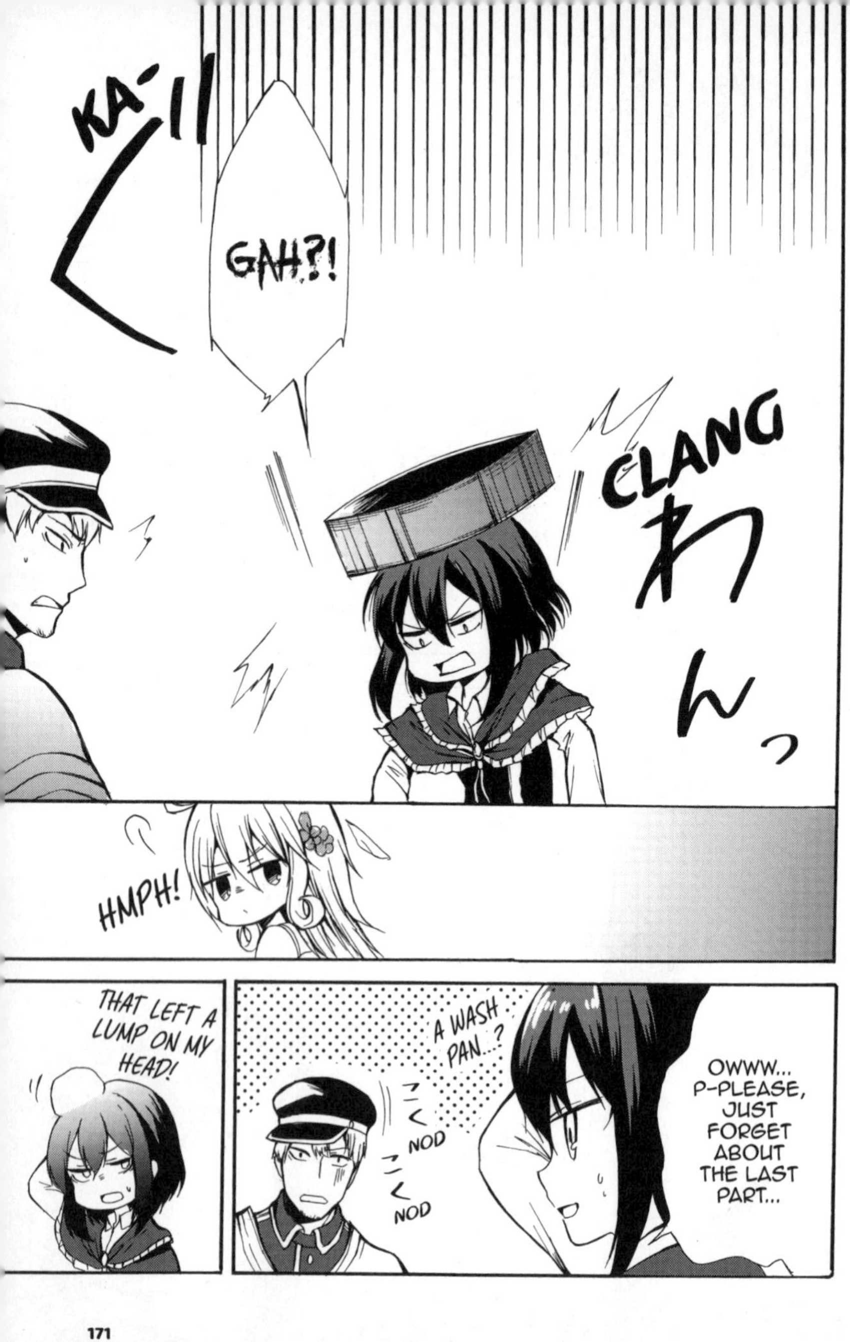
GAH?!
CLANG
わんっ
KA-I
HMPH!
OWWW... P-PLEASE, JUST FORGET ABOUT THE LAST PART...
A WASH PAN...?
NOD
NOD
THAT LEFT A LUMP ON MY HEAD!

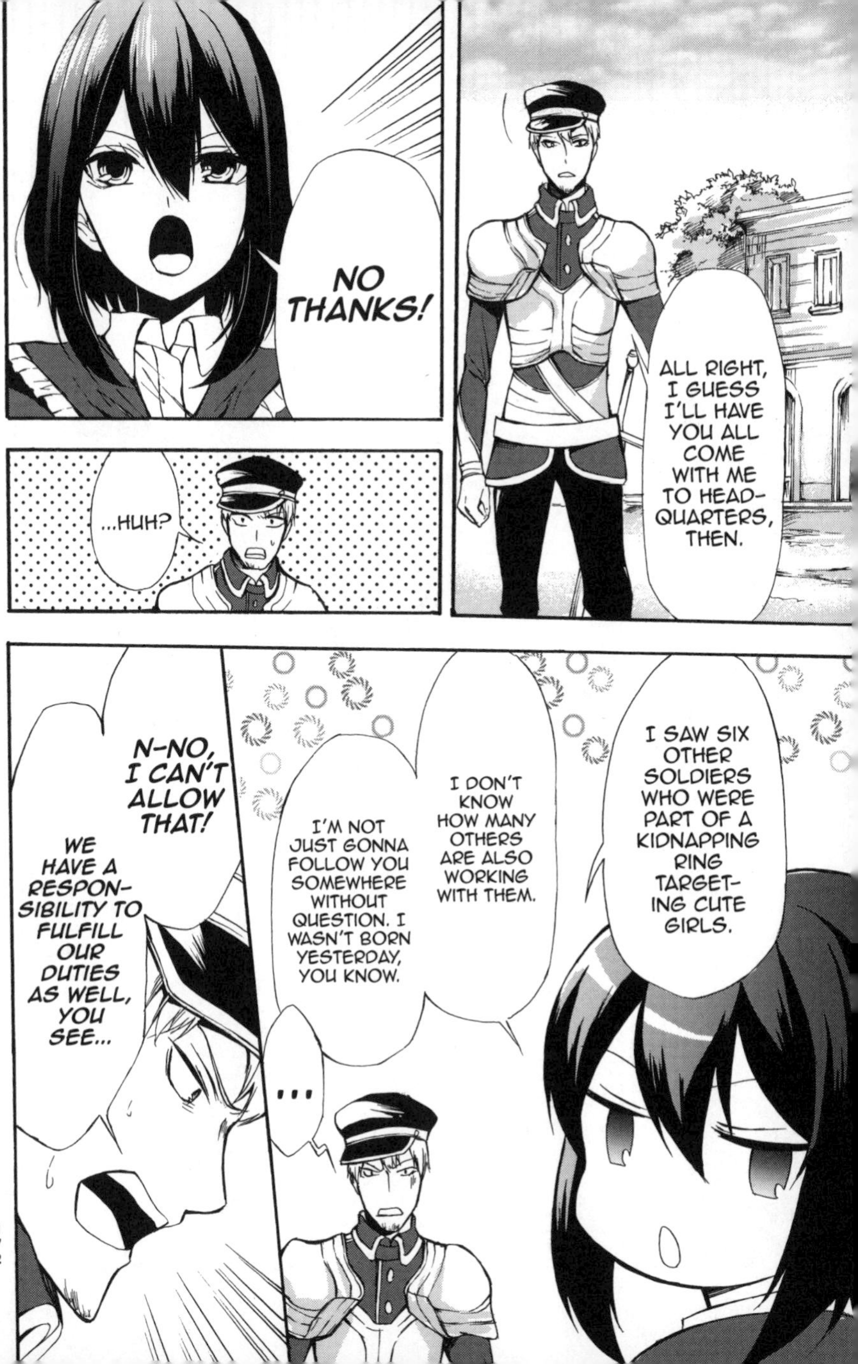
ALL RIGHT, I GUESS I'LL HAVE YOU ALL COME WITH ME TO HEAD-QUARTERS, THEN.
NO THANKS!
...HUH?
I SAW SIX OTHER SOLDIERS WHO WERE PART OF A KIDNAPPING RING TARGET-ING CUTE GIRLS.
I DON'T KNOW HOW MANY OTHERS ARE ALSO WORKING WITH THEM.
I'M NOT JUST GONNA FOLLOW YOU SOMEWHERE WITHOUT QUESTION. I WASN'T BORN YESTERDAY, YOU KNOW.
...
N-NO, I CAN'T ALLOW THAT!
WE HAVE A RESPON-SIBILITY TO FULFILL OUR DUTIES AS WELL, YOU SEE...

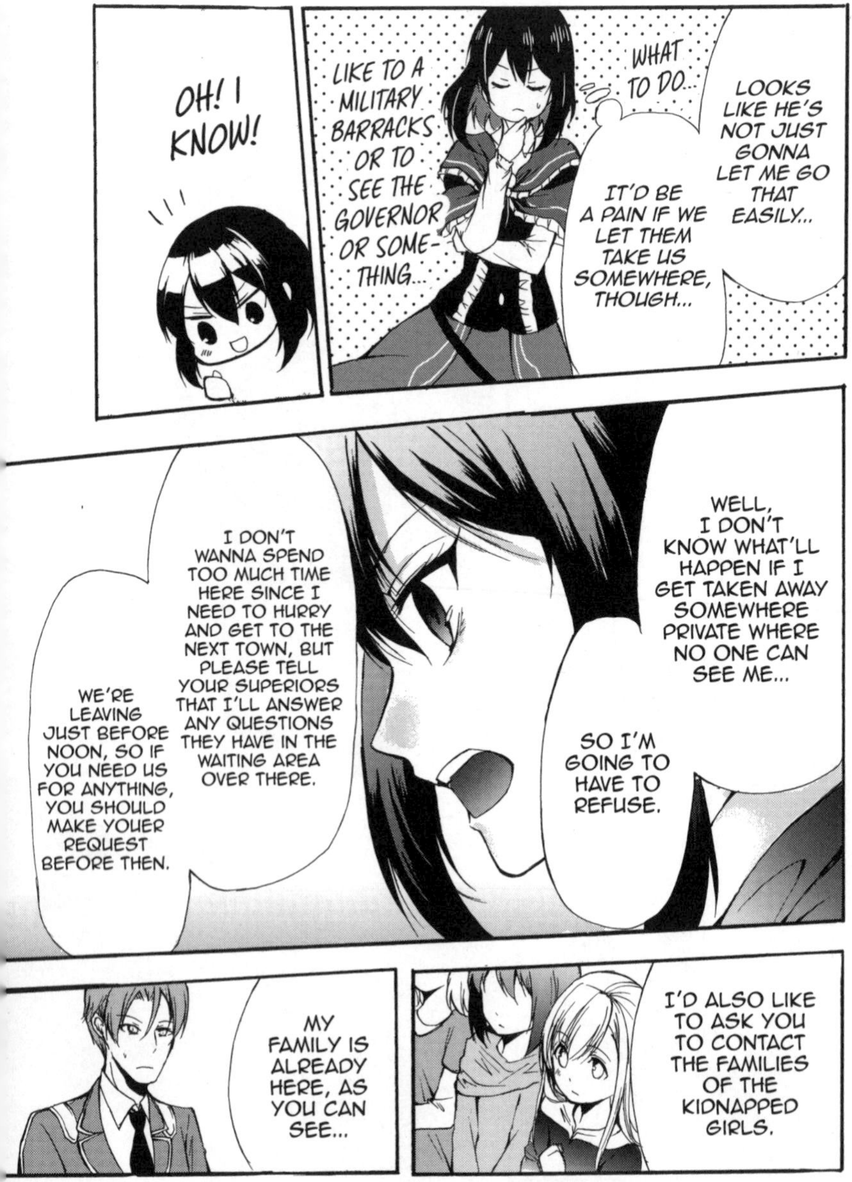
LOOKS LIKE HE'S NOT JUST GONNA LET ME GO THAT EASILY...
WHAT TO DO...
IT'D BE A PAIN IF WE LET THEM TAKE US SOMEWHERE, THOUGH...
LIKE TO A MILITARY BARRACKS OR TO SEE THE GOVERNOR OR SOME-THING...
OH! I KNOW!
WELL, I DON'T KNOW WHAT'LL HAPPEN IF I GET TAKEN AWAY SOMEWHERE PRIVATE WHERE NO ONE CAN SEE ME...
SO I'M GOING TO HAVE TO REFUSE.
I DON'T WANNA SPEND TOO MUCH TIME HERE SINCE I NEED TO HURRY AND GET TO THE NEXT TOWN, BUT PLEASE TELL YOUR SUPERIORS THAT I'LL ANSWER ANY QUESTIONS THEY HAVE IN THE WAITING AREA OVER THERE.
WE'RE LEAVING JUST BEFORE NOON, SO IF YOU NEED US FOR ANYTHING, YOU SHOULD MAKE YOUER REQUEST BEFORE THEN.
I'D ALSO LIKE TO ASK YOU TO CONTACT THE FAMILIES OF THE KIDNAPPED GIRLS.
MY FAMILY IS ALREADY HERE, AS YOU CAN SEE...

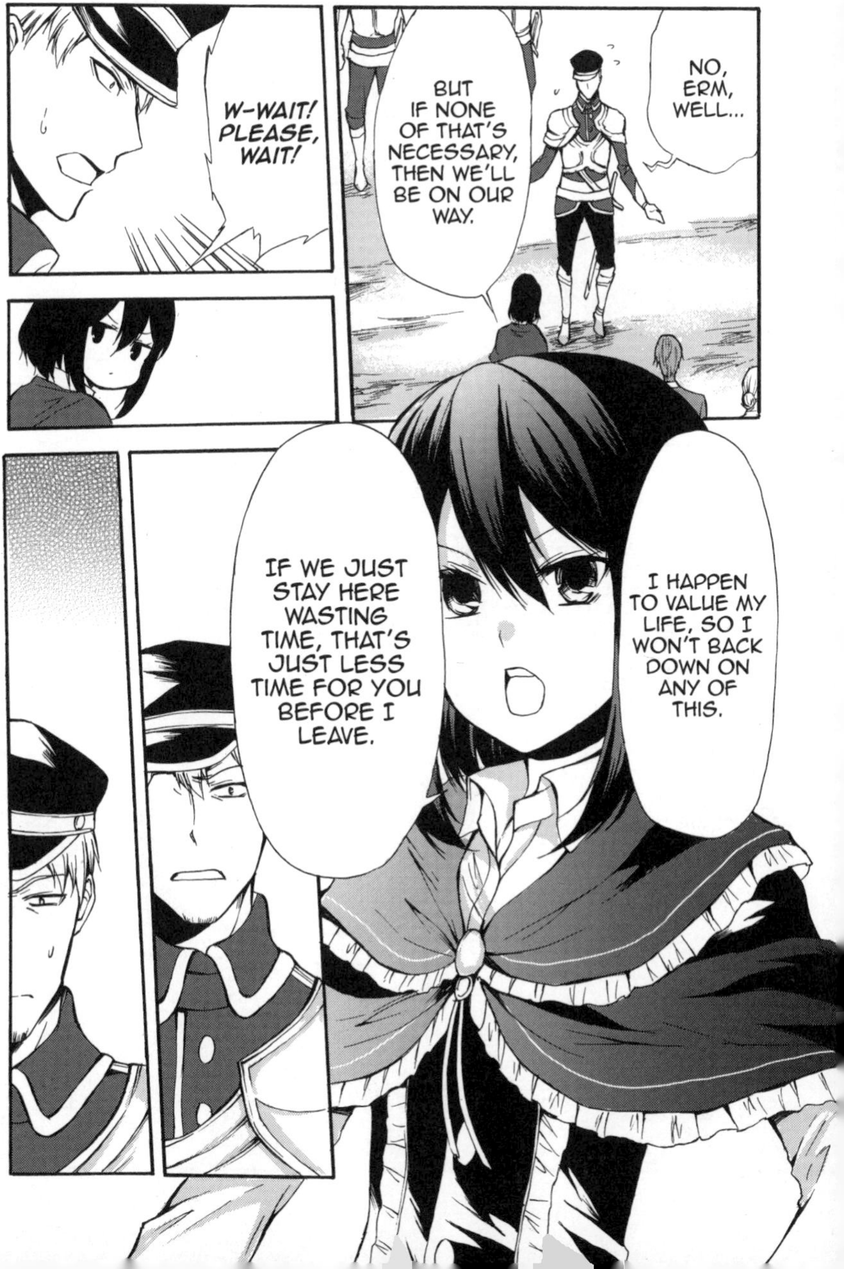
NO, ERM, WELL...
BUT IF NONE OF THAT'S NECESSARY, THEN WE'LL BE ON OUR WAY.
W-WAIT! PLEASE, WAIT!
I HAPPEN TO VALUE MY LIFE, SO I WON'T BACK DOWN ON ANY OF THIS.
IF WE JUST STAY HERE WASTING TIME, THAT'S JUST LESS TIME FOR YOU BEFORE I LEAVE.

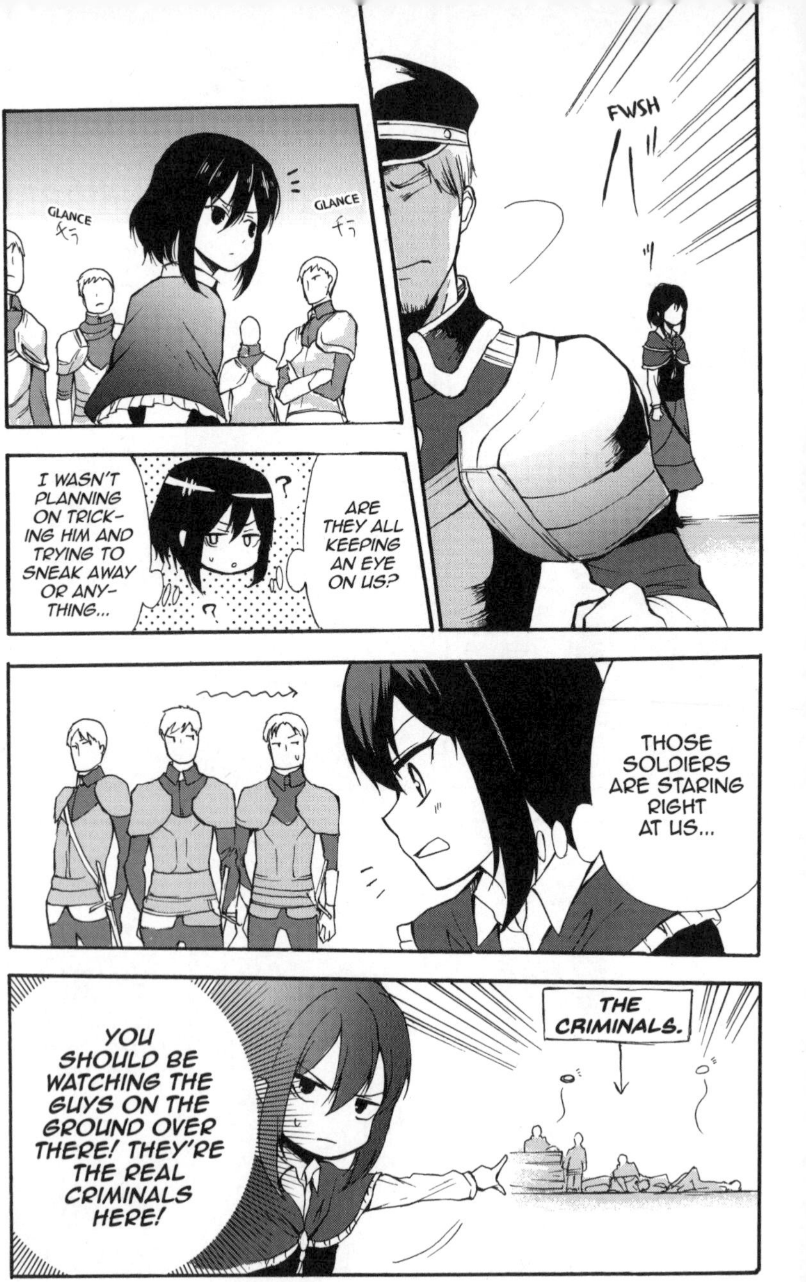
FWSH
GLANCE
チラ
GLANCE
チラ
ARE THEY ALL KEEPING AN EYE ON US?
I WASN'T PLANNING ON TRICKING HIM AND TRYING TO SNEAK AWAY OR ANYTHING...
THOSE SOLDIERS ARE STARING RIGHT AT US...
THE CRIMINALS.
YOU SHOULD BE WATCHING THE GUYS ON THE GROUND OVER THERE! THEY'RE THE REAL CRIMINALS HERE!

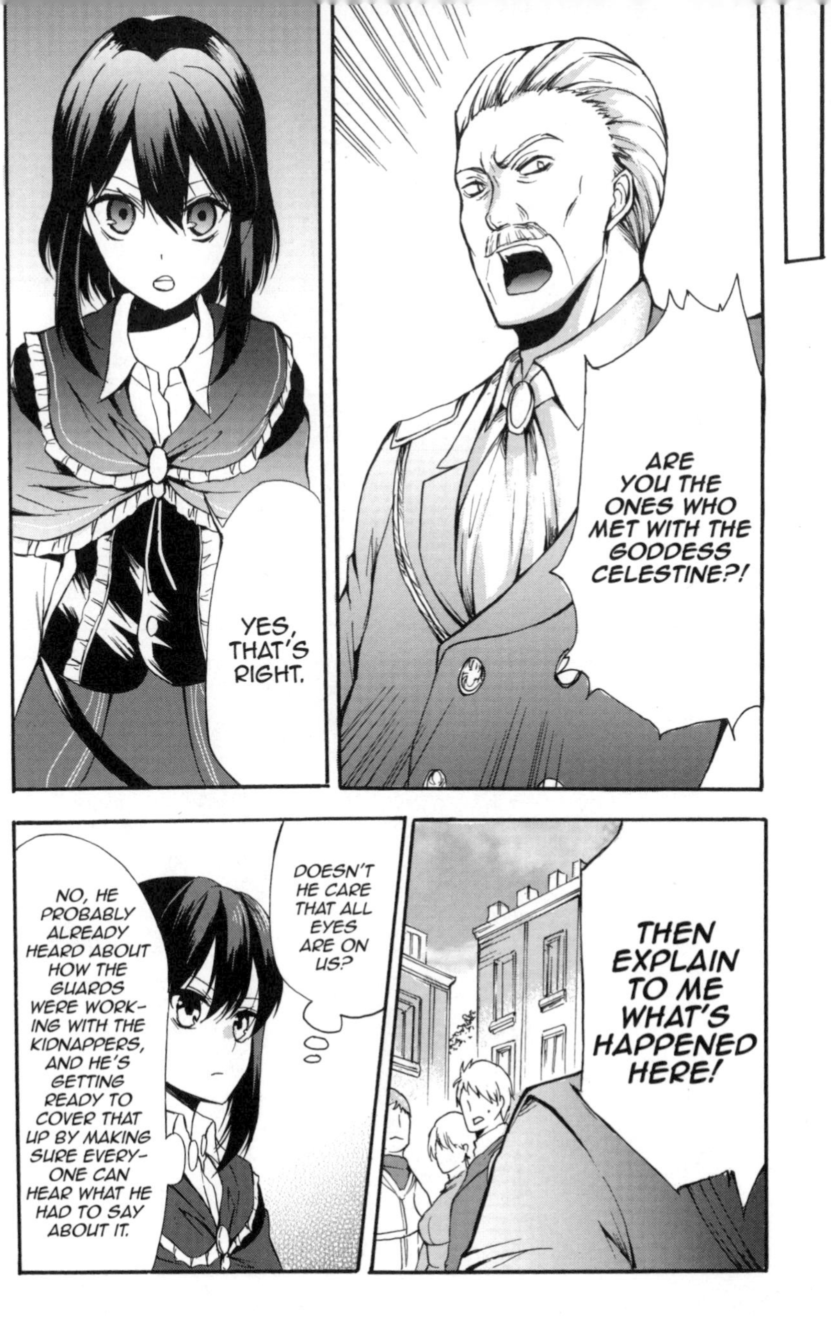
ARE YOU THE ONES WHO MET WITH THE GODDESS CELESTINE?!
YES, THAT'S RIGHT.
THEN EXPLAIN TO ME WHAT'S HAPPENED HERE!
DOESN'T HE CARE THAT ALL EYES ARE ON US?
NO, HE PROBABLY ALREADY HEARD ABOUT HOW THE GUARDS WERE WORKING WITH THE KIDNAPPERS, AND HE'S GETTING READY TO COVER THAT UP BY MAKING SURE EVERYONE CAN HEAR WHAT HE HAD TO SAY ABOUT IT.

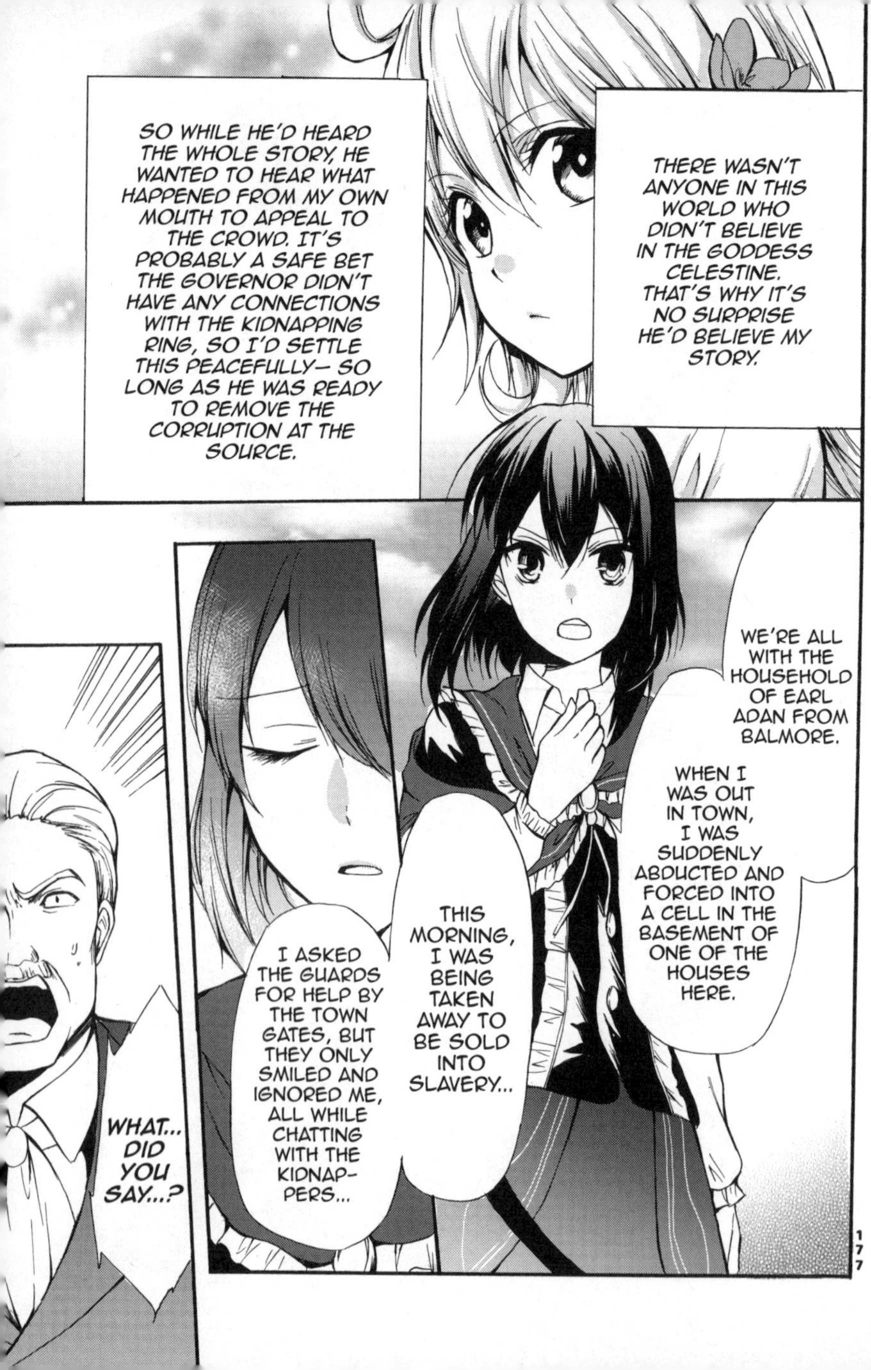
THERE WASN'T ANYONE IN THIS WORLD WHO DIDN'T BELIEVE IN THE GODDESS CELESTINE. THAT'S WHY IT'S NO SURPRISE HE'D BELIEVE MY STORY.
SO WHILE HE'D HEARD THE WHOLE STORY, HE WANTED TO HEAR WHAT HAPPENED FROM MY OWN MOUTH TO APPEAL TO THE CROWD. IT'S PROBABLY A SAFE BET THE GOVERNOR DIDN'T HAVE ANY CONNECTIONS WITH THE KIDNAPPING RING, SO I'D SETTLE THIS PEACEFULLY— SO LONG AS HE WAS READY TO REMOVE THE CORRUPTION AT THE SOURCE.
WE'RE ALL WITH THE HOUSEHOLD OF EARL ADAN FROM BALMORE.
WHEN I WAS OUT IN TOWN, I WAS SUDDENLY ABDUCTED AND FORCED INTO A CELL IN THE BASEMENT OF ONE OF THE HOUSES HERE.
THIS MORNING, I WAS BEING TAKEN AWAY TO BE SOLD INTO SLAVERY...
I ASKED THE GUARDS FOR HELP BY THE TOWN GATES, BUT THEY ONLY SMILED AND IGNORED ME, ALL WHILE CHATTING WITH THE KIDNAP-PERS...
WHAT... DID YOU SAY...?

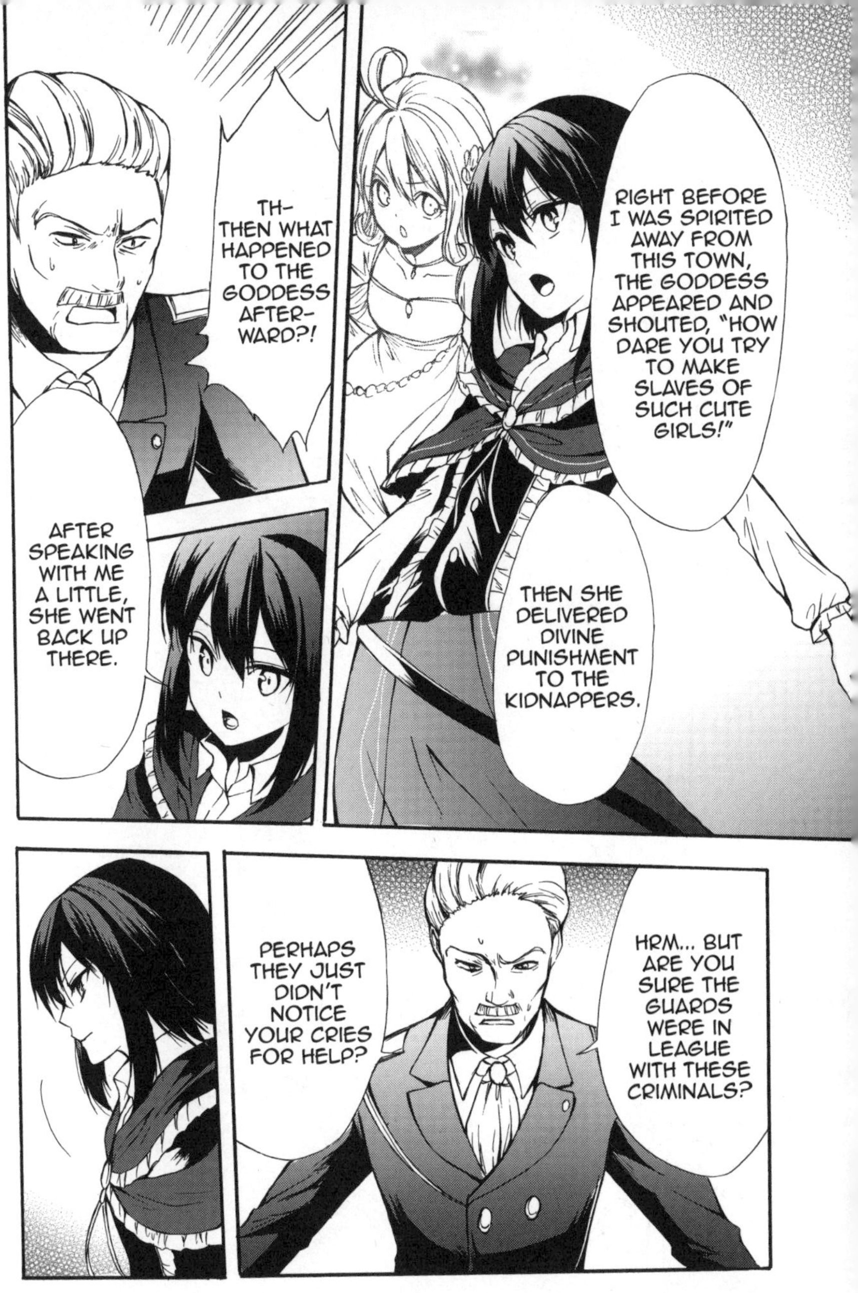
RIGHT BEFORE I WAS SPIRITED AWAY FROM THIS TOWN, THE GODDESS APPEARED AND SHOUTED, "HOW DARE YOU TRY TO MAKE SLAVES OF SUCH CUTE GIRLS!"
THEN SHE DELIVERED DIVINE PUNISHMENT TO THE KIDNAPPERS.
TH- THEN WHAT HAPPENED TO THE GODDESS AFTER-WARD?!
AFTER SPEAKING WITH ME A LITTLE, SHE WENT BACK UP THERE.
HRM... BUT ARE YOU SURE THE GUARDS WERE IN LEAGUE WITH THESE CRIMINALS?
PERHAPS THEY JUST DIDN'T NOTICE YOUR CRIES FOR HELP?

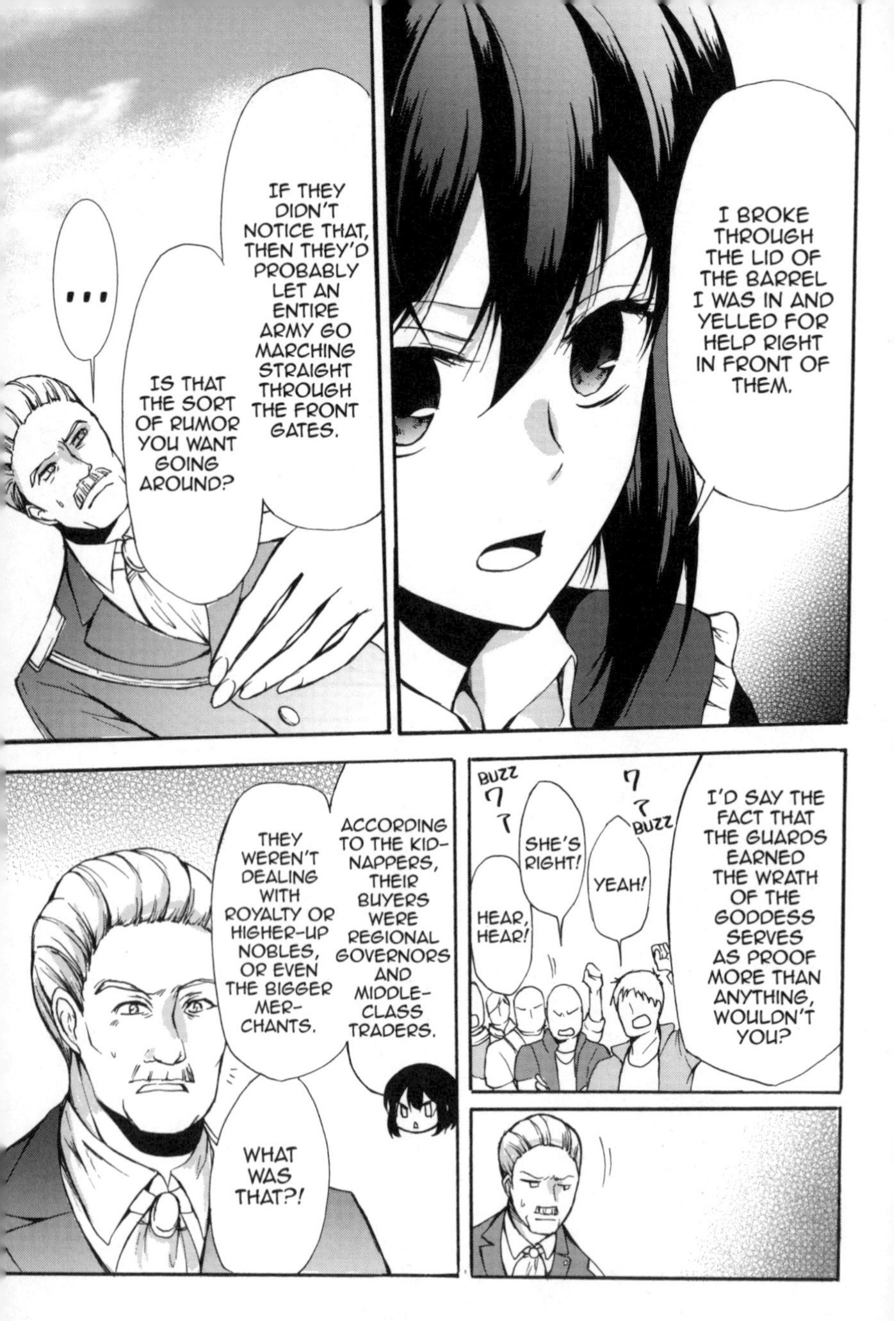
I BROKE THROUGH THE LID OF THE BARREL I WAS IN AND YELLED FOR HELP RIGHT IN FRONT OF THEM.
IF THEY DIDN'T NOTICE THAT, THEN THEY'D PROBABLY LET AN ENTIRE ARMY GO MARCHING STRAIGHT THROUGH THE FRONT GATES.
IS THAT THE SORT OF RUMOR YOU WANT GOING AROUND?
...
I'D SAY THE FACT THAT THE GUARDS EARNED THE WRATH OF THE GODDESS SERVES AS PROOF MORE THAN ANYTHING, WOULDN'T YOU?
BUZZ
SHE'S RIGHT!
YEAH!
BUZZ
HEAR, HEAR!
ACCORDING TO THE KID-NAPPERS, THEIR BUYERS WERE REGIONAL GOVERNORS AND MIDDLE-CLASS TRADERS.
THEY WEREN'T DEALING WITH ROYALTY OR HIGHER-UP NOBLES, OR EVEN THE BIGGER MER-CHANTS.
WHAT WAS THAT?!

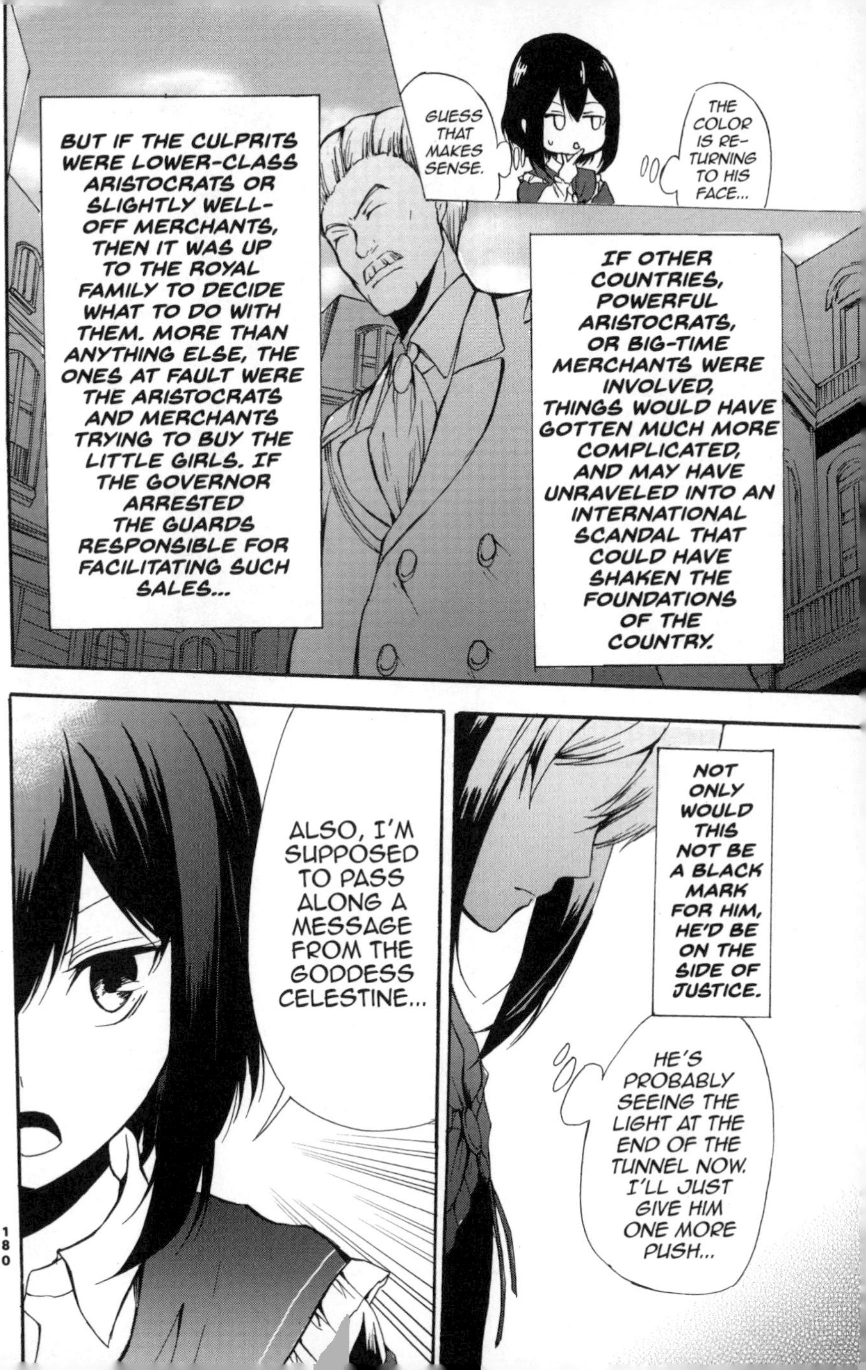
THE COLOR IS RE-TURNING TO HIS FACE...
GUESS THAT MAKES SENSE.
IF OTHER COUNTRIES, POWERFUL ARISTOCRATS, OR BIG-TIME MERCHANTS WERE INVOLVED, THINGS WOULD HAVE GOTTEN MUCH MORE COMPLICATED, AND MAY HAVE UNRAVELED INTO AN INTERNATIONAL SCANDAL THAT COULD HAVE SHAKEN THE FOUNDATIONS OF THE COUNTRY.
BUT IF THE CULPRITS WERE LOWER-CLASS ARISTOCRATS OR SLIGHTLY WELL-OFF MERCHANTS, THEN IT WAS UP TO THE ROYAL FAMILY TO DECIDE WHAT TO DO WITH THEM. MORE THAN ANYTHING ELSE, THE ONES AT FAULT WERE THE ARISTOCRATS AND MERCHANTS TRYING TO BUY THE LITTLE GIRLS. IF THE GOVERNOR ARRESTED THE GUARDS RESPONSIBLE FOR FACILITATING SUCH SALES...
NOT ONLY WOULD THIS NOT BE A BLACK MARK FOR HIM, HE'D BE ON THE SIDE OF JUSTICE.
HE'S PROBABLY SEEING THE LIGHT AT THE END OF THE TUNNEL NOW. I'LL JUST GIVE HIM ONE MORE PUSH...
ALSO, I'M SUPPOSED TO PASS ALONG A MESSAGE FROM THE GODDESS CELESTINE...

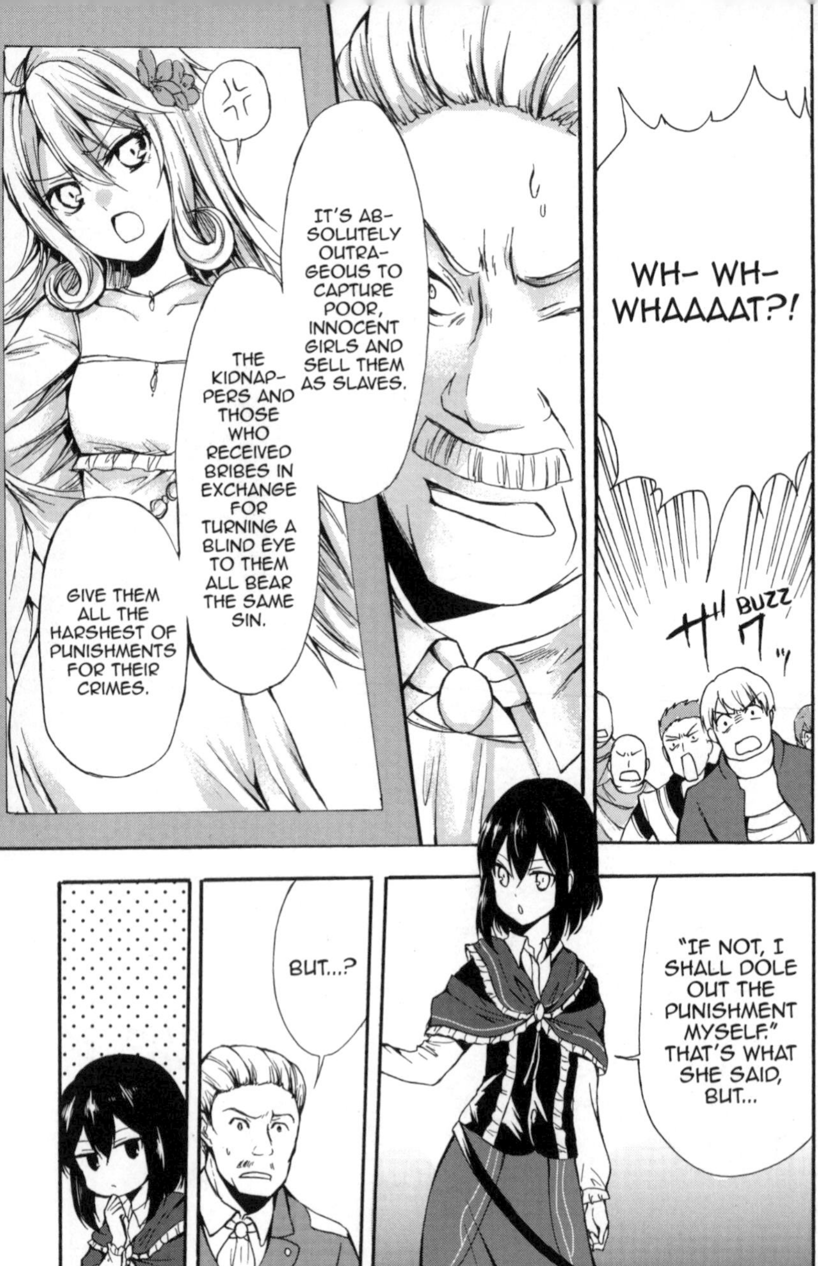
WH- WH- WHAAAAT?!
BUZZ
IT'S ABSOLUTELY OUTRAGEOUS TO CAPTURE POOR, INNOCENT GIRLS AND SELL THEM AS SLAVES.
THE KIDNAPPERS AND THOSE WHO RECEIVED BRIBES IN EXCHANGE FOR TURNING A BLIND EYE TO THEM ALL BEAR THE SAME SIN.
GIVE THEM ALL THE HARSHEST OF PUNISHMENTS FOR THEIR CRIMES.
"IF NOT, I SHALL DOLE OUT THE PUNISHMENT MYSELF." THAT'S WHAT SHE SAID, BUT...
BUT...?

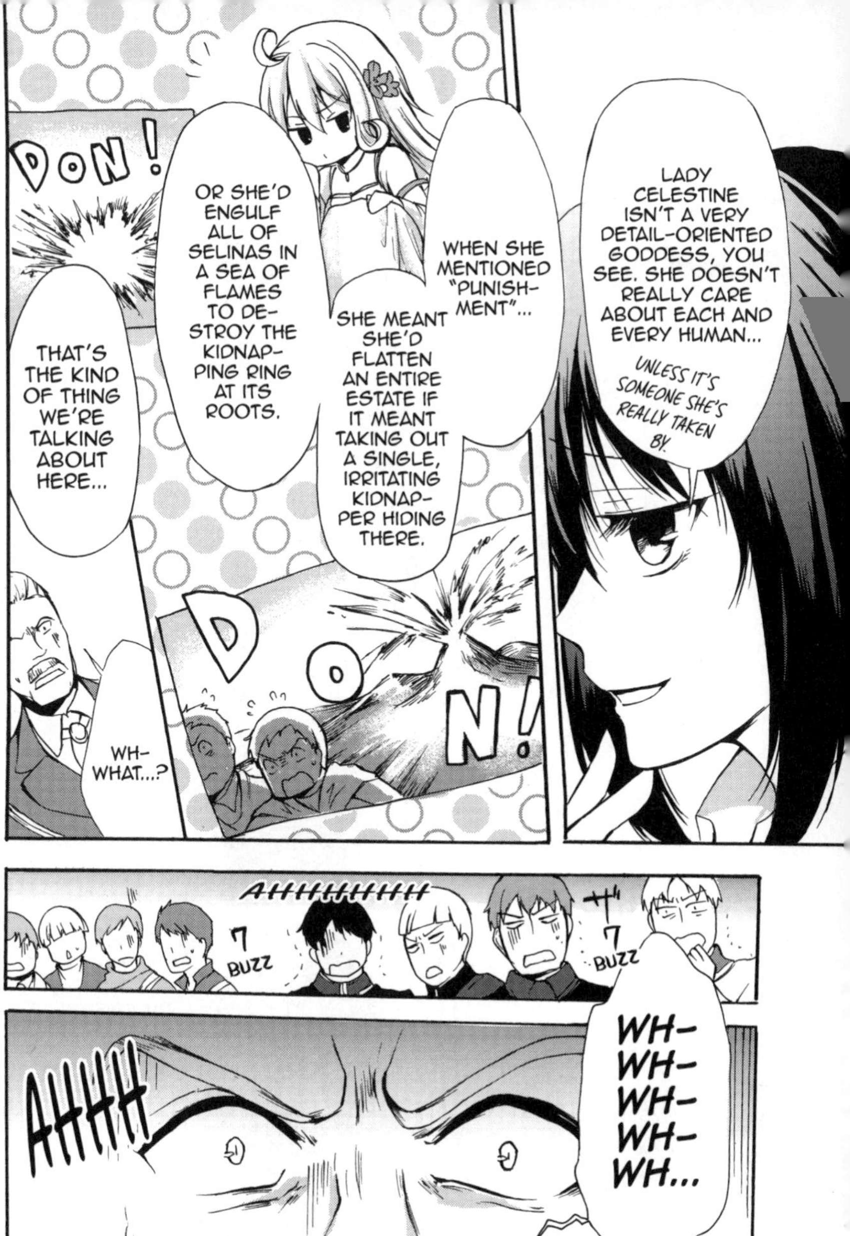
LADY CELESTINE ISN'T A VERY DETAIL-ORIENTED GODDESS, YOU SEE. SHE DOESN'T REALLY CARE ABOUT EACH AND EVERY HUMAN...
UNLESS IT'S SOMEONE SHE'S REALLY TAKEN BY.
WHEN SHE MENTIONED "PUNISHMENT"...
SHE MEANT SHE'D FLATTEN AN ENTIRE ESTATE IF IT MEANT TAKING OUT A SINGLE, IRRITATING KIDNAPPER HIDING THERE.
DON!
OR SHE'D ENGULF ALL OF SELINAS IN A SEA OF FLAMES TO DESTROY THE KIDNAPPING RING AT ITS ROOTS.
DON!
THAT'S THE KIND OF THING WE'RE TALKING ABOUT HERE...
WH- WHAT...?
BUZZ
AHHHHHHHH
BUZZ
WH- WH- WH- WH- WH...
AHHH

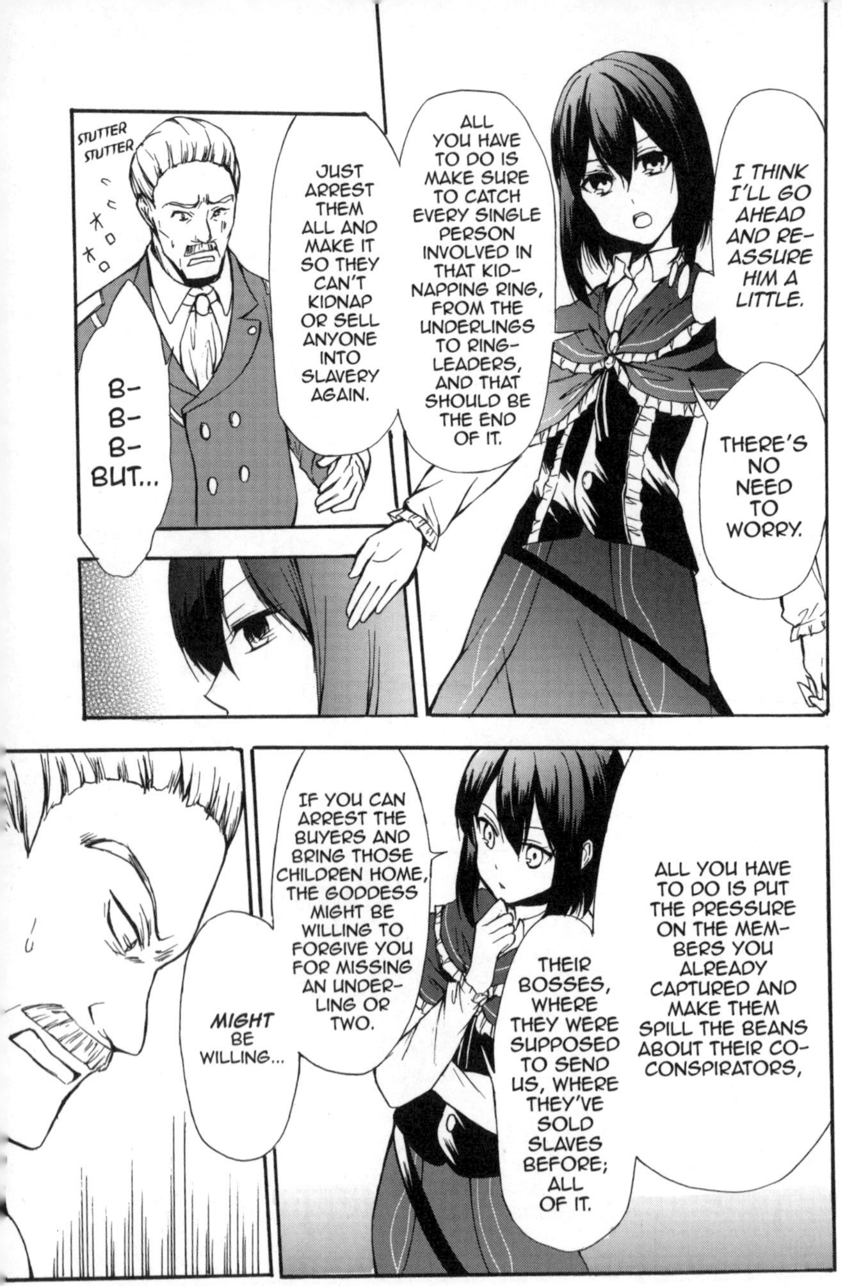
I THINK I'LL GO AHEAD AND RE-ASSURE HIM A LITTLE.
THERE'S NO NEED TO WORRY.
ALL YOU HAVE TO DO IS MAKE SURE TO CATCH EVERY SINGLE PERSON INVOLVED IN THAT KID-NAPPING RING, FROM THE UNDERLINGS TO RING-LEADERS, AND THAT SHOULD BE THE END OF IT.
JUST ARREST THEM ALL AND MAKE IT SO THEY CAN'T KIDNAP OR SELL ANYONE INTO SLAVERY AGAIN.
STUTTER STUTTER
B-B-B-BUT...
ALL YOU HAVE TO DO IS PUT THE PRESSURE ON THE MEM-BERS YOU ALREADY CAPTURED AND MAKE THEM SPILL THE BEANS ABOUT THEIR CO-CONSPIRATORS,
THEIR BOSSES, WHERE THEY WERE SUPPOSED TO SEND US, WHERE THEY'VE SOLD SLAVES BEFORE; ALL OF IT.
IF YOU CAN ARREST THE BUYERS AND BRING THOSE CHILDREN HOME, THE GODDESS MIGHT BE WILLING TO FORGIVE YOU FOR MISSING AN UNDER-LING OR TWO.
MIGHT BE WILLING...

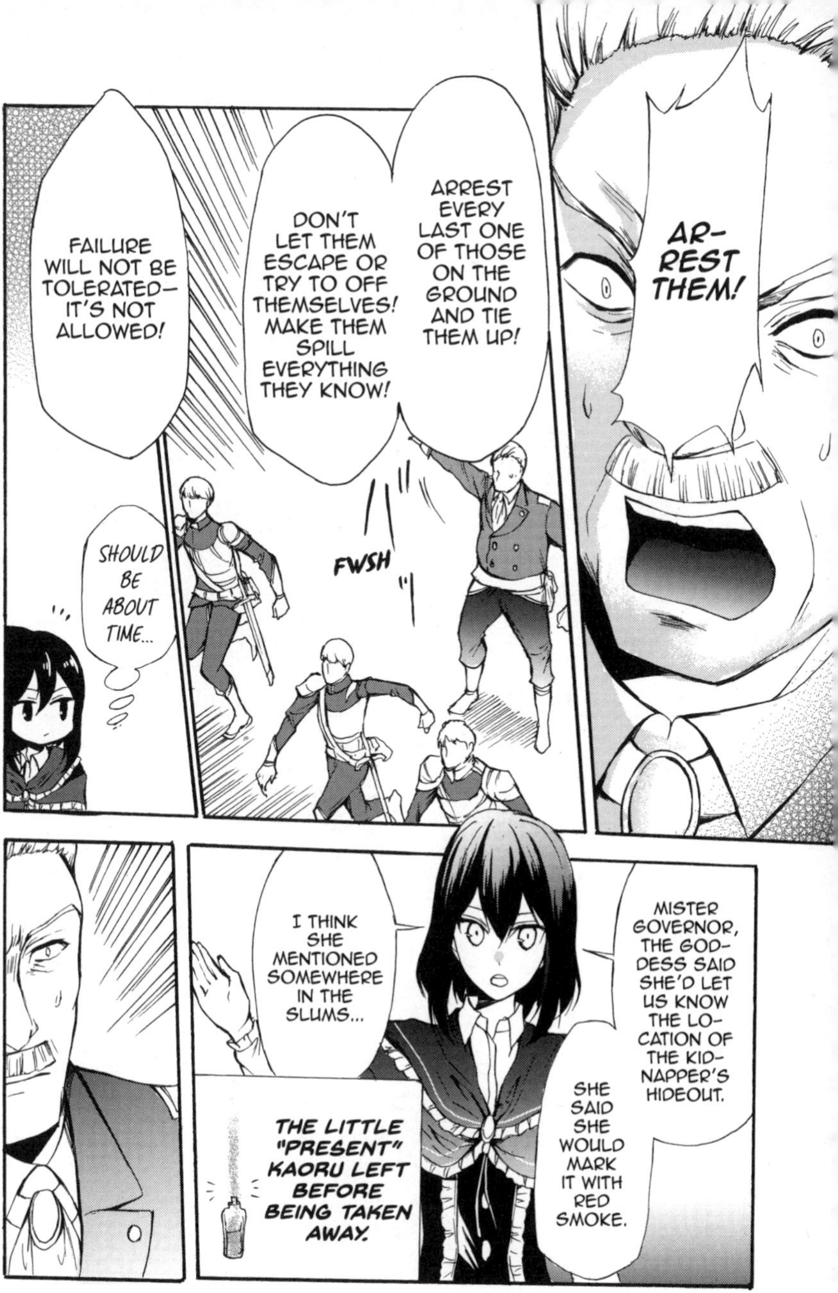
AR-REST THEM!
ARREST EVERY LAST ONE OF THOSE ON THE GROUND AND TIE THEM UP!
DON'T LET THEM ESCAPE OR TRY TO OFF THEMSELVES! MAKE THEM SPILL EVERYTHING THEY KNOW!
FAILURE WILL NOT BE TOLERATED—IT'S NOT ALLOWED!
FWSH
SHOULD BE ABOUT TIME...
MISTER GOVERNOR, THE GOD-DESS SAID SHE'D LET US KNOW THE LO-CATION OF THE KID-NAPPER'S HIDEOUT.
SHE SAID SHE WOULD MARK IT WITH RED SMOKE.
I THINK SHE MENTIONED SOMEWHERE IN THE SLUMS...
THE LITTLE "PRESENT" KAORU LEFT BEFORE BEING TAKEN AWAY.

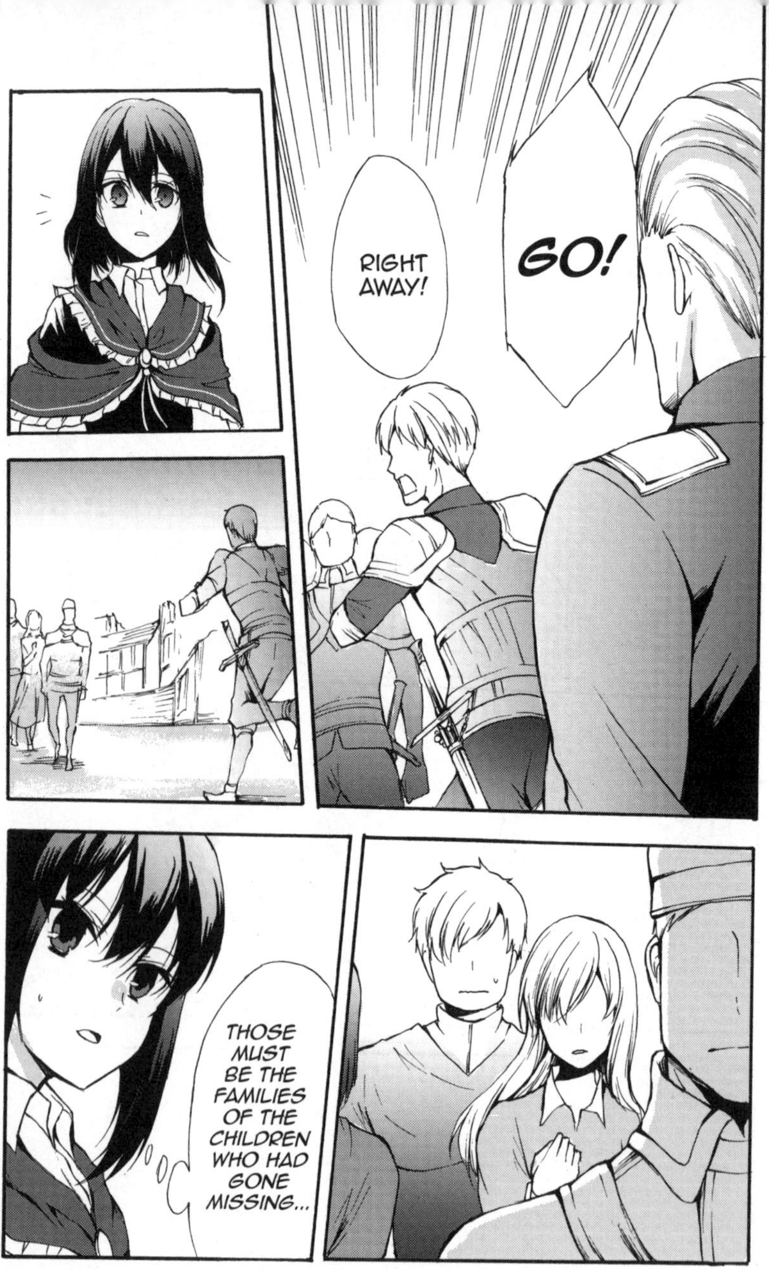
GO!
RIGHT AWAY!
THOSE MUST BE THE FAMILIES OF THE CHILDREN WHO HAD GONE MISSING...

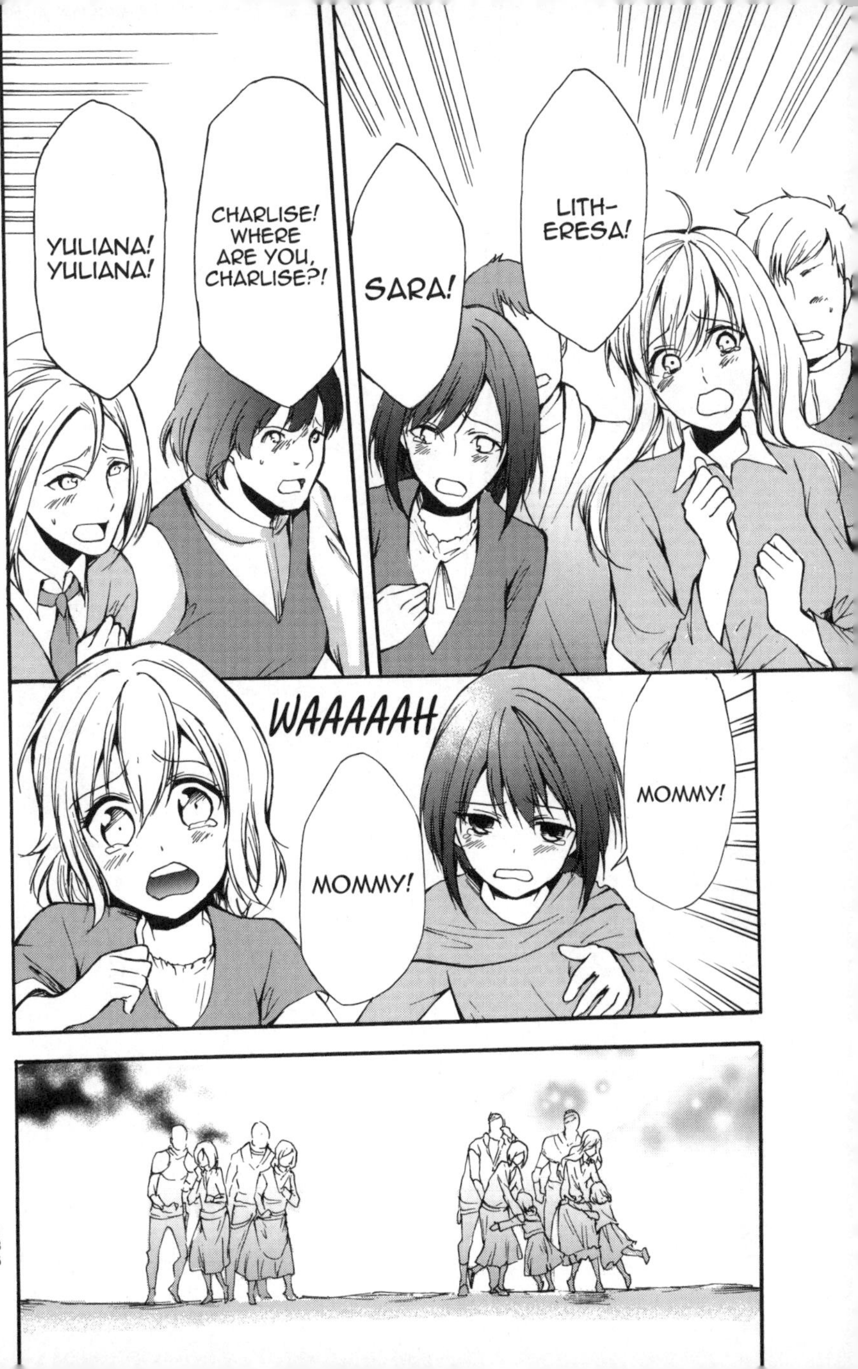
LITH-
ERESA!
SARA!
CHARLISE! WHERE ARE YOU, CHARLISE?!
YULIANA! YULIANA!
MOMMY!
WAAAAAH
MOMMY!

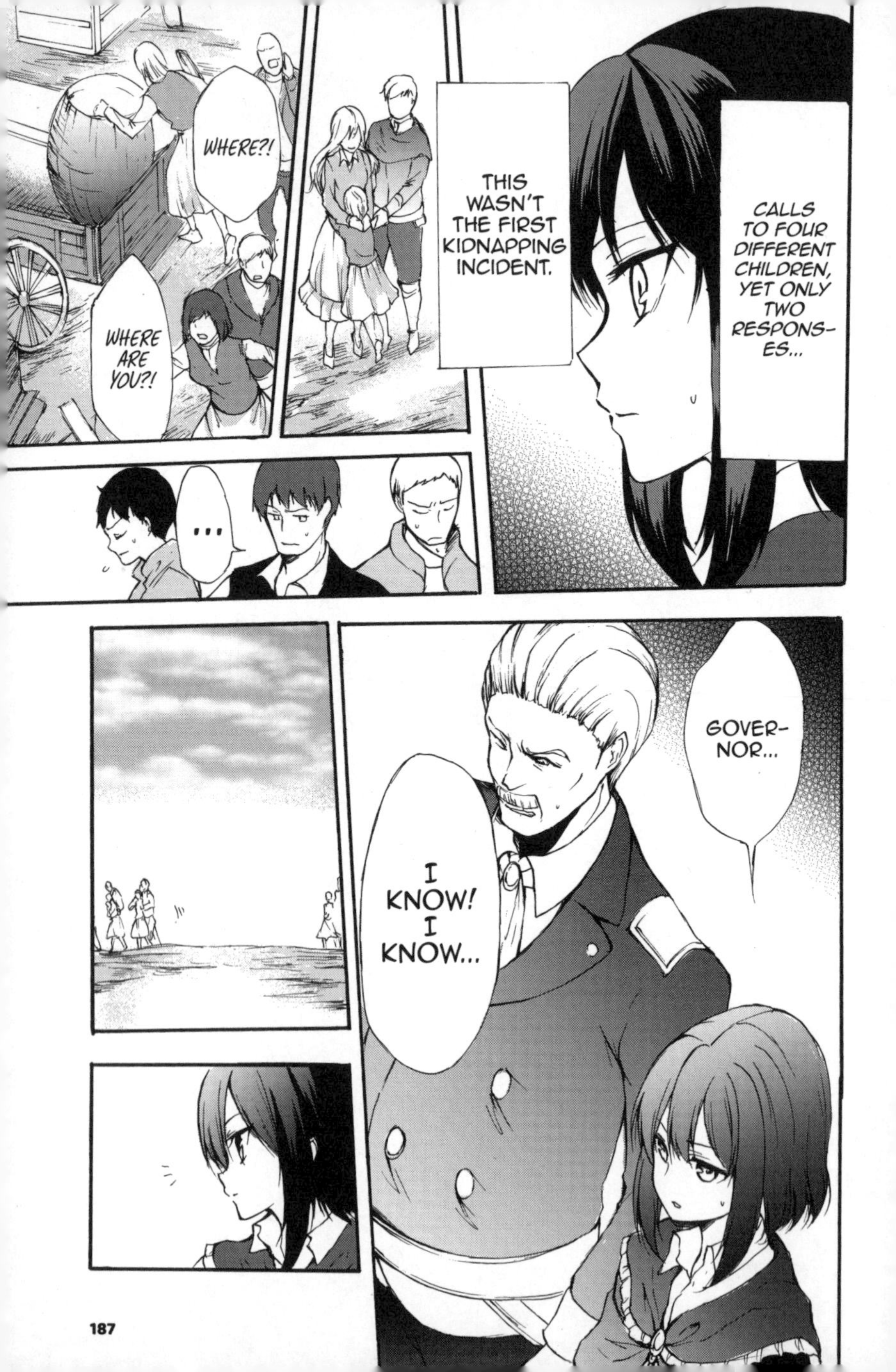
CALLS TO FOUR DIFFERENT CHILDREN, YET ONLY TWO RESPONSES...
THIS WASN'T THE FIRST KIDNAPPING INCIDENT.
WHERE?!
WHERE ARE YOU?!
...
GOVERNOR...
I KNOW! I KNOW...

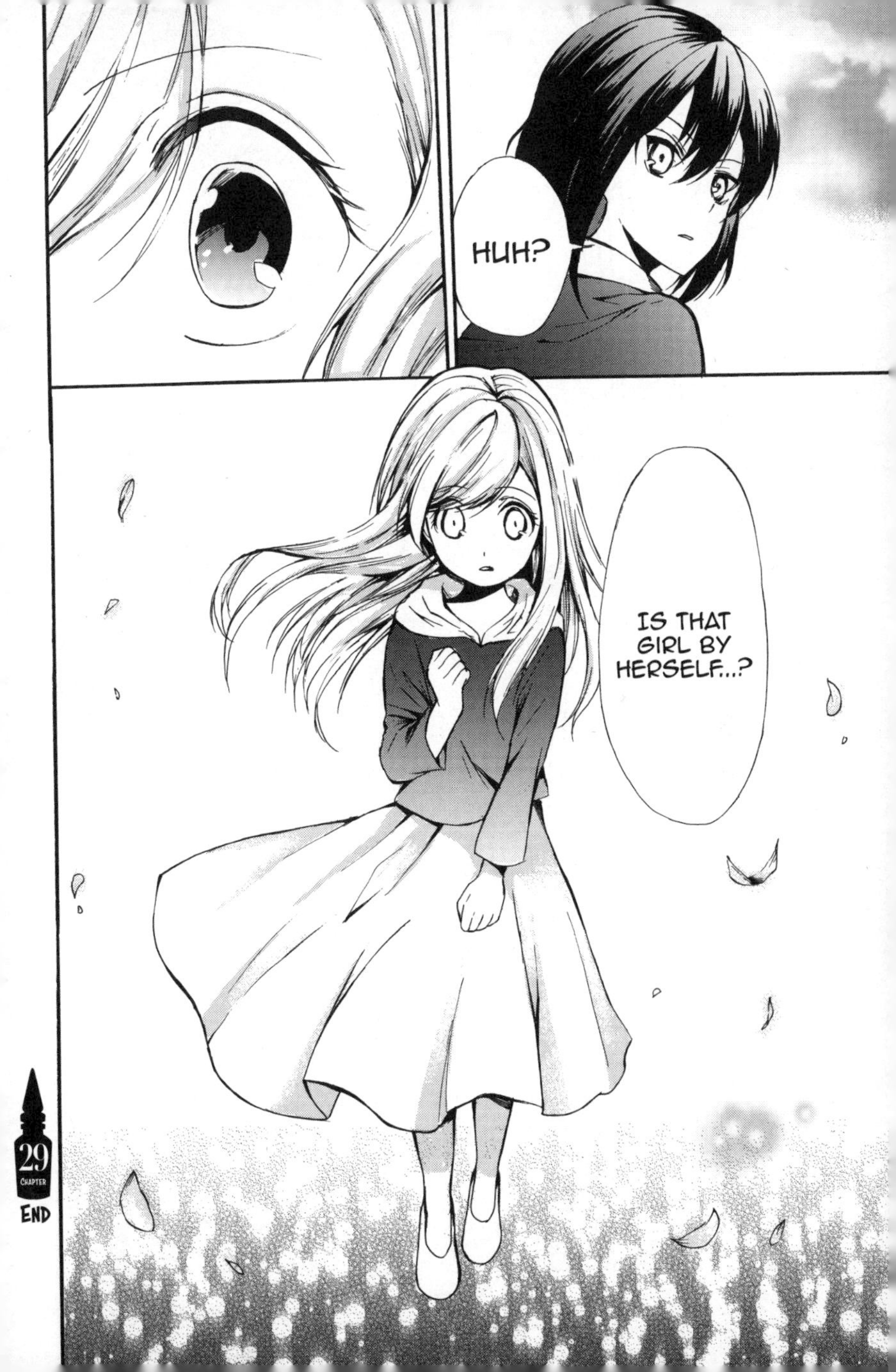
HUH?
IS THAT GIRL BY HERSELF...?
29 CHAPTER END

END OF VOLUME 5

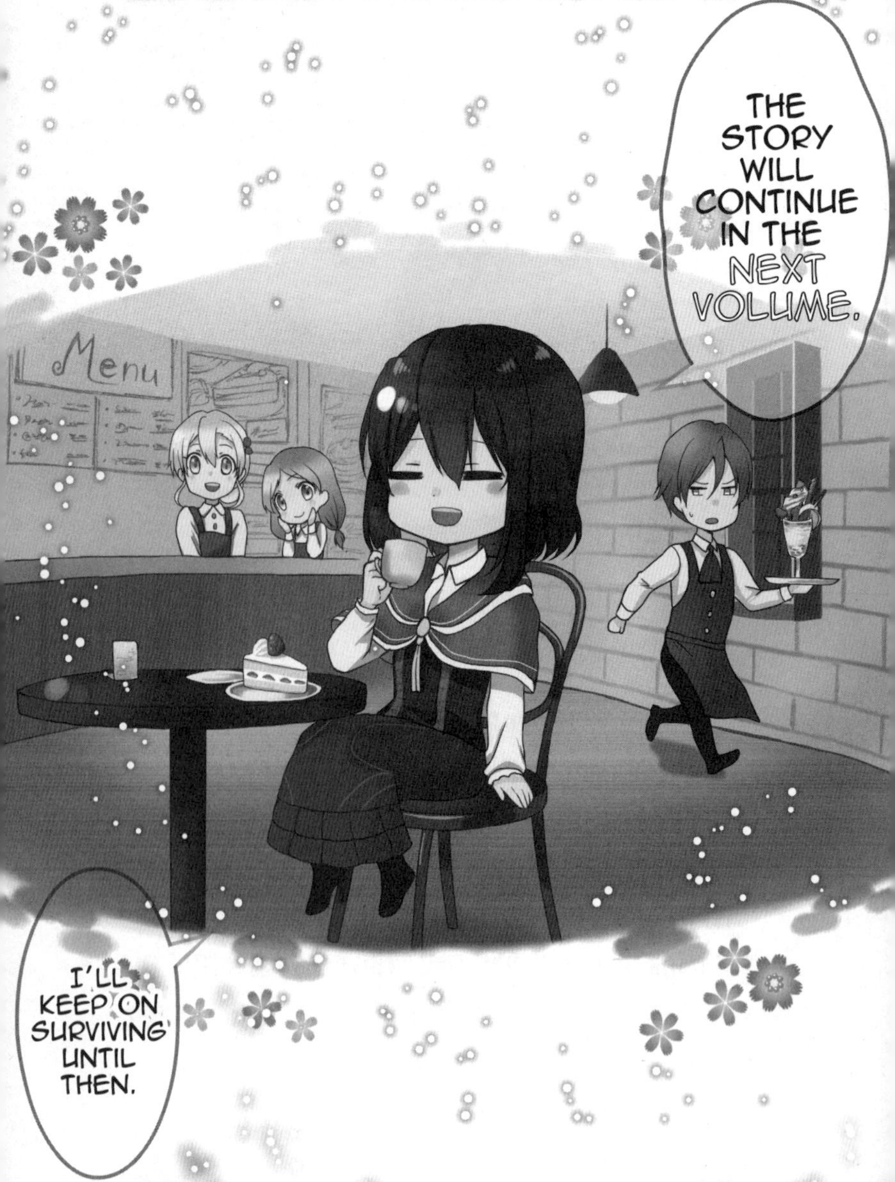
THE STORY WILL CONTINUE IN THE NEXT VOLUME.
Menu
I'LL KEEP ON SURVIVING UNTIL THEN.

CONTINUED IN VOLUME 6

AFTERWORD

MANGA **HIBIKI KOKONOE** -SENSEI

I hope you enjoyed volume 5! Things are starting to get even more exciting as new companions join in! I hope to see you in the next chapter! I want to get better at drawing...

FUNA-sensei, Sukima-sensei, and to my coordinator... Thank you.

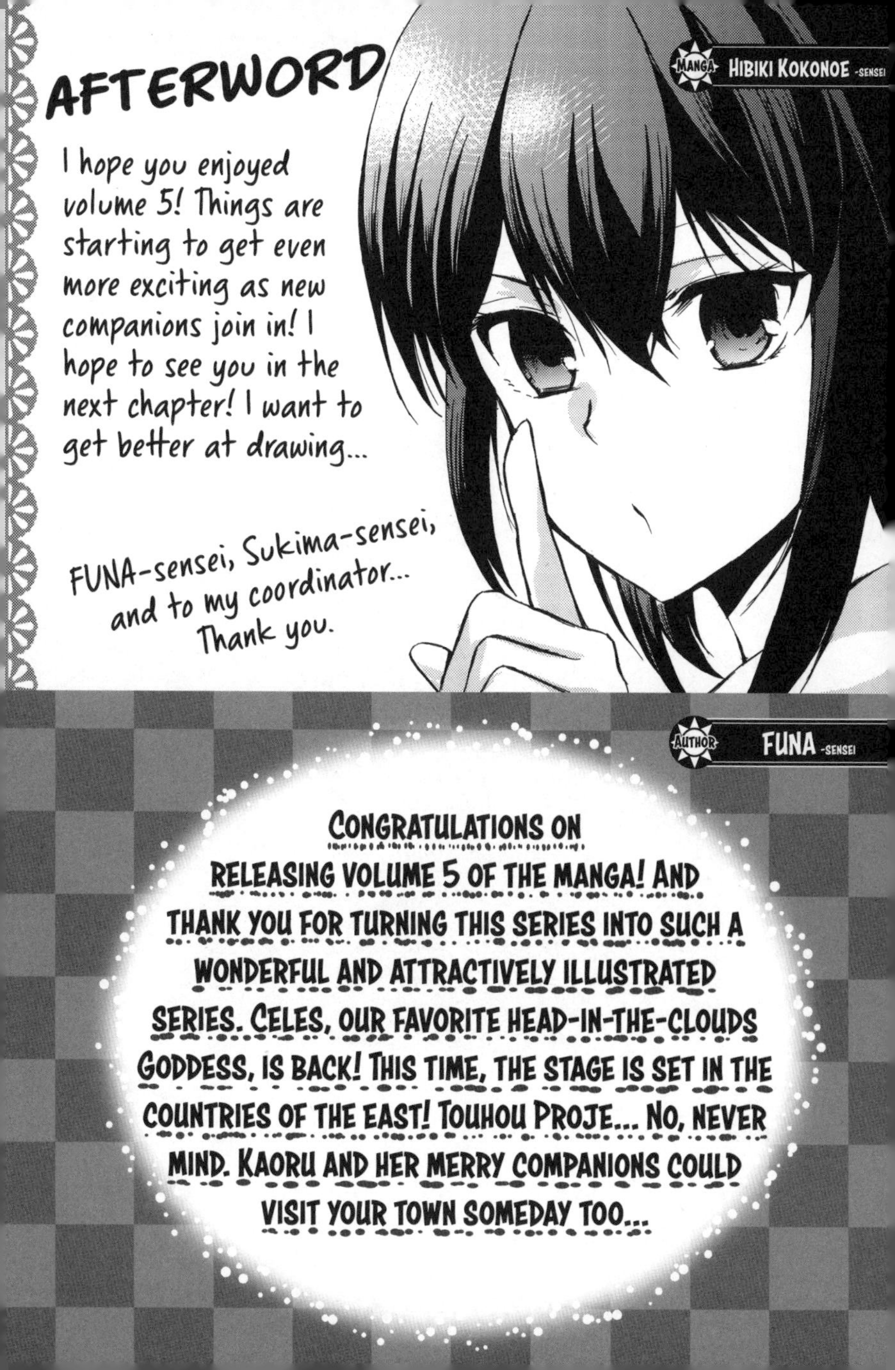

AUTHOR **FUNA** -SENSEI

CONGRATULATIONS ON RELEASING VOLUME 5 OF THE MANGA! AND THANK YOU FOR TURNING THIS SERIES INTO SUCH A WONDERFUL AND ATTRACTIVELY ILLUSTRATED SERIES. CELES, OUR FAVORITE HEAD-IN-THE-CLOUDS GODDESS, IS BACK! THIS TIME, THE STAGE IS SET IN THE COUNTRIES OF THE EAST! TOUHOU PROJE... NO, NEVER MIND. KAORU AND HER MERRY COMPANIONS COULD VISIT YOUR TOWN SOMEDAY TOO...

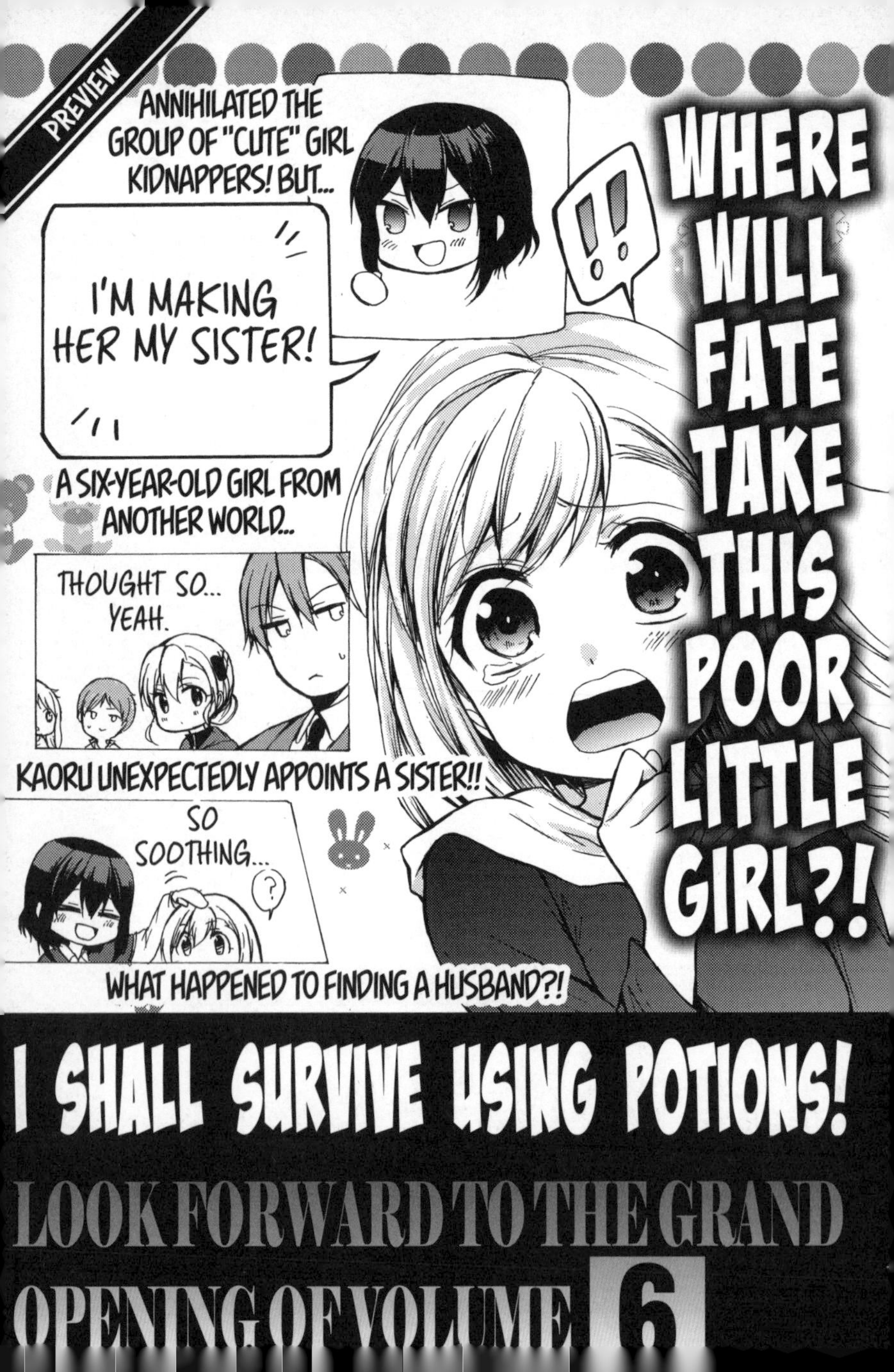
PREVIEW
WHERE WILL FATE TAKE THIS POOR LITTLE GIRL?!
ANNIHILATED THE GROUP OF "CUTE" GIRL KIDNAPPERS! BUT...
!!
I'M MAKING HER MY SISTER!
A SIX-YEAR-OLD GIRL FROM ANOTHER WORLD...
THOUGHT SO... YEAH.
KAORU UNEXPECTEDLY APPOINTS A SISTER!!
SO SOOTHING...
?
WHAT HAPPENED TO FINDING A HUSBAND?!
I SHALL SURVIVE USING POTIONS!
LOOK FORWARD TO THE GRAND OPENING OF VOLUME 6

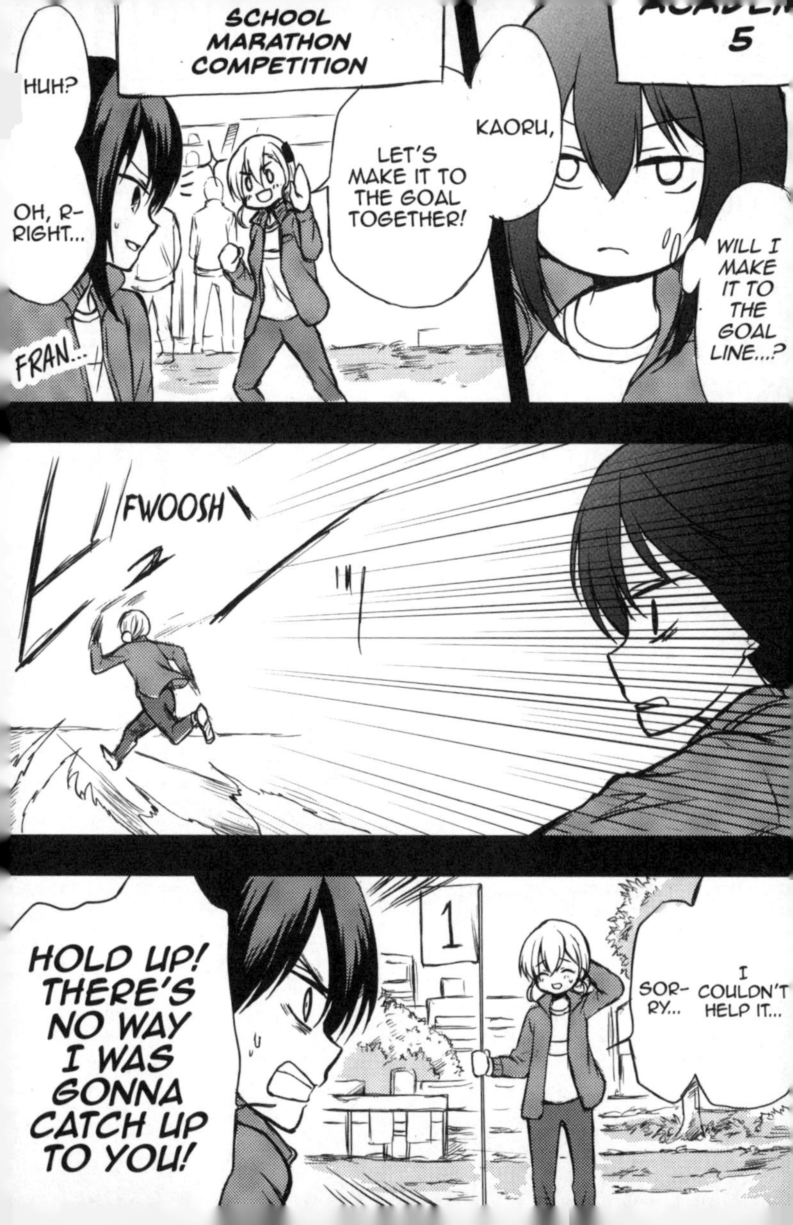
5
KAORU,
WILL I MAKE IT TO THE GOAL LINE...?
SCHOOL MARATHON COMPETITION
LET'S MAKE IT TO THE GOAL TOGETHER!
HUH?
OH, R-RIGHT...
FRAN...
FWOOSH
1
I COULDN'T HELP IT...
SORRY...
HOLD UP! THERE'S NO WAY I WAS GONNA CATCH UP TO YOU!

I SHALL SURVIVE USING POTIONS! (MANGA)VOLUME 5
by FUNA (story) and Hibiki Kokonoe (artwork)
Original character designs by Sukima

Translated by Hiro Watanabe
Edited by William Haggard
Lettered by Richard Brown

This book is a work of fiction. Names, characters, places, and incidents are the product of the author's imagination or are used fictitiously. Any resemblance to actual events, locales, or persons, living or dead, is coincidental.

First published in Japan in 2019 by Kodansha Ltd., Tokyo..
Publication rights for this English edition arranged through Kodansha Ltd., Tokyo.

Find more books like this one at www.j-novel.club!

Managing Director: Samuel Pinansky
Manga Line Manager: J. Collis
Managing Editor: Jan Mitsuko Cash
Managing Translator: Kristi Fernandez
QA Manager: Hannah N. Carter
Marketing Manager: Stephanie Hii

ISBN: 978-1-7183-7234-4
Printed in Korea
First Printing: November 2021
10 9 8 7 6 5 4 3 2 1

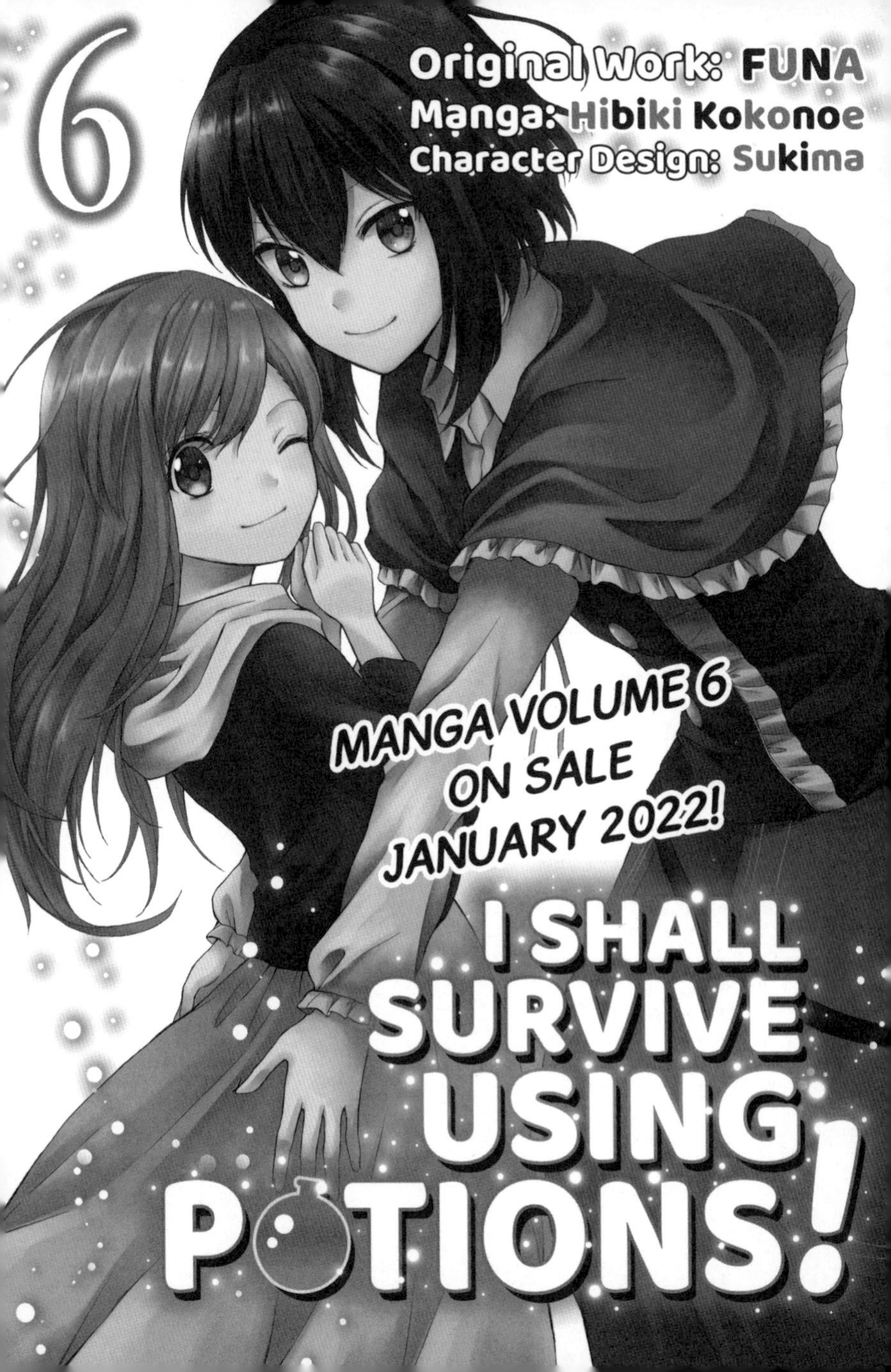
6
Original Work: FUNA
Manga: Hibiki Kokonoe
Character Design: Sukima
MANGA VOLUME 6
ON SALE
JANUARY 2022!
I SHALL SURVIVE USING POTIONS!

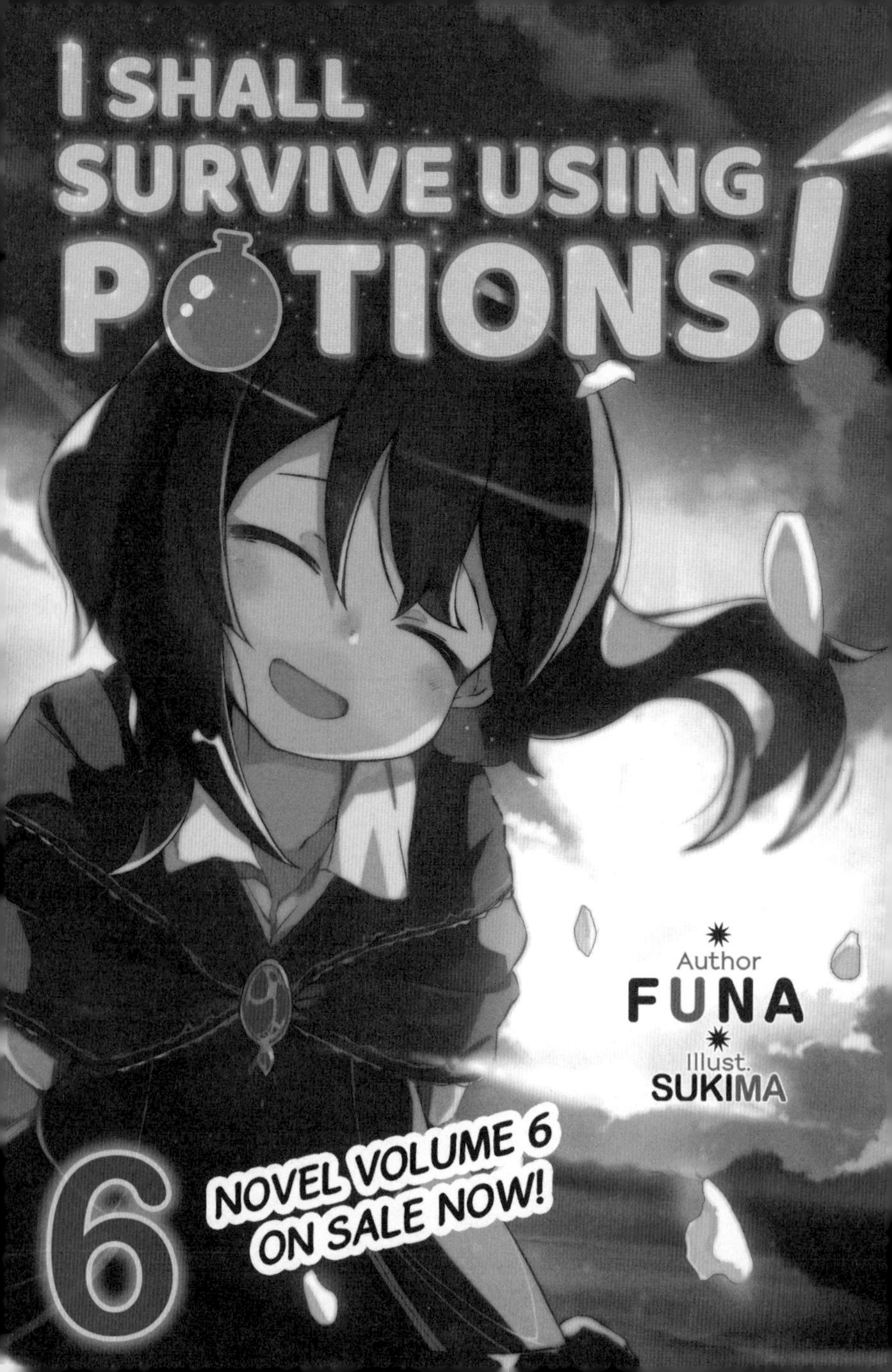
I SHALL SURVIVE USING POTIONS!
Author
FUNA
Illust.
SUKIMA
6
NOVEL VOLUME 6 ON SALE NOW!

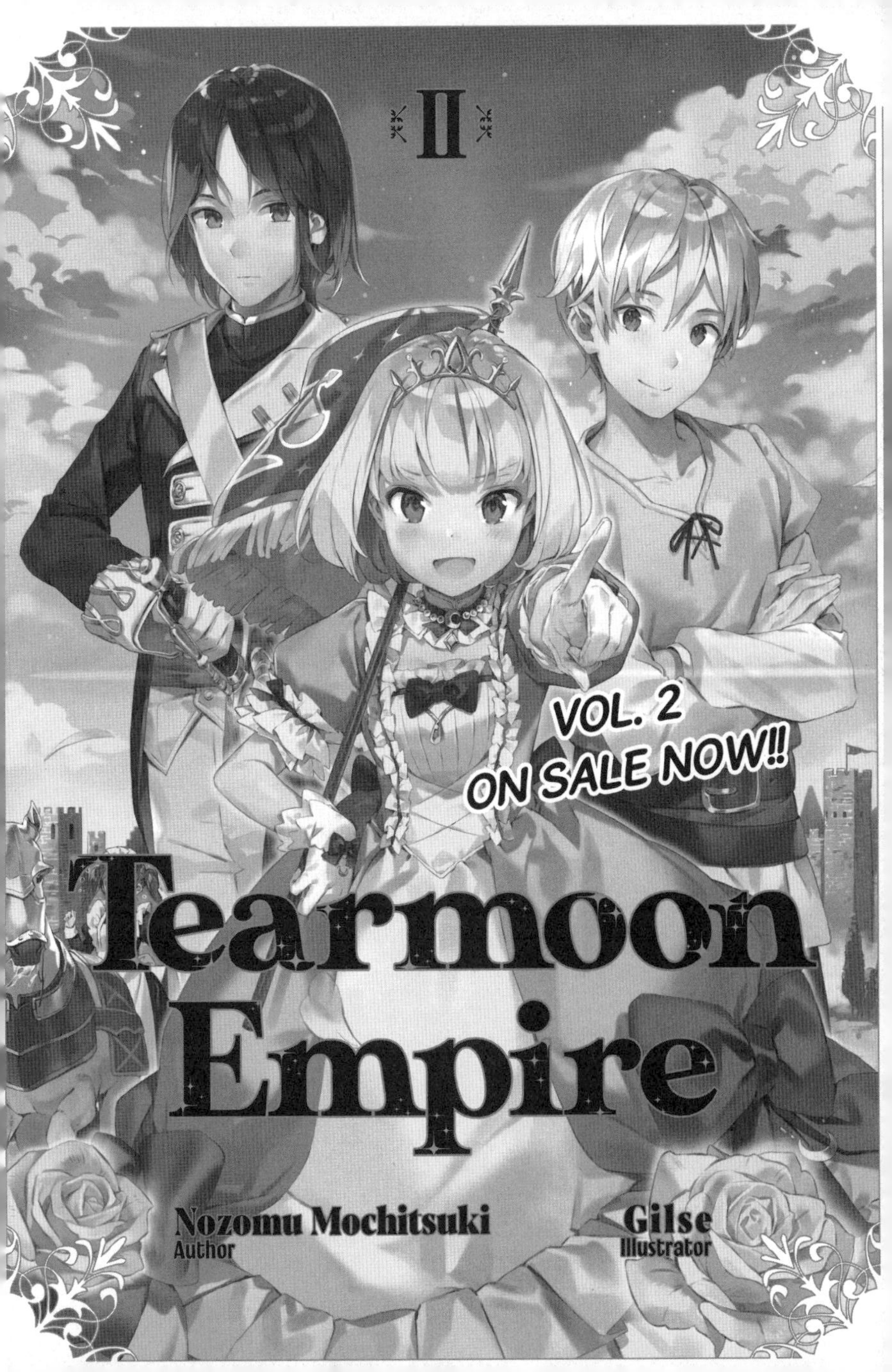
II
VOL. 2
ON SALE NOW!!
Tearmoon Empire
Nozomu Mochitsuki
Author
Gilse
Illustrator

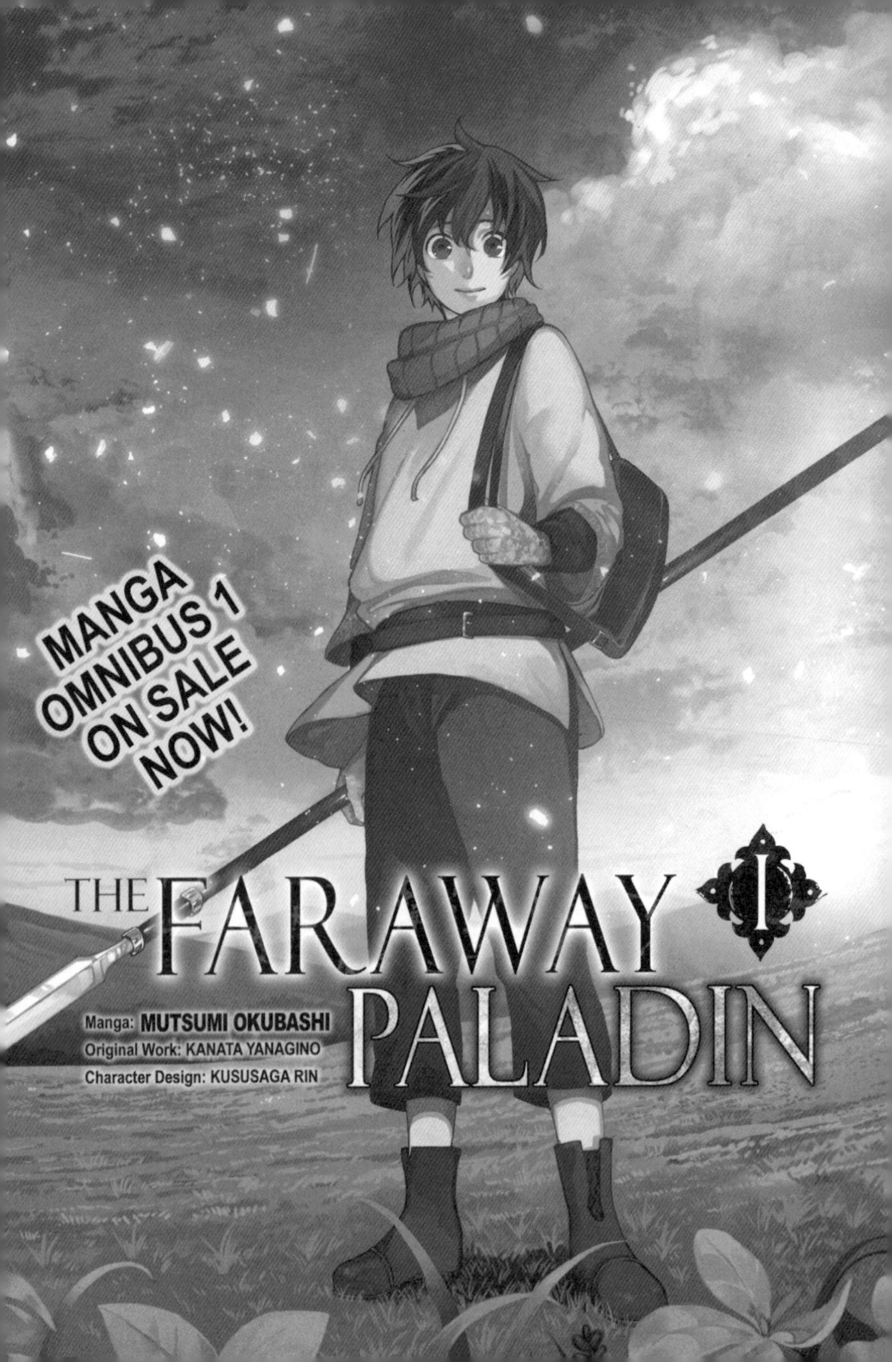

MANGA OMNIBUS 1 ON SALE NOW!
THE FARAWAY PALADIN I
Manga: MUTSUMI OKUBASHI
Original Work: KANATA YANAGINO
Character Design: KUSUSAGA RIN

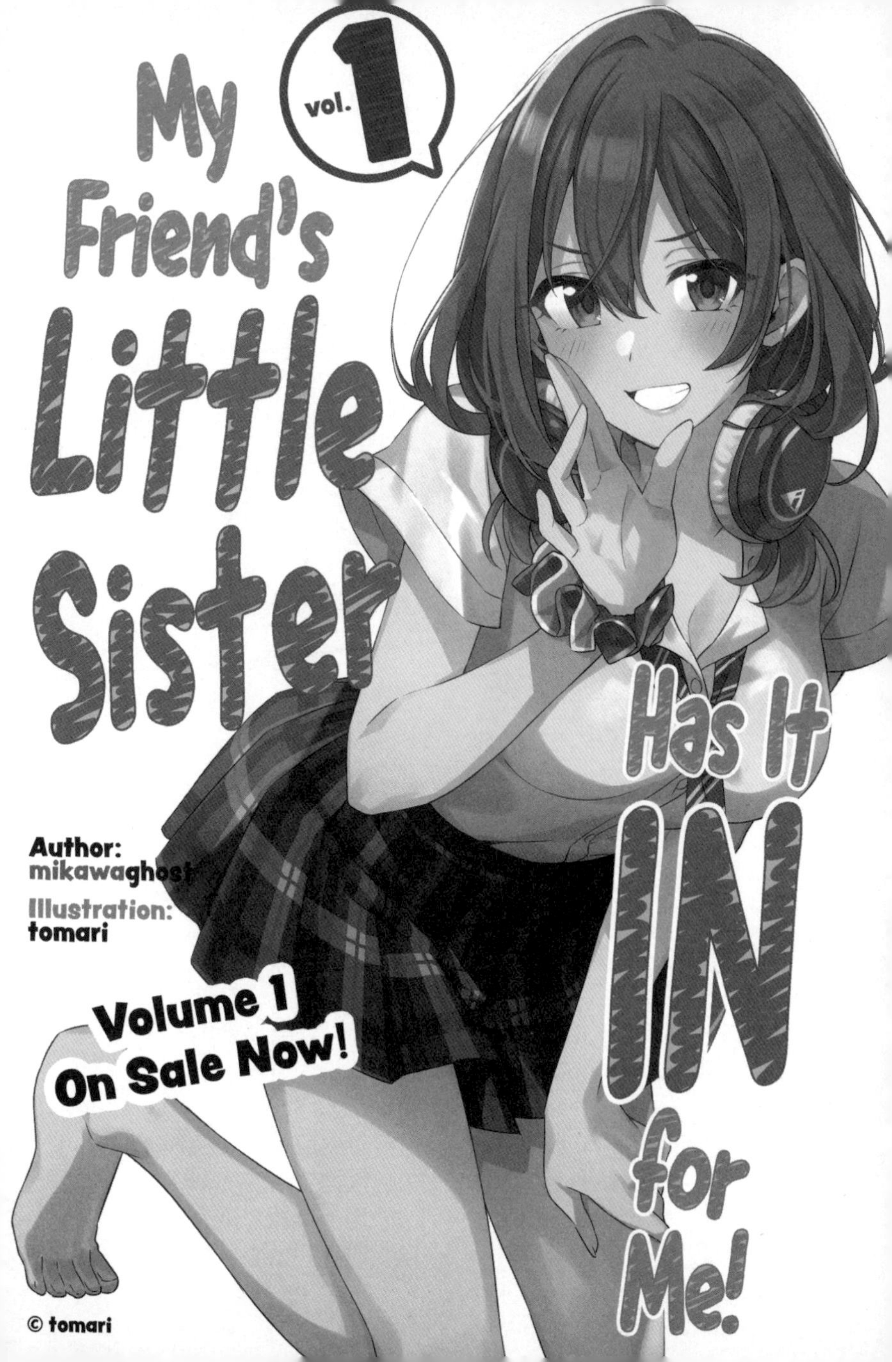

My Friend's Little Sister Has It IN for Me!
vol. 1
Author: mikawaghost
Illustration: tomari
Volume 1 On Sale Now!
© tomari

j-novel club

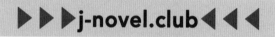

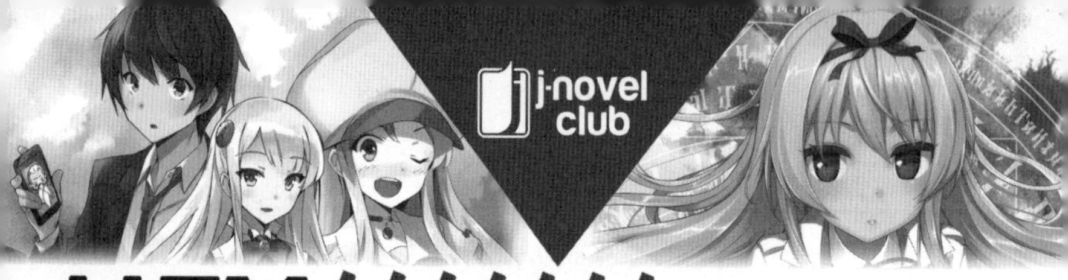

J-Novel Club Lineup

Ebook Releases Series List

A Lily Blooms in Another World
A Very Fairy Apartment**
A Wild Last Boss Appeared!
Altina the Sword Princess
Amagi Brilliant Park
An Archdemon's Dilemma: How to Love Your Elf Bride*
Animeta!**
The Apothecary Diaries
Are You Okay With a Slightly Older Girlfriend?
Arifureta: From Commonplace to World's Strongest
Arifureta Zero
Ascendance of a Bookworm*
Banner of the Stars
Bibliophile Princess*
Black Summoner*
The Bloodline
By the Grace of the Gods
Campfire Cooking in Another World with My Absurd Skill*
Can Someone Please Explain What's Going On?!
The Combat Baker and Automaton Waitress
Cooking with Wild Game*
Culinary Chronicles of the Court Flower
Deathbound Duke's Daughter
Demon Lord, Retry!*
Der Werwolf: The Annals of Veight*
Discommunication**
Dungeon Busters
The Emperor's Lady-in-Waiting is Wanted as a Bride*
The Economics of Prophecy
The Epic Tale of the Reincarnated Prince Herscherik
The Extraordinary, the Ordinary, and SOAP!
The Faraway Paladin*
Full Metal Panic!
Fushi no Kami: Rebuilding Civilization Starts With a Village
The Great Cleric
The Greatest Magicmaster's Retirement Plan
Girls Kingdom
Grimgar of Fantasy and Ash
Guide to the Perfect Otaku Girlfriend: Roomies & Romance

Her Majesty's Swarm
Holmes of Kyoto
The Holy Knight's Dark Road
How a Realist Hero Rebuilt the Kingdom*
How NOT to Summon a Demon Lord
I Love Yuri and I Got Bodyswapped with a Fujoshi!**
I Refuse to Be Your Enemy!
I Saved Too Many Girls and Caused the Apocalypse
I Shall Survive Using Potions!*
I'll Never Set Foot in That House Again!
The Ideal Sponger Life
If It's for My Daughter, I'd Even Defeat a Demon Lord
In Another World With My Smartphone
Infinite Dendrogram*
Infinite Stratos
Invaders of the Rokujouma!?
Jessica Bannister
JK Haru is a Sex Worker in Another World
John Sinclair: Demon Hunter
Kobold King
Kokoro Connect
Lazy Dungeon Master
The Magic in this Other World is Too Far Behind!*
The Magician Who Rose From Failure
Mapping: The Trash-Tier Skill That Got Me Into a Top-Tier Party*
Marginal Operation**
The Master of Ragnarok & Blesser of Einherjar*
Middle-Aged Businessman, Arise in Another World!
Monster Tamer
My Big Sister Lives in a Fantasy World
My Friend's Little Sister Has It In for Me!
My Instant Death Ability is So Overpowered, No One in This Other World Stands a Chance Against Me!
My Next Life as a Villainess: All Routes Lead to Doom!

Our Crappy Social Game Club Is Gonna Make the Most Epic Game
Otherside Picnic
Outbreak Company
Perry Rhodan NEO
Reborn to Master the Blade: From Hero-King to Extraordinary Squire ♀
Record of Wortenia War*
Reincarnated as the Piggy Duke: This Time I'm Gonna Tell Her How I Feel!
Seirei Gensouki: Spirit Chronicles*
Sexiled: My Sexist Party Leader Kicked Me Out, So I Teamed Up With a Mythical Sorceress!
She's the Cutest... But We're Just Friends!
The Sidekick Never Gets the Girl, Let Alone the Protag's Sister!
Slayers
The Sorcerer's Receptionist
Sorcerous Stabber Orphen*
Sweet Reincarnation**
The Tales of Marielle Clarac*
Tearmoon Empire
Teogonia
The Underdog of the Eight Greater Tribes
The Unwanted Undead Adventurer*
Villainess: Reloaded! Blowing Away Bad Ends with Modern Weapons*
Welcome to Japan, Ms. Elf!*
When the Clock Strikes Z
The White Cat's Revenge as Plotted from the Dragon King's Lap
Wild Times with a Fake Fake Princess
The World's Least Interesting Master Swordsman

* Novel and Manga Editions
** Manga Only
Keep an eye out at j-novel.club for further new title announcements!